NOLO Products & Services

⇨ Books & Software

Get in-depth information. Nolo publishes hundreds of great books and software programs for consumers and business owners. Order a copy—or download an ebook version instantly—at Nolo.com.

⇨ Legal Encyclopedia

Free at Nolo.com. Here are more than 1,400 free articles and answers to common questions about everyday legal issues including wills, bankruptcy, small business formation, divorce, patents, employment and much more.

⇨ Plain-English Legal Dictionary

Free at Nolo.com. Stumped by jargon? Look it up in America's most up-to-date source for definitions of legal terms.

⇨ Online Legal Documents

Create documents at your computer. Go to Nolo.com to make a will or living trust, form an LLC or corporation or obtain a trademark or provisional patent. For simpler matters, download one of our hundreds of high-quality legal forms, including bills of sale, promissory notes, nondisclosure agreements and many more.

⇨ Lawyer Directory

Find an attorney at Nolo.com. Nolo's consumer-friendly lawyer directory provides in-depth profiles of lawyers all over America. From fees and experience to education and expertise, you'll find all the information you need to choose and contact the right lawyer.

⇨ Free Legal Updates

Keep up to date. Check for free updates at Nolo.com. Under "Products," find this book and click "Legal Updates." You can also sign up for our free e-newsletters at Nolo.com/newsletters.

8th Edition

Home Business Tax Deductions

Keep What You Earn

Stephen Fishman, J.D.

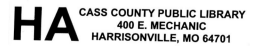

EIGHTH EDITION	JANUARY 2012
Editor	DIANA FITZPATRICK
Cover Design & Production	SUSAN PUTNEY
Proofreading	CATHERINE CAPUTO
Index	JEAN MANN
Printing	BANG PRINTING

International Standard Serial Number (ISSN): 1932-2402
ISBN-13: 978-1-4133-1639-1

Please note

We believe accurate, plain-English legal information should help you solve many of your own legal problems. But this text is not a substitute for personalized advice from a knowledgeable lawyer. If you want the help of a trained professional—and we'll always point out situations in which we think that's a good idea—consult an attorney licensed to practice in your state.

Acknowledgments

Many thanks to:

Lisa Guerin and Diana Fitzpatrick for their superb editing

Terri Hearsh for her outstanding book design

Table of Contents

Your Home Business Tax Deductions Companion 1

1   Some Tax Basics 3

How Tax Deductions Work 4

How Businesses Are Taxed 7

What Businesses Can Deduct 14

Adding It All Up: The Value of Tax Deductions 16

2   Is Your Home Business Really a Business? 23

Proving That You Are in Business 24

Tax Consequences of Engaging in a Hobby 34

Investing and Other Income-Producing Activities 35

3   Getting Your Business Up and Running 45

What Are Start-Up Expenses? 46

When Does a Business Begin? 51

Claiming the Deduction 53

If Your Business Doesn't Last 15 Years 53

Expenses for Businesses That Never Begin 55

Avoiding the Start-Up Tax Rule's Bite 56

4 Home Business Operating Expenses 59

Requirements for Deducting Operating Expenses 60

Operating Expenses That Are Not Deductible 68

How to Report Operating Expense Deductions 69

5 Deducting Long-Term Assets 71

Long-Term Assets 73

Section 179 Deductions 84

Bonus Depreciation 95

Regular Depreciation 100

When You Can't Use Section 179 101

Tax Reporting and Record Keeping for Section 179 and Depreciation 115

Leasing Long-Term Assets 117

6 The Home Office Deduction 121

Qualifying for the Home Office Deduction 122

Corporation Employees 135

Calculating the Home Office Deduction 136

IRS Reporting Requirements 154

Audit-Proofing Your Home Office Deduction 155

7 Eating Out and Going Out: Deducting Meal and Entertainment Expenses 157

What Is Business Entertainment? 158

Who You Can Entertain 160

Deducting Entertainment Expenses 160

Calculating Your Deduction 166

Reporting Entertainment Expenses on Your Tax Return 173

8 Getting Around Town: Car and Local Travel Expenses 175

Deductible Local Transportation Expenses 176

The Standard Mileage Rate 179

The Actual Expense Method 183

How to Maximize Your Car Expense Deduction 199

Other Local Transportation Expenses 201

Reporting Transportation Expenses on Your Tax Return 201

When Clients or Customers Reimburse You 203

9 Leaving Town: Business Travel 205

What Is Business Travel? 206

Deductible Travel Expenses 214

How Much You Can Deduct 216

Maximizing Your Business Travel Deductions 228

Travel Expenses Reimbursed by Clients or Customers 230

10 Inventory 233

What Is Inventory? 234

Maintaining an Inventory 237

Deducting Inventory Costs 239

IRS Reporting 245

11 Hiring Help: Employees and Independent Contractors 247

Employees Versus Independent Contractors 248

Tax Deductions for Employee Pay and Benefits 252

Reimbursing Employees for Business-Related Expenditures 262

Employing Your Family or Yourself 268

Tax Deductions When You Hire Independent Contractors 278

12 What If You Get Sick? Deducting Medical Expenses 283

The Health Care Reform Act 284

The Personal Deduction for Medical Expenses 287

Deducting Health Insurance Premiums 288

Tax Credits for Employee Health Insurance 296

Medical Reimbursement Plans 300

Health Savings Accounts 309

13 Deductions That Can Help You Retire 321

Why You Need a Retirement Plan (or Plans) 323

Individual Retirement Accounts (IRAs) 326

Employer IRAs 332

Keogh Plans 334

Solo 401(k) Plans 336

14 More Home Business Deductions 339

Advertising 341

Business Bad Debts 343

Casualty Losses 349

Charitable Contributions 353

Dues and Subscriptions 354

Education Expenses 355

Gifts 358

Insurance for Your Business 359

Interest on Business Loans 361

Legal and Professional Services 366

Taxes and Licenses 367

15 Record Keeping and Accounting 373

Basic Record Keeping for Tax Deductions 374

Records Required for Specific Expenses 387

How Long to Keep Records 401

What If You Don't Have Proper Tax Records? 403

Accounting Methods 404

Tax Years 413

16 Claiming Tax Deductions for Prior Years 415

Reasons for Amending Your Tax Return 416

Time Limits for Filing Amended Returns 420

How to Amend Your Return 423

How the IRS Processes Refund Claims 424

17 Staying Out of Trouble With the IRS 425

What Every Home Business Owner Needs to Know About the IRS 426

Ten Tips for Avoiding an Audit 434

18 Help Beyond This Book 441

Secondary Sources of Tax Information 442

The Tax Law 449

Consulting a Tax Professional 457

Index 461

Your Home Business Tax Deductions Companion

This is a book about income tax deductions for home business owners. A tax deduction is money on which you don't have to pay taxes. The government has decided that business owners don't have to pay tax on income they spend for certain business purposes. So, the trick to paying lower taxes—and keeping more of your hard-earned dollars—is to take advantage of every tax deduction you can.

If you have a legitimate home business, you may be able to deduct:

- a portion of your rent or mortgage
- expenses for local and business trips
- half the cost of business-related meals and entertainment, and
- medical expenses for yourself and your family.

All of these deductions—and many others—can add up to substantial tax savings. Depending on your income tax bracket and the state where you live, every $1,000 you take in tax deductions can save you from about $280 to more than $400 in taxes.

Business owners—whether they work at home or in outside offices—live in a different tax universe from wage earners—those who work for other people's businesses or for the government. Wage earners have their income taxes withheld from their paychecks and can take relatively few deductions. The vast majority of business owners have no taxes withheld from their earnings and can take advantage of a huge array of tax deductions unavailable to employees.

To take advantage of the benefits tax deductions offer, you'll have to figure out which deductions you are entitled to take—and keep proper records documenting your expenses. The IRS will never complain if you don't take all the deductions available to you. In fact, the majority of home business owners miss out on many deductions every year simply because they aren't aware of them—or because they neglect to keep the records necessary to back them up.

That's where this book comes in. It shows you how you can deduct all or most of your business expenses from your federal taxes. This book is not a tax preparation guide—it does not show you how to fill out your tax forms. (By the time you do your taxes, it may be too late to take deductions you could have taken if you had planned the prior year's business spending wisely and kept proper records.) Instead, this book gives you all the information you need to maximize your deductible expenses—and avoid common deduction mistakes. You can (and should) use this book all year long, so that you're ready to take advantage of every available deduction opportunity come April 15.

Even if you work with an accountant or another tax professional, you need to learn about home business tax deductions. No tax professional will ever know as much about your business as you do, and you can't expect a hired professional to search high and low for every deduction you might be able to take, especially during the busy tax preparation season. The information in this book will help you provide your tax professional with better records, ask better questions, and obtain better advice. It will also help you evaluate the advice you get from tax professionals, websites, and other sources, so you can make smart decisions about your taxes.

If you do your taxes yourself (as more and more home business-people are doing, especially with the help of tax preparation software), your need for knowledge is even greater. Not even the most sophisti-cated tax preparation program can decide which tax deductions you should take or tell you whether you've overlooked a valuable deduction. This book can be your guide—providing you with practical advice and information so you can rest assured you are taking full advantage of the many deductions available to home business owners.

Get Updates and More Online

When there are important changes to the information in this book, we'll post updates online, on a page dedicated to this book: **www.nolo.com/back-of-book/DEHB8.html**. You'll find other useful information there, too, including author blogs, podcasts, and videos.

Some Tax Basics

How Tax Deductions Work..4

    Types of Tax Deductions..4

    You Pay Taxes Only on Your Business Profits..5

    Claiming Your Deductions..6

    Make Sure You Are in Business...6

How Businesses Are Taxed..7

    Basic Business Forms...7

    Sole Proprietorship—The Most Popular Home Business Entity....................7

    Tax Treatment...11

What Businesses Can Deduct...14

    Start-Up Expenses..14

    Operating Expenses...15

    Capital Expenses..15

    Inventory..16

Adding It All Up: The Value of Tax Deductions..16

    Federal and State Income Taxes..16

    Self-Employment Taxes..18

    Total Tax Savings..20

Once you start your own business, you can begin taking advantage of the many tax deductions available only to business owners. The tax code is full of deductions for businesses—and you are entitled to take them whether you work from home or from a fancy outside office. Before you can start using these deductions to hang on to more of your hard-earned money, however, you need a basic understanding of how businesses pay taxes and how tax deductions work. This chapter gives you all the information you need to get started. It covers:

- how tax deductions work
- how businesses are taxed
- what expenses businesses can deduct, and
- how to calculate the value of a tax deduction.

How Tax Deductions Work

A tax deduction (also called a write-off) is an amount of money you are entitled to subtract from your gross income (all the money you make) to determine your taxable income (the amount on which you must pay tax). The more deductions you have, the lower your taxable income will be and the less tax you will have to pay.

Types of Tax Deductions

There are three basic types of tax deductions: personal deductions, investment deductions, and business deductions. This book covers only business deductions—the large array of write-offs available to business owners, including those who work out of their homes.

Personal Deductions

For the most part, your personal, living, and family expenses are not tax deductible. For example, you can't deduct the food that you buy for yourself and your family. There are, however, special categories of personal expenses that may be deducted, subject to strict limitations. These include items such as home mortgage interest, state and local taxes, charitable contributions, medical expenses above a threshold amount, interest on education loans, and alimony. This book does not cover these personal deductions.

Investment Deductions

Many people try to make money by investing money. For example, they might invest in real estate or play the stock market. These people incur all kinds of expenses, such as fees paid to money managers or financial planners, legal and accounting fees, and interest on money borrowed to buy investment property. These and other investment expenses (also called expenses for the production of income) are tax deductible, subject to some important limitations. (See "Investing and Other Income-Producing Activities" in Chapter 2 for more on investment deductions.)

Business Deductions

Home business owners usually have to spend money on their businesses—for example, for equipment, supplies, or business travel. Most business expenses are deductible sooner or later. It makes no difference for tax deduction purposes whether you run your business from home or from an outside office or workplace—either way, you are entitled to deduct your legitimate business expenses. This book is about the many deductions available to people who are in business and who happen to work from home.

You Pay Taxes Only on Your Business Profits

The federal income tax law recognizes that you must spend money to make money. Virtually every home business, however small, incurs some expenses. Even someone with a low-overhead business (such as a freelance writer) must buy paper, computer equipment, and office supplies. Some home businesses incur substantial expenses, even exceeding their income.

You are not legally required to pay tax on every dollar your business takes in (your gross business income). Instead, you owe tax only on the amount left over after your business's deductible expenses are subtracted from your gross income (this remaining amount is called your net profit). Although some tax deduction calculations can get a bit complicated, the basic math is simple: The more deductions you take, the lower your net profit will be, and the less tax you will have to pay.

EXAMPLE: Karen, a sole proprietor, earned $50,000 this year from her consulting business, which she operates from her home office. Fortunately, she doesn't have to pay income tax on the entire $50,000—her gross income. Instead, she can deduct various business expenses, including a $5,000 home office deduction (see Chapter 6) and a $5,000 deduction for equipment expenses (see Chapter 5). She deducts these expenses from her $50,000 gross income to arrive at her net profit: $40,000. She pays income tax only on this net profit amount.

Claiming Your Deductions

All tax deductions are a matter of legislative grace, which means that you can take a deduction only if it is specifically allowed by one or more provisions of the tax law. You usually do not have to indicate on your tax return which tax law provision gives you the right to take a particular deduction. If you are audited by the IRS, however, you'll have to provide a legal basis for every deduction you take. If the IRS concludes that your deduction wasn't justified, it will deny the deduction and charge you back taxes, interest, in some cases, and penalties.

Make Sure You Are in Business

Only businesses can claim business tax deductions. This probably seems like a simple concept, but it can get tricky. Even though you might believe you are running a business, the IRS may beg to differ. If your home business doesn't turn a profit for several years in a row, the IRS might decide that you are engaged in a hobby rather than a business. This may not sound like a big deal, but it could have disastrous tax consequences: People engaged in hobbies are entitled to very limited tax deductions, while businesses can deduct all kinds of expenses. Fortunately, careful taxpayers can usually avoid this unhappy outcome. (See Chapter 2 for tips that will help you convince the IRS that you really are running a business.)

How Businesses Are Taxed

If your home business earns money (as you undoubtedly hope it will), you will have to pay taxes on your profits. How you pay those taxes will depend on how you have structured your business. So before getting further into the details of tax deductions, it's important to understand what type of business you have formed (a sole proprietorship, partnership, limited liability company, or corporation), and how you will pay tax on your business's profit.

 RESOURCE

Need help figuring out how to structure your business? Although most home businesses are sole proprietorships, that may not be the best business form for you. If you need to decide how to organize a new business or you want to know whether you should change your current business form, refer to *LLC or Corporation? How to Choose the Right Form for Your Business*, by Anthony Mancuso (Nolo).

Basic Business Forms

Every business, from a part-time operation you run from home while in your jammies to a Fortune 500 multinational company housed in a gleaming skyscraper, has a legal structure. If you're running a business right now, it has a legal form—even if you never made a conscious decision about how it should be legally organized.

Sole Proprietorship—The Most Popular Home Business Entity

A sole proprietorship is a one-owner business. According to the Small Business Administration, 90% of all home businesses are sole proprietorships. Unlike the other business forms, a sole proprietorship has no legal existence separate from the business owner. It cannot sue or be sued, own property in its own name, or file its own tax returns. The business owner (proprietor) personally owns all of the assets of the business and controls its operations. If you're running a one-person home business and you haven't incorporated or formed a limited liability company, you are a sole proprietor. However, you can't be a sole proprietor if two or more people own your home business, unless you are one of two spouses who jointly own and run their home business together (see "Spouses Who Co-Own a Business," below).

Other Business Forms You Can Use

Only about 10% of home businesses adopt a business form other than a sole proprietorship. These other forms include:

- **Partnerships.** A partnership is a form of shared ownership and management of a business. The partners contribute money, property, or services to the partnership; in return, they receive a share of the profits it earns, if any. The partners jointly manage the partnership business. A partnership automatically comes into existence whenever two or more people enter into business together to earn a profit and don't incorporate or form a limited liability company. Thus, if you're running a home business with somebody else, you are in a partnership right now (unless you've formed an LLC or a corporation). Although many partners enter into written partnership agreements, no written agreement is required to form a partnership.

- **Corporations.** Unlike a sole proprietorship or partnership, a corporation cannot simply spring into existence—it can only be created by filing incorporation documents with your state government. A corporation is a legal entity distinct from its owners. It can hold title to property, sue and be sued, have bank accounts, borrow money, hire employees, and perform other business functions. For tax purposes, there are two types of corporations: S corporations (also called small business corporations) and C corporations (also called regular corporations). The most important difference between the two types of corporations is how they are taxed. An S corporation pays no taxes itself—instead, its income or loss is passed on to its owners, who must pay personal income taxes on their share of the corporation's profits. A C corporation is a separate taxpaying entity that pays taxes on its profits (see "Tax Treatment," below).

- **Limited Liability Companies.** The limited liability company (LLC) is like a sole proprietorship or partnership in that its owners (called members) jointly own and manage the business and share in the profits. However, an LLC is also like a corporation. Because its owners must file papers with the state to create the LLC, it exists as a separate legal entity, and the LLC structure gives owners some protection from liability for business debts.

Spouses Who Co-Own a Business

Prior to 2007, spouses who co-owned a business were classified as a partnership for federal tax purposes (unless they formed a corporation or LLC, or lived in a community property state—see below). Now, married couples in any state who own a home business together may be able to elect to be taxed as sole proprietors. This does not reduce their taxes, but it does result in a much simpler tax return.

The rules for electing sole proprietor tax status differ depending on whether you live in a community property state or not. If a couple doesn't qualify for or choose sole proprietor status, their jointly-owned home business will be classified as a partnership for federal tax purposes, assuming they have not formed an LLC or corporation. This means they must file a partnership tax return for the business. Each spouse should carry his or her share of the partnership income or loss from Form 1065, Schedule K-1, to their joint or separate Form 1040. Each spouse should also include his or her share of self-employment income on a separate Form 1040, Schedule SE.

Spouses in all states. Spouses in all states who jointly own and manage a business together can elect to be taxed as a "qualified joint venture" and treated as sole proprietors for tax purposes. To qualify as co-sole proprietors, the married couple must be the only owners of the business and they must both "materially participate" in the business—be involved with the business's day-to-day operations on a regular, continuous, and substantial basis. Working more than 500 hours during the year meets this requirement. So does working over 100 hours if no one else works more. It's likely that many couples will not be able to satisfy the material participation requirement.

A couple elects to be treated as a qualified joint venture by filing a joint tax return (IRS Form 1040). Each spouse files a separate Schedule C to report their share of the business's profits and losses, and a separate Schedule SE to report their share of self-employment tax. That way, each spouse gets credit for Social Security and Medicare coverage purposes. If, as is usually the case, each spouse owns 50% of the business, they equally share the business income or loss on their individual Schedule Cs. The couple must also share any deductions and credits according to their individual ownership interest in the business. If the business has employees, either spouse may report and pay the employment taxes due on any wages paid to the employees using the EIN of that spouse's sole proprietorship.

Spouses in community property states. Spouses in any of the nine community property states (Arizona, California, Idaho, Louisiana, Nevada, New Mexico, Texas, Washington, and Wisconsin) may elect qualified joint venture status as described above. However, couples in these states can also choose to classify their business as a sole proprietorship simply by filing a single Schedule C listing one spouse as the sole proprietor. For many couples, this is easier to do than the qualified joint venture status because there is no material participation requirement. The only requirements are that:

- the business is wholly owned by the husband and wife as community property
- no person other than one or both spouses would be considered an owner for federal tax purposes, and
- the business entity is not treated as a corporation. (Rev. Proc. 2002-69).

One drawback to this election is that only one spouse (the one listed in the Schedule C) receives credit for Social Security and Medicare coverage purposes.

What if Your Spouse Is Your Employee?

Instead of being co-owners of a business, spouses can have an employer-employee relationship—that is, one spouse solely owns the business (usually as a sole proprietor) and the other spouse works as his or her employee. In this event, there is no need to worry about having to file a partnership tax return. One Schedule C would be filed in the name of the owner-spouse. The non-owner spouse's income would be employee salary subject to income tax and FICA (Social Security and Medicare) withholding. (See Chapter 11.)

However, a spouse is considered an employee only if there is an employer/employee type of relationship—that is, the first spouse substantially controls the business in terms of management decisions and the second spouse is under the direction and control of the first spouse. If the second spouse has an equal say in the affairs of the business, provides substantially equal services to the business, and contributes capital to the business, that spouse cannot be treated as an employee.

Tax Treatment

Your business's legal form will determine how it is treated for tax purposes. There are two different ways that business entities can be taxed: The business itself can be taxed as a separate entity, or the business's profits and losses can be passed through to the owners, who include these amounts on their individual tax returns.

Pass-Through Entities: Sole Proprietorships, Partnerships, LLCs, and S Corporations

Sole proprietorships and S corporations are always pass-through entities. LLCs and partnerships are almost always pass-through entities as well—partnerships and multiowner LLCs are automatically taxed as partnerships when they are created. One-owner LLCs are automatically taxed like sole proprietorships. However, LLC and partnership owners have the option of choosing to have their entity taxed as a C corporation or S corporation by filing an election with the IRS. This is rarely done.

A pass-through entity does not pay any taxes itself. Instead, the business's profits or losses are passed through to its owners, who include them on their own personal tax returns (IRS Form 1040). If a profit is passed through to the owner, the owner must add that money to any income from other sources, and pay tax on the total amount. If a loss is passed through, the owner can generally use it to offset income from other sources—for example, salary from a job, interest, investment income, or a spouse's income (as long as the couple files a joint tax return). The owner can subtract the business loss from this other income, which leaves a lower total subject to tax.

> **EXAMPLE:** Lisa is a sole proprietor who works part-time from home doing engineering consulting. During her first year in business, she incurs $10,000 in expenses and earns $5,000, giving her a $5,000 loss from her business. She reports this loss on IRS Schedule C, which she files with her personal income tax return (Form 1040). Because Lisa is a sole proprietor, she can deduct this $5,000 loss from any income she has, including her $100,000 annual salary from her engineering job. This saves her about $2,000 in total taxes for the year.

Although pass-through entities don't pay taxes, their income and expenses must still be reported to the IRS as follows:

- **Sole proprietors** must file IRS Schedule C, *Profit or Loss From Business*, with their tax returns. This form lists all the proprietor's business income and deductible expenses.
- **Partnerships** are required to file an annual tax form (Form 1065, *U.S. Return of Partnership Income*) with the IRS. Form 1065 is used to report partnership revenues, expenses, gains, and losses. The partnership must also provide each partner with an IRS Schedule K-1, *Partner's Share of Income, Credits, Deductions, etc.*, listing the partner's share of partnership income and expenses (copies of these schedules must also be attached to IRS Form 1065). Partners must then file IRS Schedule E, *Supplemental*

Income and Loss, with their individual income tax returns, showing their partnership income and deductions.

- **S corporations** must file information returns with the IRS on Form 1120S, *U.S. Income Tax Return for an S Corporation*, showing how much the business earned or lost and each shareholder's portion of the corporate income or loss.

- **LLCs** with only one member are treated like a sole proprietorship for tax purposes. The member reports profits, losses, and deductions on Schedule C—just like a sole proprietor. An LLC with two or more members is ordinarily treated like a partnership: The LLC must prepare and file IRS Form 1065, *Partnership Return of Income*, showing the allocation of profits, losses, credits, and deductions passed through to the members. The LLC must also prepare and distribute to each member a Schedule K-1 showing the member's allocations of profits, losses, credits, and deductions.

Regular C Corporations—Creating Two Taxable Entities

A regular C corporation is the only business form that is not a pass-through entity. Instead, a C corporation is taxed separately from its owners. C corporations must pay income taxes on their net income and file corporate tax returns with the IRS, using Form 1120, *U.S. Corporation Income Tax Return,* or Form 1120-A, *U.S. Corporation Short-Form Income Tax Return*. They also have their own income tax rates (which are lower than individual rates at some income levels).

When you form a C corporation, you have to take charge of two separate taxpayers: your corporation and yourself. Your C corporation must pay tax on all of its income. You pay personal income tax on C corporation income only when it is distributed to you in the form of salary, bonuses, or dividends. However, you might have to pay special penalty taxes if you keep too much money in your corporation to avoid having to pay personal income tax on it.

C corporations can take all the same business tax deductions that pass-through entities take. In addition, because a C corporation is a separate tax-paying entity, it may provide its employees with tax-free fringe benefits, then deduct the entire cost of the benefits from the corporation's income as a business expense. No other form of business entity can do this. (Although they are corporations, S corporations cannot deduct the cost of benefits provided to shareholders who hold more than 2% of the corporate stock.)

What Businesses Can Deduct

Business owners, whether they work at home or elsewhere, can deduct four broad categories of business expenses:

- start-up expenses
- operating expenses
- capital expenses, and
- inventory costs.

This section provides an introduction to each of these categories (they are covered in greater detail in later chapters).

 TIP

You must keep track of your expenses. You may deduct only those expenses that you actually incur. You need to keep records of these expenses to (1) know for sure how much you actually spent, and (2) prove to the IRS that you really spent the money you deducted on your tax return, in case you are audited. Accounting and bookkeeping are discussed in detail in Chapter 15.

Start-Up Expenses

Start-up expenses are expenses you incur to get your home business up and running—such as license fees, advertising costs, attorney and accounting fees, market research, and office supplies expenses. Start-up costs are not currently deductible—that is, you cannot deduct them all in the year in which you incur them. However, you can deduct up to $5,000 in start-up costs in the first year your new business is in operation. You must deduct amounts over $5,000 over the next 15 years. Most home business owners should be able to avoid incurring substantial start-up expenses. (See Chapter 3 for a detailed discussion of deducting start-up expenses.)

Operating Expenses

Operating expenses are the ongoing day-to-day costs a business incurs to stay in business. They include such things as rent, utilities, salaries, supplies, travel expenses, car expenses, and repairs and maintenance. These expenses (unlike start-up expenses) are currently deductible— that is, you can deduct them all in the year when you pay them. (See Chapter 4 for more on operating expenses.)

Capital Expenses

Capital assets are things you buy for your business that have a useful life of more than one year, such as equipment, vehicles, books, office furniture, machinery, and patents you buy from others. These costs, called capital expenses, are considered to be part of your investment in your business, not day-to-day operating expenses.

Large businesses—those that buy at least several hundred thousand dollars of capital assets in a year—must deduct these costs by using depreciation. To depreciate an item, you deduct a portion of the cost in each year of the item's useful life. Depending on the asset, this could be anywhere from three to 39 years (the IRS decides the asset's useful life).

Small businesses can also use depreciation, but they have another option available for deducting many capital expenses—they can deduct a certain amount in capital expenses per year under a provision of the tax code called Section 179. In 2010 and 2011, the Section 179 deduction ceiling was $500,000. This is scheduled to go down to $125,000 in 2012. Section 179 and depreciation are discussed in detail in Chapter 5.

Certain capital assets, such as land and corporate stock, never wear out. What you spend to purchase and improve capital assets is not deductible; you have to wait until you sell the asset (or it becomes worthless) to recover these costs. (See Chapter 5 for more on deducting capital assets.)

Inventory

If your home business involves making or buying products, you'll have an inventory. Inventory includes almost anything you make or buy to resell to customers. It doesn't matter whether you manufacture the goods yourself or buy finished goods from someone else and resell them to customers. Inventory doesn't include tools, equipment, or other items that you use in your business; it refers only to items that you buy or make to sell.

You must deduct inventory costs separately from all other business expenses—you deduct inventory costs as you sell the inventory. Inventory that remains unsold at the end of the year is a business asset, not a deductible expense. (See Chapter 10 for more on deducting inventory.)

Adding It All Up: The Value of Tax Deductions

Most taxpayers, even sophisticated businesspeople, don't fully appreciate just how much money they can save with tax deductions. Of course, only part of any deduction will end up back in your pocket as money saved. Because a deduction represents income on which you don't have to pay tax, the value of any deduction is the amount of tax you would have had to pay on that income had you not deducted it. So a deduction of $1,000 won't save you $1,000—it will save you whatever you would otherwise have had to pay as tax on that $1,000 of income.

Federal and State Income Taxes

To determine how much income tax a deduction will save you, you must first figure out your income tax bracket. The United States has a progressive income tax system for individual taxpayers with six different tax rates (called tax brackets), ranging from 10% of taxable income to 35% (see the chart below). The higher your income, the higher your tax rate.

You move from one bracket to the next only when your taxable income exceeds the bracket amount. For example, if you are a single taxpayer, you pay 10% income tax on all your taxable income up to $8,500 in 2011. If your taxable income exceeds that amount, the next tax rate (15%) applies to all your income over $8,500—but the 10% rate still applies to the first $8,500. If your income exceeds the 15% bracket amount, the next tax rate (25%) applies to the excess amount, and so on until the top bracket of 35% is reached.

The tax bracket in which the last dollar you earn for the year falls is called your marginal tax bracket. For example, if you have $70,000 in taxable income, your marginal tax bracket is 25%. To determine how much federal income tax a deduction will save you, multiply the amount of the deduction by your marginal tax bracket. For example, if your marginal tax bracket is 25%, you will save 25¢ in federal income taxes for every dollar you are able to claim as a deductible business expense (25% × $1 = 25¢).

The following table lists the 2011 federal income tax brackets for single and married individual taxpayers and shows the federal income tax savings for each dollar of deductions.

Income tax brackets are adjusted each year for inflation. For current brackets, see IRS Publication 505, *Tax Withholding and Estimated Tax.*

2011 Federal Personal Income Tax Rates		
Tax Bracket	Income If Single	Income If Married Filing Jointly
10%	Up to $8,500	Up to $17,000
15%	From $8,501 to $34,500	$17,001 to $69,000
25%	$34,501 to $83,600	$69,001 to $139,350
28%	$83,601 to $174,400	$139,351 to $212,300
33%	$174,401 to $379,150	$212,301 to $379,150
35%	All over $379,150	All over $379,150

You can also deduct your business expenses from any state income tax you must pay. The average state income tax rate is about 6%, although seven states (Alaska, Florida, Nevada, South Dakota, Texas,

Washington, and Wyoming) don't have an income tax. You can find your state's tax rates at the Federation of Tax Administrators website at www.taxadmin.org.

State Income Tax Deductions May Differ

Generally, you may deduct the same business expenses for state tax purposes as you do for your federal taxes. However, there are some exceptions. You should contact your state tax agency for details. Every state tax agency has a website; you can find links to all of them at www.taxsites.com/state.

Self-Employment Taxes

Everyone who works—business owner and employee alike—is required to pay Social Security and Medicare taxes. Employees pay one-half of these taxes through payroll deductions; the employer must pony up the other half and send the entire payment to the IRS. Business owners must pay all of these taxes themselves. Business owners' Social Security and Medicare contributions are called self-employment taxes.

Ordinarily, self-employment taxes consist of a 12.4% Social Security tax on income up to an annual ceiling; however, for 2011, this amount has been reduced to 10.4%. In 2011, the annual Social Security ceiling was $106,800. Medicare taxes are not subject to any income ceiling and are levied at a 2.9% rate. For 2011, this combines to a total 13.3% tax on employment or self-employment income up to the Social Security tax ceiling. For all other years, the total tax is 15.3%.

However, the effective self-employment tax rate is lower because (1) you are allowed to deduct half of your self-employment taxes from your net income for income tax purposes and (2) you pay self-employment tax on only 92.35% of your net self-employment income.

Like income taxes, self-employment taxes are paid on the net profit you earn from a business. Thus, deductible business expenses reduce the amount of self-employment tax you have to pay by lowering your net profit. This makes business tax deductions doubly valuable.

Higher Medicare Taxes in 2013

Starting in 2013, Medicare taxes for high income taxpayers will go up by 0.9% to 3.8%. The increase applies to self-employed people with net self-employment income over $200,000. If the taxpayer is married and files a joint return, the increase kicks in at $250,000. Thus, for example, a single person with self-employment income of $300,000 would pay a 2.9% Medicare tax on the first $200,000 in income and 3.8% on the remaining $100,000.

Unlike the other self-employment taxes discussed above, you can't deduct the increased Medicare payments from your income taxes.

The increase applies to employees as well as to the self-employed. Employees will have to pay the entire increase out of their own pockets. Thus, employers will continue to pay a 1.45% Medicare tax on their employees' wages. Employees will continue to pay 1.45% until their wages reach the $200,000 or $250,000 ceiling. Then they will pay the additional 2.35%.

In addition, also starting in 2013, Medicare taxes will have to be paid by high income taxpayers on investment income as well as on wages and self-employment income. A 3.8% Medicare contributions tax will be imposed on the lesser of (1) the taxpayer's net investment income, or (2) any excess of modified adjusted gross income over $200,000 ($250,000 for married taxpayers filing jointly). Net investment income consists of gross income from interest, dividends, royalties, annuities, and rents not derived from an active trade or business.

Total Tax Savings

When you add up your savings in federal, state, and self-employment taxes, you can see the true value of a business tax deduction. For example, if you're in the 25% federal income tax bracket, a business deduction can be worth as much as 25% (in federal taxes) + 13.3% (in self-employment taxes) + 6% (in state taxes). That adds up to a whopping 44.3% savings. (If you itemize your personal deductions, your actual tax savings from a business deduction is a bit less because it reduces your state income tax and therefore reduces the federal income tax savings from this itemized deduction.) If you buy a $1,000 computer for your business and you deduct the expense, you save about $443 in taxes. In effect, the government is paying for almost half of your business expenses. This is why it's so important to know all of the business deductions to which you are entitled—and to take advantage of every one.

> **CAUTION**
>
> **Don't buy things just to get a tax deduction.** Although tax deductions can be worth a lot, it doesn't make sense to buy something you don't need just to get a deduction. After all, you still have to pay for the item, and the tax deduction you get in return will only cover a portion of the cost. If you buy a $1,000 computer, you'll probably be able to deduct less than half the cost. That means you're still out over $500—money you've spent for something you don't need. On the other hand, if you really do need a computer, the deduction you're entitled to is like found money—and it may help you buy a better computer than you could otherwise afford.

The Value of Common Tax Deductions
(Sole Proprietors Earning $25,000–$100,000 (2001))

The following table lists the 15 most common tax deductions, and the average amounts taken for each in 2001 by sole proprietor businesses with annual earnings of $25,000 to $100,000.

Expense	Average Amount	Income Tax Savings (25% bracket)	Self-Employment Tax Savings	Total Federal Tax Savings
1. Car and truck expenses	$6,100	$1,525	$933	$2,458
2. Utilities	$2,100	$525	$321	$856
3. Supplies (other than office supplies)	$3,000	$750	$459	$1,209
4. Office supplies	$1,300	$325	$199	$524
5. Legal and professional services	$700	$175	$107	$282
6. Insurance	$1,600	$400	$245	$645
7. Depreciation	$4,300	$1,075	$658	$1,733
8. Taxes	$1,000	$250	$153	$403
9. Meals and entertainment	$1,000	$250	$153	$403
10. Advertising	$1,600	$400	$245	$645
11. Repairs	$2,200	$530	$337	$867
12. Travel	$2,300	$575	$352	$927
13. Rent on business property	$6,400	$1,600	$979	$2,579
14. Home office	$3,000	$750	$459	$1,209
15. Rent on equipment and machinery	$3,100	$775	$474	$1,249

Source: *Information on Expenses Claimed by Sole Proprietorships,* Government Accountability Office (GAO-04-304; January 2004).

Is Your Home Business Really a Business?

Proving That You Are in Business..24

    Profit Test..27

    Behavior Test..29

Tax Consequences of Engaging in a Hobby.. 34

Investing and Other Income-Producing Activities...35

    Tax Consequences of Income-Producing Activities.. 36

    Types of Income-Producing Activities..38

    Trading in Stocks as a Business..39

    Real Estate as a Business...42

Y ou must operate a bona fide business (in the eyes of the IRS) to take business deductions. This point may seem obvious, but it has gotten more home businesspeople in trouble with the IRS than almost any other provision of the tax law. By declaring your home activity to be a hobby rather than a business, the IRS can, at one fell swoop, eliminate all of your tax deductions for the activity. Because hobbies are ordinarily carried on at home, home ventures are especially vulnerable to being viewed as hobbies by the IRS. That's why it's so important for you to be able to show the IRS that your home activity is a real business.

Proving That You Are in Business

For tax purposes, a business is an activity you regularly and continuously engage in primarily to earn a profit. You don't have to show a profit every year to qualify as a business. As long as your primary purpose is to make money, you should qualify as a business (even if you show a loss when you're first starting out, and even afterward, depending on the circumstances). Your business can be conducted from home, full-time or part-time, as long as you work at it regularly and continuously. And you can have more than one business at the same time. However, if your primary purpose is something other than making a profit—for example, to incur deductible expenses or just to have fun—the IRS may find that your activity is a hobby rather than a business. If this happens, you'll face some potentially disastrous tax consequences.

> EXAMPLE: Jorge and Vivian Lopez thought that they had found an ideal way to save on their income taxes (and enjoy themselves as well). They started an Amway distributorship as a sideline business. They ran the distributorship out of their home. While they had a lot of fun socializing with family and friends, they never came close to earning a profit. They claimed a loss from this business of over $18,000 a year for two straight years. They deducted this loss from Jorge's salary as a full-time petroleum engineer, which saved them thousands of dollars in

income taxes. Things were going great tax-wise, until the IRS audited the Lopezes' tax returns and concluded that the Amway distributorship was a hobby rather than a business. This meant the Lopezes could no longer deduct their Amway losses from Jorge's salary, and they owed the IRS over $17,000 in back taxes for the deductions they had already taken. (*Lopez v. Comm'r.*, TC Memo 2003-142.)

CAUTION

Beware of home business tax scams. Many self-proclaimed tax experts market tax avoidance scams on the Internet and elsewhere. According to the IRS, one of the top 12 tax scams involves setting up a phony business at home and then deducting personal expenses, such as rent or mortgage payments, as business expenses. This scam has been around for years and the IRS is well aware of it—which means you won't get away with it if you're audited. You'll have to pay back the value of any tax deductions you claimed, plus penalties.

Popular home business scams include processing medical insurance claims, online schemes, mail-order scams, envelope stuffing, assembling craft items or sewing, multilevel marketing distributorships, and chain letters. Be extremely skeptical about work-at-home promotions that claim you'll be able to reap substantial tax deductions without making a substantial monetary investment in your home business, working at it regularly, or turning a profit.

Your home-based activity can be a business for tax purposes only if you can show that you are engaged in it to earn a profit, not simply to have fun or pursue a personal interest. If you can't prove a profit motive for the activity, you will be considered a hobbyist and forced to enter tax hell.

The IRS has established two tests to determine whether someone has a profit motive. One is a simple mechanical test that looks at whether you have earned a profit in three of the last five years. The other is a more complex test designed to determine whether you act like you want to earn a profit.

Portrait of a Tax Scam Artist

Linda Borden ran a Florida-based income tax preparation service. According to the U.S. Justice Department, she promised her clients that they could legally pay zero taxes by using home business deductions. Claiming that she had found a "secret loophole" in the Internal Revenue Code, she told her customers that they could deduct personal expenses as business expenses by creating a fictitious home business. Among other things, she advised her customers (incorrectly) that:

- thinking about a business is the same as starting a business
- helping friends and relatives with their computer problems free of charge was a computer consulting business
- their "businesses" could pay $1,000 per month to them as rent for their homes and deduct the amount as a business expense
- they could characterize Thanksgiving and Christmas parties held at home as business "functions" and deduct the costs as business expenses, and
- they could deduct personal expenses such as haircuts, manicures, and cosmetics because a businessperson must look his or her best.

Borden charged her customers a $2,899 fee to prepare their tax returns. She had them provide a list of their personal assets and values. She then listed the value of these assets, including such items as dining room furniture and home entertainment equipment, as "office expenses" on IRS Schedule C. If necessary, she made up other expenses such as "advertising costs." When she was done, the losses on the customer's Schedule C roughly equaled his or her income from salary, investments, and other sources, so little or no tax was due.

Borden marketed her scheme through radio ads, the Internet, and recruiting seminars held in Florida, New Jersey, and Georgia. She had clients in 22 states. The Justice Department claimed that her tax preparation activities resulted in her customers underpaying their taxes by at least $15 million.

Eventually, the law caught up with Borden. In 2004, the Justice Department obtained an injunction (court order) permanently barring Borden from preparing federal income tax returns for others. She was also required to provide a list of her customers to the Justice Department. (*United States v. Borden*, Civil No. 6:03cv01705, M.D. Fla., April 26, 2004.)

> ⓘ **CAUTION**
>
> **Personal investing is not a business.** Personal investing, whether in stocks, real estate, collectibles, or anything else that makes money, is not a business, even though most people do it to earn a profit. See "Investing and Other Income-Producing Activities," later in this chapter.

Profit Test

If your venture earns a profit in three of five consecutive years, the IRS will presume that you have a profit motive. The IRS and courts look at your tax returns for each year you claim to be in business to see whether you turned a profit. Any legitimate profit—no matter how small—qualifies; you don't have to earn a particular amount or percentage. Careful year-end planning can help your business show a profit for the year. If clients owe you money, for example, you can press for payment before the end of the year. You can also put off paying expenses or buying new equipment until the new year.

Even if you meet the three-of-five test, the IRS can still try to claim that your activity is a hobby, but it will have to prove that you don't have a profit motive. In practice, the IRS usually doesn't attack ventures that pass the profit test unless the numbers have clearly been manipulated just to meet the standard.

The presumption that you are in business applies to your third profitable year and extends to all later years within the five-year period beginning with your first profitable year.

> **EXAMPLE:** Tom began to work as a self-employed graphic designer in 2008. Due to economic conditions and the difficulty of establishing a new business, his income varied dramatically from year to year. However, as the chart below shows, he managed to earn a profit in three of the first five years that he was in business.

Year	Losses	Profits
2008	$10,000	
2009		$5,500
2010	$6,000	
2011		$9,000
2012		$18,000

If the IRS audits Tom's taxes for 2012, it must presume that he was in business during that year because he earned a profit during three of the five consecutive years ending with 2012. The presumption that Tom is in business extends through 2014, five years after his first profitable year (2009).

The IRS doesn't have to wait for five years after you start your activity to decide whether it is a business or hobby—it can audit you and classify your venture as a business or hobby at any time. However, you can give yourself some breathing room by filing IRS Form 5213, *Election to Postpone Determination as to Whether the Presumption Applies That an Activity Is Engaged in for Profit*, which requires the IRS to postpone its determination until you've been in business for at least five years.

Although this may sound like a good idea, it can backfire. Filing the election alerts the IRS to the fact that you might be a good candidate to audit on the hobby loss issue after five years. It also adds two years to the statute of limitations—the period in which the IRS can audit you and assess a tax deficiency. For this reason, almost no one ever files Form 5213. Also, you can't wait five years and then file the election once you know that you will pass the profit test. You must make the election within three years after the due date for the tax return for the first year you were in business—that is, within three years after the first April 15 following your first business year. So if you started doing business in 2011, you would have to make the election by April 15, 2015 (three years after the April 15, 2012 due date for your 2011 tax return).

There is one situation in which it might make sense to file Form 5213. If the IRS has already told you that you will be audited, you may want to file the election to postpone the audit for two years. However, you can do this only if the IRS audit notice is sent to you within three years after the due date for your first business tax return. If you're notified after this time, it's too late to file the election. In addition, you must file your election within 60 days after you receive an IRS audit notice, whenever it is given, or you'll lose the right to make the election.

Behavior Test

If you keep incurring losses and can't satisfy the profit test, don't panic. Millions of business owners are in the same boat, whether they work at home or in outside offices. The sad fact is that many businesses don't earn profits every year or even for many years in a row, especially when they're first starting out. Indeed, over *four million* sole proprietors file a Schedule C tax form each year showing a loss from their business, yet the IRS does not categorize all of these ventures as hobbies.

You can continue to treat your activity as a business and fully deduct your losses, even if you have yet to earn a profit. However, you must take steps to demonstrate that your business isn't a hobby, in case you ever face an audit. You must be able to convince the IRS that earning a profit—not having fun or accumulating tax deductions—is your primary motive for doing what you do. This will require some time and effort on your part. It will be especially difficult if you're engaged in a home-based activity that could objectively be considered fun—such as creating artwork, antique collecting, photography, or writing—but it can be done. People who have incurred losses for seven, eight, or nine years in a row have been able to convince the IRS that they were running businesses.

How does the IRS figure out whether you really want to earn a profit? IRS auditors can't read your mind to establish your motives, and they certainly aren't going to take your word for it. Instead, they look at whether you behave as though you want to make money.

Factors the IRS Considers

The IRS looks at the following objective factors to determine whether you are behaving like a person who wants to earn a profit (and therefore, should be classified as a business). You don't have to satisfy all of these factors to pass the test—the first three listed below (acting like a business, expertise, and time and effort expended) are the most important by far. Studies demonstrate that taxpayers who meet these three factors are always found to be in business, regardless of how they do on the rest of the criteria. (See "How to Pass the Behavior Test," below, for tips on satisfying these factors.)

- **Whether you act like a business.** Among other things, acting like a business means you keep good books and other records and carry on your activities in a professional manner.
- **Your expertise.** People who are trying to make money usually have some knowledge and skill in the field of their endeavor.
- **The time and effort you spend.** People who want to make profits work regularly and continuously. You don't have to work full time, but you must work regularly.
- **Your track record.** Having a track record of success in other businesses—whether or not they are related to your current business—helps show that you are trying to make money in your most recent venture.
- **Your history of profit and losses.** Even if you can't satisfy the profit test described in "Profit Test," above, earning a profit in at least some years helps show that you have a profit motive. This is especially true if you're engaged in a business that tends to be cyclical—that is, where one or two good years are typically followed by one or more bad years.
- **Your profits.** Earning a substantial profit, even after years of losses, can help show that you are trying to make a go of it. On the other hand, earning only small or occasional yearly profits when you have years of large losses and/or a large investment in the activity tends to show that you aren't in it for the money.
- **Your business assets.** Your profit includes money you make through the appreciation (increase in value) of your business assets. Even if you don't make any profit from your business's day-to-day operations, you can still show a profit motive if you stand to earn substantial profits when you sell your assets. Of course, this rule applies only to ventures that purchase assets

that increase in value over time, such as land, collectibles, or buildings.

- **Your personal wealth.** The IRS figures that you probably have a profit motive if you don't have substantial income from other sources. After all, you'll need to earn money from your venture to survive. On the other hand, the IRS may be suspicious if you have substantial income from other sources (particularly if the losses from your venture generate substantial tax deductions).

- **The nature of your activity.** If your venture is inherently fun or recreational, the IRS may doubt that you are in it for the money. This means that you'll have a harder time convincing the IRS that you're in business if your venture involves activities such as art, crafts or sewing, photography, writing, antique or stamp collecting, or training and showing dogs or horses, for example. However, these activities can still be businesses, if you carry them on in a businesslike manner. Even if they don't qualify as businesses, they can still be classified as income-producing activities, which is better than being a hobby.

How to Pass the Behavior Test

Almost anyone with a home business can pass the behavior test, but it takes time, effort, and careful planning. Focus your efforts on the first three factors listed above. As noted earlier, a venture that can meet these three criteria will always be classified as a business. Here are some tips that will help you satisfy these crucial factors—and ultimately ace the behavior test.

Act Like a Businessperson

First and foremost, you must show that you carry on your activity in a businesslike manner. Doing the things outlined below will not only help you with the IRS, but will also help you actually earn a profit someday (or at least help you figure out that your business will not be profitable).

- **Keep good business records.** Keeping good records of your expenses and income from your activity is the single most important thing you can do to show that you want to earn a profit. Without good records, you'll never have an accurate idea of where you stand financially. Lack of records shows that you don't really care whether you make money or not—and it is almost always fatal in an IRS audit. You don't necessarily need an elaborate set of books; a simple record of your expenses and income will usually suffice. (See Chapter 15 for a detailed discussion of record keeping.)

EXAMPLE: A computer consultant who sold software on the side (at a loss) was found not to be profit motivated because he didn't keep adequate records. The tax court found that his failure to keep records meant that he was "unaware of the amount of revenue he could expect and had no concept of what his ultimate costs might be or how he might achieve any degree of cost efficiency." (*Flanagin v. Comm'r.*, TC Memo 1999-116.)

- **Keep a separate checking account.** Open up a separate checking account for your business. This will help you keep your personal and business expenses separate—another factor that shows you want to make money.
- **Create a business plan.** Draw up a business plan with a realistic profit and loss forecast—a projection of how much money your business will bring in, your expenses, and how much profit you expect to make. The forecast should cover the next five or ten years. It should show you earning a profit some time in the future (although it doesn't have to be within five years). Both the IRS and courts are usually impressed by good business plans.

RESOURCE

Need help drawing up a business plan? If you are really serious about making money, you will need a business plan. A business plan is useful not only to show the IRS that you are running a business, but also to convince others—such as lenders and investors—that they should support your venture financially. For detailed guidance on putting together a business plan, see *How to Write a Business Plan*, by Mike McKeever (Nolo).

- **Get business cards and letterhead.** It may seem like a minor matter, but obtaining business stationery and business cards shows that you think you are in business. Hobbyists ordinarily don't have such things. You can use software programs to create your own inexpensive stationery and cards.
- **Create a website.** Most businesses today have some sort of website that, at a minimum, provides contact information. Not having a website indicates you're not serious about being in business.
- **Obtain all necessary business licenses and permits.** Getting the required licenses and permits for your activities will show that you are acting like a business. For example, a home-based inventor who attempted to build a wind-powered ethanol generator in his backyard was found to be a hobbyist partly because he failed to get a permit to produce alcohol from the federal Bureau of Alcohol, Tobacco and Firearms.
- **Obtain a separate phone line for your home office.** Set up a separate phone line for your business (which may be a cell phone). This helps separate the personal from the professional and reinforces the idea that you're serious about making money.
- **Join professional organizations and associations.** Taking part in professional groups and organizations will help you make valuable contacts and obtain useful advice and expertise. This helps to show that you're motivated to earn a profit.

Expertise

If you're already an expert in your field, you're a step ahead of the game. But if you lack the necessary expertise, you can develop it by attending educational seminars and similar activities and/or consulting with other experts. Keep records of your efforts (for example, a certificate for completing a training course or your notes documenting your attendance at a seminar or convention).

Work Steadily

You don't have to work full time to show that you want to earn a profit. It's fine to hold a full-time job and work at your sideline business only part of the time. However, you must work regularly and continuously rather than sporadically. You may establish any schedule you want, as long as you work regularly. For example, you could work at your business an hour every day, or one day a week, as long as you stick to your schedule.

Although there is no minimum amount of time you must work, you'll have a hard time convincing the IRS that you want to make money if you work fewer than five or ten hours a week. Keep a log showing how much time you spend working. Your log doesn't have to be fancy—you can just mark down your hours and a summary of your activities each day on your calendar or appointment book.

Tax Consequences of Engaging in a Hobby

A hobby is something you do primarily for a purpose other than to make a profit—for example, to have fun, learn something, help your community, or impress your neighbors. Almost anything can be a hobby; common examples include creating artwork or crafts, photography, writing, or collecting coins, stamps, or other objects.

You do not want what you consider business activities to be deemed a hobby by the IRS. Because hobbies are not businesses, hobbyists cannot take the tax deductions to which businesspeople are entitled. Instead, hobbyists can deduct their hobby-related expenses only from the income the hobby generates. If you have no income from the hobby, you get no deduction. And you can't carry over the deductions to use in future years when you earn income—you lose them forever.

> **EXAMPLE:** Charles collects antiques from his home. This year, he spent $10,000 buying antiques and earned no income from the activity. The IRS determines that this activity is a hobby. As a result, his $10,000 in expenses can be deducted only from any income he earned from his hobby. Because he earned no money from antique collecting during the year, he can't deduct any of these expenses this year—and he can't carry over the deduction to any future years.

Even if you have income from your hobby, you must deduct your expenses in a way that is less advantageous (and more complicated) than regular business deductions. Hobby expenses are deductible only as a Miscellaneous Itemized Deduction on IRS Schedule A, *Itemized Deductions* (the form that you file with your Form 1040 to itemize your deductions). This means that you can deduct your hobby expenses only if you itemize your deductions instead of taking the standard deduction. You can itemize deductions only if your total deductions are greater than the standard deduction—in 2011, the standard deduction was $5,800 for single people and $11,600 for married people filing jointly. If you do itemize, your hobby expenses can be used to offset your hobby income—but only to the extent that your expenses plus your other miscellaneous itemized deductions exceed 2% of your adjusted gross income (your total income minus business expenses and a few other deductions).

> **EXAMPLE:** Assume that Charles, a single taxpayer, earned $5,000 from his antique collecting hobby this year, and had $10,000 in expenses. He could deduct $5,000 of these expenses—the amount equal to his antique collecting income—as an itemized deduction. However, Charles can only deduct those expenses that, together with his other miscellaneous itemized deductions, exceed 2% of Charles's adjusted gross income (AGI) for the year. If Charles's AGI was $100,000 and he had no other miscellaneous itemized deductions, he could not deduct the first $2,000 in expenses (2% × $100,000 = $2,000). So Charles can deduct only $3,000 of his antique collecting expenses on his Schedule A.

You don't need to understand all of this in great detail. Just be aware that an IRS finding that your activities are a hobby will probably result in tax disaster if you claimed business deductions for your expenses.

Investing and Other Income-Producing Activities

You can earn money without being in business. Many people do this all the time (or try to) by engaging in personal investing—for example, by having personal bank accounts that pay interest or investing in stocks that pay dividends and appreciate in value over time (hopefully). Activities like these—that are pursued primarily for profit but aren't businesses—are called income-producing activities. They are neither businesses nor hobbies, and receive their own special income tax treatment.

Many of the moneymaking activities people engage in at home are income-producing activities, not businesses. The distinction is crucial because income-producing activities generally receive less favorable tax treatment than businesses. Thus, you'll want to avoid this classification, if possible.

Tax Consequences of Income-Producing Activities

You are entitled to deduct the ordinary and necessary expenses you incur to produce income, or to manage property held for the production of income—for example, real estate rentals. (I.R.C. § 212.) These include many of the same expenses that businesspeople are allowed (many are covered in later chapters). For example, a person with a real estate rental may deduct maintenance and repair costs, and an investor in the stock market may deduct fees for investment advice or accounting services.

However, there are some crucial limitations on deductions for income-producing activities (these restrictions do not apply to businesses):

- **No home office deduction.** You can't take a home office deduction for an income-producing activity. This important deduction is available only for businesses conducted from home. Obviously, this is a significant benefit to having your venture classified as a business.
- **No Section 179 expensing.** In addition, taxpayers involved in income-producing activities may not take advantage of Section 179, the tax code provision that allows businesspeople to deduct a substantial amount of long-term asset purchases in a single year—$500,000 for 2010 and 2011, scheduled to go down to $125,000 in 2012. (See Chapter 5 for more on Section 179.)

- **No seminar or convention deductions.** People with income-producing activities can't deduct their expenses for attending conventions, seminars, or similar events. Thus, for example, you can't deduct the cost of attending a stock market investment seminar.

- **Limit on deducting investment interest.** Interest on money you borrow to use for a business is fully deductible (see "Interest on Business Loans" in Chapter 14). However, interest paid on money borrowed to make an investment is deductible only up to the amount of income you earn from the investment. If you earn no income from the investment, you get no deduction.

- **No deduction for start-up expenses.** Most of the expenses you incur in starting up a business are deductible (see Chapter 3). You get no deduction at all for expenses incurred to start up an income-producing activity.

- **Limit on deductions.** If, in the course of an income-producing activity, you incur expenses to produce rents or royalties, you can deduct these expenses directly from your gross income (just like business expenses). What are rents and royalties? Rent is what you earn from renting real estate. Thus, landlords who don't qualify as businesspeople may still fully deduct their expenses. Royalties are income from things like copyrights or patents, or mineral leases.

  However, expenses incurred from any other income-producing activity—for example, investing—are miscellaneous itemized deductions. As such, they are deductible only to the extent they exceed 2% of your adjusted gross income—the same standard used for hobbies. If all your itemized deductions don't exceed the standard deductions, you can't itemize and you get no deduction at all. This is perhaps the unkindest cut of all.

- **Only individuals can deduct expenses from income-producing activities.** Corporations, partnerships, and limited liability companies cannot deduct these expenses.

- **No self-employment tax.** One good tax effect of having an income-producing activity is that you don't have to pay any self-employment tax on your income from the activity. Only people in business have to pay self-employment taxes. This is a substantial savings, because the self-employment tax is 13.3% (2011) of your net self-employment income, up to an annual ceiling amount.

When you have an income-producing activity, you don't file an IRS Schedule C, *Profit or Loss From Business*, with your tax return. You don't have a business, so that schedule doesn't apply. Instead, you list your expenses on Schedule A, *Itemized Deductions*. However, if your income comes from real estate or royalties, you list it and your expenses on Schedule E, *Supplemental Income and Loss*. Investors who incur capital gains or losses must file Schedule D, *Capital Gains and Losses*.

RESOURCE
Need more information on investment deductions? For detailed guidance on tax deductions for investments, refer to IRS Publication 550, *Investment Income and Expenses*. Like all IRS publications, you can download it from the IRS website at www.irs.gov, or obtain it by calling the IRS at 800-829-3676.

Types of Income-Producing Activities

Anything you do primarily to earn a profit is an income-producing activity, unless it constitutes a business. You determine whether an activity is done primarily for profit by applying the three-of-five-year profit test or the behavioral test discussed in "Proving That You Are in Business," above—the same tests used for businesses.

Personal Investing

Personal investing is by far the most common income-producing activity. Investing means making money in ways other than running a business—for example:
- you put your money in a bank and earn interest
- you buy stocks, bonds, or other securities in publicly traded corporations and earn money from dividends or from the securities' appreciation in value over time

- you buy commodities like gold or pork bellies and earn money from their appreciation in value over time
- you buy real estate and earn money from rents or from appreciation in the property's value over time, or
- you purchase an interest in a privately owned business run by someone else and earn money from the increase in the business's value over time or payments from the business.

What all these activities have in common is that you are not engaged in the active, continuous, and regular management or control of a business. You are passive—you put your money in somebody else's business and hope your investment will increase in value due to their efforts, not yours. Or, you buy an item like gold, and then sit and wait for it to increase in value.

Personal investing is always an income-producing activity for tax purposes, not a business. It makes no difference whether you invest from home or an outside office. Thus, for example, you can't take a home office deduction when you direct your investments from a home office.

Other Activities

Investing is by far the most common and important income-producing activity, but it is by no means the only one. Almost any activity can qualify if your primary motive for engaging in it is making money, but you don't work at it enough for it to rise to the level of a business. You must work continuously and regularly at an activity for it to be a business.

Trading in Stocks as a Business

People who buy stocks, bonds, and other securities as personal investments are not in business for tax purposes. But professional securities dealers and traders in securities are in business because they are not investors.

Such people are not subject to the restrictions on deductions listed in "Tax Consequences of Income-Producing Activities," above. Thus, for example, a professional stock trader may take a home office deduction (provided, of course, that the other requirements for the deduction are met; see Chapter 6). Professional dealers and traders may not deduct the commissions they pay to buy stocks or other securities; these are added to the basis (value) of the securities for purposes of calculating gain or loss when they are sold. Traders who are sole proprietors list their expenses on Schedule C, *Profit or Loss From Business*. However, they list their income or loss from trading on Schedule D, *Capital Gains and Losses*.

Securities Dealers

A securities dealer is someone who maintains an inventory of stocks, bonds, or other securities and offers them for sale to buyers. Dealers make their money from the fees they charge buyers, not from dividends or appreciation in the value of the securities. Dealers include stock brokers and people who buy and sell securities on the floors of stock exchanges. If you're a dealer in securities, you undoubtedly already know it.

Professional Stock Traders

Most people who buy and sell stocks and other securities do it as an investment. Professional stock traders do it as a business. What's the difference between a stock market investor and a professional trader? A trader's profits come from the *very act of trading*; an investor's come from dividends or from the increase in value of his or her holdings over time. The IRS says that to qualify as a professional trader, you must meet these requirements:

- you must seek to profit from daily market movements in the price of securities, not from dividends, interest, or capital appreciation
- your trading must be substantial, and
- your trading must be continuous and regular.

Key factors the IRS examines are:

- **How long you hold your securities before you sell them.** Professional traders usually don't hold on to most stocks for long, often selling them the same day they buy them. You don't have to be a day trader to be in business. But if you have a "buy and hold" portfolio, you are not a professional trader. Indeed, you're probably in trouble if you hold on to your stocks for more than two or three months on average.

- **How often you trade.** Professionals trade frequently. Many accountants use the rule of thumb that a professional investor must execute at least ten trades a day, five days a week; this adds up to at least 3,000 trades a year. However, people who do fewer trades a year may still qualify as professional investors.

- **Whether you pursue trading to earn a living.** Professionals usually trade to make a living (though they may have other sources of income).

- **How much time you devote to trading.** Professional traders spend a lot of time trading, though not necessarily all of their time. Another accountant's rule of thumb is that a professional trader must trade at least five hours a day, five days a week. Moreover, you must trade continuously throughout the year. Thus, for example, a person who did 303 stock trades during February, March, and April, but almost none the rest of the year, did not qualify as a professional stock trader. (*Chen v. Comm'r.*, TC Memo 2004-132.)

Before the advent of the Internet, few people could afford to engage in the frequent trading required to be a professional trader because the commissions and other transaction costs were too great. Today, however, with inexpensive online trading, millions of people are making frequent stock trades from their homes. However, simply calling yourself a day trader will not make you a businessperson. You must meet the criteria listed above.

Note that being an investor or a professional trader is not an either/or proposition. You can be both. That is, you can hold on to some stocks as personal investments, while you actively trade others as your business. If you do this, be sure to keep the two categories separate.

Any Type of Buying and Selling Can Be a Business

Buying and selling anything can be a business—it doesn't have to involve stock or other securities. If you earn your money from the activity of buying and selling and you engage in it regularly and continuously, you can qualify as a business. For example, thousands of people now have businesses buying and selling items on eBay. However, sporadic buying and selling is not a business, even though it is profitable—for example, occasionally selling items on eBay won't qualify as a business.

Real Estate as a Business

Another way people commonly earn money without running a business is by investing in real estate. However, real estate can also qualify as a business if you are actively and regularly involved.

Real Estate Dealers

A real estate dealer is anyone who holds property primarily for sale to customers, such as builders or developers. Numerous and frequent sales over an extended time period are the hallmark of a dealer who is engaged in a business, not an income-producing activity.

Being classified as a dealer is often a tax disadvantage because gains from sales of real property by a dealer are usually subject to ordinary income tax rates. In contrast, gains realized by an investor are usually taxed at capital gains rates, which are lower. However, dealers are better off if real estate proves to be a money-losing proposition: A dealer is typically permitted to deduct the full amount of a loss, while an investor's deductions for losses may be strictly limited.

Managing Rental Property

You don't have to be a big shot developer to be in the business of real estate. You can also run a business actively managing rental real estate. But the key word here is active. You can't just sit back and collect rent checks while someone else does all the work of being a landlord. You, or an employee or agent who works on your behalf, must be actively involved on a regular, systematic, and continuous basis.

> **EXAMPLE 1:** Carolyn Anderson, a nurse, owned an 80-acre farm that she rented to a tenant farmer. She attempted to deduct her home office expenses by claiming that the rental activity was a business. The IRS and tax court disagreed because Carolyn's landlord activities involved little more than depositing rent checks and occasionally talking to her tenant on the telephone. (*Anderson v. Comm'r.*, TC Memo 1982-0576.)

> **EXAMPLE 2:** Edwin Curphey, a dermatologist, owned six rental properties in Hawaii. He converted a bedroom in his home into an office for his real estate activities. Curphey personally managed his rentals, which included seeking new tenants, supplying furnishings, and cleaning and otherwise preparing the units for new tenants. The court held that these activities were sufficiently systematic and continuous to place him in the business of real estate rental. As a result, Curphey was entitled to a home office deduction. (*Curphey v. Comm'r.*, 73 TC 766 (1980).)

If managing real estate is a business, you ordinarily don't file Schedule C, *Profit or Loss From Business,* to report your income and expenses. Instead, you file Schedule E, *Supplemental Income and Loss.* However, you must file Schedule C if you run a hotel, motel, or apartment building where you provide hotel-type services to the occupants (such as maid services).

RESOURCE

Need more help with real estate taxation? Taxation of activities relating to real estate is a complex subject that is beyond the scope of this book. For a detailed guide to tax deductions for residential landlords, refer to *Every Landlord's Tax Deduction Guide,* by Stephen Fishman (Nolo).

Getting Your Business Up and Running

What Are Start-Up Expenses?.. 46

    Common Start-Up Expenses 47

    Special Rules for Some Expenses 48

    Buying an Existing Business 50

    Expanding an Existing Business..50

When Does a Business Begin? 51

    Home Manufacturers...51

    Knowledge Workers...51

    Service Providers 52

    Existing Businesses 53

Claiming the Deduction...53

If Your Business Doesn't Last 15 Years..53

Expenses for Businesses That Never Begin..55

    General Start-Up Costs...55

    Costs to Start or Acquire a Specific Business.. 56

Avoiding the Start-Up Tax Rule's Bite 56

E veryone knows that it costs money to get a new business up and running. But many people don't know that these costs—called start-up expenses—are subject to special tax rules. This chapter explains what types of costs are start-up expenses and how you can deduct them as quickly as possible.

What Are Start-Up Expenses?

To take business deductions, you must actually be running a business (see Chapter 2). This commonsense rule can lead to problems if you want to start (or buy) a new business. The money you spend to get your business up and running is not a currently deductible business operating expense because your business hasn't yet begun.

Instead, business start-up expenses are capital expenses—costs that you incur to acquire an asset (a business) that will benefit you for more than one year. Normally, you can't deduct these types of expenses until you sell or otherwise dispose of the business. However, a special tax rule allows you to deduct up to $5,000 in start-up expenses the first year you are in business, and then deduct the remainder, if any, in equal amounts over the next 15 years. (I.R.C. § 195.) Without this special rule for start-up expenses, these costs (capital expenses) would not be deductible until you sold or otherwise disposed of your business.

Once your business begins, the same expenses that were start-up expenses before your business began become currently deductible business operating expenses. For example, supplies you purchase *after* your home business starts are currently deductible operating expenses, but supplies you buy *before* your business begins are start-up expenses.

> EXAMPLE: Diana Drudge is sick of her office job. She decides to start a business as a home-based independent travel agent. Before her business begins, she spends $20,000 of her life savings on advertising. Her business finally starts on July 1, 2011. Because advertising is a start-up expense, she can't deduct the full cost in her first year of business—instead, she can deduct $5,000 of the

expenses the first year she's in business and the remaining $15,000 in equal installments over 15 years (assuming she's in business that long).

This means she may deduct $1,000 of the remaining $15,000 for each full year she's in business, starting with the first year. However, Diana's business is open for only six months her first year, so she may deduct only $500 of the $15,000 that year, plus the initial $5,000 she's entitled to. Her total first year total deduction is $5,500.

Obviously, you want to spend no more than the first-year ceiling on start-up expenses so you don't have to wait 15 years to get all your money back. There are ways you can avoid spending more than the first-year threshold amount. These are described in "Avoiding the Start-Up Tax Rule's Bite," at the end of this chapter.

> **CAUTION**
>
> **Your business must actually start to have start-up expenses.** If your business never gets started, many of your expenses will not be deductible. So think carefully before spending your hard-earned money to investigate starting a new business venture (see "Avoiding the Start-Up Tax Rule's Bite," at the end of this chapter).

Common Start-Up Expenses

The vast majority of home business owners (87%, according to a Small Business Administration study) start new businesses rather than buying an existing venture. Most of the costs of investigating whether, where, and how to start a new business, as well as the cost of actually creating it, qualify as business start-up expenses.

Here are some common types of deductible start-up expenses:

- operating expenses incurred before the business begins, such as home office rent, telephone service, utilities, office supplies, equipment rental, and repairs

- the cost of investigating what it would take to create a successful business, including research on potential markets or products
- advertising costs, including advertising for your business opening
- costs for employee training before the business opens
- expenses related to obtaining financing, suppliers, customers, or distributors
- licenses, permits, and other fees, and
- fees paid to lawyers, accountants, consultants, and others for professional services.

Special Rules for Some Expenses

There are some costs related to opening a business that are not considered start-up expenses. Many of these costs are still deductible, but different rules and restrictions apply to the way they are deducted.

Expenses That Wouldn't Qualify as Business Operating Expenses

You get no deduction at all for preopening operating expenses that are not ordinary, necessary, directly related to the business, and reasonable in amount. (See Chapter 4 for a discussion of business operating expenses.) For example, you can't deduct the cost of pleasure travel or entertainment *unrelated* to your business. These expenses would not be deductible as operating expenses by an ongoing business, so you can't deduct them as start-up expenses either.

Inventory

The largest expense many home businesspeople incur before they start their business is for inventory—that is, buying the goods (or the materials to make them) that they will sell to customers. For example, if you decide to start an eBay business selling items you buy at flea markets, you would treat the items you purchase for resale as inventory. (See Chapter 10 for more on deducting inventory costs.)

Long-Term Assets

Long-term assets are things you purchase for your business that will last for more than one year, such as computers, office equipment, cars, and machinery. Long-term assets you buy before your business begins are not considered part of your start-up costs. Instead, you must treat these purchases like any other long-term asset you buy *after* your business begins—you must either depreciate the item over several years or deduct the cost in one year under Section 179. (Chapter 5 explains how to deduct long-term assets.) However, you can't take depreciation or Section 179 deductions until after your business begins.

Research and Development Costs

The tax law includes a special category for research and development expenses. These are costs a business incurs to discover something new (in the laboratory or experimental sense), such as a new invention, formula, prototype, or process. They include laboratory and computer supplies, salaries, rent, utilities, other overhead expenses, and equipment rental, but not the cost of purchasing long-term assets. Research and development costs are currently deductible under Section 174 of the Internal Revenue Code, even if you incur them before the business begins operations. This tax rule is a particular benefit to home-based inventors.

Organizational Costs

Costs you incur to form a partnership, limited liability company, or corporation are technically not part of your start-up costs. However, the rule for deducting these costs is the same as for start-up expenses. (I.R.C. § 248.)

Buying an Existing Business

Different (and harsher) rules apply if you buy an existing business rather than creating a new one. The money you pay to actually purchase the existing business is not deductible. Instead, it is a capital expense that becomes part of the tax basis of your business. If and when you sell the business, you will be able to deduct this amount from any profit you make on the sale before taxes are assessed. The expenses you incur to decide *whether* to purchase a business and *which* business you should buy are start-up expenses. Few home business owners (only 13%, according to the Small Business Administration) buy existing businesses, so this rule probably won't apply to you.

What's Tax Basis?

Tax basis is accounting lingo for your investment in property for tax purposes. Generally, your tax basis is the amount you paid for the property plus the costs of any improvements you make to it. You need to know your basis to figure your gain or loss on a sale, whether you sell a single item of property or an entire business. Chapter 5 explains how to figure out your tax basis.

Expanding an Existing Business

What if you already have a home business and decide to expand your operation? The cost of expanding an existing business is considered a business operating expense, not a start-up expense. As long as these costs are ordinary and necessary, they are currently deductible. However, this rule applies only when the expansion involves a business that is the same as—or similar to—the existing business. The costs of expanding into a new business are start-up costs, not operating expenses.

When Does a Business Begin?

The date when your home business begins for tax purposes marks an important turning point. Operating expenses you incur after your business starts are currently deductible, while expenses you incur before this crucial date may have to be deducted over many years.

A new business begins for tax purposes when it starts to function as a going concern and performs the activities for which it was organized. (*Richmond Television Corp. v. U.S.*, 345 F.2d 901 (4th Cir. 1965).) The IRS says that a venture becomes a going concern when it acquires all of the assets necessary to perform its intended functions and puts those assets to work. In other words, your business begins when you start doing business, whether or not you are actually earning any money.

This is usually not a difficult test to apply. Here are the rules for some common types of home businesses.

Home Manufacturers

A manufacturing or other business that produces goods begins when it starts using its assets to make saleable products. The products don't have to be completed, nor do sales have to be solicited or made. For example, a home crafts business begins when materials and equipment are acquired and work is begun on the crafts. If it takes several days to create a completed craft item (and to find someone willing to buy it), that doesn't matter—the business begins when the process of creating the crafts starts.

Knowledge Workers

Writers, artists, photographers, graphic designers, computer programmers, and similar knowledge workers might not think of themselves as manufacturers, but the courts do. For example, courts have held that a home-based writer's business begins when he or she starts working on a writing project. (*Gestrich v. Comm'r.*, 74 TC 525 (1982).) Just like a manufacturing business, a writer's business begins when the necessary materials are in place and the work starts—not when the work is finished or sold. Similarly, an inventor's business begins when he or she starts working on an invention in earnest, not when the invention is completed, patented, or sold.

Proving When Your Business Begins

Your business begins when you make your services available to the public (or are ready to sell and/or produce a product). There are many ways you can do this. Being able to show the IRS a copy of an advertisement or website for your business is a great way to prove you were open for business. You can also mail out brochures or other promotional materials. If you don't want to pay for postage, you can leave them on your neighbors' doors or car windshields.

You don't have to advertise to show you are open for business—simply handing out business cards is sufficient. Have cards made up and start giving them out. Give your first cards to friends and associates who could testify for you if you're audited by the IRS.

Establish your home office to show you are ready to take on clients or customers. Take a photo of it with a digital camera (which will be date stamped).

If you're selling a product, you can start with a small inventory. Keep invoices and other documents showing the date you purchased the inventory. Photograph your equipment and inventory with your digital camera.

If you are making a product at home, your business begins when you have all the equipment and materials ready to start production. Keep invoices and other documents showing when you obtained these items.

Service Providers

If your business involves providing a service to customers or clients—for example, accounting, consulting, financial planning, or law—your business begins when you first offer your services to the public. No one has to hire you; you just have to be available for hire. For example, a consultant's business begins when he or she is available for hire by clients.

Existing Businesses

If you buy an existing business, your business is deemed to begin for tax purposes when the purchase is complete—that is, when you take over ownership.

Claiming the Deduction

If you have more than $50,000 of start-up expenses in one year, you are not entitled to the full first-year deduction. You must reduce your first-year $5,000 deduction by the amount that your start-up expenditures exceed the $50,000 threshold amount. For example, if you have $53,000 in start-up expenses, you may only deduct $2,000 the first year, instead of $5,000. If you have $55,000 or more in start-up expenses, you get no current deduction for start-up expenses. Instead, you must deduct the entire amount over the first 180 months (15 years) you're in business. This process is called amortization. One hundred and eighty months is the minimum amortization period; you can choose a longer period if you wish (almost no one does).

You used to have to attach a separate written statement to your tax return electing to claim start-up expenses as a current deduction. This is no longer required. Instead, you are automatically deemed to have made the election for the year in which your business began. All you must do is list your start-up costs as "Other expenses" on your Schedule C (or other appropriate return if you are not a sole proprietor). You don't have to specifically identify the deducted amounts as start-up expenditures for the election to be effective.

One reason for this change is that you can't include a separate written statement with an electronically filed return, and the IRS is trying to encourage electronic filing.

If Your Business Doesn't Last 15 Years

Not all home businesses last for 15 years. In fact, most small businesses don't last this long. If you had more than $5,000 in start-up expenses and are in the process of deducting the excess amount, you don't lose the value of your deductions if you sell or close your business before you have had a chance to deduct all of your start-up expenses. You can deduct any leftover start-up expenses as ordinary business losses. (I.R.C. § 195(b)(2).) This means that you may be able to deduct these losses from any income you have that year, deduct them in future years, or deduct them from previous years' taxes.

If you sell your business or its assets, your leftover start-up costs will be added to your tax basis in the business. This is just as good as getting a tax deduction. If you sell your business at a profit, you can subtract the remaining start-up costs from your profits before taxes are assessed, which reduces your taxable gain. If you sell at a loss, you can add the start-up costs to the money you lost—because this shortfall is deductible, a larger loss means a larger deduction, and therefore lower taxes.

If you simply go out of business with no assets to sell, you can deduct your leftover start-up expenses as ordinary business losses. This means that you can deduct them from any income you have that year, deduct them in future years, or deduct them from previous years' taxes.

Keep Good Expense Records

Whether you intend to start a new business or buy an existing one, you should keep careful track of every expense you incur before the business begins. Obviously, you should keep receipts and canceled checks. You should also keep evidence that will help show that the money went to investigate a new business—for example, correspondence and emails with accountants, attorneys, and consultants; marketing or financial reports; and copies of advertisements. You will need these records to calculate your deductions and to prove your expenses to the IRS if you face an audit.

Expenses for Businesses That Never Begin

Many people investigate starting a home business, but the venture never gets off the ground. While this is no doubt disappointing, you might be able to recoup some of your expenses in the form of tax deductions.

General Start-Up Costs

General start-up costs are expenses you incur *before* you decide to start a new business or acquire a specific existing business. They include all of the costs of doing a general search for, or preliminary investigation of, a business—for example, costs you incur analyzing potential markets. If you never start the business, these costs are personal and not deductible. In other words, they are a dead loss.

> EXAMPLE: Bruno would like to start his own home business as a fashion designer. He buys several books on fashion, attends a fashion design course, and travels to New York City, where he stays several nights in a hotel, to speak to people in the fashion industry. However, he ultimately decides to keep his day job. None of the expenses he incurred in investigating the fashion design business idea are deductible.

One intended effect of this rule is that you can't deduct travel, entertainment, or other "fun" expenses by claiming that you incurred them to investigate a business *unless you actually start the business.* Otherwise, it would be pretty tough for the IRS to figure out whether you were really considering a new venture or just having a good time.

> EXAMPLE: Kim spends $5,000 on a two-week Hawaii vacation. While there, she attends a one-hour seminar on how to make money by stuffing envelopes at home. However, she never starts the business. The cost of her trip is not a start-up expense.

> **TIP**
>
> **Corporations can deduct general start-up costs.** A corporation can deduct general start-up expenses as a business loss, even if the business never gets going.

Costs to Start or Acquire a Specific Business

The expenses you incur to actually start or acquire a particular business (that ultimately never begins operations) are not deductible as start-up expenses. Expenses such as accounting and legal fees may be deducted as investment expenses, which are generally deductible only as itemized miscellaneous deductions (I.R.C. § 165; see Chapter 2 for more information on deducting investment expenses). Costs incurred to acquire a specific asset for your future business—for example, equipment—are capital expenses. You get no direct tax deduction for these costs, but you may recover them when you sell or otherwise dispose of the asset.

Avoiding the Start-Up Tax Rule's Bite

You will be adversely affected by the start-up tax rule only if you spend more than $5,000 on start-up costs before your business begins. If you spend less, you can deduct all your start-up expenses during the first year you are in business. You will need to keep track of what you spend and, if you get near the threshold amount, cut back on your spending until your business begins. If you are at or near the threshold and need to keep spending, you could try to postpone paying for an item until after your business begins. Deductible start-up costs always qualify as currently deductible business operating expenses once a business begins. Postponing payment will only work, though, if you're a cash basis taxpayer—someone who reports income and expenses on the date they are actually paid, not on the date when an agreement to pay is made.

If you need to spend more than $5,000, go ahead and do it—you will still be able to deduct those expenses. You'll just have to deduct them over 15 years instead of one. Try to keep your total start-up expenses below $50,000 though. If you go above the limit, your first-year deduction will be reduced by the amount you exceed the limit.

Home Business Operating Expenses

Requirements for Deducting Operating Expenses 60

Ordinary and Necessary 60

Current Expense 63

Business Related 64

Reasonable in Amount 68

Operating Expenses That Are Not Deductible 68

How to Report Operating Expense Deductions 69

This chapter covers the basic rules for deducting business operating expenses—the bread and butter expenses virtually every home business incurs for things like home office expenses, supplies, and business-related travel. If you don't maintain an inventory or buy expensive equipment, these day-to-day costs will probably be your largest category of business expenses (and your largest source of deductions).

Requirements for Deducting Operating Expenses

There are so many different kinds of business operating expenses that the tax code couldn't possibly list them all. Instead, if you want to deduct an item as a business operating expense, you must make sure the expenditure meets certain requirements. If it does, it will qualify as a deductible business operating expense. To qualify, the expense must be:

- ordinary and necessary
- current
- directly related to your business, and
- reasonable in amount. (I.R.C. § 162.)

Ordinary and Necessary

The first requirement is that the expense must be ordinary and necessary. This means that the cost is common and "helpful and appropriate" for your business. (*Welch v. Helvering*, 290 U.S. 111 (1933).) The expense doesn't have to be indispensable to be necessary; it needs only to help your business in some way—even if it's minor. A one-time expenditure can be ordinary and necessary.

> EXAMPLE: Bill, a home-based marketing consultant, hires a freelance researcher for two weeks to help him write a marketing report for a client. Hiring such assistance is a common and accepted practice among consultants. The researcher's fee is deductible as an ordinary and necessary expense for Bill's business.

It's usually fairly easy to figure out whether an expense passes the ordinary and necessary test. Some of the most common types of operating expenses include:

- home office expenses
- equipment rental
- legal and accounting fees
- car and truck expenses
- travel expenses
- meal and entertainment expenses
- supplies and materials
- business websites
- publications
- subscriptions
- repair and maintenance expenses
- business taxes
- interest on business loans
- licenses
- banking fees
- advertising costs
- business-related education expenses
- postage
- professional association dues
- business liability and property insurance
- payments to independent contractors, and
- software used for business.

Generally, the IRS won't second-guess your claim that an expense is ordinary and necessary, unless the item or service clearly has no legitimate business purpose.

> **EXAMPLE:** An insurance agent claimed a business deduction for part of his handgun collection because he had to go to "unsafe job sites" to settle insurance claims, and there was an unsolved murder in his neighborhood. The tax court disallowed the deduction explaining, "A handgun simply does not qualify as an ordinary and necessary business expense for an insurance agent, even a bold and brave Wyatt Earp type with a fast draw who is willing to risk injury or death in the service of his clients." (*Samp v. Comm'r.*, TC Memo 1981-1986.)

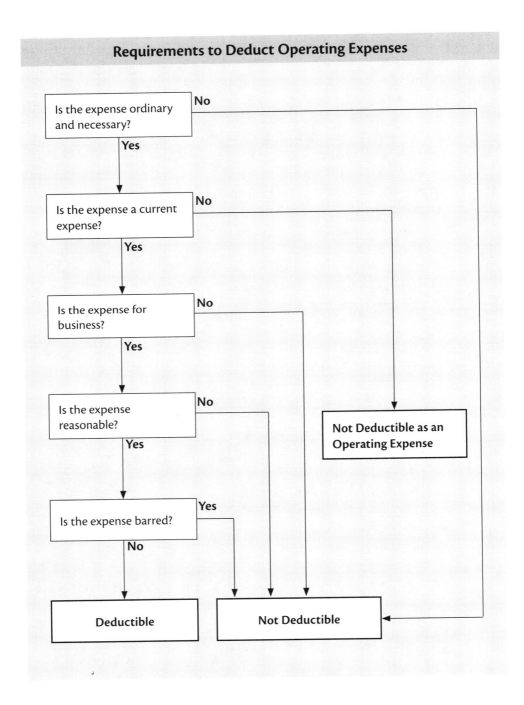

Requirements to Deduct Operating Expenses

The chart below lists the 15 most common operating expenses claimed by sole proprietor business owners who earned $25,000 to $100,000 that year.

15 Most Common Operating Expenses for Small Businesses	
Expense	Percentage of Business Owners Who Claimed the Expense
1. Car and truck expenses	81%
2. Utilities	68%
3. Supplies (other than office supplies)	60%
4. Office supplies	60%
5. Legal and professional services	60%
6. Insurance	54%
7. Taxes	51%
8. Meals and entertainment	47%
9. Advertising	43%
10. Repairs	40%
11. Travel	31%
12. Rent on business property	26%
13. Home office	21%
14. Rent on equipment and machinery	21%
15. Interest	18%

Source: *Information on Expenses Claimed by Small Business Sole Proprietorships,* General Accounting Office (GAO-04-304; January 2004).

Current Expense

Only current expenses are deductible as business operating expenses. Current expenses are for items that will benefit your business for less than one year. These are the costs of keeping your business going on a day-to-day basis, including money you spend on items or services that get used up, wear out, or become obsolete in less than one year. A good example of a current expense is your business's monthly phone bill, which benefits your business for one month. In contrast, buying a telephone for your business would be a capital expense (not a current expense) because the phone will benefit your business for more than one year. Other common capital expenses include cars, business equipment, computers, and real estate. (For more on deducting capital expenses, see Chapter 5.)

Current expenses are currently deductible—that is, they are fully deductible in the year when you incur them. Because all business operating expenses are current expenses, they are also all currently deductible. However, your total annual deduction for some operating expenses (notably home office costs) cannot exceed the profits you earn from the business in that year. (See Chapter 6 for more on the home office deduction.)

Business Related

An expenditure must be *directly related to your business* to be deductible as a business operating expense. This means that you cannot deduct personal expenses. For example, the cost of a personal computer is a deductible operating expense only if you use the computer for business purposes; it is not deductible if you use it to pay personal bills or play computer games. If you buy something for both personal and business use, you can deduct only the business portion of the expense. For example, if you buy a cellular phone and use it half of the time for business calls and half of the time for personal calls, you can deduct only half of the cost of the phone as a business expense.

A business expense for one person can be a personal expense for another, and vice versa. For example, a professional screenwriter could probably deduct the cost of going to movies—seeing movies is an essential part of the screenwriting business. But a salesperson could not deduct this type of expense.

Many expenses have both a personal and a business component, which can make it difficult to tell if an expense is business related. Even the most straightforward costs can present difficulties. For example, it's usually easy to tell whether postage is a personal or business expense. If you mail something for your business, it's a business expense; if you mail something unrelated to your business, it's a personal expense. But even here, there can be questions. For example, should a doctor be allowed to deduct the postage for postcards he sends to his patients while he is on vacation in Europe? (The tax court thinks so—it said the doctor's postage was deductible as an advertising expense.) (*Duncan v. Comm'r.*, 30 TC 386 (1958).)

The IRS has created rules and regulations for some operating expenses that commonly involve a crossover of personal and business use. Some of these rules lay out guidelines to help you figure out when an expense is and isn't deductible. Others impose record-keeping and other requirements to prevent abuses by dishonest taxpayers. Most of the complexity in determining whether an expense is deductible as a business operating expense involves understanding and applying these special rules and regulations.

The expenses that present the most common problems (and are therefore subject to the most comprehensive IRS rules and regulations) include:

- home office expenses (see Chapter 6)
- meals and entertainment (see Chapter 7)
- travel (see Chapter 9)
- car and truck expenses (see Chapter 8)
- business gifts (see Chapter 14)
- bad debts (see Chapter 14)
- employee benefits (see Chapter 11)
- interest payments (see Chapter 14)
- health insurance (see Chapter 12)
- casualty losses (see Chapter 14)
- taxes (see Chapter 14), and
- education expenses (see Chapter 14).

Through these rules and regulations, the IRS provides guidance on the following types of questions:

- If you rent an apartment and use part of one room as a business office, should you be allowed to deduct all or a portion of the rent as a business operating expense? How much of the room must you use as an office (and for what period of time) to convince the IRS that you're using the room for business rather than personal purposes? (See Chapter 6 for information on the home office deduction.)

- Can you deduct the money you spend on a nice suit to wear when you visit business clients? (See Chapter 14 for information about deducting business clothing.)

- Can you deduct the cost of going out of town for a business meeting? Does it matter if you spend part of the time sightseeing? (See Chapter 9 for rules about deducting business travel expenses.)

- Can you deduct the cost of lunch with a former client or customer? Does it matter whether you actually talk about business during lunch? (See Chapter 7 for rules about deducting meals and entertainment.)

Writer's Brothel Expenses Not Deductible

Vitale, a retired federal government budget analyst, decided to write a book about two men who travel cross-country to patronize a legal brothel in Nevada. To authenticate the story and develop characters for the book, he visited numerous legal brothels in Nevada by acting as a customer for prostitutes. He kept a detailed journal describing his experiences at the brothels, including the dates (and sometimes the hours) of his visits, the prostitutes he met, and the amount of cash he paid each one. He wrote and published the book, called *Searchlight, Nevada*, and later claimed a deduction of $3,480 on his tax return for cash payments to prostitutes. The tax court denied the deduction for prostitutes, declaring that the expenditures were "so personal in nature as to preclude their deductibility." (*Vitale v. Comm'r*, TC Memo 1999-131.)

A Deductible Day in the Life of a Home Business Owner

Gina is a full-time suburban mom who runs a part-time baby photography business from her home office. On October 1, 2011, she gets up, makes breakfast, and drives her two kids to school. On the way, she drops off some photos at the home of a client. Later that morning, she drives to the grocery store, where she buys food for her family and a box of envelopes for her business. She then drives to a fancy restaurant, where she has lunch with an old friend who recently had a baby.

Along with personal chitchat, they arrange a date for Gina to photograph the friend's baby. Gina pays for the lunch. That afternoon, Gina enrolls in a class on photographic printmaking at a local college. She plans to use this skill to expand her photography business. Later that day, the maid comes to clean the house, including Gina's home office (which takes up 20% of her home). That evening, Gina and her husband go to a baby photo exhibition at a local art gallery, where they pay for parking.

It pays to get into the habit of looking for possible operating expense deductions whenever you spend money on anything related to your business. Here are tax deductions that Gina can take:

Activity	Type of Business Expense	Amount of Business Expense	
Driving to drop off photos to clients	Business transportation	5 miles at 55.5 cents per mile	$ 2.78
Driving to grocery store	Business transportation	7 miles at 55.5 cents per mile	3.89
Buying envelopes	Business supplies		5.00
Lunch	Business meal	50% of cost of lunch	25.00
Driving to lunch	Business transportation	3 miles at 55.5 cents per mile	1.67
Registering for photography class	Business-related education		200.00
Cleaning home office	Business operating expense	20% of $75 housecleaning fee	15.00
Parking fee to visit photo exhibition	Business-related transportation costs		10.00
Total Deductions			$263.44

Reasonable in Amount

Subject to some important exceptions, there is no limit on how much you can deduct, as long as the amount is reasonable and you don't deduct more than you spend. As a rule of thumb, an expense is reasonable unless there are more economical and practical ways to achieve the same result. If the IRS finds that your deductions are unreasonably large, it will disallow them or at least disallow the portion it finds unreasonable.

Certain areas are hot buttons for the IRS—especially entertainment, travel, and meal expenses. You will have to follow strict rules requiring you to fully document these deductions. (See Chapters 7 and 9.) The reasonableness issue also comes up when a business pays excessive salaries to employees to obtain a large tax deduction. For example, a home business owner might hire his 12-year-old son to answer phones and pay him $50 an hour—clearly an excessive wage for this type of work.

For a few types of operating expenses, the IRS limits how much you can deduct. These include:

- the home office deduction, which is limited to the profit from your business (although you can carry over and deduct any excess amount in future years) (see Chapter 6)
- business meals and entertainment, which are only 50% deductible (see Chapter 7)
- travel expenses, which are limited depending on the length of your trip and the time you spend on business while away (see Chapter 9), and
- business gifts, which are subject to a $25 maximum deduction per individual per year (see Chapter 14).

Operating Expenses That Are Not Deductible

Even though they might be ordinary and necessary, some types of operating expenses are not deductible under any circumstances. In some cases, this is because Congress has declared that it would be morally wrong or otherwise contrary to sound public policy to allow people to deduct these costs. In other cases, Congress simply doesn't want to allow the deduction. These nondeductible expenses include:

- fines and penalties paid to the government for violation of any law—for example, tax penalties, parking tickets, or fines for violating city housing codes (I.R.C. § 162(f))
- illegal bribes or kickbacks to private parties or government officials (I.R.C. § 162(c))
- lobbying expenses or political contributions; however, a business may deduct up to $2,000 per year in expenses to influence local legislation (state, county, or city), not including the expense of hiring a professional lobbyist (such lobbyist expenses are not deductible)
- two-thirds of any damages paid for violation of the federal antitrust laws (I.R.C. § 162(g))
- bar or professional examination fees
- charitable donations by any business other than a C corporation (these donations are deductible only as personal expenses; see Chapter 14)
- country club, social club, or athletic club dues (see Chapter 14)
- federal income taxes you pay on your business income (see Chapter 14), and
- certain interest payments (see Chapter 14).

How to Report Operating Expense Deductions

It's very easy to deduct operating expenses from your income taxes. Simply keep track of everything you buy (or spend money on) for your business during the year, including the amount you spend on each item. Then, record the expenses on your tax return. If, like the vast majority of home business owners, you are a sole proprietor, you do this on IRS Schedule C, *Profit or Loss From Business*. To make this task easy, Schedule C lists common current expense categories—you just need to fill in the amount for each category. For example, if you spend $1,000 for business advertising during the year, you would fill in this amount in the box for the advertising category. You add up all of your current expenses on Schedule C and deduct the total from your gross business income to determine your net business income—the amount on which you are taxed.

If you are a limited liability company owner, partner in a partnership, or an S corporation owner, the process is very similar, except you don't use Schedule C. LLCs and partnerships file IRS Form 1065, *U.S. Return of Partnership Income,* and their owners' shares of expenses is reported on Schedule K-1, *Partner's Share of Income, Credits, Deductions, etc.* S corporations use Form 1120S, *U.S. Income Tax Return for an S Corporation.* Each partner, LLC member, and S corporation shareholder's share of these deductions passes through the entity and is deducted on the owners' individual tax returns on Schedule E. Regular C corporations file their own corporate tax returns.

Deducting Long-Term Assets

Long-Term Assets 73

    Capital Expenses Versus Current Expenses 73

    Methods for Deducting Long-Term Assets...75

    Real Property..76

    Repairs and Improvements...76

    Rules for Deducting Any Long-Term Asset 78

Section 179 Deductions... 84

    Property You Can Deduct 85

    Property Used Primarily (51%) for Business.. 86

    Calculating Your Deduction 87

    Recapture Under Section 179 93

Bonus Depreciation 95

    Property that Qualifies for Bonus Depreciation 97

    Placed In Service Date..97

    Class-Wide Requirement 98

    Calculating the Bonus Amount 98

    Opting Out of the Bonus.. 100

Regular Depreciation 100

    When to Use Regular Depreciation 101

    Depreciation Period 103

    First-Year Depreciation... 103

    Depreciation Methods.. 106

    Depreciation Rules for Listed Property 109

    Computer Software... 111

    Real Property.. 112

    Intangible Assets 113

Depreciation Recapture 114

Tax Reporting and Record Keeping 115

Leasing Long-Term Assets 117

Leasing Versus Purchasing 117

Leases Versus Installment Purchases 118

D o you like to go shopping? How would you like to get a 45% discount on what you buy? Sound impossible? It's not. Consider this example: Sid and Sally each buy the same $2,000 computer at their local computer store. Sid uses his computer to play games and balance his personal checkbook. Sally uses her computer in her graphic design business. Sid's net cost for his computer—that is, his cost after he pays his taxes for the year—is $2,000. Sally's net cost for her computer is $1,100.

Why the difference in cost? Because Sally uses her computer for business, she is allowed to deduct its cost from her taxable income, which saves her $900 in federal and state taxes. Thanks to tax laws designed to help people who own businesses, Sally gets a 45% discount on the computer.

This chapter explains how you can take advantage of these tax laws whenever you purchase long-term property for your business. You will need to be aware of, and follow, some tax rules that at times may seem complicated. But it's worth the effort. After all, by allowing these deductions, the government is effectively offering to help pay for your equipment and other business assets. All you have to do is take advantage of the offer.

Long-Term Assets

This chapter explains how to deduct long-term assets—business property that you reasonably expect to last for more than one year. Long-term assets are also called capital expenses (the terms are used interchangeably in this book).

Capital Expenses Versus Current Expenses

Whether an item is a capital expense or not depends on its useful life. The useful life of an asset is not its physical life, but rather the period during which it may reasonably be expected to be useful in your business—and the IRS, not you, makes this call. Anything you buy that will benefit your business for *more than one year* is a long-term asset or capital expense. For home businesses, this typically includes items such as computers, office furniture, office equipment such as telephones and copiers, books, vehicles, and software. Anything you buy that will benefit your business for less than one year is a current expense. This includes expenses such as utility bills, travel, and office supplies.

EXAMPLE: Doug pays $3,000 for office furniture for his home office. Because furniture can reasonably be expected to be useful for several years, it is a capital expense. The $50 per month that Doug spends on utilities for his home office, however, is a current expense.

The difference between current and capital expenses is important for tax purposes because current expenses (also called operating expenses) can always be deducted in the year you pay for them, assuming you're a cash basis taxpayer. In contrast, the cost of long-term assets may have to be deducted over several years.

Are Paper Clips Long-Term Assets?

Are paper clips and other inexpensive items that you buy for your business long-term assets for tax purposes? No. Although paper clips and similar items might be expected to last more than one year, you can treat their cost as a current expense for tax purposes. Most businesses establish a cost threshold for assets—things that cost more are treated like long-term assets, while items that cost less are treated as currently deductible business expenses. Proposed IRS regulations provide that a business may currently deduct materials and supplies that cost less than $100. (Prop Reg Sec. 1.162-3.) For example, you could treat a $50 bookcase you buy for your business as a currently deductible operating expense, but a $500 bookcase would be a long-term asset. Although this proposed regulation doesn't have the force of law, and the IRS is not bound by it, it does illustrate the IRS's current position on the issue.

Methods for Deducting Long-Term Assets

Traditionally, there have long been two ways to deduct capital expenses:

- depreciate them, deducting some of the cost each year over the asset's useful life, or
- deduct all or most of the cost in one year under Section 179 of the Internal Revenue Code (I.R.C.).

Since 2008, there has been a third way to deduct the cost of long-term business property: a special first-year bonus depreciation for new personal property. For 2011 (and the end of 2010), bonus depreciation allows you to deduct 100% of the cost of qualifying property in the first year the property is purchased. Bonus depreciation is limited to 50% for 2012 (and prior years). This makes 2011 a banner year for deducting long-term personal property used in your business.

You get to decide which depreciation method you use. You don't have to use the same method for all your property. (However, as discussed below, bonus depreciation must be used for all property in the same asset class.) Many small business owners choose Section 179 and/or bonus depreciation whenever they can because these methods provide the largest deduction possible in the first year you buy the asset. Regular depreciation, on the other hand, forces you to spread your deduction over several years. Because of inflation and the time value of money, it is often better to get the largest possible deduction the first year you own an asset. There are some circumstances, however, when it may be more advantageous to use regular depreciation instead. (See "When to Use Depreciation," below.)

Often, but not always, the same asset will qualify for Section 179 expensing and bonus depreciation. In this event, you decide which method to use or you may choose to combine depreciation methods. If you decide to claim Section 179 expensing and bonus depreciation for the same asset, you must use Section 179 first, then bonus depreciation, and then regular depreciation (if needed). The biggest difference between the two is that Section 179 can be used for both new and used property and bonus depreciation is limited to new property. For this reason, many taxpayers use Section 179 expensing for their used property and bonus depreciation for their new property.

Section 179 Versus 100% Bonus Depreciation	
Section 179	**Bonus Depreciation**
Limited to annual business profit	No profit limitation
Can use for new and used property	Can use only for new property
Cannot create net operating loss to be carried back to prior years	Can create a net operating loss to be carried back to prior years and result in an immediate tax refund
$500,000 annual limit for 2011	No annual limit: 100% of cost of qualified property placed in service during 2011 can be deducted in one year; 50% in 2012
Must use property for business more than 50% of the time	No minimum percentage business use of property required (except for listed property)
Recapture of deduction if business use falls below 50%	No recapture
Does not apply class wide	Applies class wide
Optional	Optional, but must opt out not to take

Real Property

Real property consists of buildings and other structures, including their components, and land and land improvements. There is only one way to deduct the cost of real property you use in your real estate business—you must use regular depreciation to deduct a portion of the cost each year over many years. These rules are discussed below in "Regular Depreciation."

Repairs and Improvements

When you make repairs or improvements to long-term assets, it can be hard to tell if the cost is a capital or an operating expense. The rule is that ordinary repairs and maintenance for long-term assets are operating expenses that can be currently deducted. However, you must treat a repair or replacement as a capital expense if it:

- increases the value of your property
- makes it more useful
- lengthens its useful life, or
- is part of a general plan of improvement.

EXAMPLE 1: Doug spends $100 to repair the carburetor on his car, which he uses for his sales business. This is a current expense because the repair doesn't increase the value of his car or lengthen its useful life. The repair merely allows the car to last for its expected life span.

EXAMPLE 2: Doug spends $1,500 on a brand new engine for his car. This is a capital expense because the new engine increases the car's value and useful life.

This rule can be difficult to apply because virtually all repairs increase the value of the property being repaired. A repair becomes a capital improvement when it makes the property *more valuable, long-lived, or useful than it was before the repair.* Individual repairs made as part of a general plan of improvement are also capital expenses.

EXAMPLE: Larry buys an old house and fixes up one of the bedrooms to use as the office for his architecture business. He pays to repaint and replaster the walls and ceilings, repair the floor, put in new wiring, and install an outside door. The plastering, painting, and floor work are repairs, but because they are part of a general plan to alter the home for business use, they are capital expenses.

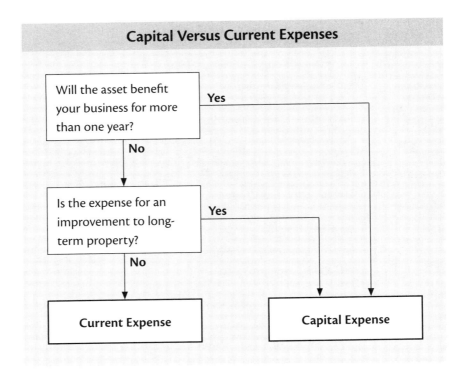

Capital Versus Current Expenses

Will the asset benefit your business for more than one year? — Yes → Capital Expense

No ↓

Is the expense for an improvement to long-term property? — Yes → Capital Expense

No ↓

Current Expense

CAUTION

Inventory is not a business expense. This chapter covers the tax treatment of things you buy to use in your business. It does not cover the cost of items you buy or make to sell to others. Such items are called inventory. Inventory is neither a current nor a capital expense. Rather, businesses deduct the cost of inventory as it is sold. (See Chapter 10 for information on deducting inventory.)

Rules for Deducting Any Long-Term Asset

Certain rules apply when you deduct long-term assets, regardless of which method you use. We will go over those rules and then discuss in more detail the three different methods for deducting long-term business assets and the rules for each.

What You Can Deduct

You can only depreciate or expense the cost of purchasing long-term business property that wears out, deteriorates, or gets used up over time. You cannot deduct:

- property that doesn't wear out, including land (whether undeveloped or with structures on it), stocks, securities, or gold
- property you use solely for personal purposes
- property purchased and disposed of in the same year
- inventory, or
- collectibles that appreciate in value over time, such as antiques and artwork.

If you use nondepreciable property in your business, you get no tax deduction while you own it. But if you sell it, you get to deduct its tax basis from the sales price to calculate your taxable profit. If the basis exceeds the sales price, you'll have a deductible loss on the property. If the price exceeds the basis, you'll have a taxable gain. (See "How Much You Can Deduct," below, for how to figure an asset's basis.)

> **EXAMPLE:** Amy bought a digital camera for her architecture business in January for $1,000 and sold it in December of the same year for $600. It was purchased and disposed of in the same year so it can't be depreciated or expensed. Instead, the property's basis (its original cost) is deducted from the sale price. This results in a loss of $400, which is a deductible business loss.

You also may not depreciate or expense property that you do not own. For example, you get no depreciation or expensing deduction for property you lease. The person who owns the property—the lessor—gets to depreciate it. (However, you may deduct your lease payments as current business expenses.) Leasing may be preferable to buying and depreciating equipment that wears out or becomes obsolete quickly. (See "Leasing Long-Term Assets," below.)

Mixed-Use Property

In order to deduct a long-term asset, you must have used the property in your business. You can't deduct an asset you use solely for personal purposes.

> **EXAMPLE:** Jill, a freelance writer, bought a computer for $2,000. She used it to play games, manage her checkbook, and surf the Internet for fun. In other words, she used it only for personal purposes. The computer is not deductible.

However, you need not use an asset 100% of the time for business to claim a deduction. You can use it for personal purposes part of the time. In this event, your deduction is reduced by the percentage of your personal use. This will, of course, reduce the amount of your deduction.

> **EXAMPLE:** Miranda buys a $400 camera for her real estate business. She uses the camera 75% of the time for business and 25% for personal use. Her deduction is reduced by 25%, so Miranda can deduct only $300 of the camera's $400 cost.

You can take a regular or bonus depreciation deduction even if you use an asset only 1% of the time for business, as long as it's not listed property. This is one advantage of depreciation over the Section 179 deduction, which is available only for property you use more than 50% of the time for business.

If you use property for both business and personal purposes, you must keep a diary or log with the dates, times, and reasons the property was used to distinguish business from personal use. Moreover, special rules apply if you use cars and other types of listed property less than 50% of the time for business.

Listed Property

The IRS imposes special rules on certain personal property items that can easily be used for personal as well as business purposes. These items, called "listed property," include cars and other passenger vehicles below 6,000 pounds; motorcycles, boats, and airplanes; computers;

and any other property generally used for entertainment, recreation, or amusement—for example, VCRs, cameras, stereos, and camcorders.

As long as you use listed property more than 50% of the time for business, you may deduct its cost just like any other long-term business property under Section 179 or using bonus depreciation or regular depreciation. However, if you use listed property 50% or less of the time for business, you can only use the slowest method of regular depreciation: straight-line depreciation. (See "Depreciation Rules for Listed Property," below, for more on these special rules for deducting listed property).

When Depreciation Starts and Ends

You begin to depreciate and/or expense your property when it is placed in service—that is, when it's ready and available for use in your business. As long as it is available for use, you don't have to actually use the property for business during the year to take depreciation.

> EXAMPLE: Tom, a publicist, purchased a copy machine for his office. He had the device ready for use in his office on December 31, 2011, but he didn't actually use it until January 2, 2012. Tom may take a depreciation deduction for the copier for 2011 because it was available for use that year.

You stop depreciating property either when you have fully recovered your cost or other basis or when you retire it from service, whichever occurs first. Property is retired from service when you stop using it for business, sell it, destroy it, or otherwise dispose of it.

> EXAMPLE: Tom depreciates the $5,000 cost of his copier a portion at a time over seven years. At the end of that time, he has recovered his $5,000 basis and depreciation ends. He is free to continue using the machine, but he can't get any more depreciation deductions for it.

CAUTION

You must *actually be in business* to take depreciation or expensing deductions. In other words, you cannot depreciate or expense an asset until your business is up and running. This is one important reason why it is a good idea to postpone large property purchases until your business has begun. (See Chapter 3 for a detailed discussion of tax deductions for business start-up expenses.)

EXAMPLE: In 2011, Julia buys $10,000 worth of equipment for a new restaurant she plans to open. However, the restaurant does not open its doors for business until 2012. Julia may not take a depreciation deduction for the equipment in 2011, but she can in 2012 and later years.

How Much You Can Deduct

You are allowed to deduct your total investment in a long-term asset that you buy for your business, up to your business use percentage of the property. In tax lingo, your investment is called your basis or tax basis. Basis is a word you'll hear over and over again when the subject of depreciation comes up. Don't let it confuse you; it just means the amount of your total investment in the property.

Usually, your basis in long-term property is whatever you paid for it. This includes not only the purchase price, but also sales tax, delivery charges, installation, and testing fees, if any. You may deduct the entire cost, no matter how you paid for the property—in cash, with a credit card, or with a bank loan.

EXAMPLE: The ABC Web Design Co. buys ten computers for its office. They are used 100% for business. ABC pays $20,000 cash, $1,800 in sales tax, and $500 for delivery and installation. Its basis in the property is $22,300.

Whenever you use Section 179 expensing or bonus or regular depreciation, you must subtract the amount of your deduction from the property's basis—this is true regardless of whether you actually claimed any depreciation on your tax return. This new basis is called the adjusted basis, because it reflects adjustments from your starting basis. When your adjusted basis is reduced to zero, you can no longer deduct any of the property's cost.

> **EXAMPLE:** The ABC Web Design Co. (from the above example) bought ten computers in 2011. Its starting basis was $22,300. It expenses the entire cost in 2011 using Section 179. The computer's' adjusted basis is zero, and ABC gets no more deductions for the property.

If you sell long-term property, your gain or loss on the sale is determined by subtracting the property's adjusted basis from the sales price.

> **EXAMPLE:** ABC sells its ten computers for $5,000 in 2012. Because its adjusted basis in the computers is zero, its taxable gain on the sale will be $5,000.

If you abandon long-term business property instead of selling it, you may deduct its adjusted basis as a business loss. Of course, if your adjusted basis in the property is zero, you get no deduction. You abandon property when you voluntarily and permanently give up possessing and using it with the intention of ending your ownership and without passing it on to anyone else. Loss from abandonment of business property is deductible as an ordinary loss, even if the property is a capital asset.

For more information on the tax implications of selling or otherwise disposing of business property, refer to IRS Publication 544, *Sales and Other Dispositions of Assets*.

Section 179 Deductions

If you learn only one section number in the tax code, it should be Section 179. This provision is one of the greatest tax boons ever for small business owners. Section 179 doesn't increase the total amount you can deduct, but it allows you to take your entire depreciation deduction in one year, rather than taking it a little at a time over the term of an asset's useful life—which can be up to 39 years. This is called first-year expensing or Section 179 expensing. (Expensing is an accounting term that means currently deducting a long-term asset.)

> EXAMPLE: In 2011, Ginger buys a $5,000 computer system for her home business. Under the regular depreciation rules (using the straight-line depreciation method—see "Depreciation Methods"), Ginger would have to deduct a portion of the cost each year over its five-year useful life, as follows:

Year	Depreciation Deduction
2011	$500
2012	$1,000
2013	$1,000
2014	$1,000
2015	$1,000
2016	$500

By using Section 179 instead, Ginger can deduct the entire $5,000 expense from her income taxes in 2011. This is $4,500 more than she could have deducted for the year using depreciation.

TIP
You might want to save your deductions for later. Because of inflation and the time value of money, it is often better to use Section 179 if you can, to get the largest possible deduction for the current year. There are some circumstances, however, when it may be more advantageous to use depreciation instead. (See "When to Use Regular Depreciation," below.)

Property You Can Deduct

You qualify for the Section 179 deduction only if you buy long-term, tangible personal property that you use in your business more than 50% of the time.

Tangible Personal Property

Under Section 179, you can deduct the cost of tangible personal property (new or used) that you buy for your business, if the IRS has determined that the property will last more than one year. Examples of tangible personal property include computers, business equipment, and office furniture. Although it's not really tangible property, computer software can also be deducted under Section 179 (see "Computer Software," below, for more on deducting software).

You can't use Section 179 to deduct the cost of:

- land
- permanent structures attached to land, including buildings and their structural components, fences, swimming pools, or paved parking areas
- inventory (see Chapter 10)
- intangible property such as patents, copyrights, and trademarks
- property used outside the United States, or
- air conditioning and heating units.

However, nonpermanent property attached to a building is deductible. For example, refrigerators, grocery store counters, printing presses, testing equipment, and signs are all deductible under Section 179. Structures such as barns and greenhouses that are specifically designed and used for agriculture or horticulture are also deductible, as is livestock (including horses). Special rules apply to cars. (See Chapter 8.)

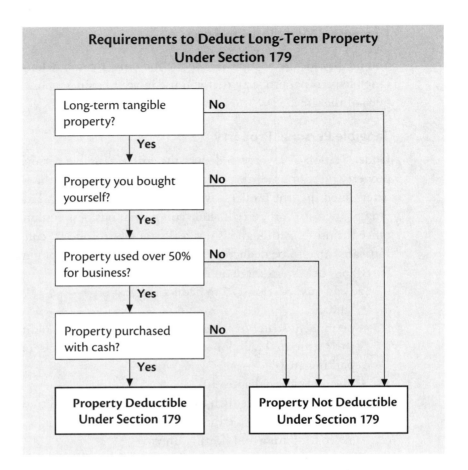

Requirements to Deduct Long-Term Property Under Section 179

Long-term tangible property? — **No** →
↓ **Yes**

Property you bought yourself? — **No** →
↓ **Yes**

Property used over 50% for business? — **No** →
↓ **Yes**

Property purchased with cash? — **No** →
↓ **Yes**

Property Deductible Under Section 179

Property Not Deductible Under Section 179

Property Used Primarily (51%) for Business

To deduct the cost of property under Section 179, you must use the property primarily for your business—that is, to provide your professional services. You can take a Section 179 deduction for property you use for both personal and business purposes, as long as you use it for your practice more than half of the time. The amount of your deduction is reduced by the percentage of your personal use. (See "Calculating Your Deduction," below.) You'll need to keep records showing your business use of the property. If you use an item for business less than half the time, you will have to use bonus or regular depreciation instead.

There is another important limitation regarding the business use of property. You must use the property over half the time for business in the year in which you buy it. You can't convert property you previously used for personal use to business use and claim a Section 179 deduction for the cost.

> **EXAMPLE:** Kim, an interior designer, bought a $2,000 digital camera in 2009 and used it to take family and other personal pictures. In 2011, Kim starts using her digital camera 75% of the time for her business. She may not deduct the cost under Section 179 because she didn't use the camera for business until two years after she bought it.

Property That You Purchase

You can use Section 179 expensing only for property that you purchase—not for leased property or property you inherit or receive as a gift. You also can't use it for property that you buy from a relative or from a corporation or an organization that you control. The property you purchase may be used or new.

Calculating Your Deduction

There are several limitations on the amount you can deduct each year under Section 179. Your total annual deduction will depend on:
- what you paid for the property
- how much you use the property for business
- how much Section 179 property you buy during the year, and
- your annual business income.

Cost of Property

The amount you can deduct for Section 179 property is initially based on the property's cost: what you paid for the property, plus sales tax, delivery, and installation charges. It doesn't matter if you pay cash or finance the purchase with a credit card or bank loan. However, if you pay for property with both cash and a trade-in, the value of the trade-in is not deductible under Section 179. You must depreciate the amount of the trade-in.

> **EXAMPLE:** Stuart buys a $5,000 computer system to use for his home-based graphic design business. He pays $4,000 cash and receives a $1,000 trade-in for an older computer that he owns. He may deduct $4,000 of the $5,000 purchase under Section 179; he must depreciate the remaining $1,000.

Percentage of Business Use

If you use Section 179 property solely for business, you can deduct 100% of the cost (subject to the other limitations discussed below). However, if you use property for both business and personal purposes, you must reduce your deduction by the percentage of the time that you use the property for personal purposes.

> **EXAMPLE:** Max buys a $4,000 computer. The year he buys it, he uses it for his consulting business 75% of the time and for personal purposes 25% of the time. He may currently deduct 75% of the computer's cost ($3,000) under Section 179 that year. The remaining $1,000 is not deductible as a business expense.

You must continue to use property that you deduct under Section 179 for business at least 50% of the time for as many years as it would take to depreciate the item under the normal depreciation rules. For example, computers have a five-year depreciation period. If you deduct a computer's cost under Section 179, you must use the computer at least 50% of the time for business for five years.

If you don't meet these rules, you'll have to report as income (and pay tax on) part of the deduction you took under Section 179. This is called recapture, which is discussed in more detail in "Recapture Under Section 179," below.

Annual Deduction Limit

There is a limit on the total amount of business property expense you can deduct each year under Section 179. The Section 179 limit was $128,000 in 2007. In an effort to prevent an economic downturn, the limit was increased to a whopping $250,000 in 2008. Due to the continuing bad economy, the $250,000 limit was extended through 2009. The limit was increased again to $500,000 for 2010 and 2011. Then, in 2012, the Section 179 limit is scheduled to go to $125,000. The limit is scheduled to go down to $25,000 in 2013 and later.

Congress could decide to make the higher limit permanent, but at this point no one knows what will happen. If you're planning on buying more than $125,000 worth of property for your business in one year and you want to deduct the whole amount under Section 179, your best bet is to make your purchases before 2012.

The annual deduction limit applies to all of your businesses combined, not to each business you own and run.

> **EXAMPLE:** Britney owns a successful website that provides invest-ment advice. She also works as a financial consultant. On the side, she works part-time as a boudoir photographer. Because the Section 179 limit applies to all her businesses together, she may expense a total maximum of $500,000 in long-term asset purchases in 2011.

You don't have to claim the full amount—it's up to you to decide how much to deduct under Section 179. Whatever amount you don't claim under Section 179 must be depreciated instead. (Depreciation *is not* optional—see "Depreciation," below.)

Because Section 179 is intended to help smaller businesses, there is also a limit on the total amount of Section 179 property you can purchase each year. You must reduce your Section 179 deduction by one dollar for every dollar your annual purchases exceed the applicable limit. The limit is $2 million for 2010 and 2011. The limit will go down to $500,000 in 2012, and is scheduled to be reduced to $200,000 in 2013 and later. Few home businesses will ever reach these limits.

Currently, the Section 179 limit is so high that few home business owners need worry about ever reaching it. However, if you purchase enough business property in one year to go over the limit, you can divide the deduction among the items you purchase in any way you want, as long as the total deduction doesn't exceed the Section 179 limit. It's usually best to apply Section 179 to property that has the longest useful life—and therefore the longest depreciation period. This reduces the total time you will have to wait to get your deductions, which usually works to your financial benefit.

Year	Section 179 Deduction Limit	Property Value Limit
2008-2009	$250,000	$800,000
2010-2011	$500,000	$2 million
2012	$125,000	$500,000
2013	$25,000	$200,000

Business Profit Limitation

You can't use Section 179 to deduct more in one year than your net taxable business income for the year. To figure out what this is, you subtract your business deductions from your business income. However, do not subtract your Section 179 deduction, the deduction for 50% of self-employment tax, or any net operating losses you are carrying back or forward.

If you have a net loss for the year, you get no Section 179 deduction for that year. If your net taxable income is less than the cost of the property you wish to deduct under Section 179, your deduction for the year is limited to the amount of your income. Any amount you cannot deduct in the current year, you can carry forward and deduct the next year (or any other year in the future).

> **EXAMPLE:** In 2011, Rich had $15,000 in net income from his home business recording audiobooks. He spent $20,000 buying equipment to set up his home recording studio. Even though

the Section 179 maximum limit is $500,000, Rich's deduction is limited to $15,000. He can carry forward the remaining $5,000 to the following year and deduct it then (provided he has sufficient income).

This limitation is particularly important to home business owners because many earn very small incomes. A study sponsored by the Small Business Administration found that 57% of all home businesses earned less than $10,000 in profits per year. Only 16% earned more than $10,000 in profit, while 27% incurred losses. (See *Homebased Business: The Hidden Economy*, by Joanne H. Pratt (Office of Advocacy, United States Small Business Administration).)

Fortunately, if you are a sole proprietor (like most home business owners), you can count your salary from a regular job as business income if you work in addition to running your home business. If you're a married sole proprietor and file a joint tax return, you can include your spouse's salary and business income in this total as well. You can't count investment income—for example, interest you earn on your personal savings account—as business income. But you can include interest you earn on your business working capital—for example, interest you earn on your business bank account.

EXAMPLE 1: In 2011, Amelia earned $5,000 in profit from her engineering consulting business and $10,000 in salary from a part-time job. She spent $17,000 for a computer and office equipment. She can use Section 179 to deduct $15,000 of this expense for 2011. She can deduct the remaining $2,000 the following year.

EXAMPLE 2: In 2011, James purchased $100,000 of recording equipment for his fledgling commercial voiceover business, but earned only $5,000 from the venture. James's wife, however, earned $75,000 from her job as a college professor. Because James and his wife file a joint return, they may take a Section 179 deduction for up to $80,000 for 2011 ($5,000 + $75,000 = $80,000). Thus, James may deduct $80,000 of his equipment purchases under Section 179 and deduct the remaining $20,000 in a future year.

If you're a partner in a partnership, member of a limited liability company (LLC), or shareholder in an S corporation, the Section 179 limit applies both to the business entity and to each owner personally.

> EXAMPLE: Dean, a builder, is a partner in the ABC Partnership. He also runs his own part-time home repair business as a sole proprietor. In 2011, ABC purchases $100,000 in construction equipment that it elects to expense under Section 179. Its business income for the year is $120,000, so it can deduct the full $100,000. ABC allocates $50,000 of its purchases and $50,000 of its income to Dean. Dean also purchases $10,000 of equipment for his sole proprietor home business that he would like to expense under Section 179. However, Dean's home business incurs a $5,000 loss for the year. His purchases for the year total $60,000 ($50,000 from the partnership plus $10,000 for equipment for his home business). His total business income for the year is $45,000 ($50,000 from the partnership minus the $5,000 loss from his home repair business). Thus, Dean may expense only $45,000 of the equipment purchases for that year. He must carry the remaining $15,000 over to deduct in future years.

Date of Purchase

As long as you meet the requirements, you can deduct the cost of Section 179 property up to the limits discussed above, no matter when you place the property in service during the year (that is, when you buy the property and make it available for use in your ongoing business). This differs from regular depreciation rules, by which property bought later in the year may be subject to a smaller deduction for the first year. (See "First-Year Depreciation," below.) This is yet another advantage of taking a Section 179 deduction rather than using regular depreciation.

EXAMPLE: John buys a $5,000 computer for his home business on January 1, 2011, and $5,000 of office furniture on December 31, 2011. Both purchases are fully deductible in 2011 under Section 179.

Use It or Lose It—Make Your Section 179 Claims

Section 179 deductions are not automatic. You must claim a Section 179 deduction on your tax return by completing Part 1 of IRS Form 4562, *Depreciation and Amortization,* and checking a specific box. If you neglect to do this, you may lose your deduction. If you filed your return for the year without making the election to use Section 179, you can file an amended return within six months after your tax return was due for the year—April 15 (October 15 if you obtain an extension to file). Once this deadline passes, however, you lose your right to a Section 179 deduction forever—you can't file an amended return in a later year to claim the deduction. (See Chapter 16 for detailed guidance on amending tax returns.)

Recapture Under Section 179

Recapture is a nasty tax trap for unwary business owners. It requires you to give back part of a tax deduction that you took in a previous year. You may have to recapture part of a Section 179 tax deduction if, during the property's recovery period, either:

- your business use of the property drops below 51%, or
- you sell the property.

The recovery period is the property's useful life as determined under IRS rules. The IRS has determined the useful life of all types of property that can be depreciated. The useful life is the time period over which you must depreciate the asset. For personal property that can be expensed under Section 179, the useful life ranges from three years for computer software to seven years for office furniture and business equipment. If you deduct property under Section 179, you must continue to use it in your business at least 51% of the time for each year of its useful life. For example, if you buy office furniture, you must use it more than half of the time for business for at least seven years.

If your business use falls below 51% or you sell the property before the recovery period ends, you become subject to recapture. This means that you have to give back to the IRS all of the accelerated deductions you took under Section 179. You get to keep the amount you would have been entitled to under regular depreciation (using the fastest method available), but you must include the rest of your Section 179 deduction in your ordinary income for the year—and pay tax on it.

> EXAMPLE: In 2009, Paul purchases office equipment worth $10,000 and deducts the entire amount under Section 179. He uses the property 100% for business during 2009 and 2010, but in 2011, he uses it only 40% for business. The equipment has a seven-year recovery period, so Paul is subject to recapture. He figures the recapture amount as follows:
>
> First, he figures all the annual depreciation he would have been entitled to during 2009 through 2011 had he depreciated the property under the regular depreciation rules. He calculates this using the fastest depreciation method available—the 200% double declining balance method. (If he had purchased listed property, he would have had to use the slowest method—straight-line depreciation; see "Depreciation Methods" and "Listed Property," below.)
>
> | | | |
> |---|---|---|
> | 2009 | $1,429 | |
> | 2010 | 2,449 | |
> | 2011 | 700 | ($1,749 × 40% business use) |
> | Total | $4,578 | |

He then deducts this amount from the $10,000 Section 179 deduction he claimed in 2009: $10,000 − $4,578 = $5,422.

Thus, Paul's recapture amount is $5,422. Paul must add $5,422 to his income for 2011. He can continue to depreciate the equipment for the next four years.

You eventually get back through depreciation any recapture amount you have to pay. But recapture can spike your tax bill for the year, so it's best to avoid the problem by making sure that you use property you deduct under Section 179 for business more than half of the time for every year of its recovery period.

You can maximize your Section 179 deduction by keeping your percentage of business use of Section 179 property as high as possible during the year that you buy the property. After the first year, you can reduce your business use—as long as it stays above 50%—and avoid recapture.

> EXAMPLE: Paul buys $10,000 worth of office equipment and uses it 90% of the time for business in 2008. He would have been entitled to currently deduct $9,000 of the cost under Section 179 (90% business use × $10,000 cost = $9,000 deduction). In 2009 and 2010, he uses the equipment for business only 60% of the time. Nevertheless, he need not recapture any of his Section 179 deduction because his business use is still more than 50%.

Bonus Depreciation

In an ongoing effort to help jumpstart the faltering economy, business owners have been allowed to claim bonus depreciation for qualifying personal property. Using bonus depreciation, a business owner can deduct a specified percentage of a long-term asset's cost the first year it's placed in service. For 2008, 2009, most of 2010, and 2012, the percentage you can claim is 50%; that is, you can deduct 50% of the cost of the asset in the first year, with the remaining cost deducted over several years using regular depreciation and/or Section 179 expensing. However, for assets placed in service from September 8, 2010 through December 31, 2011, the deductible first-year percentage is 100%, meaning the entire cost of the asset can be deducted the first year, without limit. This has never been possible before, and likely never will be again.

Year Qualified Property Placed In Service	Amount of Bonus Depreciation
2008 through 9/7/2010	50%
9/8/2010 - 12/31/2011	100%
2012	50%

EXAMPLE: Barry is a successful pawnbroker who owns the building housing his business. During 2011, he spends $10,000 to purchase a fancy new sign for his building. He can't deduct this expense in 2011 using Section 179 because it is an improvement to real property. However, he can deduct it in 2011 using 100% bonus depreciation, which may be used for any property with a useful life of less than 20 years. For tax purposes, the sign has a useful life of 15 years. Barry may claim a $10,000 bonus depreciation deduction for the sign in 2011. Without bonus depreciation, he'd have to deduct the $10,000 over 15 years using regular depreciation.

Bonus depreciation is optional—you don't have to take it if you don't want to. But if you want to get the largest depreciation deduction you can during the year that you buy a long-term asset, take advantage of it whenever you can.

 CAUTION

Bonus depreciation is scheduled to end after 2012. Bonus depreciation was enacted as a temporary measure to help the ailing U.S. economy. It was originally scheduled to end on December 31, 2008. However, due to the continuing bad economy, it was extended through the end of 2012. This means that, unless Congress acts to extend it again, you won't be able to use bonus depreciation for long-term personal property that you place in service starting in 2013.

Property that Qualifies for Bonus Depreciation

Property qualifies for bonus depreciation only if:

- it is new (if the newly purchased property contains used parts, it is still treated as new if the cost of the used parts is less than 20% of the total cost of the property)
- it has a useful life of 20 years or less (this includes all types of tangible personal business property and software you buy, but not real property—see above), and
- you purchase it from someone who is unrelated to you (it can't be a gift or inheritance).

In addition, if the asset is listed property, it must be used over 50% of the time for business to qualify for bonus depreciation. (Listed property consists of automobiles and computers and certain other personal property—see "Listed Property," above.)

In contrast, you can use the Section 179 deduction and regular depreciation for both used and new personal property. And, you can use regular depreciation for any long-term business property, including listed property, without any restrictions on the percentage of business use.

Placed In Service Date

Bonus depreciation is available only for personal business use property purchased and placed in service during 2008 through 2012. In other words, you won't be able to take bonus depreciation for property purchased and placed in service during 2013 or later, or before 2008. Property is "placed in service" when it's ready and available for use in your business. As long as it is available for use, you don't have to actually use the property for business during the year to take depreciation.

> EXAMPLE: Tom, a real estate agent, purchased a digital camera to take photos of properties for sale. He had the device ready for use in his office on November 1, 2011. However, he had no properties to photograph until 2012. Tom may take a

depreciation deduction for the camera for 2011, even though he didn't actually use it that year, because it was ready and available for use then.

If a binding contract to acquire the property existed before January 1, 2008, the property does not qualify for bonus depreciation.

There are certain exceptions to the time period rules. For example, if the property is purchased to repair or replace business property damaged by a federally declared disaster that occurred during 2008 through 2009, then the time period is extended through December 31, 2012. There are other exceptions for airplanes and certain other property that costs more than $1 million and takes more than one year to produce.

Class-Wide Requirement

If you use bonus depreciation, you must use it for all assets that fall within the same class. Unlike Section 179 expensing, you may not pick and choose the assets you want to apply it to within a class. For example, if you buy a car and take bonus depreciation, you must take bonus depreciation for any other property you buy that year within the same class. Cars are five-year property, so you must take bonus depreciation that year for any other five-year property—for example, computers and office equipment. (See "IRS Depreciation Periods," below, for a list of the various classes of property.)

Calculating the Bonus Amount

You use bonus depreciation to figure out your depreciation deduction for the first year that you own an asset. You figure the deduction by multiplying the depreciable basis of the asset by the applicable bonus percentage. (See "How Much You Can Deduct," above, for how to figure an asset's depreciable basis.) For property placed in service from September 8, 2010 through December 31, 2012, this calculation is easy because the bonus percentage is 100%.

EXAMPLE: Stan, a printer, purchased and placed into service $10,000 in equipment for his business during 2011. He claims 100% bonus depreciation, which allows him to deduct the entire $10,000 cost for 2011. (He couldn't use Section 179 to deduct the expense in 2011 because his business lost money that year and the Section 179 deduction is limited to a business owner's annual net income.)

If the property was placed in service during 2012, or from January 1, 2008 through September 7, 2010, the bonus percentage is 50%. The remaining 50% cost of the property is deducted over several years using regular depreciation.

Assume that Stan purchases $10,000 of printing equipment and places it into service for his business during 2012. He may deduct 50% of the cost using bonus depreciation in 2012, and deduct the remaining $5,000 using regular depreciation. His regular depreciation for 2012 is $1,000 (20% x $5,000). Thus, his total deduction in 2012 is $6,000.

If you want to claim the Section 179 deduction and 50% bonus depreciation for the same asset, you first use Section 179, then 50% bonus depreciation, and then regular depreciation, in that order. This can give you an enormous deduction.

EXAMPLE: During 2012, Mark purchases and places in service $250,000 worth of furnishings and equipment for his three home businesses. Mark had $500,000 in net taxable income in 2012. First, he may take the maximum $125,000 Section 179 deduction for 2012—that is, he may currently deduct this entire amount from his business income. Next, he may take a 50% bonus depreciation deduction on the remaining $125,000 cost of the equipment—this amounts to a $62,500 deduction. He may then deduct the remaining $62,500 of the equipment's cost under the normal depreciation rules. Using the 200% double declining balance method, he gets $15,000 in regular depreciation (20% × $62,500 = $15,000). His total deduction for the year is $202,500: $125,000 Section 179 deduction + $62,500 bonus depreciation + $15,000 regular depreciation. The next year, he'll get a regular depreciation deduction of $16,000 (32% × $62,500 = $16,000).

Opting Out of the Bonus

Bonus depreciation deduction is applied automatically to all taxpayers who qualify for it. However, the deduction is optional. You need not take it if you don't want to. You can elect not to take the deduction by attaching a note to your tax return. It may be advantageous to do this if you expect your income to go up substantially in future years, placing you in a higher tax bracket.

> CAUTION
>
> **When you opt out, you do so for the entire class of assets.** It's very important to understand that if you opt out of the bonus, you must do so for the entire class of assets, not just one asset within a class. This is the same rule that applies when you decide to take the bonus. (See "Class-Wide Requirement," above.)

Regular Depreciation

The traditional method of getting back the money you spend on long-term business assets is to deduct the cost a little at a time over several years (exactly how many years is determined by the IRS). This process is called depreciation.

Depreciation is a complicated subject. The IRS instruction booklet, Publication 946, *How to Depreciate Property*, is over 100 pages long. For a comprehensive discussion of depreciation, read Section 1, "Overview of Depreciation." This section covers the depreciation basics that all business owners should know.

> CAUTION
> **Regular depreciation is not optional.** Unlike the Section 179 deduction and bonus depreciation, regular depreciation is not optional. You *must* take a depreciation deduction if you qualify for it and you don't deduct the property under Section 179. If you fail to take it, the IRS will treat you as if you had taken it. This means that you could be subject to depreciation recapture when you sell the asset—even if you never took a depreciation deduction. This would increase your taxable income by the amount of the deduction you failed to take. (See "Depreciation Recapture," below.) So if you don't expense a depreciable asset under Section 179 or claim bonus depreciation, be sure to take the proper depreciation deductions for it. If you realize later that you failed to take a depreciation deduction that you should have taken, you may file an amended tax return to claim any deductions that you should have taken in prior years. (See Chapter 16 for guidance about filing amended returns.)

When to Use Regular Depreciation

With the Section 179 deduction at $500,000 for 2010 through 2012, and 100% first-year bonus depreciation for 2011, you might not need to use regular depreciation for the foreseeable future. However, you may need to use regular depreciation to write off the cost of long-term assets that don't qualify for Section 179 expensing or bonus depreciation. Also, under some circumstances, it may be better to use depreciation and draw out your deduction over several years instead of getting your deductions all at once under Section 179 and/or bonus depreciation.

When You Can't Use Section 179

There are many more limitations on using Section 179 than there are for regular depreciation. For example, you can't use Section 179 to deduct the cost of something that you use less than 50% of the time for business. There is no such minimum percentage business use for regular depreciation—you can use and deduct 1% of an item's cost if that's your business use. Other restrictions that apply to Section 179 that don't apply to regular depreciation include the following. Under Section 179, you can't deduct:

- personal property items that you convert to business use
- structures, such as a building or building component
- items financed with a trade-in (the value of the trade-in must be depreciated)
- intangible assets, such a patent, copyright, trademark, or business goodwill
- items purchased from a relative
- property inherited or received as a gift
- air conditioning or heating units, or
- personal property used inside rental property--for example, kitchen appliances, carpets, drapes, or blinds.

None of these limitations apply to regular depreciation.

In addition, your Section 179 deduction may not exceed your business income. If you're married and file a joint return, your spouse's income can be included. But if your business is making little or no money and you have little or no income from wages or your spouse, you may not be able take a Section 179 deduction for the current year. In contrast, there is no income limitation on regular or bonus depreciation deductions. You can deduct regular or bonus depreciation from your business income; if this results in a net loss for a year, you can deduct the loss from income taxes you paid in prior years.

You will also have to use depreciation instead of Section 179 to the extent you exceed the Section 179 annual limit.

When You Can't Use Bonus Depreciation

There are also rules that limit the availability of bonus depreciation that don't apply to regular depreciation. With bonus depreciation, you can't deduct:

- used property, including property you convert to business use
- real property
- listed property used less than 51% of the time for business
- property received as a gift or inheritance, and
- intangible assets such patents, copyrights, trademarks, or business goodwill.

None of these limitations apply to regular depreciation so there may be instances when you can't use bonus depreciation but the property is still eligible for regular depreciation.

Depreciation Period

The depreciation period (also called the recovery period) is the time over which you must take your depreciation deductions for an asset. The tax code has assigned depreciation periods to all types of business assets, ranging from three to 39 years. These periods are somewhat arbitrary. However, property that can be expected to last a long time generally has a longer recovery period than property that has a short life—for example, nonresidential real property has a 39-year recovery period, while software has only a three-year period. Most of the property that you buy for your business will probably have a five- or seven-year depreciation period.

The major depreciation periods are listed below. These periods are also called recovery classes; all property that comes within a period is said to belong to that class. For example, computers have a five-year depreciation period and thus fall within the five-year class, along with automobiles and office equipment.

First-Year Depreciation

Sid and Sam are identical twins who have competing horse breeding businesses, which they operate from adjoining ranches. Sid buys a horse on January 2, 2011, and Sam buys one on December 30, 2011. How much depreciation should each be allowed for the first year they own their horses? Should Sid get a full year and Sam just a day?

The IRS has established certain rules (called "conventions") that govern how many months of depreciation you can take for the first year that you own an asset.

Half-Year Convention

The basic rule is that, no matter when you buy an asset, you treat it as being placed in service on July 1—the midpoint of the year. This means that you can take half a year of depreciation for the first year that you own an asset.

> **EXAMPLE:** If Sam buys one horse in January, one in March, and one in December, he treats them all as having been placed in service on July 1.

Midquarter Convention

You are not allowed to use the half-year convention if more than 40% of the long-term personal property you buy during the year is placed in service during the last three months of the year. The 40% figure is determined by adding together the basis of all the depreciable property you bought during the year and comparing that to the basis of all of the property you bought during the fourth quarter.

If you exceed the 40% ceiling, you must use the midquarter convention. You must group all of the property that you purchased during the year by quarter (depending on when you bought it) and treat it as if you had placed it in service at the midpoint of that quarter. (A quarter is a three-month period: The first quarter is January through March; the second quarter is April through June; the third quarter is July through September; and the fourth quarter is October through December.)

> **EXAMPLE:** Sam buys one horse in January, one in October, and one in December. Each horse costs $25,000, so the basis for all the horses he bought during the year is $75,000. He paid $50,000 of this amount during the fourth quarter, so more than 40% of his purchases were made in the fourth quarter of the year. Sam must use the midquarter convention. He must treat the first horse he bought as being placed in service on February 15—the midpoint of the first quarter. The second and last horses must be treated as being placed in service on November 15—the midpoint of the fourth quarter. As a result, Sam gets very little depreciation that year for the horses he bought in October and December.

Depreciation Periods

Depreciation Period	Type of Property
3 years	Computer software
	Tractor units for over-the-road use
	Any race horse over 2 years old when placed in service
	Any other horse over 12 years old when placed in service
5 years	Automobiles, taxis, buses, and trucks
	Computers and peripheral equipment
	Office machinery (such as typewriters, calculators, and copiers)
	Any property used in research and experimentation
	Breeding cattle and dairy cattle
	Appliances, carpets, furniture, and so on used in a residential rental real estate activity
7 years	Office furniture and fixtures (such as desks, files, and safes)
	Agricultural machinery and equipment
	Any property that does not have a class life and has not been designated by law as being in any other class
10 years	Vessels, barges, tugs, and similar water transportation equipment
	Any single-purpose agricultural or horticultural structure
	Any tree or vine bearing fruits or nuts
15 years	Improvements made directly to land or added to it (such as shrubbery, fences, roads, and bridges)
	Interior improvements to leased nonresidential property and certain restaurant property placed in service during October 22, 2004 through December 31, 2009
	Any retail motor fuels outlet, such as a convenience store
20 years	Farm buildings (other than single-purpose agricultural or horticultural structures)
27.5 years	Residential rental property—for example, an apartment building
39 years	Nonresidential real property, such as a home office, office building, store, or warehouse

It's usually best to avoid having to use the midquarter convention, which means you'll want to buy more than 60% of your total depreciable assets before September 30 of the year. Assets you currently deduct using Section 179 do not count toward the 40% limitation, so you can avoid the midquarter convention by using Section 179 to deduct most or all of your purchases in the last three months of the year.

Depreciation Methods

There are several ways to calculate depreciation. However, most tangible property is depreciated using the Modified Accelerated Cost Recovery System, or MACRS. (A slightly different system, called ADS, applies to certain listed property (see "Listed Property," below), property used outside the United States, and certain farm property and imported property.)

You can ordinarily use three different methods to calculate the depreciation deduction under MACRS: straight-line depreciation or one of two accelerated depreciation methods. Once you choose your method, you're stuck with it for the entire life of the asset.

In addition, you must use the same method for all property of the same class that you purchase during the year. For example, if you use the straight-line method to depreciate a computer, you must use that method to depreciate any other property in the same class as computers. Computers fall within the five-year class, so you must use the straight-line method for all other five-year property you buy during the year, such as office equipment.

Straight-Line Method

Using the straight-line depreciation method, you deduct an equal amount each year over the useful life of an asset. However, if the midyear convention applies (as it often does), you deduct only a half-year's worth of depreciation in the first year. You make up for this by taking an extra one-half year of depreciation at the end. You can use the straight-line method to depreciate any type of depreciable property.

> **EXAMPLE:** Sally buys a $1,000 printer-fax-copy machine for her home business in 2011. It has a useful life of five years. (See

"Depreciation Period," above.) Sally bought more than 60% of her depreciable property for the year before September 30, so she can use the midyear convention. Using the straight-line method, she can depreciate the asset over six years—the five years of the printer's useful life, plus an extra year to allow her to make up for the partial deduction she takes for the first year. Her annual depreciation deductions are as follows:

2011	$ 100
2012	200
2013	200
2014	200
2015	200
2016	100
Total	$ 1,000

If the midquarter convention applies, you don't get a half year's worth of depreciation the first year. Instead, your first year depreciation amount depends on the month of the year when you bought the property. Whatever you can't depreciate in the first year is tacked on to the last year. For example, if Sally bought her machine in September, she could deduct $75 depreciation in 2011, $200 in 2012 through 2015, and $125 in 2016. If she bought it in December, she would get $25 in 2011 and $175 in 2016. If she bought it in January, she would get $175 in 2011 and $25 in 2016.

Accelerated Depreciation Methods

There is nothing wrong with straight-line depreciation, but the tax law provides an alternative that most businesses prefer: accelerated depreciation. As the name implies, this method provides faster depreciation than the straight-line method. It does not increase your total depreciation deduction, but it permits you to take larger deductions in the first few years after you buy an asset. You make up for this by taking smaller deductions in later years.

The fastest and most commonly used form of accelerated depreciation is the double declining balance method. This is a confusing name, but all it means is that you get double the deduction that you would get for the first full year under the straight-line method. You then get less in later years. However, in later years, you may switch to the straight-line method (which will give you a larger deduction). This is built into the IRS depreciation tables. You may use this method to depreciate virtually all tangible personal property you buy for your business, except for listed property you use less than half the time for business (see "Listed Property," below).

The following table is from IRS Publication 946, *How to Depreciate Property*. It shows you the percentage of the cost of an asset you may deduct each year using the double (200%) declining balance method.

200% Declining Balance Depreciation Method						
Convention: Half-year						
If the recovery period is:						
Year	**3-year**	**5-year**	**7-year**	**10-year**	**15-year**	**20-year**
1	33.33%	20.00%	14.29%	10.00%	5.00%	3.750%
2	44.45%	32.00%	24.49%	18.00%	9.50%	7.219%
3	14.81%	19.20%	17.49%	14.40%	8.55%	6.677%
4	7.41%	11.52%	12.49%	11.52%	7.70%	6.177%
5		11.52%	8.93%	9.22%	6.93%	5.713%
6		5.76%	8.92%	7.37%	6.23%	5.285%
7			8.93%	6.55%	5.90%	4.888%
8			4.46%	6.55%	5.90%	4.522%
9				6.56%	5.91%	4.462%
10				6.55%	5.90%	4.461%
11				3.28%	5.91%	4.462%
12					5.90%	4.461%
13					5.91%	4.462%
14					5.90%	4.461%
15					5.91%	4.462%
16					2.95%	4.461%
17						4.462%
18						4.461%
19						4.462%
20						4.461%
21						2.231%

EXAMPLE: Sally decides to use the double declining balance method to depreciate her $1,000 printer-fax-copier machine. Her annual depreciation deductions are as follows:

2011	$ 200.00
2012	320.00
2013	192.00
2014	115.20
2015	115.20
2016	57.60
Total	$1,000.00

Using this method, she takes a $200 deduction in 2010 instead of the $100 deduction she'd get using straight-line depreciation. But starting in 2013, she'll get smaller deductions than she would using the straight-line method.

Using accelerated depreciation is not necessarily a good idea if you expect your income to go up in future years. There are also some restrictions on when you can use accelerated depreciation. For example, you can't use it for cars, computers, and certain other property that you use for business less than 50% of the time (see "Listed Property," below).

Depreciation Tables

Figuring out your annual depreciation deduction might seem to require some complicated calculations, but actually it's not that difficult. Of course, if you use a tax preparation computer program, it will do the math for you. However, if you want to do it yourself, you can use depreciation tables prepared by the IRS. These tables factor in the depreciation convention and method. They are all available in IRS Publication 946, *How to Depreciate Property*.

Depreciation Rules for Listed Property

The IRS imposes special record keeping rules on listed property—items that can easily be used for personal as well as business purposes. (See

"Listed Property" in Chapter 15.) If you use listed property for business more than 50% of the time, you may deduct its cost just like any other long-term business property (under Section 179 or using bonus or regular depreciation rules).

However, if you use listed property 50% or less for business, you may not deduct the cost under Section 179 or use bonus depreciation or accelerated depreciation. Instead, you must use the slowest method of depreciation: straight-line depreciation. In addition, you are not allowed to use the normal depreciation periods allowed under the MACRS depreciation system. Instead, you must use the depreciation periods provided for by the Alternative Depreciation System (ADS for short). These are generally longer than the ordinary MACRS periods. However, you may still depreciate cars, trucks, and computers over five years. The main ADS depreciation periods for listed property are provided in the chart below.

ADS Depreciation Periods	
Property	**Depreciation Period**
Cars and light trucks	5 years
Computers and peripheral equipment	5 years
Communication equipment	10 years
Personal property with no class life	12 years

If you start out using accelerated depreciation and in a later year your business use drops to 50% or less, you have to switch to the straight-line method and ADS period for that year and subsequent years. In addition, you are subject to depreciation recapture for the prior years—that is, you must calculate how much more depreciation you got in the prior years by using accelerated depreciation and count that amount as ordinary taxable income for the current year (see "Recapture Under Section 179," above). This will, of course, increase your tax bill for the year.

Computer Software

Most businesses buy computer software; some also create it themselves. The tax law favors the latter group.

Software You Buy

The software you buy comes in two basic types for tax purposes: software that comes already installed on a computer that you buy and software you purchase separately and install yourself (often called "off-the-shelf" software).

Software that comes with a computer you buy and is included in the price—for example, your operating system—is depreciated as part of the computer, unless you're billed separately for the software.

You must depreciate off-the-shelf software over three years using the straight-line method.

In the past, Section 179 expensing was not available for computer software. However, Congress temporarily changed the law in 2003 to permit off-the-shelf software to be currently deducted under Section 179. However, this exception applies only to software placed in service from January 1, 2003 through December 31, 2011. Starting in 2012, Section 179 will once again be prohibited for off-the-shelf software (unless, of course, the law is changed again).

If you acquire software that is not off-the-shelf, by buying another business or its assets, the rules discussed above don't apply. You must depreciate this software over 15 years using the straight-line method; this type of depreciation is called amortization (see I.R.C. § 197).

Software You Create

If you create software yourself, you can currently deduct the cost under Section 174 of the Internal Revenue Code. This provision allows deductions for research and experimentation expenses incurred in developing an invention, patent, process, prototype, formula, technique, or similar product.

You may currently deduct the costs under Section 174 whether you develop the software for your own use, or to sell or license to others. (Rev. Proc. 2000-50.) For a detailed discussion of Section 174, see

What Every Inventor Needs to Know About Business & Taxes, by Stephen Fishman (Nolo).

Real Property

Land cannot be depreciated because it never wears out. However, this doesn't mean you never get a tax deduction for land. When you sell it, you may deduct the cost of the land from the sale price to determine your taxable gain, if any. The costs of clearing, grading, landscaping, or demolishing buildings on land are not depreciable. They are added to the tax basis of the land—that is, to its cost—and subtracted from the money you get when you sell the land, to calculate your taxable loss or gain.

Unlike land, buildings do wear out over time and therefore may be depreciated. This means that when you buy property with buildings on it, you must separate the cost of the buildings from the total cost of the property to calculate your depreciation.

As you might expect, the depreciation periods for buildings are quite long (after all, buildings usually last a long time). The depreciation period for nonresidential buildings placed in service after May 12, 1993 is 39 years. Nonresidential buildings include office buildings, stores, workshops, and factories. Residential real property—an apartment building, for example—is depreciated over 27.5 years. Different periods apply to property purchased before 1993. For detailed guidance on how to depreciate residential real property, refer to *Every Landlord's Tax Deduction Guide,* by Stephen Fishman (Nolo).

You must use the straight-line method to depreciate real property. This means you'll only be able to deduct a small fraction of its value each year—$1/39$ of its value annually if the 39-year period applies.

If you have an office or other workplace in your home that you use solely for your business, you are entitled to depreciate the business portion of the home. For example, if you use 10% of your home for your business, you may depreciate 10% of the home's cost (excluding the cost of the land). In the unlikely event your home has gone down in value since you bought it, you must use its fair market value on the date you began using your home office as your tax basis. You depreciate a home office over 39 years—the term used for nonresidential property.

(A home office is nonresidential property because you don't live in that portion of your home.)

Intangible Assets

Tangible things like equipment and computers aren't the only business assets that wear out or get used up. Intangible assets can also get used up or become obsolete. Intangible assets are things you can't see or touch. They include intellectual property—patents, copyrights, trade secrets, and trademarks—and business goodwill.

The cost of intangible assets that get used up may be deducted over the useful life of the asset. This process is called amortization, but it works just like straight-line depreciation. You deduct an equal amount of the cost of the asset each year over its useful life.

If you buy an intangible asset from someone else, you may deduct its cost over its useful life. Except for trademarks, which are amortized over 15 years, the IRS has not established any set time periods for the useful lives of intangible assets. The taxpayer determines the useful life, subject to review by the IRS. The useful life of an invention or copyright for tax purposes can be complex to determine: It could be the entire legal duration of the copyright or patent (at least 70 years for copyrights, and up to 20 years for patents) or a shorter time if the asset will become worthless or obsolete more quickly.

Patents and copyrights that you obtain through the purchase of another business or its assets are depreciated over 15 years using the straight-line method. (I.R.C. § 197.)

Generally, if you create an intangible asset (such as an invention or a copyrighted work of authorship like a book or film) yourself, you may currently deduct the cost. Any costs that you can't currently deduct may be amortized as described above.

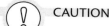 CAUTION

Amortization can be tricky. This is a complex area of taxation. Consult with a knowledgeable tax pro if you need to amortize an intangible asset.

> **RESOURCE**
>
> **Need more information on deductions for inventors?** For a detailed discussion of the tax deductions involved in creating inventions, see *What Every Inventor Needs to Know About Business & Taxes,* by Stephen Fishman (Nolo).

Depreciation Recapture

To deduct long-term property under Section 179 or depreciate listed property using bonus or accelerated depreciation, you must use the property for your business at least 51% of the time. If your business use falls to 50% or less, you'll have to give back part of the Section 179 or bonus or accelerated depreciation deductions you received. This is called "recapture" because the IRS is getting back—recapturing—part of your deduction. (See "Recapture Under Section 179," above.)

Recapture is required for listed property and for property for which you took a Section 179 deduction. It is not required for nonlisted property for which you took no Section 179 deduction. For example, it is not required for a building or factory machine.

Recapture may be triggered when you sell a long-term asset for a gain—that is, for more than your adjusted basis.

> **EXAMPLE:** Sam buys a computer for $5,000 for his home business in 2009. By 2011, he has taken $3,470 in depreciation deductions, leaving an adjusted basis of $1,530. He resells the computer in 2012 for $2,500. This gives Sam a gain of $970. This $970 gain is taxable as ordinary income.

You can't avoid recapture by not taking a Section 179 or depreciation deduction to which you were entitled. The IRS will treat you as though you took the deduction for recapture purposes, even if you didn't.

> **EXAMPLE:** If Sam fails to depreciate his computer and then sells it in 2012 for $2,500, the IRS will figure that his adjusted basis is $1,530 because he could have taken $3,470 in depreciation for it. So, he still has a taxable gain of $970.

Tax Reporting and Record Keeping

You must report depreciation and Section 179 deductions on IRS Form 4562, *Depreciation and Amortization*. If you have more than one business for which you're claiming depreciation, you must use a separate Form 4562 for each business. If you're a sole proprietor, you carry over the amount of your depreciation and Section 179 deductions to your Schedule C and subtract them from your gross business income along with your other business expenses.

> **TIP**
>
> **Let your computer handle the fine print.** Form 4562 is one of the most complex and confusing IRS forms. If you want to complete it yourself, do yourself a favor and use a tax preparation program.

You need to keep accurate records for each asset you depreciate or expense under Section 179, showing:
- a description of the asset
- when and how you purchased the property
- the date it was placed in service
- its original cost
- the percentage of time you use it for business
- whether and how much you deducted under Section 179
- the amount of depreciation you took for the asset in prior years, if any
- the asset's depreciable basis
- the depreciation method used
- the length of the depreciation period, and
- the amount of depreciation you deducted for the year.

If you use tax preparation software, it should create a worksheet containing this information. Be sure to check this carefully and save it. You can also use an accounting program, such as *QuickBooks*, to keep track of your depreciating assets. (Simple checkbook programs like *Quicken* are not designed to track depreciation.) You may also use a spreadsheet program to create your own depreciation worksheet.

Spreadsheet templates are available for this purpose. Of course, you can also do the job by hand.

The instructions to IRS Form 4562 contain a worksheet you can use. An example of a filled-out worksheet prepared by the IRS appears below.

Depreciation Worksheet

Description of Property	Date Placed in Service	Cost or Other Basics	Business/Investment Use Percentage	Section 179 Deduction and Special Allowance	Depreciation in Prior Years	Basis for Depreciation	Method/Convention	Recovery Period	Rate or Table Percentage	Depreciation Deduction
Used Equipment —Transmission Jack	1-3	3,000	100%	—	—	3,000	200 DB/HY	7	14.29%	$ 429
Used Pickup Truck	1-3	8,000	100%	—	—	8,000	200 DB/HY	5	20%	1,600
Used Heavy Duty Tow Truck	1-3	30,000	100%	—	—	30,000	200 DB/HY	5	20%	6,000
Used Equipment —Engine Hoist	1-3	4,000	100%	—	—	4,000	200 DB/HY	7	14.29%	572
										$8,601

For listed property, you'll also have to keep records showing how much time you spend using it for business and personal purposes. You should also keep proof of the amount you paid for the asset—receipts, canceled checks, and purchase documents. You need not file these records with your tax return, but you must have them available to back up your deductions if you're audited.

Leasing Long-Term Assets

When you're acquiring a long-term asset for your business, you should consider whether it makes more sense to lease the item rather than purchase it. Almost everything a business needs can be leased —computers, office furniture, equipment. And leasing can be an attractive alternative to buying. However, when making your decision it's important to understand the tax consequences of leasing.

Leasing Versus Purchasing

So which is better, leasing or buying? It depends. Leasing equipment and other long-term assets can be a better option for small business owners who have limited capital or who need equipment that must be upgraded every few years. Purchasing equipment can be a better option for businesses with ample capital or for equipment that has a long usable life. Each business's situation is unique, and the decision to buy or lease must be made on a case-by-case basis. The following chart summarizes the major tax and nontax differences between leasing and buying equipment.

Before deciding whether to purchase or lease an expensive item, it's a good idea to determine the total actual costs of each option. This depends on many factors, including:

- the cost of the lease
- the purchase price for the item
- the item's useful life
- the interest rate on a loan to purchase the item
- the item's residual value—how much it would be worth at the end of the lease term
- whether you will purchase the item at the end of the lease and how much this would cost
- how much it would cost to dispose of the item
- your income tax bracket
- whether the item qualifies for one-year Section 179 expensing or must be depreciated, and
- if the item must be depreciated, the length of the depreciation period.

There are several lease-versus-buy calculators on the Internet that you can use to compare the costs of leasing versus buying, including www.lease-vs-buy.com. Commercial software and computer spreadsheets can also be used for this purpose.

	Leasing	Buying
Tax Treatment	Lease payments are a currently deductible business operating expense. No depreciation or Section 179 deductions.	Up to $500,000 (2011) in equipment purchases can be deducted in one year under Section 179 (if requirements satisfied). 100% can be deducted in 2011 using bonus depreciation, 50% in 2012. Otherwise, cost is depreciated over several years (usually 5 to 7). Interest on loans to buy equipment is currently deductible.
Initial Cash Outlay	Small. No down payment required. Deposit ordinarily required.	Large. At least a 20% down payment usually required. Bank loan may be required to finance the remaining cost.
Ownership	You own nothing at end of lease term.	You own the equipment.
Costs of Equipment Obsolescence	Borne by lessor because it owns equipment. Lessee may lease new equipment when lease expires.	Borne by buyer because buyer owns equipment, which may have little resale value.

Leases Versus Installment Purchases

An installment purchase (also called a conditional sales contract) is different from a lease—although the two can seem very similar. With an installment purchase, you end up owning all or part of the property, whereas with a lease you own nothing when the lease ends.

The distinction between a lease and an installment purchase is important because installment purchases are treated very differently for tax purposes. Payments for installment purchases are not rent and cannot be deducted as a business operating expense. The purchaser may deduct installment purchase payments under Section 179 (if applicable) or depreciate the property's value over several years, except that any portion of the payments that represent interest may be currently deducted as an interest expense.

You can't simply label a transaction a lease or installment purchase depending on which is more advantageous. A lease must really be a lease (often called a true lease or tax lease) to pass muster with the IRS. A lease that is really just a way of financing a purchase is a financial lease, not a true lease, and will be treated as an installment purchase by the IRS.

Whether a transaction is a lease or installment purchase depends on the parties' intent. The IRS will conclude that a conditional sales contract exists if any of the following are true.

- The agreement applies part of each payment toward an ownership interest that you will receive.
- You get title to the property upon the payment of a stated amount required under the contract.
- The amount you pay to use the property for a short time is a large part of the amount you would pay to get title to the property.
- You pay much more than the current fair rental value for the property.
- You have an option to buy the property at a nominal price compared to the value of the property when you may exercise the option.
- You have an option to buy the property at a nominal price compared to the total amount you have to pay under the lease.
- The lease designates some part of the payments as interest, or part of the payments are easy to recognize as interest.

A transaction will also look like an installment purchase to the IRS (even if it's labeled a lease) if:

- the lease term is about equal to the functional or economic life of the property
- the lease may not be canceled, and
- the lessee is responsible for maintaining the property.

The Home Office Deduction

Qualifying for the Home Office Deduction.. 122

   Threshold Requirements: Regular and Exclusive Business Use...................... 123

   Additional Requirements 129

Corporation Employees.. 135

Calculating the Home Office Deduction 136

   How Much of Your Home Is Used for Business?... 136

   What Expenses Can You Deduct?.. 140

IRS Reporting Requirements.. 154

Audit-Proofing Your Home Office Deduction... 155

   Prove That You Are Following the Rules.. 155

   Keep Good Expense Records... 156

Т he home office deduction allows you to deduct many of the costs associated with running a business from your home. If you're a renter, this may be your single largest tax deduction. It won't save you nearly as much if you own your home, but you'll still be able to recoup some of your business-related costs by using this deduction.

Qualifying for the Home Office Deduction

The federal government helps out home business owners by letting them deduct their home office expenses from their taxable income. This is true whether you own your home or apartment or are a renter. Although this tax deduction is commonly called the home office deduction, it applies not only to space devoted to office work, but also to a workshop, lab, studio, or any other home workspace that you use for your business.

> **EXAMPLE:** Rich, a professional musician and freelance writer, uses the basement of his San Francisco rental home as his writing office and recording studio. He can deduct his home office expenses, including a portion of his rent, from his business income. This saves him over $2,000 per year on his income and self-employment taxes.

If you've heard stories about how difficult it is to qualify for the home office deduction, you can breathe more easily. Changes in the tax law that took effect in 1999 make it much easier for businesspeople to qualify for the deduction. So even if you haven't qualified for the deduction in the past, you may be entitled to take it now.

Some people believe that taking the home office deduction invites an IRS audit. The IRS denies this. But even if taking the deduction increases your audit chances, the risk of an audit is still low (see Chapter 17). Moreover, you have nothing to fear from an audit if you're entitled to take the deduction and you keep good records to prove it. Unfortunately, because of these fears, only about one third of all taxpayers who qualify for the home office deduction actually take it—as many as 5 million taxpayers who could take the deduction, don't.

However, if you plan on taking the deduction, you need to learn how to do it properly. There are strict requirements you must meet in order to qualify for the home office deduction. You are entitled to the home office deduction if you:

- are in business
- use your home office exclusively for business (unless you store inventory or run a day care center in your home—see "Additional Requirements," below), and
- use your home office for business on a regular basis.

These are the three threshold requirements that everyone must meet. If you get past this first hurdle, then you must also meet *any one* of the following requirements:

- your home office is your principal place of business
- you regularly and exclusively use your home office for administrative or management activities for your business and have no other fixed location where you perform such activities
- you meet clients or customers at home
- you use a separate structure on your property exclusively for business purposes
- you store inventory or product samples at home, or
- you run a day care center at home.

These rules apply whether you are a sole proprietor, partner in a partnership, limited liability company (LLC) owner, or an S corporation owner. If you're one of the few home business people who has formed a regular C corporation that you own and operate, and you work as its employee, however, you must meet some additional requirements (see "Corporation Employees," below).

Threshold Requirements: Regular and Exclusive Business Use

To take the home office deduction, you must have a home office—that is, an office or other workplace in your home that you use regularly and exclusively for business. Your home may be a house, apartment, condominium, mobile home, or even a boat. You can also take the deduction for separate structures on your property that you use for business, such as an unattached garage, workshop, studio, barn, or greenhouse.

Requirements for Home Office Deduction

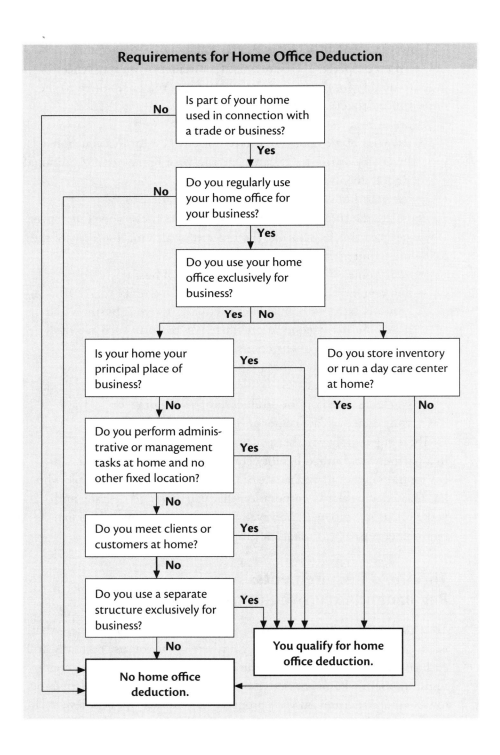

You Must Be in Business

You must be in business to take the home office deduction. You can't take the deduction for a hobby or other nonbusiness activity that you conduct out of your home. Nor can you take it if you perform personal investment activities at home—for example, researching the stock market. (See Chapter 2 for information on what constitutes a business for tax purposes.)

You don't have to work full time in a business to qualify for the home office deduction. If you satisfy the requirements, you can take the deduction for a side business that you run from a home office. However, you must use your home office regularly, and the total amount you deduct cannot exceed your profit from the business. (See "What Expenses Can You Deduct?" later in this chapter, for more on the profit limitation.)

> **EXAMPLE:** Barbara works full time as an editor for a publishing company. An avid bowler, she also spends about 15 hours a week writing and publishing a bowling newsletter. She does all the work on the newsletter from an office in her apartment. Barbara may take the home office deduction, but she can't deduct more than she earns from the newsletter.

If you have more than one business, each business must qualify separately for the home office deduction. Depending on where you do your work, it's possible that one of your businesses will qualify while the other does not.

> **EXAMPLE:** Jim has two businesses: He runs a bookkeeping service and also works as a professional magician, performing at birthdays, conventions, and similar events. He performs all of his bookkeeping work at home, so he can take a home office deduction for his bookkeeping business. However, because he does not work on his magic business at home, he gets no home office deduction for that income.

This rule can be important because of the profit limit on the amount of the home office deduction—that is, your deduction may not exceed the net profit you earn from your home office business or businesses. You'll want to make sure that your most profitable enterprises qualify for the deduction.

You Must Use Your Home Office Exclusively for Business

You can't take the home office deduction unless you use part of your home exclusively for your business. In other words, you must use your home office *only for your business*. The more space you devote exclusively to your business, the more your home office deduction will be worth. (See "Calculating the Home Office Deduction," below.) This requirement doesn't apply if you store inventory at home or run a home day care center. (See "Additional Requirements," below.)

If you use part of your home—such as a room or studio—as your business office, but you also use that space for personal purposes, you won't qualify for the home office deduction.

> EXAMPLE: Johnny, a home-based professional fundraiser, has a den at home furnished with a desk, chair, bookshelf, filing cabinet, and a bed for visiting guests. He uses the desk and chair for both business and personal reasons. The bookshelf contains both personal and business books, the filing cabinet contains both personal and business files, and the bed is used only for personal reasons. Johnny can't claim a business deduction for the den because he does not use it, or any part of it, exclusively for business purposes.

The easiest way to meet the exclusive use test is to devote an entire room in your home to your business—for example, by using an extra bedroom as your office. However, not everybody has a room to spare— and the IRS recognizes this. You can still claim the deduction even if you use just part of a room as your office, as long as you devote that portion of the room exclusively to your business.

> EXAMPLE: Paul, a software engineer, keeps his desk, chair, bookshelf, computer, and filing cabinet in one part of his den and uses them exclusively for business. The remainder of

the room—one-third of the space—is used to store a bed for houseguests. Paul can take a home office deduction for the two-thirds of the room that he uses exclusively as an office.

How Big (or Small) Can Your Home Office Be?

Your home office can be as big or small as you want or need. You are not required to use as small a space as possible. If you like plenty of office space, you can spread out and even use more than one room. But remember, you may use your home office space only for business. You aren't even supposed to use it for personal business, such as writing personal checks.

Although the IRS probably won't be inspecting your home office, your deduction must still make sense in the event you are audited. If you live in a one-bedroom apartment and claim the entire bedroom as a home office, you'll have to have an answer ready when the IRS asks where you sleep.

In one case, for example, a psychologist who lived in San Francisco claimed a home office deduction for one-quarter of her apartment. However, the entire apartment was a 400-square-foot studio, consisting of an open area (approximately 13 feet by 15 feet) furnished with a desk and a couch, and a small dining area and kitchen (each approximately seven feet by eight feet). Given the layout of this tiny apartment, neither the IRS nor the tax court bought the psychologist's claim that she used 100 square feet exclusively for her psychology practice. (*Mullin v. Comm'r.,* TC Memo 2001-121.) On the other hand, a home-based entrepreneur who lived in a studio apartment in Detroit was allowed to take the home office deduction for a walk-in closet he claimed to use exclusively to store corporate books and records. In this case, it was plausible that he used the closet only for business. (*Hughes v. Comm'r.,* TC Memo 1981-140.)

If you use the same room (or rooms) for your office and for other purposes, you'll have to arrange your furniture and belongings so that a portion of the room is devoted exclusively to your business. Place only your business furniture and other business items in the office portion of the room. Business furniture includes anything that you use for your business, such as standard office furniture like a desk and chair. Depending on your business, it could include other items as well—for example, a psychologist might need a couch, an artist might need work tables and easels, and a consultant might need a seating area to meet with clients. One court held that a financial planner was entitled to have a television in his home office because he used it to keep up on financial news. Be careful what you put in this space, however. In another case, the IRS disallowed the deduction for a doctor because he had a television in the part of his living room that he claimed as his home office. The court wouldn't buy the doctor's claim that he used the TV only to watch medical programs.

The IRS does not require you to physically separate the space you use for business from the rest of the room. However, doing so will help you satisfy the exclusive use test. For example, if you use part of your living room as an office, you could separate it from the rest of the room with folding screens or bookcases.

Although you must use your home office exclusively for business, you and other family members or visitors may walk through it to get to other rooms in your residence.

As a practical matter, the IRS doesn't have spies checking to see whether you're using your home office just for business. However, complying with the rules from the beginning means you won't have to worry if you are audited.

When the IRS Can Enter Your Home

IRS auditors may not enter your home unless you or another lawful occupant gives them permission. The only exception is if the IRS obtains a court order to enter your home, which is very rare. In the absence of such a court order, an IRS auditor must ask permission to come to your home to verify your home office deduction. You don't have to grant permission for the visit—but if you don't, the auditor will probably disallow your deduction.

You Must Use Your Home Office Regularly

It's not enough to use a part of your home exclusively for business; you must also use it regularly. For example, you can't place a desk in a corner of a room and claim the home office deduction if you almost never use the desk for your business.

Unfortunately, the IRS doesn't offer a clear definition of regular use. The agency has stated only that you must use a portion of your home for business on a continuing basis—not just for occasional or incidental business. One court has held that 12 hours of use a week is sufficient. (*Green v. Comm'r.*, 79 TC 428 (1982).) You might be able to qualify with less use—for example, an hour a day—but no one knows for sure.

Additional Requirements

Using a home office exclusively and regularly for business is not enough to qualify for the home office deduction: You also must satisfy at least one of the additional tests described below.

Your Home Is Your Principal Place of Business

The most common way to satisfy the additional home office deduction requirement is to show that you use your home as your principal place of business. How you accomplish this depends on where you do most of your work and what type of work you do at home.

If you work only at home. If, like many home business owners, you do all or almost all of your work in your home office, your home is clearly your principal place of business, and you'll have no trouble qualifying for the home office deduction. This would be the case, for example, for a writer who writes only at home or a salesperson who sells by phone and makes sales calls from home.

If you work in multiple locations. If you work in more than one location, your home office still qualifies as your principal place of business if you perform your most important business activities—those activities that most directly generate your income—at home.

> **EXAMPLE:** Charles is a self-employed author who uses a home office to write. He spends 30 to 35 hours per week in his home

office writing and another ten to 15 hours a week at other locations conducting research, meeting with publishers, and attending promotional events. The essence of Charles's business is writing—this is how he generates his income. Therefore, his home qualifies as his principal place of business because that's where he writes.

If you perform equally important business activities in several locations, your principal place of business is where you spend more than half of your time. If there is no such location, you don't have a principal place of business.

> **EXAMPLE:** Sue sells costume jewelry over eBay from her home office, at crafts fairs, and through consignments to craft shops. She spends 25 hours per week in her home office and 15 hours at fairs and crafts shops. Her home office qualifies as her principal place of business.

You Conduct Administrative or Management Activities From Home

Of course, many businesspeople spend the bulk of their time working away from home. This is the case, for example, for:

- building contractors who work primarily on building sites
- doctors who work primarily in hospitals
- traveling salespeople who visit clients at their places of business, and
- housepainters, gardeners, and home repair people who work primarily in their customers' homes.

Fortunately, legal changes that took effect in 1999 make it possible for these people to qualify for the home office deduction. Under the rules, your home office qualifies as your principal place of business, even if you work primarily outside your home, if:

- you use the office to conduct administrative or management activities for your business, and
- there is no other fixed location where you conduct substantial administrative or management activities.

Administrative or management activities include, but are not limited to:

- billing clients or patients
- keeping books and records
- ordering supplies
- setting up appointments, and
- writing reports.

This means that you can qualify for the home office deduction even if your home office is not where you generate most of your business income. It's sufficient that you regularly use your office to administer or manage your business—for example, to keep your books, schedule appointments, do research, write reports, forward orders, or order supplies. As long as you have no other fixed location where you regularly do these things—for example, an outside office—you'll get the deduction.

Because of these rules, almost any home business owner can qualify for the home office deduction. All you have to do is set up a home office that you regularly use to manage or administer your business. Even people who spend most of their work time away from home can usually find plenty of business-related work to do in a home office.

> EXAMPLE: Sally, a self-employed handyperson, performs home repair work for clients in their homes. She also has a home office that she uses regularly and exclusively to keep her books, arrange appointments, and order supplies. Sally is entitled to a home office deduction.

Under these rules, you may have an outside office or workplace and still qualify for the home office deduction as long as you use your home office to perform administrative or management tasks and you don't perform substantial administrative tasks at your outside office.

> EXAMPLE: Bill, a self-employed goldsmith, maintains a workshop in an industrial park where he performs his goldsmithing. He also has a home office where he takes care of all the administrative

functions for his business, including taking orders and record keeping. Bill may take the home office deduction.

You may occasionally conduct minimal administrative or management activities at your outside office (or other fixed location). You may also perform some administrative tasks in a place other than a fixed location, such as your car, hotel room, or clients' offices (a client's office is a fixed location only for the client, not for you).

EXAMPLE: Millie sells Bibles door-to-door. She stores order forms and keeps tracks of appointments in her car. She regularly uses her home office to forward orders and perform other administrative tasks. Millie is entitled to take a home office deduction.

All the administrative or management activities for your business don't have to be done at home to qualify for the home office deduction. Your home office can qualify for the deduction even if you have others conduct your administrative or management activities at locations other than your home—for example, an outside company does your billing from its place of business.

Moreover, you can qualify for the deduction even if you have suitable space to conduct administrative or management activities outside your home, but choose to use your home office for those activities instead.

EXAMPLE: Paul, a self-employed anesthesiologist, spends most of his time administering anesthesia and postoperative care in three local hospitals. One of the hospitals provides him with a small shared office where he could conduct administrative or management activities, but rarely does. Instead, he uses a room in his home that he has converted to an office. He uses this room exclusively and regularly to contact patients, surgeons, and hospitals regarding scheduling; prepare for treatments and presentations; maintain billing records and patient logs; satisfy continuing medical education requirements; and read medical journals and books. Paul qualifies for the home office deduction even though he could use the office provided by the hospital.

You Meet Clients or Customers at Home

Even if your home office is not your principal place of business, you may deduct your expenses for any part of your home that you use exclusively to meet with clients, customers, or patients. You must physically meet with others in this home location; phoning them from there is not sufficient. And the meetings must be a regular part of your business; occasional meetings don't qualify.

It's not entirely clear how often you must meet clients at home for those meetings to be considered regular. However, the IRS has indicated that meeting clients one or two days a week is sufficient. Exclusive use means you use the space where you meet clients only for business. You are free to use the space for business purposes other than meeting clients—for example, doing your business bookkeeping or other paperwork. But you cannot use the space for personal purposes, such as watching television.

> EXAMPLE: June, an attorney, works three days a week in her city office and two days in her home office, which she uses only for business. She meets clients at her home office at least once a week. Because she regularly meets clients at her home office, she qualifies for the home office deduction even though her city office is her principal place of business.

If you want to qualify under this part of the rule, encourage clients or customers to visit you at home and keep a log or appointment book showing all of their visits.

You Use a Separate Structure for Business

You can also deduct expenses for a separate freestanding structure, such as a studio, garage, or barn, if you use it exclusively and regularly for your business. The structure does not have to be your principal place of business, and you do not have to meet patients, clients, or customers there.

Exclusive use means that you use the structure only for business—for example, you can't use it to store gardening equipment or as a guesthouse. Regular use is not precisely defined, but it's probably sufficient to use the structure ten or 15 hours a week.

> EXAMPLE: Deborah is a freelance graphic designer. She has her main office in a downtown office building, but also works every weekend in a small studio in her backyard. Because she uses the studio regularly and exclusively for her design work, she qualifies for the home office deduction.

You Store Inventory or Product Samples at Home

You can also take the home office deduction if you are in the business of selling retail or wholesale products and you store inventory or product samples at home. To qualify, you can't have an office or other business location outside your home. And you must store your inventory in a particular place in your home—for example, a garage, closet, or bedroom. You can't move your inventory from one room to the other. You don't have to use the storage space exclusively to store your inventory to take the deduction—you just have to regularly use it for that purpose.

> EXAMPLE: Lisa sells costume jewelry door to door. She rents a home and regularly uses half of her attached garage to store her jewelry inventory; she also parks her Harley Davidson motorcycle there. Lisa can deduct the expenses for the storage space even though she does not use her entire garage exclusively to store inventory.

You Operate a Day Care Center at Home

You're also entitled to a home office deduction if you operate a day care center at home. This is a place where you care for children, people who are at least 65 years old, or people who are physically or mentally unable to care for themselves. Your day care must be licensed by the appropriate licensing agency, unless it's exempt. You must regularly use part of your home for day care, but your day care use need not be exclusive—for example, you could use your living room for day care during the day and for personal reasons at night.

Corporation Employees

If you form a corporation to own and operate your business, you'll probably work as its employee. You'll be entitled to deduct your home office expenses only if you meet the requirements discussed above and you maintain your home office for the convenience of your employer— that is, your corporation. An employee's home office is deemed to be for an employer's convenience if it is:

- a condition of employment
- necessary for the employer's business to properly function, or
- needed to allow the employee to properly perform his or her duties.

When you own the business that employs you, you ordinarily won't be able to successfully claim that a home office is a condition of your employment—after all, as the owner of the business, you're the person who sets the conditions for employees, including yourself. If there is no other office where you do your work, however, you should be able to establish that your home office is necessary for your business to properly function and/or for you to perform your employee duties.

It will be more difficult to establish convenience if you have separate corporate offices. Nevertheless, business owners in this situation have successfully argued that their home offices were necessary—for example, because their corporate offices were not open or not usable during evenings, weekends, or other nonbusiness hours, or were too far from home to use during off-hours.

Calculating the Home Office Deduction

This is the fun part—figuring out how much the home office deduction will save you in taxes.

How Much of Your Home Is Used for Business?

To calculate your home office deduction, you need to determine what percentage of your home you use for business. The law says you can use "any reasonable method" to do this. Obviously, you want to use the method that will give you the largest home office deduction. To do this, you want to maximize the percentage of your home that you claim as your office. There is no single way to do this for every home office. Try both methods described below, the square footage and the room, and use the one that gives you the largest deduction.

Renting Your Home Office to Your Corporation

If you've incorporated your business as a C corporation and you can't meet the convenience of the employer test or the other requirements for the home office deduction, you have another option: Forget about the home office deduction and rent your home office to your C corporation. You won't save any income tax this way, but you can still save on Social Security and Medicare taxes.

Here's how it works.

- You rent your home office to your C corporation for a fair market rental.
- Your C corporation deducts the rent as a business expense on its tax return (Form 1120).
- You report the rent you receive as ordinary income on your personal tax return, and pay income tax on it.

Ordinarily, a landlord may deduct his rental expenses such as mortgage interest, depreciation, and utilities. However, a special tax rule prohibits an employee who rents part of his home to his employer from deducting

Renting Your Home Office to Your Corporation (cont'd)

such expenses. (I.R.C. § 280A(c)(6).) So, you can forget about taking any deductions for your rental expenses to reduce your income taxes.

However, you still save on Social Security and Medicare taxes because the rental income you receive is not subject to these taxes. For the rent to be deductible by the corporation, however, there must be a legitimate business reason for this rental arrangement. This would be the case if your home office was your only office, or if you could otherwise show a legitimate need for it.

> EXAMPLE: Rod, an accountant who works out of his home, formed a C corporation. Rod does not qualify for the home office deduction because he does not use his office exclusively for his accounting business. He charges his corporation $10,000 per year for the use he makes of his office for his accounting business. Rod gets no home office deduction, but his corporation deducts the rent on its own tax return. He reports the $10,000 on his personal tax return as rental income, but takes no deductions for rental expenses such as depreciation and utilities. Rod saves nothing on his income taxes, but he and his corporation need not pay Social Security and Medicare taxes on the $10,000 rental payment. This saves Rod $1,530 in taxes that he would have had to pay if the $10,000 were paid to him as employee salary.

This strategy only works for C corporations because they are not subject to the home office deduction rules (although their employees are). It won't work with an S corporation because the home office rules apply to pass-through entities. As a result, an S corporation can't deduct rent paid for a home office that doesn't satisfy all the rules discussed above.

You need to be careful not to charge your corporation too much rent. Amounts the IRS deems excessive may be recharacterized as constructive dividends that are not deductible by the corporation. They will, therefore, be subject to corporate income tax which professional corporations usually pay at a 35% rate. To avoid this, the rent you charge your corporation should be the same as what you would charge a stranger.

Some tax experts advise not to claim more than 20% to 25% of your home as an office unless you store inventory at home. However, home business owners have successfully claimed much more. In one case, for example, an interior decorator claimed 74% of his apartment (850 of 1,150 square feet) as a home office. He was audited by the IRS, but the Service did not object to the amount of space he claimed for his office. (*Visin v. Comm'r.*, TC Memo 2003-246.) And a professional violinist successfully claimed a home office deduction for her entire living room, which took up 40% of her one-bedroom apartment. She used the room solely for violin practice. (*Popov v. Comm'r.*, 246 F.3d 1190 (9th Cir. 2002).) It is probably true, though, that the larger your home office deduction, the greater your chances of being audited.

When Is an Office Part of a Home?

Kenneth Burkhart, a professional photographer, purchased a two-story building with a full basement. The building was originally constructed and used as a three-flat apartment building with a separate apartment in the basement and on each of the two upper floors. Burkhart converted the upper two floors into a single residence for his use and converted the basement into a studio and darkroom for his photography business.

Was the studio part of his residence or a separate apartment? This was not an idle question. The home office deduction rules apply only to offices or other workspaces that are part of a business owner's "dwelling."

Courts faced with this issue look at whether the area used for business is physically and functionally part of the business owner's residence. In this case, the court noted that Burkhart had removed the basement's outside entrance, kitchen, bathroom, and sleeping area. Because the basement could only be reached from the upper floors of the building, the court reasoned that the upper floors and the basement had become a single "house," similar to millions of other family homes with two upper floors and a basement. Thus, Burkhart's studio was part of his dwelling and was subject to the home office deduction rules. (*Burkhart v. Comm'r.*, TC Memo 1989-417.)

> **CAUTION**
> **The day care center deduction amount is calculated differently.**
> If you operate a day care center at home but you don't devote a portion of your home exclusively to day care, your home office deduction is calculated differently than described here. You need to compare the time you use the space for day care with the time you use it for personal purposes—for example, if you use 50% of your house as a day care center for 25% of the hours in a year, you can claim a deduction for 12.5% of your housing costs (50% × 25% = 12.5%). See IRS Publication 587, *Business Use of Your Home*, for more information.

Square Footage Method

The most precise method of measuring your office space is to divide the square footage of your home office by the total square footage of your home. For example, if your home is 1,600 square feet and you use 400 square feet for your home office, 25% of the total area is used for business. Of course, you must know the square footage of your entire home and your office to make this calculation. Your home's total square footage may be listed on real estate documents or plans; you'll have to measure your office space yourself. You don't need to use a tape measure; you can just pace off the measurements.

You are allowed to subtract the square footage of common areas—such as hallways, entries, stairs, and landings—from the total area that you are measuring. You can also exclude attics and garages from your total space if you don't use them for business purposes. You aren't required to measure this way, but doing so will give you a larger deduction because your overall percentage of business use will be higher.

Room Method

Another way to measure is the room method. You can use this method only if all of the rooms in your home are about the same size. Using this method, you divide the number of rooms used for business by the total number of rooms in the home. Don't include bathrooms, closets, or other storage areas. You may also leave out garages and attics if you don't use them for business. For example, if you use one room in a five-room house for business, your office takes up 20% of your home.

TIP

The room method often yields a larger deduction. Even though IRS Form 8829, *Expenses for Business Use of Your Home* (the form sole proprietors file to claim the home office deduction), seems to require you to use the square footage method, this isn't the case. As long as all of the rooms in your home are about the same size, you can use the room method. Using the room method will often result in a larger deduction.

> **EXAMPLE:** Rich rents a six-room house in San Francisco and uses one bedroom as his home office. Using the square footage method, Rich measures his entire house and finds it is 2,000 square feet. His home office is 250 square feet. Using these figures, his home office percentage is 12.5% (250 divided by 2,000 = 12.5%). However, he wants to do better than this, so he measures his common areas, such as hallways and stairways, which amount to 200 square feet. He subtracts this amount from the 2,000 total square feet, which leaves 1,800 square feet. This gives him a home office percentage of 14% (250 divided by 1,800 = 14%).
>
> Rich then tries the room method to see whether this provides a better result. His house has six rooms—three bedrooms, a living room, a dining room, and a kitchen. He doesn't count the bathroom, garage, or attic. Because he uses one entire room as his home office, he divides one by six, leaving 16.7% as his home office percentage. Rich uses this amount to figure his home office deduction.

What Expenses Can You Deduct?

The home office deduction is not one deduction, but many. Most costs associated with maintaining and running your home office are deductible. However, because your office is in your home, some of

Square Footage Method (Total Area)

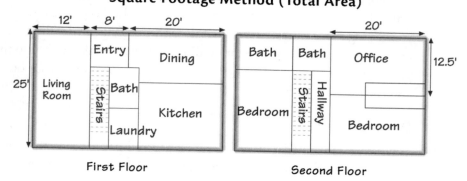

First Floor

Second Floor

Square Footage Method (Excluding Common Areas)

First Floor

Second Floor

Room Method

First Floor

Second Floor

the money you spend also benefits you personally. For example, your utility bill pays to heat your home office, but it also keeps the rest of your living space warm. The IRS deals with this issue by dividing home office expenses into two categories: direct expenses, which benefit only your home office; and indirect expenses, which benefit both your office and the rest of your home.

Direct Expenses

You have a direct home office expense when you pay for something just for the home office portion of your home. This includes, for example, the cost of painting your home office, carpeting it, or hiring someone to clean it. The entire amount of a direct home office expense is deductible.

> **EXAMPLE:** Jean pays a housepainter $400 to paint her home office. She may deduct this entire amount as a home office deduction.

Virtually anything you buy for your office that wears out, becomes obsolete, or gets used up is deductible. However, you may have to depreciate permanent improvements to your home office over 39 years, rather than deduct them in the year when you pay for them. Permanent improvements are changes that go beyond simple repairs, such as adding a new room to your home to serve as your office. (See Chapter 5 for more information.)

Indirect Expenses

An indirect expense is a payment for something that benefits your *entire home*, including both the home office portion and your personal space. You may deduct only a portion of this expense—the home office percentage of the total.

> **EXAMPLE:** Instead of just painting her home office, Jean decides to paint her entire home for $1,600. She uses 25% of her home as an office, so she may deduct 25% of the cost, or $400.

Most of your home office expenses will be indirect expenses, including:

- **Rent.** If you rent your home or apartment, you can use the home office deduction to deduct part of your rent—a substantial expense that is ordinarily not deductible. Your tax savings will be particularly great if you live in a high-rent area.

   > **EXAMPLE:** Sam uses 20% of his Manhattan studio apartment as a home office for his consulting business. He pays $2,000 per month in rent, and may therefore deduct $400 of his rent per month ($4,800 per year) as a home office expense. This saves him over $2,000 in federal, state, and self-employment taxes.

- **Mortgage interest and property taxes.** Whether or not you have a home office, you can deduct your monthly mortgage interest and property tax payments as a personal itemized income tax deduction on your Schedule A, *Itemized Deductions* (the tax form where you list your personal income tax deductions). But if you have a home office, you have the option of deducting the home office percentage of your mortgage interest and property tax payments as part of your home office deduction. If you do this, you may not deduct this amount on your Schedule A (you can't deduct the same item twice). The advantage of deducting the home office percentage of your monthly mortgage interest and real estate tax payments as part of your home office deduction is that it is a business deduction, not a personal deduction; as such, it reduces the amount of your business income subject to self-employment taxes, as well as reducing your income taxes. The self-employment tax is 15.3% (13.3% for 2011), so you save $153 ($133 for 2011) in self-employment taxes for every $1,000 in mortgage interest and property taxes you deduct as part of your home office deduction.

You Can Deduct Business Expenses Even If You Don't Qualify for the Home Office Deduction

Many business owners believe that they can't deduct any expenses they incur while working at home unless they qualify for the home office deduction. This is a myth that has cost many taxpayers valuable deductions. Even if you don't qualify for or take the home office deduction, you can still take tax deductions for expenses you incur while doing business at home. These are expenses that arise from the fact that you are doing business, not from your use of the home itself.

These include:

- Telephone expenses: You can't deduct the basic cost of a single telephone line into your home, but you can deduct the cost of long-distance business calls and special phone services that you use for your business (such as call waiting or message center). You can also deduct the entire cost of a second phone line that you use just for business, including a cell phone.

- Business equipment and furniture: The cost of office furniture, copiers, fax machines, and other personal property you use for your business and keep at home is deductible, whether or not you qualify for the home office deduction. If you purchase these items specifically for your home business, you can expense them (deduct them in one year) under Section 179 or depreciate them over several years. If you convert personal property you already own to business use, you may depreciate the fair market value. If you're a sole proprietor, you deduct these costs directly on Schedule C, *Profit or Loss From Business.* You don't have to list them on the special tax form used for the home office deduction. If you use the property for both business and personal reasons, the IRS requires you to keep records showing when the item was used for business or personal reasons—for example, a diary or log with the dates, times, and reasons the item was used. See Chapter 5 for a detailed discussion of these rules.

- Supplies: Supplies for your business are currently deductible as an operating expense if they have a useful life of less than one year (see Chapter 4). Otherwise, you must depreciate them or expense them under Section 179, as explained in Chapter 5.

EXAMPLE: Suzy, a self-employed medical record transcriber, uses 20% of her three-bedroom Tulsa home as a home office. She pays $10,000 per year in mortgage interest and property taxes. When she does her taxes for the year, she may deduct $2,000 of her interest and taxes as part of her home office deduction (20% of $10,000). She adds this amount to her other home office expenses and decreases her business income for both income tax and self-employment tax purposes. The extra $2,000 business deduction saves her $306 in self-employment tax (15.3% × $2,000) ($266 for 2011). She may deduct the remaining $8,000 of mortgage interest and property tax as a personal deduction on her Schedule A.

- **Depreciation.** If you own your home, you're also entitled to a depreciation deduction for the office portion of your home. See Chapter 5 for a detailed discussion of depreciation.
- **Utilities.** You may deduct your home office percentage of your utility bills for your entire home, including electricity, gas, water, heating oil, and trash removal. If you use a disproportionately large amount of electricity for your home office, you may be able to deduct more.

EXAMPLE: Sheila, a pottery maker, works out of a home workshop that takes up 25% of the space in her home. Her work requires a substantial amount of electricity. About 50% of her monthly electricity bill is for her home workshop. She may deduct 50% of her electricity costs as a home office expense, instead of just 25%. However, to prove that she isn't deducting too much, she should keep electricity bills for her home before she began using the workshop, or for periods when she doesn't use the workshop, to show that her bills for these months are about 50% lower than the bills for her working months.

- **Insurance.** Both homeowner's and renter's insurance are partly deductible as indirect home office expenses. However, special insurance coverage you buy just for your home office—for example, insurance for your computer or other business equipment—is fully deductible as a direct expense.

- **Home maintenance.** You can deduct the home office percentage of home maintenance expenses that benefit your entire home, such as housecleaning of your entire house, roof and furnace repairs, and exterior painting. These costs are deductible whether you hire someone or do them yourself. If you do the work yourself, however, you can only deduct the cost of materials, not the cost of your own labor. Termite inspection, pest extermination fees, and snow removal costs are also deductible. However, the IRS won't let you deduct lawn care unless you regularly use your home to meet clients or customers. Home maintenance costs that don't benefit your home office—for example, painting your kitchen—are not deductible at all.

- **Casualty losses.** Casualty losses are damage to your home caused by such things as fire, floods, or theft. Casualty losses that affect your entire house—for example, a leak that floods your entire home—are deductible in the amount of your home office percentage. Casualty losses that affect only your home office—for example, a leak that floods only the home office area of the house—are fully deductible direct expenses. Casualty losses that don't affect your home office—for example, if only your kitchen floods—are not deductible as business expenses. However, they may be deductible as itemized personal deductions. (See Chapter 14 for a detailed discussion of casualty losses.)

- **Condominium association fees.** These fees (often substantial) are partly deductible as an indirect expense if you have a home office.

- **Security system costs.** Security system costs are partly deductible as an indirect expense if your security system protects your entire home. If you have a security system that protects only your home office, the cost is a fully deductible direct expense.

- **Computer equipment.** Computers and peripheral equipment (such as printers) are deductible whether or not you qualify for the home office deduction. However, if you don't qualify for the home office deduction, you must prove that you use your computer more than half of the time for business by keeping a log of your usage. (See Chapter 5 for more information on this requirement.) If you qualify for the home office deduction, you don't need to keep track of how much time you spend using your computer for business.

- **Supplies and materials.** Office supplies and materials you use for your home business are not part of the home office deduction. They are deductible whether or not you qualify for the home office deduction.

Mileage Deductions for Leaving the House

If your home office is your principal place of business, you can deduct the cost of traveling from your home to other work locations for your business. For example, you can deduct the cost of driving to perform work at a client's or customer's office. The value of this deduction often exceeds the value of the home business deduction itself. If you don't have a home office, these costs are not deductible. See Chapter 8 for a detailed discussion of the business mileage deduction.

Profit Limit on Deductions

Gilbert Parker worked full time for a large accounting firm, but in his spare time he was writing a book. Parker set aside a portion of his home as an office he used exclusively for writing. Like many beginning authors, he earned no money from writing. But he thought that he could at least get a tax deduction for his writing efforts by deducting his home office expenses, totaling $6,571, $4,904, and $5,444 over three years. He used these deductions to reduce the income tax he had to pay on his salary from his day job. However, both the IRS and the tax court held he could not deduct these expenses. Although he had a legitimate home office, Parker wasn't entitled to a home office deduction because he earned no money from writing. (*Parker v. Comm'r.*, TC Memo 1984-233.)

Gilbert Parker ran afoul of the most significant limitation on the home office deduction: You cannot deduct more than the net profit you earn from your home office. If you run a successful business out of your home office, this won't pose a problem. But if your business earns very little or loses money, the limitation could prevent you from deducting part or even all of your home office expenses in the current year.

If your deductions exceed your profits, you can deduct the excess in the following year and in each succeeding year until you deduct the entire amount. There is no limit on how far into the future you can deduct these expenses; you can claim them even if you are no longer living in the home where they were incurred.

So, whether or not your business is making money, you should keep track of your home office expenses and claim the deduction on your tax return. You do this by filing IRS Form 8829, *Expenses for Business Use of Your Home* (see "IRS Reporting Requirements," below). When you complete the form by plugging in the figures for your business income and home office expenses, it will show you how much you can deduct in the current year and how much you must carry over to the next year.

The profit limitation applies only to the home office deduction. It does not apply to business expenses that you can deduct under other provisions of the tax code.

For these purposes, your profit is the gross income you earn from your business minus your business deductions other than your home office deduction. You must also subtract the home office portion of your mortgage interest, real estate taxes, and casualty losses.

Tax preparation software can calculate your profit for home office deduction purposes, but it's a good idea to understand how it works. First, start with your gross income from your business—if you sell goods, this is the total sales of your business minus the cost of goods sold; if you sell services, it's all the money you earn. You must list this amount on line 7 of your Schedule C. Next, figure out how much money you earn from using your home office. If you do all of your work at home, this will be 100% of your business income. But if you work in several locations, you must determine the portion of your gross income that comes from working in your home office. To do this, consider how much time you spend working in your home office and the type of work you do at home.

Then, subtract from this amount:

- the business percentage of your mortgage interest and real estate taxes (you'll have these expenses only if you own your home), plus any casualty losses, and

- all of your business expenses that are not part of the home office deduction; these are all the deductions listed in Part II of your Schedule C—for example, car expenses, travel, insurance, depreciation of business equipment, business phone, supplies, or salaries. You must deduct these separately from the home office deduction, even if you incurred them while doing business at home.

The remainder is your net profit—the most you can deduct for using your home office.

Types of Home Expenses		
Expense	**Description**	**Deductibility**
Direct	Things you buy only for your home office	Deductible in full
Indirect	Things you buy to keep your entire home up and running	Deductible based on the percentage of your home used as a business office
Unrelated	Things you buy only for parts of your home that are not used for business	Not deductible

Sam Creates a Home Office

Sam starts a part-time home business to help people repair bad credit. He converts one of the bedrooms of his two-bedroom condominium into a home office. He goes on something of a shopping spree, purchasing the following items:

- carpeting for his office and living room
- a separate telephone for the office
- office supplies, such as stapler and paper
- a new desk for his office, and
- a new computer for his office (and one for his family).

He also moves a fancy chair he already owns to his office and uses it solely for his business. In the meantime, Sam's wife has their kitchen repainted and hires a maid to clean the entire condo twice a month. Sam and his wife pay $2,000 each month on mortgage interest, real estate taxes, and homeowner's insurance.

The chart below shows which of these expenses are direct and indirect home office expenses, business operating expenses that are deductible whether or not Sam qualifies for the home office deduction, long-term asset expenses that are also deductible without regard to the home office deduction, and expenses that are not deductible.

Direct Home Office Expenses (100% Deductible)	Indirect Home Office Expense (Deductible in Amount of Home Office Percentage)	Business Operating Expenses	Long-Term Asset Expenses	Not Deductible
Carpet for home office	Mortgage interest and real estate taxes	Office supplies	Office desk	Carpet for living room
	Utilities (electricity and heat)	Business telephone	Office chair	Computer for family
	Maid service		Computer for business	
	Homeowner's insurance			

EXAMPLE: Sam runs a part-time consulting business out of his home office, which occupies 20% of his home. In one year, his gross income from the business was $4,000 and he had $1,000 in expenses separate from his home office deduction. He paid $10,000 in mortgage interest and real estate taxes for the year. His home office deduction for the year is limited to $1,000. He calculates this as follows:

Gross income from business		$4,000
Minus business portion of mortgage interest and taxes ($10,000 × 20%)	–	2,000
Balance	=	2,000
Minus direct business expenses	–	1,000
Home office deduction limit	=	$1,000

Sam's total home office expenses for the year amount to $4,000; this includes $2,000 in mortgage interest and real estate taxes, plus $2,000 in other expenses, such as utilities and depreciation of his home. Sam first deducts those home office expenses that are not deductible as personal itemized deductions—everything other than mortgage interest, real estate taxes, and casualty losses. These expenses were $2,000; he may deduct only $1,000 of this amount because his home office deduction profit limit is $1,000. Because he has reached his profit limit, Sam can't deduct as a home office deduction any portion of his $2,000 mortgage interest and real estate tax expenses. However, he may deduct these amounts as personal itemized deductions on Schedule A. Sam may deduct the $1,000 in unused home office expenses the following year, if he has sufficient income from his business.

Special Concerns for Homeowners

Until recently, homeowners who took the home office deduction were subject to a special tax trap: If they took a home office deduction for more than three of the five years before they sold their house, they had to pay capital gains taxes on the profit from the home office portion of their home. For example, if you made a $50,000 profit on the sale of your house, but your home office took up 20% of the space, you would have had to pay a tax on $10,000 of your profit (20% × $50,000 = $10,000).

Fortunately, IRS rules no longer require this. As long as you live in your home for at least two out of the five years before you sell it, the profit you make on the sale—up to $250,000 for single taxpayers and $500,000 for married taxpayers filing jointly—is not taxable. (See IRS Publication 523, *Selling Your Home.*) If you sold your house after May 6, 1997 and paid capital gains tax on the home office portion, you may be entitled to amend your return for the year you sold the house and receive a tax refund from the IRS. (See Chapter 16 for information on amending tax returns for prior years.)

However, you will have to pay a capital gains tax on the depreciation deductions you took after May 6, 1997 for your home office. This is the deduction you are allowed for the yearly decline in value due to wear and tear of the portion of the building that contains your home office. (See Chapter 5 for more information on depreciation deductions.) These recaptured deductions are taxed at a 25% rate (unless your income tax bracket is lower than 25%).

> EXAMPLE: Sally bought a $200,000 home six years ago and used one of her bedrooms as her home office. She sold her home this year for $300,000, realizing a $100,000 gain (profit). Her depreciation deductions for her home office for the last six years totaled $2,000. She must pay a tax of 25% of $2,000, or $500.

Having to pay a 25% tax on the depreciation deductions you took in the years before you sold your house is actually not a bad deal. This is probably no more—and is often less—tax than you would have had to pay if you hadn't taken the deductions in the first place and instead paid tax on your additional taxable income at ordinary income tax rates.

Additional Limitations for Corporation Employees

If you form a regular corporation to own and operate your business, you will probably be its employee. In this event, you can take home office deductions only as miscellaneous itemized deductions on Schedule A of your tax return. This means you may deduct home office expenses only to the extent that they, along with your other miscellaneous deductions (if any), exceed 2% of your adjusted gross income (AGI). For example, if your AGI was $100,000, you would get a tax benefit only on the amount of your miscellaneous deductions that exceed $2,000. This rule greatly reduces the value of the home office deduction for corporation employees.

Make Your Corporation Reimburse You

There is a better way to recoup your office expenses if you're a corporate employee. Instead of claiming these expenses as miscellaneous itemized deductions, get your C corporation to reimburse you directly for your home office expenses. The corporation can then deduct this amount as an ordinary business expense.

The reimbursement will not be taxable to you personally if:

- you keep careful track of your home office expenses and can prove them with receipts or other records
- your corporation formally approves reimbursement of your home office expenses and the approval is documented in its corporate minutes, and
- you have an "accountable reimbursement plan"—a written agreement in which the corporation agrees to reimburse you if you provide proper substantiation for your expenses. (Reimbursement plans are covered in Chapter 11.)

For more information, see *Tax Deductions for Professionals*, by Stephen Fishman (Nolo), and IRS Publication 334, *Tax Guide for Small Business*.

IRS Reporting Requirements

If, like the vast majority of home business owners, you are a sole proprietor, you deduct your business operating expenses by listing them on IRS Schedule C, *Profit or Loss From Business*. You must list your home office deduction on Schedule C, but you also have to file a special tax form to show how you calculated the home office deduction: Form 8829, *Expenses for Business Use of Your Home*. This form tells the IRS that you're taking the deduction and shows how you calculated it. You should file this form even if you can't currently deduct your home office expenses because your business has no profits. By filing, you can apply the deduction to a future year in which you earn a profit. For detailed guidance on how to fill out Form 8829, see IRS Publication 587, *Business Use of Your Home*.

If you organize your business as a partnership, multimember LLC, or an S corporation, you don't have to file Form 8829. Instead, you deduct your unreimbursed home office expenses (and any other unreimbursed business expenses) on IRS Schedule E (Part II) and attach it to your personal tax return. However, these expenses are deductible only if you have a written partnership or an LLC agreement that requires you to pay these expenses. You must attach a separate schedule to Schedule E listing the home office and other business expenses you're deducting. Any home office expense for which your partnership or LLC reimbursed you must be listed on the partnership or LLC tax return, IRS Form 1065, *U.S. Return of Partnership Income*. These deductions pass through to you along with other partnership deductions.

If you're a renter and take the home office deduction, you should file an IRS Form 1099-MISC each year, reporting the amount of your rental payments attributable to your home office.

> **EXAMPLE:** Bill rents a house and takes the home office deduction. He spends $12,000 per year on rent and uses 25% of his house as a home office. He should file Form 1099, reporting $3,000 of his rental payments.

You should file three copies of Form 1099:

- file one copy with the IRS by February 28
- give one copy to your landlord by January 31, and
- file one copy with your state tax department, if your state imposes income taxes.

Your landlord may not appreciate receiving a Form 1099 from you, but it will definitely be helpful if you're audited by the IRS and your home office deduction is questioned. It helps to show that you really were conducting a business out of your home.

You don't have to file Form 1099 if your landlord is a corporation. Form 1099 is also not required in the unlikely event that your rental payments for your home office total less than $600 for the year.

Audit-Proofing Your Home Office Deduction

If you are audited by the IRS and your home office deduction is questioned, you want to be able to prove that you:

- qualify for the deduction, and
- have correctly reported the amount of your home office expenses.

If you can do both those things, you should be home free.

Prove That You Are Following the Rules

Here are some ways to convince the IRS that you qualify for the home office deduction:

- Take a picture of your home office and draw up a diagram showing your home office as a portion of your home. Do not send the photo or diagram to the IRS. Just keep it in your files to use in case you're audited. The picture should have a date on it—this can be done with a digital camera, or you can have your film date-stamped by a developer.
- Have all of your business mail sent to your home office.
- Use your home office address on all of your business cards, stationery, and advertising.
- Obtain a separate phone line for your business and keep that phone in your home office.

- Encourage clients or customers to regularly visit your home office, and keep a log of their visits.
- To make the most of the time you spend in your home office, communicate with clients by phone, fax, or electronic mail instead of going to their offices. Use a mail or messenger service to deliver your work to customers.
- Keep a log of the time you spend working in your home office. This doesn't have to be fancy; notes on your calendar will do.

Keep Good Expense Records

Be sure to keep copies of your bills and receipts for home office expenses, including:

- IRS Form 1098, *Mortgage Interest Statement* (sent by whoever holds your mortgage), showing the interest you paid on your mortgage for the year
- property tax bills and your canceled checks as proof of payment
- utility bills, insurance bills, and receipts for payments for repairs to your office area, along with your canceled checks paying for these items, and
- a copy of your lease and your canceled rent checks, if you're a renter.

Eating Out and Going Out: Deducting Meal and Entertainment Expenses

What Is Business Entertainment? 158

    Activities That Aren't Entertainment 158

    Meals Can Be Travel or Entertainment 159

Who You Can Entertain 160

Deducting Entertainment Expenses 160

    Business Discussions Before or After Entertainment 161

    Business Discussions During Entertainment 162

    Entertaining at Home 164

    Entertainment in Business Settings 166

Calculating Your Deduction 166

    Expenses Must Be Reasonable 167

    Going "Dutch" 167

    Expenses You Can't Deduct 167

    Entertainment Tickets 170

    Reimbursed Expenses 171

Reporting Entertainment Expenses on Your Tax Return 173

Even though you don't have an outside office, you may do a significant amount of work away from home. Some of your most important business meetings, client contacts, and marketing efforts may take place at restaurants, golf courses, or sporting events. The tax law recognizes that much business is mixed with pleasure—in the form of meals and social events—and permits you to deduct part of the cost of business-related entertainment. However, because many taxpayers have abused this deduction in the past, the IRS has imposed strict rules limiting the types of entertainment expenses you can deduct and the size of the deduction.

What Is Business Entertainment?

You may deduct only half of the total amount you spend on business entertainment activities. Because ordinary and necessary business activities are usually fully deductible, you'll need to know how the IRS distinguishes between regular business activities and entertainment.

The basic rule is that entertainment involves something fun, such as:

- dining out
- going to a nightclub
- attending a sporting event
- going to a concert, movie, or the theater
- visiting a vacation spot (a ski area or beach resort, for example), or
- taking a hunting, yachting, or fishing trip.

Although eating out might fall into other categories of business operating expenses (depending on the circumstances), it is by far the number one business entertainment expense—that is, it is claimed more often than any other entertainment expense and makes up the largest dollar portion of most taxpayers' entertainment deductions.

Activities That Aren't Entertainment

Anything you do as a regular part of your business does not count as entertainment. This is true even though these same activities might constitute entertainment for others. For example, the cost of going to the theater would not be an entertainment expense for a professional theater critic. But if a salesperson invited a client to the theater following an important business meeting, the outing would constitute entertainment. The critic could deduct the entire cost of the theater tickets as a business operating expense (see Chapter 4), while the salesperson could deduct only 50% of the cost as an entertainment expense.

Entertainment does not include activities that are for business purposes only and don't involve any fun or amusement, such as:

- the cost of a hotel room used while traveling on business
- automobile expenses incurred while conducting business, or
- supper money paid to an employee working overtime.

In addition, meals or other entertainment expenses related to advertising or promotions are not considered entertainment. As a rule, an expense for a meal or other entertainment item will qualify as advertising if you make it available to the general public—for example, if a wine importer holds wine tastings where he provides customers with free wine and food to promote his business, the costs of the events would not be considered entertainment expenses. These kinds of advertising and promotion costs are fully deductible as business operating expenses. (See Chapter 14 for more on deducting advertising costs.)

Meals Can Be Travel or Entertainment

A meal can be a travel expense, an entertainment expense, or both. The distinction won't affect how much you can deduct—both travel (overnight) and entertainment expenses are only 50% deductible. But different rules apply to the two categories.

A meal is a travel expense if you eat out of necessity while away on a business trip. For example, any meal you eat alone while on the road for business is a travel expense. On the other hand, a meal is an entertainment expense if you treat a client, customer, or other business associate, and the purpose of the meal is to benefit your business. A meal is both a travel and an entertainment expense if you treat a client or other business associate to a meal while on the road. However, you may only deduct this cost once—whether you choose to do it as an entertainment or a travel expense, only 50% of the cost is deductible (see "Calculating Your Deduction," below).

Who You Can Entertain

You must be with at least one person who can benefit your business in some way to claim an entertainment expense. This could include current or potential:

- customers
- clients
- suppliers
- employees (see Chapter 11 for special tax rules for employees)
- independent contractors
- agents
- partners, or
- professional advisers.

This list includes almost anyone you're likely to meet for business reasons. Although you can invite family members or friends along, you can't deduct the costs of entertaining them, except in certain limited situations (see "Calculating Your Deduction," below).

Deducting Entertainment Expenses

Entertainment expenses, like all business operating expenses, are deductible only if they are ordinary and necessary. This means that the entertainment expense must be common, helpful, and appropriate for your business. Taxpayers used to have to show only that the entertainment wasn't purely for fun, and that it benefited their business in some way. This standard was so easy to satisfy that the IRS came up with a few additional requirements.

Before the IRS made the standard tougher, you could deduct ordinary and necessary entertainment expenses even if business was never discussed. For example, you could deduct the cost of taking a client to a restaurant, even if you spent the whole time drinking martinis and talking about sports (the infamous "three-martini lunch"). This is no longer the case—now you must discuss business with one or more business associates either before, during, or after a social activity if you want to claim an entertainment deduction (subject to one exception: see "Entertainment in Business Settings," below).

> **CAUTION**
>
> **Who's going to know?** The IRS doesn't have spies lurking in restaurants, theaters, or other places of entertainment, so it has no way of knowing whether you really discuss business with a client or other business associate. You're pretty much on the honor system here. However, be aware that if you're audited, the IRS closely scrutinizes this deduction because many taxpayers cheat when they take it. You'll also have to comply with stringent record-keeping requirements. (See Chapter 15 for tips on record keeping.)

Business Discussions Before or After Entertainment

The easiest way to get a deduction for entertainment is to discuss business before or after the activity. To meet this requirement, the discussion must be "associated" with your business—that is, it must have a clear business purpose, such as developing new business or encouraging existing business relationships. You don't, however, have to expect to get a specific business benefit from the discussion. Your business discussion can involve planning, advice, or simply exchanging useful information with a business associate.

You automatically satisfy the business discussion requirement if you attend a business-related convention or meeting to further your business. Business activities—not socializing—must be the main purpose for the convention. Save a copy of the program or agenda to prove this.

Generally, the entertainment should occur on the same day as the business discussion. However, if your business guests are from out of town, the entertainment can occur the day before or the day after the business talk.

EXAMPLE: Mary, a home-based architect who lives in Los Angeles, has been hired to design a large home for Wayne, who lives in Las Vegas. Wayne travels to Los Angeles to discuss his ideas for the house and look at some preliminary drawings prepared by Mary. Wayne arrives on Tuesday evening and Mary treats him to dinner at a nice restaurant that night. The following morning, Wayne goes to Mary's home office to discuss the home building project. Mary can deduct half of the cost of the dinner they had the night before as an entertainment expense.

You can get a deduction even if the entertainment occurs in a place like a nightclub, theater, or loud sports arena, where it's difficult or impossible to talk business. Because your business discussions can take place before or after the entertainment, the IRS won't be scrutinizing whether or not you actually could have talked business during your entertainment activity.

EXAMPLE: Following lengthy contract negotiations at a prospective client's office, you take the client to a baseball game to unwind. You can deduct half of the cost of the tickets as a business expense.

The entertainment can last longer than your business discussions, as long as you don't spend just a small fraction of your total time on business. In other words, you can't simply ask an associate "How's business?" You must have a substantial discussion. Also, your business-related discussions don't have to be face-to-face—they can occur over the telephone or even by email.

Business Discussions During Entertainment

Another way to make your entertainment expenses deductible is to discuss business during an entertainment activity. To get the deduction, you must show that:

- the main purpose of the combined business discussion and entertainment was the active conduct of business—you don't have to spend the entire time talking business, but the main character of the entertainment must be business

- you did, in fact, have a business meeting, negotiation, discussion, or other bona fide business transaction with your guest or guests during the entertainment, and

- you expect to get income or some other *specific business benefit* in the future from your discussions during the entertainment—thus, for example, a casual conversation in which the subject of business comes up won't do; you must have a specific business goal in mind.

EXAMPLE: Ivan, a home-based consultant, has had ongoing email discussions with a prospective client who is interested in hiring him. Ivan thinks he'll be able to close the deal and get a contract signed in a face-to-face meeting. He chooses a lunch meeting because it's more informal and the prospective client will like getting a free lunch. He treats the client to a $40 lunch at a nice restaurant. During the lunch, they finalize the terms of a contract for Ivan's consulting services and come to a handshake agreement. This meal clearly led to a specific business benefit for Ivan, so he can deduct half of the cost of the $40 lunch as an entertainment expense.

You don't necessarily have to close a deal, sign a contract, or otherwise obtain a specific business benefit to get a deduction. But you do have to have a *reasonable expectation* that you can get some specific business benefit through your discussions during the entertainment—for example, to make progress toward new business, sales of your product, or investment in your business.

With the possible exception of some types of home entertainment (see "Entertaining at Home," below), this deduction is limited to business discussions held during meals. In the IRS's view, it's usually not possible to engage in serious business discussions at other types of entertainment activities because of the distractions. Examples of places the IRS would probably find not conducive to serious talk include:

- nightclubs, theaters, or sporting events
- cocktail parties or other large social gatherings
- hunting or fishing trips
- yachting or other pleasure boat outings, or
- group gatherings at a cocktail lounge, golf club, athletic club, or vacation resort that includes people who are not business associates.

This means, for example, that you usually can't claim that you discussed business *during* a golf game, even if your foursome consists of you and three business associates. In the IRS's view, golfers are unable to play and talk business at the same time. On the other hand, you could have a business discussion *before or after* a golf game—for example, in the clubhouse. This might seem ridiculous, but it is the rule.

Entertaining at Home

Home business owners don't just work at home; they may entertain business associates there as well. The cost of entertaining at your home is deductible if it meets either of the above two tests. You cannot, however, deduct the costs of inviting nonbusiness guests to your house, with the possible exception of a business associate's spouse (see "Expenses You Can't Deduct," below).

Business Discussed During Home Entertainment

You are most likely to qualify for a deduction for home entertainment if you discuss business during the activity.

> EXAMPLE: Jack, a home-based venture capital entrepreneur, invites Thomas, an inventor, and his wife to his house for dinner to discuss investing in Thomas's latest invention. They have a lengthy discussion that helps Jack decide to make the investment. The dinner qualifies as a deductible entertainment expense.

However, the IRS probably won't believe that you discussed business during home entertainment if large numbers of people are involved.

EXAMPLE: Arthur invited 40 people to his house for a celebratory party after he passed the bar exam. He served a catered, buffet-style dinner and hired a bartender to serve drinks. Both the IRS and the tax court ruled that the party was not a deductible business entertainment expense. They both concluded that the party was primarily a social event at which Arthur engaged in no substantial business-related conversations. (*Ryman v. Comm'r.*, 51 TC 799.)

A quiet dinner party at home is more likely to qualify as an entertainment expense.

EXAMPLE: Jack Howard, president and managing editor of a large newspaper chain, held monthly dinner parties to which he invited eight to ten guests who were prominent in politics, business, the arts, and other fields. The tax court held that the gatherings were deductible entertainment expenses. The court believed Howard when he said that he held the dinner parties at his home to have "off the record" conversations that helped his media business. The court noted in particular that the gatherings were small and were held on weeknights. (*Howard v. Comm'r.*, TC Memo 98-250.)

Business Discussed Before or After Home Entertainment

A large home gathering (such as a cocktail party) will probably qualify as an entertainment expense only if you have business discussions before or after the event. Of course, small gatherings could qualify on this basis as well.

EXAMPLE: Sheila, a home-based public relations consultant, signs a new contract to represent the raisin growers' trade association. To celebrate and help cement her new business relationship, she invites the association's president and board of directors to her house for a catered dinner party that evening. The party is a deductible business entertainment expense.

Entertainment in Business Settings

An exception to the general rule that you must discuss business before, during, or after entertainment applies when the entertainment occurs in a clear business setting. For example, you can deduct half of the following costs as entertainment expenses:

- the price of renting a hospitality room at a convention where you display or discuss your business products
- entertainment that is mainly a price rebate on the sale of your products—for example, when a restaurant owner provides a free meal to a loyal customer, or
- entertainment that occurs under circumstances where there is no meaningful personal relationship between you and the people you entertained—for example, you entertain local business or civic leaders at the opening of a new hotel to get business publicity, rather than to form business relationships with them.

Calculating Your Deduction

Most expenses you incur for business entertainment are deductible, including meals (with beverages, tax, and tips), your transportation expenses (including parking), tickets to entertainment or sporting events, catering costs for parties, cover charges for admission to night clubs, and rent you pay for a room in which to hold a dinner or cocktail party.

You are allowed to deduct only *50%* of your entertainment expenses. For example, if you spend $50 for a meal in a restaurant, you can deduct $25. (Even though you can deduct only half of the expense, you must keep track of everything you spend and report the entire amount on your tax return.) The only exception to the 50% rule is for transportation expenses, which are 100% deductible.

If you have a single bill or receipt that includes some business entertainment and some other expenses (such as lodging or transportation), you must allocate the expense between the cost of the entertainment and the cost of the other services. For example, if your hotel bill covers meals as well as lodging, you'll have to make a reasonable estimate of the portion that covers meals. It's best to avoid this hassle by getting a separate bill for your deductible entertainment.

Expenses Must Be Reasonable

Your entertainment expenses must be reasonable—the IRS won't let you deduct entertainment expenses that it considers lavish or extravagant. There is no dollar limit on what is reasonable, nor are you necessarily barred from entertaining at deluxe restaurants, hotels, nightclubs, or resorts.

Whether your expenses will be considered reasonable depends on the particular facts and circumstances—for example, a $250 expense for dinner with a client and two business associates at a fancy restaurant would probably be considered reasonable if you closed a substantial business deal during the meal. Because there are no concrete guidelines, you have to use your common sense.

Going "Dutch"

You can deduct entertainment expenses only if you pay for the activity. If a client picks up the tab, you obviously get no deduction. If you split the expense, you must subtract what it would ordinarily cost you for the meal from the amount you actually paid, and then deduct 50% of that total. For example, if you pay $20 for lunch and you usually pay only $5, you can deduct 50% of $15, or $7.50.

If you split a lot of tabs and are worried that the IRS might challenge your deductions, you can save your grocery bills or receipts from eating out for a month to show what you usually spend. You don't need to keep track of which grocery items you eat for each meal. Instead, the IRS assumes that 50% of your total grocery receipts are for dinner, 30% for lunch, and 20% for breakfast.

Expenses You Can't Deduct

There are certain expenses that you are prohibited from deducting as entertainment.

Entertainment Facilities

You may not deduct the cost of buying, leasing, or maintaining an entertainment facility, such as a yacht, swimming pool, tennis court, hunting camp, fishing lodge, bowling alley, car, airplane, hotel suite, apartment, or home in a vacation resort. These entertainment facilities are not considered deductible business assets.

> EXAMPLE: Sue, a home-based salesperson, takes a customer for a day of fishing at a nature resort. The expenses of the outing, such as fishing licenses, bait and tackle, and boat rental are deductible if the requirements are met. However, if Sue and her customer stay overnight at a fishing lodge at the resort, the cost of the lodging is not deductible.

This rule also applies to your home if you use it for business-related entertaining. Thus, for example, you can't take a business entertainment deduction for your normal home maintenance costs just because you do business entertaining at home. You may deduct only expenses that are directly attributable to the entertainment—for example, the cost of food, liquor, caterers, bartenders, and so on.

Expenses of Nonbusiness Guests

You may not deduct the cost of entertaining people who are not business associates. If you entertain business and personal guests at an event, you must divide your entertainment expenses between the two and deduct only the business part.

> EXAMPLE: You take three business associates and six friends to dinner. Because there were ten people at dinner (including you), and only four were business related, 40% of this expense qualifies as business entertainment. If you spend $200 for the dinner, only $80 would be deductible. And because you can deduct only half of your entertainment expenses, your total deduction for the event is $40.

Ordinarily, you cannot deduct the cost of entertaining your spouse or the spouse of a business associate. However, there is an exception: You can deduct these costs if you can show that you had a clear business purpose (rather than a personal or social purpose) for bringing the spouse or spouses along.

> **EXAMPLE:** You take a client who is visiting from out of town to dinner with his wife. The client's wife joins you because it's impractical (not to mention impolite) to have dinner with the client and not include his wife. Your spouse joins the party because the client's spouse is present. You may deduct half of the cost of dinner for both spouses.

Club Dues and Membership Fees

In the good old days, you could deduct dues for belonging to a country club or similar private facility where business associates gathered. This is no longer possible. The IRS says you cannot deduct dues (including initiation fees) for membership in any club if one of the principal purposes of the club is to:

- conduct entertainment activities for members, or
- provide entertainment facilities for members to use.

Thus, you cannot deduct dues paid to country clubs, golf and athletic clubs, yacht clubs, airline clubs, hotel clubs, or clubs operated to provide members with meals. However, you can deduct the direct expenses you incur to entertain a business associate at a club.

> **EXAMPLE:** Jack, a home-based salesperson, is a member of the Golden Bear Golf Club in Columbus, Ohio. His annual membership dues are $10,000. One night, Jack invites a client to dinner at the club's dining room where they discuss whether Jack should buy the client out. Jack pays $100 for the dinner. Jack's $10,000 annual dues are not deductible, but his costs for the dinner are. Because of the 50% limitation on entertainment expenses, Jack can deduct $50 for the meal.

You can deduct dues you pay to join a business-related tax-exempt organization or civic organization as long as the organization's primary purpose isn't to provide entertainment. Examples include organizations like the Kiwanis or Rotary Club, business leagues, chambers of commerce, real estate boards, trade associations, and professional associations such as a medical or bar association.

Entertainment Tickets

You can deduct only the face value of an entertainment ticket, even if you paid a higher price for it. For example, you cannot deduct service fees that you pay to ticket agencies or brokers, or any amount over the face value of tickets that you buy from scalpers. However, you can deduct the entire amount you pay for a ticket to an amateur sporting event run by volunteers to benefit a charity.

Ordinarily, you or an employee must be present at an entertainment activity to claim it as a business entertainment expense. This is not the case, however, for entertainment tickets. You can give tickets to clients or other business associates rather than attending the event yourself, and still take a deduction. If you don't go to the event, you have the option of treating the tickets as a gift. You can get a bigger deduction this way sometimes. Gifts of up to $25 are 100% deductible (see Chapter 14), so you get a bigger deduction for tickets that cost less than $50 if you treat them as a gift. If they cost more, treat them as an entertainment expense to maximize your deduction.

> EXAMPLE: You pay $40 to a scalper for a ticket to a college basketball game; the ticket has a face value of only $30. You give the ticket to a client, but don't attend the game yourself. By treating the ticket as a gift, you may deduct $25 of the expense. If you treated it as an entertainment expense, your deduction would be limited to 50% of the face value of the ticket ($30), or $15. However, if you paid $100 for a ticket with a $60 face value, you would be better off treating it as an entertainment expense. This way you would be able to deduct 50% of $60, or $30. If you

treated the ticket as a gift, your deduction would still be limited to $25.

You may also deduct the cost of season tickets at a sports arena or theater. But if you rent a skybox or other private luxury box, your deduction is limited to the cost of a regular nonluxury box seat. The cost of season tickets must be allocated to each separate event.

> **EXAMPLE:** Jim, an investment counselor, spends $5,000 for two season tickets to his local professional football team. The tickets entitle him and a guest to attend 16 games. He must allocate the cost game by game. If, during the course of the football season, he gives tickets for half of the games to clients and uses the others for himself and his wife, half of the total cost of the season tickets is a business entertainment expense. Because entertainment expenses are only 50% deductible, Jim may deduct $1,250 (half of the cost of half of the games).

Reimbursed Expenses

If a client or customer reimburses you for entertainment expenses, you don't need to count the reimbursement that you receive as income as long as you give the client an adequate accounting of your expenses and comply with the accountable plan rules. Basically, this requires that you submit all your documentation to the client in a timely manner and return any excess payments. Accountable plans are covered in detail in Chapter 11.

If you comply with the rules, the client gets to deduct 50% of the expenses and you get 100% of your expenses paid for by somebody else. This is a lot better then getting only a 50% entertainment expense deduction. The reimbursement should not be listed by the client on any Form 1099-MISC a client is required to send to the IRS showing the amount paid to you for your services during the year.

> **EXAMPLE:** Philip, a home-based private detective, takes several people out to lunch to discuss the theft of trade secrets from a biotechnology firm. He bills his client $200 for the lunches and provides all the proper documentation. The client reimburses Philip $200. Philip gets no deduction for the lunches, but he also doesn't have to include the $200 reimbursement in his income for the year; his client may deduct $100 (50% of the expense) as a business entertainment expense.

On the other hand, if you don't properly document your expenses and obtain reimbursement from your client, you must report the amount as income on your tax return and the client should also include it in the Form 1099-MISC it submits to the IRS. You can still deduct the cost as a business entertainment expense on your own tax return, but your deduction will be subject to the 50% limit.

The client can deduct the reimbursement as compensation paid to you. The client's deduction is not subject to the 50% limit because the payment is classified as compensation, not reimbursement of entertainment expenses.

> **EXAMPLE:** Assume that Philip from the above example fails to make an adequate accounting of his meal expenses to his client, but the client still reimburses him for the full $200. The client may deduct the entire $200, and must include this amount in the 1099-MISC form it provides the IRS reporting how much it paid Philip during the year. Philip must include the $200 as income on his tax return and pay tax on it. He may list the $200 as an entertainment expense on his personal tax return, but his deduction is limited to $100.

Clearly, it's better tax-wise to get your clients to reimburse you for entertainment expenses and keep careful track of the costs.

Reporting Entertainment Expenses on Your Tax Return

If, like most home business owners, you're a sole proprietor, you must list your entertainment expenses on Schedule C, *Profit or Loss From Business*. The schedule contains a line just for this deduction. You list the total amount and then subtract from it the portion that is not deductible—50%.

If you've formed a partnership or an LLC, expenses paid with partnership or LLC funds are listed on the information return the entity files with the IRS. Your share of these and all other deductions for your entity pass through and are deducted on your individual tax return on Schedule E.

If you pay for entertainment expenses from your personal funds or credit card and are reimbursed by your business entity, the expense is handled as if the entity paid it. You do not include the amount of the reimbursement in your income for the year.

If you personally pay for entertainment expenses and are not reimbursed by your business entity, you may directly deduct the expenses on your personal tax return by listing them on Schedule E. They are not included in your business entity's information return. However, such unreimbursed expenses are deductible by you only if your partnership or LLC agreement allows it.

If you've formed a C corporation and the corporation pays for your entertainment expenses, the corporation deducts the expenses on its own tax return. If you've formed an S corporation that pays your expenses, the tax reporting is the same as for a partnership or an LLC.

Things are more complicated if you personally pay for entertainment expenses because usually you will be your corporation's employee and special rules apply to expenses paid by employees. (See Chapter 11.)

Getting Around Town:
Car and Local Travel Expenses

Deductible Local Transportation Expenses 176

    Travel Must Be for Business 177

    Trips From Your Home Office 178

    If You Have No Regular Workplace 178

The Standard Mileage Rate 179

    How the Standard Mileage Rate Works 180

    Requirements to Use the Standard Mileage Rate 181

The Actual Expense Method 183

    How the Actual Expense Method Works 183

    Record Keeping Requirements 185

    Vehicle Depreciation Deductions 185

    Leasing a Car 197

How to Maximize Your Car Expense Deduction 199

    Use the Method That Gives the Largest Deduction 199

    Use Two Cars for Business 200

    Keep Good Records 200

Other Local Transportation Expenses 201

Reporting Transportation Expenses on Your Tax Return 201

    Sole Proprietors 202

    LLCs and Partnerships 203

    Corporations 203

When Clients or Customers Reimburse You 203

T hat expensive car parked in your garage doesn't just look great—it could also give you a great tax deduction. This chapter shows you how to deduct expenses for *local transportation* —that is, business trips that don't require you to stay away from home overnight. These rules apply to local business trips using any means of transportation, but this chapter focuses primarily on car expenses, the most common type of deduction for local business travel. Overnight trips (whether by car or other means) are covered in Chapter 9.

RELATED TOPIC

Different rules apply to corporate employees. This chapter covers local transportation deductions by business owners—sole proprietors, partners in partnerships, or LLC members—not by corporate employees. If you have incorporated your business and work as its employee, you must follow special rules to deduct local transportation expenses. Those rules are covered in Chapter 11.

CAUTION

Transportation expenses are a red flag for the IRS. Transportation expenses are the number one item that IRS auditors look at when they examine small business tax returns. These expenses can be substantial—and it is easy to overstate them—so the IRS will look very carefully to make sure that you're not bending the rules. Your first line of defense against an audit is to keep good records to back up your deductions. This is something no tax preparation program or accountant can do for you—you must develop good record-keeping habits and follow them faithfully to stay out of trouble with the IRS. You can find information on record keeping in Chapter 15.

Deductible Local Transportation Expenses

Local transportation costs are deductible as business operating expenses if they are ordinary and necessary for your business, trade, or profession. The cost must be common, helpful, and appropriate for your business. (See Chapter 4 for a detailed discussion of the ordinary and necessary requirement.) It makes no difference what type of transportation you use to make the local trips—car, van, pickup, truck, motorcycle, taxi, bus, or train—or whether the vehicle you use is owned or leased. You can deduct these costs as long as they are ordinary and necessary and meet the other requirements discussed below.

Travel Must Be for Business

You can only deduct local trips that are for business—that is, travel to a business location. Personal trips—for example, to the supermarket or the gym—are not deductible as business travel expenses. A business location is any place where you perform business-related tasks, such as:

- the place where you have your principal place of business, including a home office
- other places where you work, including temporary job sites
- places where you meet with clients or customers
- the bank where you do business banking
- a local college where you take work-related classes
- the store where you buy business supplies, or
- the warehouse or other place where you keep business inventory.

Starting a New Business

The cost of local travel before you start your business, such as travel to investigate starting a new business, is not a currently deductible business operating expense. It is a start-up expense subject to special deduction rules. (See Chapter 3 for information on deducting start-up costs.)

As explained below, you can take the largest deduction for local business trip expenses if you have a home office.

Moreover, you don't have to do all the driving yourself to get a car expense deduction. Any use of your car by another person qualifies as a deductible business expense if:

- it is directly connected with your business
- it is properly reported by you as income to the other person (and, if you have to, you withhold tax on the income)—for example, where an employee uses your car (see Chapter 11), or
- you are paid a fair market rental for use of your car.

Thus, for example, you can count as business mileage a car trip your employee, spouse, or child takes to deliver an item for your business or for any other business purpose.

Trips From Your Home Office

If, like most home business people, you have a home office that qualifies as your principal place of business, you can deduct the cost of any trips you make from home to another business location. You can get a lot of travel deductions this way. For example, you can deduct the cost of driving from home to a client's office or to attend a business-related seminar.

Your home office will qualify as your principal place of business if it is the place where you earn most of your income or perform most of your business administrative or management tasks. Virtually all home businesses should be able to qualify under either or both of these criteria.

> EXAMPLE: Kim, a personal trainer, spends most of her time working with her clients at their homes or gyms. But she maintains a home office where she does the administrative work for her business, such as billing, scheduling appointments, and creating written exercise programs for her clients. She may deduct the cost of driving from home to meet with clients and back home again.

If You Have No Regular Workplace

If you have no regular office—whether inside or outside your home— the location of your first business contact of the day is considered your office for tax purposes. Transportation expenses from your home to this first business contact are commuting expenses, which are not deductible. The same is true for your last business contact of the day—your trip home is nondeductible commute travel. You can deduct the cost of all your other trips during the day between clients or customers.

> **EXAMPLE:** Jim is an encyclopedia salesman who works in the Houston metropolitan area. He works out of his car, with no office at home or anywhere else. One day, he makes ten sales calls by car. His trip from home to his first sales contact of the day is a nondeductible commuting expense. His next nine trips are deductible, and his trip home from his last sales contact is a nondeductible personal commuting expense.

There is an easy way to get around this rule about the first and last trip of the day: Open a home office. That way, all of your trips are deductible.

> **EXAMPLE:** Jim creates an office at home where he performs administrative tasks for his sales business, such as bookkeeping. He may now deduct the cost of all of his business trips during the day, including driving from home to his first business contact and back home from his last contact of the day.

The Standard Mileage Rate

If you drive a car, panel truck, van, pickup, or an SUV for business (as most people do), you have two options for deducting your vehicle expenses: You can use the standard mileage rate or you can deduct your actual expenses.

Let's start with the easy one—the standard mileage rate. This method works best for people who don't want to bother with a lot of record keeping or calculations. But this ease comes at a price—it often results in a lower deduction than you might be entitled to if you used the actual expense method. However, this isn't always the case. The standard mileage rate may give you a larger deduction if you drive many business miles each year, especially if you drive an inexpensive car. (See "The Actual Expense Method," below.)

But, even if the standard mileage rate does give you a lower deduction, the difference is often so small that it doesn't justify the extra record keeping you will have to do using the actual expense method.

How the Standard Mileage Rate Works

To use the standard mileage rate, you deduct a specified number of cents for every business mile you drive. Ordinarily, there is one standard mileage rate for the entire year. However, due to the rising cost of gas, the IRS created two rates for 2011: 51 cents per mile for business driving done January 1, 2011 through June 30, 2011, and 55.5 cents per mile for July 1, 2011 through December 31, 2011.

To figure out your deduction, simply multiply your business miles by the applicable standard mileage rate. The rate is the same whether you own or lease your car.

> **EXAMPLE:** Ed, a self-employed salesperson, drove his car 20,000 miles for business during 2011. He drove his car 10,000 business miles during the first half of the year and 10,000 miles during the second half. To determine his car expense deduction, he simply multiplies his business mileage by the applicable standard mileage rate. His deduction for the first half of 2011 is $510 (51 cents x 10,000 = $510). His deduction for the second half of the year is 545 (55.5 cents x 10,000 = $555).

The big advantage of the standard mileage rate is that it requires very little record keeping. You need only to keep track of how many business miles you drive and the dates, not the actual expenses for your car, such as gas, maintenance, or repairs.

If you choose the standard mileage rate, you cannot deduct actual car operating expenses—for example, maintenance and repairs, gasoline and its taxes, oil, insurance, and vehicle registration fees. All of these items are factored into the rate set by the IRS. And you can't deduct the cost of the car through depreciation or Section 179 expensing because the car's depreciation is also factored into the standard mileage rate (as are lease payments for a leased car).

The only actual expenses you can deduct (because these costs aren't included in the standard mileage rate) are:

- interest on a car loan
- parking fees and tolls for business trips (but you can't deduct parking ticket fines or the cost of parking your car at your place of work), and
- personal property tax you paid when you bought the vehicle, based on its value—this is often included as part of your auto registration fee.

Interest on an automobile loan is usually the largest of these expenses. Unfortunately, many people fail to deduct this because of confusion about the tax law. Taxpayers are not allowed to deduct interest on a loan for a car that is for personal use, so many people believe they also can't deduct interest on a business car. This is not the case. You may deduct interest on a loan for a car you use in your business. But there is one exception—if you're an employee, you may not deduct interest on a car loan even if you use the car 100% for your job.

If you use your car for both business and personal trips, you can deduct only the business use percentage of the above-mentioned interest and taxes.

> **EXAMPLE:** Ralph uses his car 50% for his home business and 50% for personal trips. He uses the standard mileage rate to deduct his car expenses. He pays $3,000 a year in interest on his car loan. He may deduct 50% of this amount, or $1,500, as a business operating expense, in addition to his business mileage deduction.

Requirements to Use the Standard Mileage Rate

Not everyone can use the standard mileage rate. You won't be able to use it (and will have to use the actual expense method instead) if you can't meet the following requirements.

First-Year Rule

You must use the standard mileage rate in the first year you use a car for business or you are forever foreclosed from using that method for that car. If you use the standard mileage rate the first year, you can switch to the actual expense method in a later year, and then switch back and forth between the two methods after that, provided the requirements listed below are met. For this reason, if you're not sure which method you want to use, it's a good idea to use the standard mileage rate the first year you use the car for business. This leaves all your options open for later years. However, this rule does not apply to leased cars. If you lease your car, you must use the standard mileage rate for the entire lease period if you use it in the first year.

There are some restrictions on switching back to the standard mileage rate after you have used the actual expense method. You can switch back to the standard mileage rate only if you used the straight-line method of depreciation during the years you used the actual expense method. This depreciation method gives you equal depreciation deductions every year, rather than the larger deductions you get in the early years using accelerated depreciation methods. You can't switch back to the standard mileage rate after using the actual expense method if you took accelerated depreciation, a Section 179 deduction, or bonus depreciation.

However, these restrictions on depreciation are often academic. Because of the severe annual limits on the depreciation deduction for passenger automobiles, it often makes no difference which depreciation method you use—you'll get the same total yearly deduction. So using straight-line depreciation poses no hardship. Keep in mind, however, that if you switch to the actual expense method after using the standard mileage rate, you'll have to reduce the tax basis of your car by a portion of the standard mileage rate deductions you already received. This will reduce your depreciation deduction. (See "Vehicle Depreciation Deductions," below, for more on vehicle depreciation deductions.)

The Actual Expense Method

Instead of using the standard mileage rate, you can deduct the actual cost of using your car for business. This requires more record keeping, but usually results in a higher deduction. However, you may conclude that the amount of the increased deduction may not be enough to outweigh the extra record keeping you must do to qualify for the deduction.

Business Travel by Motorcycle

You must use the actual expense method if you ride a motorcycle—the standard mileage rate is only for passenger vehicles. However, the limits on depreciation for passenger automobiles (discussed in "Vehicle Depreciation Deductions," below) do not apply to bicycles or motorcycles. You may depreciate these items just like any other business property. Or, if you wish, you can deduct the cost of a motorcycle or bicycle in the year that you purchase it under Section 179. (See Chapter 5 for more on depreciation and Section 179.)

How the Actual Expense Method Works

As the name implies, under the actual expense method, you deduct the actual costs you incur each year to operate your car, plus depreciation. If you use this method, you must keep careful track of all of your car expenses during the year, including:

- gas and oil
- repairs and maintenance
- depreciation of your original vehicle and improvements (see "Vehicle Depreciation Deductions," below)
- car repair tools
- license fees
- parking fees for business trips
- registration fees

- tires
- insurance
- garage rent
- tolls for business trips
- car washing
- lease payments
- interest on car loans
- towing charges, and
- auto club dues.

Watch Those Tickets

You may not deduct the cost of driving violations or parking tickets, even if you were on business when you got the ticket. Government fines and penalties are never deductible, as a matter of public policy.

When you do your taxes, add up the cost of all these items. For everything but parking fees and tolls, multiply the total cost of each item by the percentage of time you use your car for business. For parking fees and tolls that are business related, include (and deduct) the full cost. The total is your deductible transportation expense for the year.

> **EXAMPLE:** Laura, a salesperson, drove her car 8,000 miles for her business and 8,000 miles for personal purposes in one year. She can deduct 50% of the actual costs of operating her car, plus the full cost of any business-related tolls and parking fees. Her expenses amount to $10,000 for the year, so she gets a $5,000 deduction, plus $500 in tolls and parking for business.

If you have a car that you use only for business, you may deduct 100% of your actual car costs. Be careful here. If you own just one car, it's hard to successfully claim that you use it only for business. The IRS is not likely to believe that you walk or take public transportation everywhere, except when you're on business. Your argument might be more persuasive if you live in a city with a developed transportation system, such as Chicago, New York City, or San Francisco, and drive your car only when you go out of town on business. But be prepared for the IRS to question your deduction. (If you're a sole proprietor, the IRS will know how many cars you own; sole proprietors who claim transportation expenses must provide this information on their tax returns—see "Reporting Transportation Expenses on Your Tax Return," below).

Record Keeping Requirements

When you deduct actual car expenses, you must keep records of all the costs of owning and operating your car. This includes not only the number of business miles and total miles you drive, but also gas, repair, parking, insurance, tolls, and any other car expenses. (You'll find more information on record-keeping requirements in Chapter 15.)

Vehicle Depreciation Deductions

Using the actual expense method, you can deduct the cost of your vehicle. However, you can't deduct the entire cost in the year when you purchase your car. Instead, you must deduct the cost a portion at a time over several years, using a process called depreciation. (For more on depreciation generally, see Chapter 5.) Although the general concept of depreciation is the same for every type of property, special rules apply to depreciation deductions for cars. These rules give you a lower deduction for cars than you'd be entitled to using the normal depreciation rules.

This section focuses on the depreciation rules for passenger automobiles, as defined by the IRS. To understand the depreciation rules discussed in this section, you will need to be familiar with the general depreciation rules covered in Chapter 5.

Is Your Vehicle a Passenger Automobile?

First, you must figure out whether your vehicle is a passenger automobile as defined by the IRS. A passenger automobile is any four-wheeled vehicle made primarily for use on public streets and highways that has an unloaded gross weight of 6,000 pounds or less. The vehicle weight includes any part or item physically attached to the automobile or usually included in the purchase price of an automobile. This definition includes virtually all automobiles.

However, if your vehicle is a truck, an SUV, or a van, or has a truck base (as do most SUVs), it is a passenger automobile only if it has a gross loaded vehicle weight of 6,000 pounds or less. The gross loaded weight is based on how much the manufacturer says the vehicle can carry and is different from unloaded weight—that is, the vehicle's weight without any passengers or cargo.

You can find out your vehicle's gross loaded and unloaded weight by looking at the metal plate in the driver's side doorjamb, looking at your owner's manual, checking the manufacturer's website or sales brochure, or asking an auto dealer. The gross loaded weight is usually called the Gross Vehicle Weight Rating (GVWR for short). The gross unloaded weight is often called the curb weight.

Vehicles that would otherwise come within the passenger automobile definition are excluded if they are not likely to be used more than a minimal amount for personal purposes—for example, moving vans, construction vehicles, ambulances, hearses, tractors, and taxis or other vehicles used in a transportation business. Also excluded are trucks and vans that have been specially modified so they are not likely to be used more than a minimal amount for personal purposes—for example, by installation of permanent shelving, or painting of the vehicle to display advertising or a company's name. The restrictions on depreciation discussed in this section don't apply to these vehicles.

Passenger Automobiles Are Listed Property

All passenger automobiles are listed property—property that is often used for personal purposes. As explained in Chapter 5, the IRS imposes more stringent requirements on deductions for listed property to discourage fraudulent deduction claims. Because passenger automobiles are listed property, you must keep mileage records showing how much you use your car for business and personal purposes. You must also file IRS Form 4562, *Depreciation and Amortization*, with your annual tax return.

Other Vehicles That Are Listed Property

Passenger automobiles are not the only vehicles that are listed property. Trucks, buses, boats, airplanes, motorcycles, and any other vehicles used to transport persons or goods are also listed property. The listed property rules apply to these vehicles even if they weigh more than 6,000 pounds and therefore don't qualify as passenger automobiles. However, some types of vehicles are not subject to the listed property rules, including vehicles not likely to be used more than a minimal amount for personal purposes (as described in "Is Your Vehicle a Passenger Automobile?" above) and any vehicle with a loaded gross vehicle weight of over 14,000 pounds that is designed to carry cargo.

What You Can Depreciate

You can depreciate your entire investment in a car (also called your basis). If you buy a passenger automobile and use it for business that same year, your basis is its cost. You may depreciate the entire cost, even if you financed part of the purchase with a car loan. The cost also includes sales taxes, destination charges, and other fees the seller charges. It does not, however, include auto license and registration fees. This assumes you use the car 100% for business. If you use it less than 100%, you may only depreciate an amount equal to your percentage of business use. For example, if you use your car 50% for business, you may depreciate only 50% of the cost.

If you trade in your old car to a dealer to purchase a new car, your basis in the car you purchase is the adjusted basis of the trade-in car, plus the cash you pay (whether out of your own pocket or financed with a car loan).

EXAMPLE: Brenda buys a new pickup for her construction business. The pickup has a $20,000 sticker price. She trades in her old pickup and pays the dealer $15,000, all of which she finances with a car loan from her bank. Her trade-in has an adjusted basis of $3,000. Her basis in the new pickup is $18,000

($3,000 + $15,000), even though the sticker price on the new pickup was $20,000.

If you convert a car that you previously owned for personal use to a business car, your basis is the lower of what you originally paid for it (when you purchased it for personal use) or its fair market value at the time you convert it to business use. Your basis will usually be its fair market value, as this is usually the lower number.

You can determine the fair market value of your car on the date of conversion by checking used car value guides, such as the *Kelley Blue Book*. These guides often give more than one value—for example, the *Kelley Blue Book* gives a private party value and a retail value. Using the highest value will give you the largest deduction. The best-known used car price guides (available free on the Internet) are:

- Kelley Blue Book: www.kbb.com
- Edmunds: www.edmunds.com, and
- NADA guides: www.nadaguides.com.

Look at more than one guide, because the prices can vary.

Depreciation Limits for Passenger Automobiles

Passenger automobiles have a five-year recovery period (but it takes six calendar years to depreciate a car; see "Listed Property," in Chapter 5). As a result, you'd think it would take at most six years to fully depreciate a car. Unfortunately, this is usually not the case. Depreciating a passenger automobile is unique in one very important way: The annual depreciation deduction for automobiles is limited to a set dollar amount each year. The annual limit applies to all passenger vehicles, no matter how much they cost. Because the limits are so low, it can take many years to fully depreciate a car, far longer than the six years it takes to depreciate other assets with a five-year recovery period.

Starting in 2003, the IRS established two different sets of deduction limits for passenger automobiles: one for passenger automobiles other than trucks and vans; and slightly higher limits for trucks and vans that qualify as passenger automobiles (based on their weight) and are built on a truck chassis. This includes minivans and many sport utility vehicles (as long as they meet the weight limit).

The charts below show the maximum annual depreciation deduction allowed for passenger automobiles and trucks and vans placed in service in 2011. (You can triple these limits if you buy an electric car after May 6, 2003.) The second chart shows the limits for passenger automobiles that are trucks and vans as defined above. Both charts assume 100% business use of the vehicle. You can find the current deduction limits in IRS Publication 946, *How to Depreciate Property*, and Publication 463, *Travel, Entertainment, Gift, and Car Expenses*.

Depreciation Limits for Passenger Automobiles Placed in Service During 2011	
1st tax year	$11,060 ($3,060 + $8,000 bonus depreciation)
2nd tax year	$4,900
3rd tax year	$2,950
Each succeeding year	$1,775

Depreciation Limits for Trucks and Vans Placed in Service During 2011	
1st tax year	$11,260 ($3,260 + $8,000 bonus depreciation)
2nd tax year	$5,200
3rd tax year	$3,150
Each succeeding year	$1,875

These figures are the maximum amount you can deduct each year, regardless of what depreciation method you use or whether you use first-year bonus depreciation or Section 179 expensing.

> **EXAMPLE:** Mario pays $50,000 for a new passenger automobile on June 1, 2011 and uses it 100% for his sales business. He may deduct a maximum of $11,060 in 2011, $4,900 in 2012, $2,950 in 2013, and $1,775 each year thereafter.

The depreciation limits are not reduced if a car is in service for less than a full year. This means that the limit is not reduced when the automobile is either placed in service or disposed of during the year.

Determining Your Miles for Depreciation

Your total depreciation deduction depends on the percentage of the time you use your car for business. For example, if you drive 5,000 miles for business and 5,000 for personal purposes in a year, you'll have 50% business use and you'll only qualify for 50% of the total allowable depreciation deduction for that year. For example, if the total allowable deduction was $11,060, you'd only get $5,530. Obviously, you want to have as many business miles as possible. A little-known IRS rule can help you rack up more business mileage. When you determine your business mileage for purposes of your depreciation deduction, you may include miles you drove for investment or other income-producing purposes—for example, to visit a rental property or attend an investment seminar. This rule applies only when you figure your total allowable automobile depreciation deduction. (See "Investing and Other Income-Producing Activities," in Chapter 2, for a detailed discussion of investment or other income-producing activities.)

The first-year deduction limit is so large (compared to the other years) because of first-year bonus depreciation for 2011 (see Chapter 5). For passenger automobiles other than trucks and vans, the first-year bonus allows you to add $8,000 to the regular $3,060 depreciation limit. However, if you don't qualify for bonus depreciation or decide not to take it (it is not required), your first-year limit will be reduced to the regular $3,060 limit. To take bonus depreciation, you must buy a new car and use it more than 50% of the time for business.

The deduction limits in the above tables are based on 100% business use of the vehicle. If you don't use your car solely for business, the limits are reduced based on your percentage of personal use.

> EXAMPLE: Mario uses his new car 60% for business. His first-year deduction is limited to $6,636 (60% × $11,060 = $6,636).

You may combine Section 179 expensing with bonus and regular depreciation, in that order. However, your total deduction cannot exceed the annual limits listed in the charts above. You reduce the depreciable basis in the auto after each deduction is taken.

Given the fact that the maximum Section 179 deduction for 2011 is $500,000, it will often not be necessary to use regular depreciation because the Section 179 deduction alone will be enough to equal the maximum allowed deduction.

> EXAMPLE: In February 2011, Mario buys a $20,000 new car and uses 100% for business. His business earned $100,000 for the year. He may deduct a maximum of $11,060 of the cost for 2011. He decides to deduct the entire $11,060 of the cost the first year using Section 179. This leaves him with a depreciable basis of $8,940 to depreciate in 2012 and future years (subject to the annual limits noted above).

However, in some cases it may not be possible (or advisable) to take advantage of Section 179 because it is subject to important limitations. First, you must use the automobile for business over 50% of the time for six years (the IRS useful life for automobiles) for an automobile to qualify for Section 179. If you qualify for Section 179 the first year, but your business usage falls below 51% in a later year, you'll have to give back to the IRS any extra deduction you got the first year by using Section 179 instead of, or in addition to, regular depreciation—a process known as recapture. (See Chapter 5.) So don't use Section 179 unless you're sure you'll use the car over half the time for business over the next six years.

In addition, there is an income limit—your Section 179 deduction for a year may not exceed your business's annual income. If you have no income, or a very small one, you'll get little or no Section 179 deduction the year. The deduction will have to be carried forward to deduct from your next year's taxes. (See Chapter 5.) Moreover, you may use Section 179 to depreciate a passenger automobile's cost only if you use it at least 51% of the time for business during the year. In addition, you cannot use Section 179 if you convert a personal passenger automobile to business use.

In contrast, depreciation is not subject to an income limit. Thus, for example, you get a full deduction for the current year even if it exceeds the income from your business or you have no income. Any resulting net operating loss for the year may be used to reduce your taxable income from other sources—for example, income from a job, your spouse's income, or investment income. If there's a remaining loss, you can use it to obtain a refund for part of the tax you paid in previous years, or you can apply the loss to future years. (See "Net Operating Losses," Chapter 16.)

> **EXAMPLE:** Assume that Mario from the above example lost money from his business during 2011. Nevertheless, he purchases a $25,000 car that he uses 100% for business. He can still deduct $11,060 of the cost for 2011. However, if he uses Section 179 to deduct all or part of the cost, he won't be able to deduct any of it in 2011. Mario will have to carry it forward to deduct the following year. On the other hand, he can take full bonus and regular depreciation deductions for 2011, even though his business earned no money. He first takes bonus depreciation, which permits him to deduct 50% of the cost of the car. This amounts to $12,500, which exceeds the 2011 $11,060 auto depreciation limit. By using bonus deprecation alone, Mario gets to deduct $11,060 as a 2011 business deduction. This and his other business deductions give him a $20,000 business loss for the year which he uses this loss to help offset his wife's income for 2011 (he and his wife file a joint return).

If a car is relatively inexpensive, there may be some room left under the $11,060 cap after bonus deprecation is taken. You can depreciate this amount under the regular depreciation rules. Usually, people use the fastest form of depreciation, the 200% declining balance method. Under this method, 20% of an automobile's cost could be depreciated in the first year. (See Chapter 5.)

> **EXAMPLE:** Assume that Mario's business car that he uses 100% for business cost $20,000 in 2011. He first deducts $10,000 using bonus depreciation. Because of the $11,060 annual cap, he can only deduct an additional $1,060 in 2011. Using regular depreciation, his deduction for the remaining $10,000 basis is $2,000 (20% × $10,000 = $2,000). However, he can only deduct $1,060 of this amount, giving him a total deduction for 2011 of $11,060. He then uses regular depreciation in later years to deduct the remaining basis, subject to the annual caps.

In addition, in many cases, it won't be possible to use bonus depreciation—for example, if you use the car less than 51% for business or if you bought the car used. (See Chapter 5.) In this event, you must depreciate the entire cost under the regular rules. You'll have to use the slowest method of depreciation—the straight-line method—if you use the car less than 51% for business, and you'll have to continue with this method even if your business use rises over 50% in later years.

The following table shows how much of the cost of an automobile may be depreciated each year using the three regular depreciation methods and applying the half-year convention. (If more than 40% of all the depreciable property you placed in service during the year was placed in the service during the last quarter of the year, you must use the midquarter convention; see "Depreciations" in Chapter 5.)

	200% Declining Balance Method	150% Declining Balance Method	Straight-Line Method
Year	(midyear convention)	(midyear convention)	(midyear convention)
1	20%	15%	10%
2	32%	25.5%	20%
3	19.2%	17.85%	20%
4	11.5%	16.66%	20%
5	11.5%	16.66%	20%
6	5.76%	8.33%	10%

Automobile Depreciation Table

EXAMPLE: Assume that Mario buys a new car for $25,000 in 2011 that he uses just 20% for business. His low business use of the car means that it does not qualify for bonus depreciation or Section 179 expensing. He must depreciate the car under regular depreciation only, using the straight-line method. This gives him a deduction the first year equal to 10% of his depreciable basis. Since his depreciable basis is $5,000 (20% × $25,000 = $5,000), he qualifies for a $500 depreciation deduction in 2011 (10% × $5,000 = $500).

Depreciation Beyond the Five-Year Limit

Because of the annual limits on depreciation deductions for passenger automobiles, you often won't be able to deduct the entire cost of a car over the six-year depreciation period. Don't worry—as long as you continue to use your car for business, you can keep taking annual deductions after the six-year depreciation period ends until you recover your full basis in the car. The maximum amount you can deduct each year is determined by the date you placed the car in service and your business use percentage.

EXAMPLE: In 2011, Kim pays $50,000 for a car she uses only for business. Her depreciable basis in the car is $50,000. Her maximum depreciation deductions for the car over the next five years are as follows:

2011	$ 11,060
2012	4,900
2013	2,950
2014	1,875
2015	1,875
2016	1,875
Total	$ 24,535

At the end of the depreciation period, she has $24,465 in unrecovered basis. Even though the depreciation period is over, she may continue to deduct $1,875 each year until she recovers the remaining $24,465 (assuming she continues to use the car 100% for business). This will take another 14 years.

Heavy Deductions for Heavy Metal: Expensing SUVs and Other Weighty Vehicles

The depreciation limits discussed above apply only to passenger automobiles—that is, vehicles with a gross loaded weight of less than 6,000 pounds. (See "Is Your Vehicle a Passenger Automobile?" above.) Vehicles that weigh more than this are not subject to the limits. Using bonus depreciation and/or Section 179, this means you may be able to deduct all or most of the cost of such a vehicle in a single year—a potentially enormous deduction for businesspeople who purchase heavy SUVs and similar vehicles for their business.

Bonus Depreciation

If an over 6,000 pound vehicle is placed in service during the period from September, 8, 2010 through December 31, 2011, it will qualify for 100% first-year bonus depreciation. This means you can deduct 100% of the cost in one year if you use the vehicle 100% for business. If the vehicle is placed in service anytime during 2012 or from January 1, 2008 through September 7, 2010, bonus depreciation is limited to 50%.

Section 179

Until 2004, people who purchased SUVs and other heavy vehicles they used over 50% for business could claim the full Section 179 deduction. However, allowing these huge deductions for Hummers and other SUVs bought for business purposes caused such an uproar that Congress limited the Section 179 deduction for SUVs to $25,000. The limit applies to any SUV placed in service after October 22, 2004. For these purposes, an SUV is any four-wheeled vehicle primarily designed or used to carry passengers over public streets, roads, or highways that has a gross vehicle weight of 6,000 to 14,000 pounds.

Auto Repairs and Improvements

Auto repairs and maintenance costs are fully deductible in the year they are incurred. You add these costs to your other annual expenses when you use the actual expense method. (You get no extra deduction for repairs when you use the standard mileage rate.) If you fix your car yourself, you may deduct the cost of parts and depreciate or deduct tools, but you can't take a deduction for your time or labor.

Unlike repairs, improvements to your car must be depreciated over several years, not deducted all in the year when you pay for them. What's the difference between a repair and an improvement? Unlike a repair, an improvement:

- increases the value of your car
- makes the car more useful, or
- lengthens your car's useful life.

> EXAMPLE 1: Doug spends $100 to repair his car's carburetor. This is a current expense because the repair doesn't increase the value of his car or lengthen its useful life. The repair merely allows the car to last for a normal time.

> EXAMPLE 2: Doug spends $2,000 on a brand new engine for his car. This is a capital expense because the new engine increases the car's value and useful life.

This rule can be difficult to apply because virtually all repairs increase the value of the property being repaired. Just remember that an improvement makes your vehicle *more valuable than it was before it was worked on*, while a repair simply restores the car's value to what it was worth before it broke down.

Improvements must be depreciated separately from the vehicle itself—that is, they are treated as separate items of depreciable property. The same rules, however, apply to depreciating improvements as for regular auto depreciation. Depreciation of the original automobile and the later improvements are combined for purposes of the annual depreciation limits. The recovery period begins when the improvement is placed in service.

Deduct Your Car Repair Tools

If you work on your car yourself, you may deduct the cost of your car repair tools. You must deduct your tools separately from your auto expenses. If they are worth only $100 or so, you can currently deduct them as a business operating expense. If they are worth more, you must depreciate them or expense them under Section 179. If your tools are older or you haven't kept your receipts for tools you bought this year, you'll have to estimate their fair market value. Take a look in your garage and see what you have to deduct.

Leasing a Car

If you lease a car that you use in your business, you can use the actual expense method to deduct the portion of each lease payment that reflects the business percentage use of the car. You cannot deduct any part of a lease payment that is for commuting or personal use of the car.

> EXAMPLE: John pays $400 a month to lease a Lexus. He uses it 50% for his dental tool sales business and 50% for personal purposes. He may deduct half of his lease payments ($200 a month) as a local transportation expense for his sales business.

Leasing companies typically require you to make an advance or down payment to lease a car. You can deduct this cost as well, but you must spread the deduction out equally over the entire lease period.

 TIP

You may use either the actual expense method or the standard mileage rate when you lease a car for business. However, if you want to use the standard mileage rate, you must use it the first year you lease the car and continue to use it for the entire lease term. If you use the standard mileage method, you can't deduct any portion of your lease payments. Instead, this cost is covered by the standard mileage rate set by the IRS. (See "The Standard Mileage Rate," above.)

Should You Lease or Buy Your Car?

When you lease a car, you are paying rent for it—a set fee each month for the use of the car. At the end of the lease term, you give the car back to the leasing company and own nothing. As a general rule, leasing a car instead of buying it makes economic sense only if you absolutely must have a new car every two or three years and drive no more than 12,000 to 15,000 miles per year. If you drive more than 15,000 miles a year, leasing becomes an economic disaster because it penalizes you for higher mileage.

There are numerous financial calculators available on the Internet that can help you determine how much it will cost to lease a car compared to buying one. Be careful when you use these calculators—they are designed based on certain assumptions, and different calculators can give different answers. For a detailed consumer guide to auto leasing created by the Federal Reserve Board, go to the Board's website at www.federalreserve.gov/pubs/leasing.

Is It Really a Lease?

Some transactions that are called "auto leases" are really not leases at all. Instead, they are installment purchases—that is, you pay for the car over time, and by the end of the lease term you own all or part of the car. You cannot deduct any payments you make to buy a car, even if the payments are called lease payments. Instead, you have to depreciate the cost of the car as described in "Vehicle Depreciation Deductions," above.

Leasing Luxury Cars

If you lease what the IRS considers to be a luxury car for more than 30 days, you may have to reduce your lease deduction. The purpose of this rule is to prevent people from leasing very expensive cars to get around the limitations on depreciation deductions for cars that are purchased (see "Vehicle Depreciation Deductions," above). A luxury car is currently defined as one with a fair market value of more than $16,760.

The amount by which you must reduce your deduction (called an inclusion amount) is based on the fair market value of your car and the percentage of time that you use it for business. The IRS recalculates it each year. You can find the inclusion amount for the current year in the tables published in IRS Publication 463, *Travel, Entertainment, Gift & Car Expenses*. For example, if you leased a $40,000 car in 2011 and used it solely for business, you would have to reduce your car expense deduction by $25 for the year. If you used the car only 50% for business, the reduction would be $12.50. The inclusion amount for the first year is prorated based on the month when you start using the car for business.

How to Maximize Your Car Expense Deduction

Sam and Sue both drive their cars 10,000 miles for business each year. This year, Sam got a $4,850 auto deduction, while Sue got $5,500. Why the difference? Sue took some simple steps to maximize her deduction. You can follow her lead—and get the largest deduction possible—by following these tips.

Use the Method That Gives the Largest Deduction

Most taxpayers choose the standard mileage rate because it's easier—it requires much less record keeping than the actual expense method.

However, you may get a larger deduction if you use the actual expense method. The American Automobile Association estimated that the average cost of owning a car in 2011 was 58.6 cents per mile. This is more than the IRS allowed you to deduct under the standard mileage rate for 2011. Of course, this is just an average; your expenses could be lower, depending on the value of your car and how much you spend on repairs, gas, and other operating costs. The only way to know for sure which method gives you the largest deduction is to do the numbers.

Use Two Cars for Business

If you use the actual expense method, you might think you would always get a larger deduction by using one car 100% of the time for business rather than using two cars less than 100% for business. This is not the case, however—two cars are usually better than one because you can get a larger total depreciation deduction by depreciating two cars.

> **EXAMPLE:** Biff owns two cars. He needs to drive 20,000 miles for business during the year and 10,000 miles for personal purposes. Let's compare the deduction he could take using one car to the deduction he could take using two.

The IRS requires you to have a good reason for using two cars instead of one for your business. It shouldn't be hard to come up with one—for example, you don't want to put too many miles on each car, or one car carries more cargo and the other gets better gas mileage.

Of course, if you use the standard mileage rate, it makes no difference how many cars you drive—your deduction is based solely on your total business mileage.

Keep Good Records

More than anything else, keeping good records is the key to the local transportation deduction. The IRS knows that many people don't keep good records. When they do their taxes, they make wild guesses about how many business miles they drove the previous year. This is why IRS auditors are more suspicious of this deduction than almost any other.

Record keeping for the transportation deduction doesn't have to be overly burdensome. If keeping records of gas, oil, repairs, and all your other car expenses is too much trouble (and it can be a pain in the neck), use the standard mileage rate (assuming you qualify for it). That way, you'll only need to keep track of how many miles you drive for business. Indeed, you might not even have to keep track of your business miles for the entire year; instead you may be able to use a sample period of three months or one week a month. Remember that keeping track of your actual expenses often gives you a larger deduction. It's up to you to decide which is more important: your time or your money.

See Chapter 15 for a detailed discussion of how to keep car and mileage records.

Other Local Transportation Expenses

You don't have to drive a car or other vehicle to get a tax deduction for local business trips. You can deduct the cost of travel by bus or other public transit, taxi, train, ferry, motorcycle, bicycle, or any other means. However, all the rules limiting deductions for travel by car (discussed in "Deductible Local Transportation Expenses," above) also apply to other transportation methods. This means, for example, that you can't deduct the cost of commuting from your home to your office or other permanent work location. The same record-keeping requirements apply as well.

Reporting Transportation Expenses on Your Tax Return

How you report transportation expenses on your tax return will depend on how your business is organized. The IRS reporting requirements differ depending on what type of business you have.

Sole Proprietors

If, like most home businesspeople, you're a sole proprietor, you list your car expenses on Schedule C, *Profit or Loss From Business.* Schedule C asks more questions about this deduction than almost any other deduction (reflecting the IRS's general suspicion about auto deductions). Part IV of Schedule C is reproduced below. If you answer "yes" to question 45, you cannot claim to use your single car 100% for business. If you answer "no" to questions 47a or 47b, you do not qualify for the deduction.

You must also file IRS Form 4562, *Depreciation and Amortization,* to report your Section 179 and depreciation deductions for the vehicle.

Part IV **Information on Your Vehicle.** Complete this part **only** if you are claiming car or truck expenses on line 9 and are not required to file Form 4562 for this business. See the instructions for line 13 on page C-5 to find out if you must file Form 4562.

43 When did you place your vehicle in service for business purposes? (month, day, year) ▶ _____ / _____ / _____

44 Of the total number of miles you drove your vehicle during 2009, enter the number of miles you used your vehicle for:

a Business _____ b Commuting (see instructions) _____ c Other _____

45 Was your vehicle available for personal use during off-duty hours? . . . . ☐ Yes ☐ No

46 Do you (or your spouse) have another vehicle available for personal use?. . . . . ☐ Yes ☐ No

47a Do you have evidence to support your deduction? . . . . ☐ Yes ☐ No

b If "Yes," is the evidence written? . . . . ☐ Yes ☐ No

How to Reduce Your Schedule C Auto Deduction

If you deduct the interest you pay on a car loan, you have the option of reporting the amount in two different places on your Schedule C: You can lump it in with all your other car expenses on line 9 of the schedule, titled "Car and truck expenses," or you can list it separately on line 16b as an "other interest" cost. Reporting your interest expense separately from your other car expenses reduces the total car expense shown on your Schedule C. This can help avoid an IRS audit.

LLCs and Partnerships

If you organize your business as a partnership or an LLC, you don't file Schedule C. Instead, you deduct your unreimbursed car expenses (and any other unreimbursed business expenses) on IRS Schedule E (Part II) and attach it to your personal tax return. You must attach a separate schedule to Schedule E listing the car and other business expenses you're deducting.

Any transportation expense for which your partnership or LLC reimbursed you must be listed on the partnership or LLC tax return, IRS Form 1065, *U.S. Return of Partnership Income.* These deductions pass through to you along with other partnership deductions.

Corporations

If your business is incorporated, you will ordinarily be its employee. You can deduct any transportation expenses for which the corporation does not reimburse you as miscellaneous itemized expenses on Schedule A. However, these deductions are subject to special limitations. (See "Employing Your Family or Yourself," in Chapter 11, for more on working for your corporation.)

When Clients or Customers Reimburse You

Some small business owners have their local travel expenses reimbursed by their clients or customers. You need not include such reimbursements in your income if you provide an adequate accounting of the expenses to your client and comply with the accountable plan rules. Basically, this requires that you submit all your documentation to the client in a timely manner, and return any excess payments. Accountable plans are covered in detail in Chapter 11. Record-keeping rules for business driving are covered in Chapter 15.

> **EXAMPLE:** Erica, a sole proprietor accountant, is hired by Acme Corp. to handle an audit. She keeps a complete mileage log showing that she drove 500 miles while working on the audit.

Acme reimburses Erica $250 for the business mileage. Erica need not include this amount in her income for the year. Acme may deduct it as a business expense.

If you do not adequately account to your client for these expenses, you must include any reimbursements or allowances in your income. They should also be included in any 1099-MISC form the client provides to the IRS reporting how much you were paid. The client can still deduct the reimbursement as compensation paid to you. You may deduct the expenses on your own return, but you'll need documentation to back them up in the event of an audit.

EXAMPLE: Assume that Erica doesn't keep proper track of her mileage. At the end of the year, she estimates that she drove 500 miles on Acme's behalf. Acme reimburses Erica $250, but concludes she didn't adequately account for her expenses under the IRS rules. It deducts the $250 on its tax return as compensation paid to Erica, and includes the $250 on the 1099-MISC form it sends the IRS the following February reporting how much it paid her. Erica deducts the $250 on her return as a business expense. Two years later, Erica is audited by the IRS. When the auditor asks her for her records showing how many miles she drove while representing Acme, Erica tells him she doesn't have any. The auditor disallows the deduction.

Leaving Town: Business Travel

What Is Business Travel? 206

    Where Is Your Tax Home? 207

    Your Trip Must Be for Business 211

Deductible Travel Expenses 214

    Traveling First Class or Steerage 215

    Taking People With You 215

How Much You Can Deduct 216

    Travel Within the United States 217

    Travel Outside the United States 218

    Conventions 222

    Travel by Ship 223

    Calculating Time Spent on Business 223

    Fifty Percent Limit on Meal Expenses 225

Maximizing Your Business Travel Deductions 228

    Plan Ahead 228

    Make a Paper Trail 229

    Maximize Your Business Days 229

    Take Advantage of the Sandwich Day Rule 230

Travel Expenses Reimbursed by Clients or Customers 230

I
f you travel overnight for business, you can deduct your airfare, hotel bills, and other expenses. If you plan your trip carefully, you can even mix business with pleasure and still take a deduction. However, IRS auditors closely scrutinize deductions for overnight business travel—and many taxpayers get caught claiming these deductions without proper records to back them up. To stay within the law (and avoid unwanted attention from the IRS), you need to know how this deduction works and how to properly document your travel expenses.

What Is Business Travel?

For tax purposes, business travel occurs when you travel away from your tax home overnight for business. You don't have to travel any set distance to take a travel expense deduction. However, you can't take this deduction if you just spend the night in a motel across town. You must travel outside your city limits. If you don't live in a city, you must go outside the general area where your business is located.

You must stay away overnight or at least long enough to require a stop for sleep or rest. You cannot satisfy the rest requirement by merely napping in your car.

> EXAMPLE: Phyllis, a home-based salesperson who lives in Los Angeles, flies to San Francisco to meet potential clients, spends the night in a hotel, and returns home the following day. Her trip is a deductible travel expense.

If you don't stay overnight, your trip will not qualify as business travel. However, this does not necessarily mean that you can't take a tax deduction. Local business trips are also deductible (see Chapter 8), but you are entitled to deduct only your transportation expenses—the cost of driving or using some other means of transportation. You may not deduct meals or other expenses like you can when you travel for business and stay overnight.

EXAMPLE: Philip drives from his home office in Los Angeles to a business meeting in San Diego and returns the same day. His 200-mile round trip is a deductible local business trip. He may deduct his expenses for the 200 business miles he drove, but he can't deduct the breakfast he bought on the way to San Diego.

RELATED TOPIC

How to deduct local travel. For a detailed discussion of tax deductions for local business travel, see Chapter 8.

Where Is Your Tax Home?

Your tax home is the entire city or general area where your principal place of business is located. If you run your business out of your residence, your tax home is the city or area where you live.

The IRS doesn't care how far you travel for business. You'll get a deduction as long as you travel outside your tax home's city limits and stay overnight. Thus, even if you're just traveling across town, you'll qualify for a deduction if you manage to stay outside your city limits.

EXAMPLE: Pete, a tax adviser, works from his home in San Francisco. He travels to Oakland for an all day meeting with a client. At the end of the meeting, he decides to spend the night in an Oakland hotel rather than brave the traffic back to San Francisco. Pete's stay qualifies as a business trip even though the distance between his San Francisco office and the Oakland business meeting is only eight miles. Pete can deduct his hotel and meal expenses.

If you don't live in a city, your tax home covers the general area where you reside—typically, the area within about 40 miles of your home.

No Main Place of Business

Some people have no main place of business—for example, a sales-person who is always on the road, traveling from sales contact to sales contact. In this situation, your home (main residence) can qualify as your tax home, as long as you:

- perform part of your business there and live at home while doing business in that area
- have living expenses at your home that you must duplicate because your business requires you to travel away from home, and
- satisfy one of the following three requirements:
  - you have not abandoned the area where your home is located—that is, you work in the area or have other contacts there
  - you have family living in the home, or
  - you often live in the home yourself.

EXAMPLE: Ruth is a liquor salesperson whose territory includes the entire southern United States. She has a home in Miami, Florida, where her mother lives. Ruth's sales territory includes Florida. She uses her home for her business when she is in the Miami area and lives in it when making sales calls in the area. She spends about 12 weeks a year at home and is on the road the rest of the time. Ruth's Miami home is her tax home because she satisfies all three factors listed above: (1) She does business in the Miami area and stays in her Miami home when doing so; (2) she has duplicate living expenses; and (3) she has family living at the home.

Even if you satisfy only two of the three factors, your home may still qualify as your tax home, depending on all the facts and circumstances.

EXAMPLE: Assume that Ruth's sales territory is the Northeast, and she does no work in the Miami area, where her home is located. She fails the first factor, but satisfies the second two. Her Miami home would still probably qualify as her tax home.

If you can't satisfy at least two of the three factors, you have no tax home. You are a transient for tax purposes. This means you cannot deduct any travel expenses, because you are never considered to be traveling away from home. Obviously, this is not a good situation to find yourself in, taxwise.

> **EXAMPLE:** James Henderson was a stagehand for a travelling ice skating show. He spent most of his time on the road, but spent two to three months a year living rent-free in his parents' home in Boise, Idaho. Both the IRS and the courts found that he was a transient for tax purposes because he failed to satisfy the first two of the three criteria listed above: (1) He did no work in Boise, and (2) because he paid no rent to live in his parents' house, he had no home living expenses that he had to duplicate while on the road. Thus, Henderson was not entitled to a tax deduction for his travel expenses. (*Henderson v. Comm'r.*, 143 F.3d 497 (9th Cir. 1998).)

If you travel a lot for business, you should do everything you can to avoid being classified as a transient. This means you must take steps to satisfy at least two of the three factors listed above. For example, Henderson might have avoided his transient status if he had paid his parents for his room (thereby resulting in duplicate expenses).

Temporary Work Locations

You may regularly work both at your tax home and at another location, such as a client's office or a temporary job site. It may not always be practical to return from this other worksite to your tax home at the end of each workday. Your overnight stays at these temporary work locations qualify as business travel as long as your work there is truly temporary—that is, it is reasonably expected to last no more than one year. In this situation, your tax home does not change, and you are considered to be traveling away from home for the entire period you spend at the temporary work location.

EXAMPLE: Betty is a self-employed sexual harassment educator. She works out of her home office in Chicago, Illinois. She is hired to conduct sexual harassment training and counseling for a large company in Indianapolis, Indiana. The job is expected to last three months. Betty's assignment is temporary and Chicago remains her tax home. She may deduct the expenses she incurs traveling to and staying in Indianapolis.

Even if the job ends up lasting more than one year, the job location will be treated as temporary, and you can still take your travel deductions, if you reasonably expected the job to last less than one year when you took it. However, if at some later point the job is expected to exceed one year, then the job location will be treated as temporary only until the earlier of: (1) when your expectations changed, or (2) 12 months.

EXAMPLE: Dominic, a self-employed computer expert who lived in Louisiana, took on a project as an independent contractor for a company located in Houston, about 320 miles away from his home. The project was expected to last nine to ten months, although Dominic was hired on a month-to-month basis. Due to technological delays, the project ended up taking 13 months. Nevertheless, the tax court held that Houston was a temporary work location for Dominic because he reasonably expected the project to last less than one year when he took it. Thus, the court held he was entitled to deduct his travel expenses from Louisiana to Houston for the first 12 months. (*Senulis v. Comm'r*, T.C. Summ. Op. 2009-97 (2009).)

On the other hand, if you reasonably expect your work at the other location to last more than one year, that location becomes your new tax home and you cannot deduct your travel expenses while there.

EXAMPLE: Carl is a Seattle-based plumbing contractor. He is hired to install the plumbing in a new subdivision in Boise, Idaho, and the job is expected to take 18 months. Boise is now Carl's tax home, and he may not deduct his travel expenses while staying there.

If you return to your tax home from a temporary work location on your days off, you are not considered away from home while you are in your hometown. You cannot deduct the cost of meals and lodging there. However, you can deduct your expenses, including meals and lodging, for travel between your temporary work location and your tax home. You can claim these expenses up to the amount it would have cost you to stay at your temporary work location. In addition, if you continue to pay for your hotel room during your visit home, you can deduct that cost.

Your Trip Must Be for Business

Your trip must be primarily for business to be deductible. This means that you must have a business purpose in mind before leaving on the trip, and you must actually do some business while you're away.

You have a business purpose if the trip is intended to benefit your business in some way. Examples of business purposes include:

- finding new customers or markets for your products or services
- dealing with existing customers or clients
- learning new skills to help in your business
- contacting people who could help your business, such as potential investors, or
- checking out what the competition is doing.

EXAMPLE: A taxpayer who manufactured and sold weightlifting equipment was entitled to deduct the cost of attending the summer Olympics in Rome because the purpose of the trip was to find new customers for his product line. (*Hoffman v. Comm'r.*, 798 F.2d 784 (3d Cir. 1962).)

It's not enough to claim that you had a business purpose for your trip. You must also be able to show that you actually spent some time on business activities while at your destination. Acceptable business activities include:

- visiting or working with existing or potential clients or customers
- attending trade shows or conventions, or
- attending professional seminars or business conventions that are clearly connected to your business.

On the other hand, business activities do not include:

- sightseeing
- recreational activities that you attend by yourself or with family or friends, or
- attending personal investment seminars or political events.

Use common sense when deciding whether to claim that a trip is for business. If you're audited, the IRS is likely to question any trip that doesn't have some logical connection to your existing business.

Travel for a New Business or Location

You must actually be in business to have deductible business trips. Trips you take to investigate a potential new business or to actually start or acquire a new business are not currently deductible business travel expenses. However, they may be deductible as business start-up expenses, which means you can deduct up to $5,000 of these expenses the first year you're in business if your total start-up expenses are less than $50,000. (See Chapter 3 for more on deducting start-up costs.)

That Trip to Europe Was Not for Business

Oliver Bentley and his foster son spent approximately $7,500 for an extensive European trip. When they got back, they tried to make money off their travel by attempting to arrange student tours to Europe. They contacted travel agents and distributed flyers, but the business never got off the ground. When Bentley did his taxes for the year, he took a $5,127 tax deduction for the trip, claiming it was primarily for this business. The IRS and the tax court both disagreed. Bentley could not claim a business travel deduction because he did not have an existing business when he took the trip, and the costs of investigating a new business venture are not currently deductible. (*Bentley v. Comm'r.,* TC Memo 1988-444.)

Travel as an Education Expense

You may deduct the cost of traveling to an educational activity directly related to your business. For example, a French translator can deduct the cost of traveling to France to attend formal French language classes. However, you can't take a trip and claim that the travel itself constitutes a form of education and is therefore deductible. For example, a French translator who travels to France may not take a business travel deduction if the purpose of the trip is to see the sights and become familiar with French language and culture. (See Chapter 14 for more on education expenses.)

Visiting Business Colleagues

Visiting business colleagues or competitors may be a legitimate business purpose for a trip. But you can't just socialize with them—you must use your visit to learn new skills, check out what your competitors are doing, seek investors, or attempt to get new customers or clients.

Deductible Travel Expenses

Subject to the limits covered in "How Much You Can Deduct," below, virtually all of your business travel expenses are deductible. These costs fall into two broad categories: your transportation expenses and the expenses you incur at your destination.

Transportation expenses are the costs of getting to and from your destination—for example:

- fares for airplanes, trains, or buses
- driving expenses, including car rentals
- shipping costs for your personal luggage or samples, displays, or other things you need for your business, and
- 50% of meals and beverages, and 100% of lodging expenses you incur while en route to your final destination.

If you drive your own car to your destination, you may deduct your costs by using the standard mileage rate or by deducting your actual expenses. You may also deduct your mileage while at your destination. (See Chapter 8 for more on mileage deductions.)

You may also deduct the expenses you incur to stay alive (food and lodging) and to do business while at your destination. Destination expenses include:

- hotel or other lodging expenses for business days
- 50% of meal and beverage expenses (see "How Much You Can Deduct," below)
- taxi, public transportation, and car rental expenses at your destination
- telephone, Internet, and fax expenses
- computer rental fees
- laundry and dry cleaning expenses, and
- tips you pay on any of the other costs.

You may deduct 50% of your entertainment expenses if you incur them for business purposes. You can't deduct entertainment expenses for activities that you attend alone; this solo entertainment obviously wouldn't be for business purposes. If you want to deduct the cost of a nightclub or ball game while on the road, be sure to take a business associate along. (See Chapter 7 for a detailed discussion of the special rules that apply to deductions for entertainment expenses.)

Traveling First Class or Steerage

To be deductible, business travel expenses must be ordinary and necessary. This means that the trip and the expenses you incur must be helpful and appropriate for your business, not necessarily indispensable. You may not deduct lavish or extravagant expenses, but the IRS gives you a great deal of leeway here. You may, if you wish, travel first class, stay at four-star hotels, and eat at expensive restaurants. On the other hand, you're also entitled to be a cheapskate—for example, you could stay with a friend or relative at your destination to save on hotel charges and still deduct your meals and other expenses.

Taking People With You

You may deduct the expenses you pay for a person who travels with you only if he or she:

- is your employee
- has a genuine business reason for going on the trip with you, and
- would otherwise be allowed to deduct the travel expenses.

These rules apply to your family as well. This means you can deduct the expense of taking your spouse, child, or other relative only if the person is your employee and has a genuine business reason for going on a trip with you. Typing notes or assisting in entertaining customers is not enough to warrant a deduction; the work must be essential to your business. For example, if you hire your son as a salesperson for your product or service and he calls on prospective customers during the trip, both your expenses and his are deductible.

If you bring your family along simply to enjoy the trip, you may still deduct your own business expenses as if you were traveling alone—and you don't have to reduce your deductions, even if others get a free ride with you. For example, if you drive to your destination, you can deduct the entire cost of the drive, even if your family rides along with you. Similarly, you can deduct the full cost of a single hotel room even if you obtain a larger, more expensive room for your whole family.

EXAMPLE: Yamiko travels from New Orleans to Sydney, Australia, for her landscape design business. She takes her husband and young son with her. The total airfare expense for her and her family is $2,500. She may deduct the cost of a single ticket—$1,000. She spends $250 per night for a two-bedroom hotel suite in Sydney. She may deduct the cost of a single room for one person—$100 per night.

How Much You Can Deduct

If you spend all of your time at your destination on business, you may deduct 100% of your expenses (except meal expenses, which are only 50% deductible—see "Fifty Percent Limit on Meal Expenses," below). However, things get more complicated if you mix business and pleasure. Different rules apply to your transportation expenses and the expenses you incur while at your destination ("destination expenses"). The rules also depend on whether you travel to another country or remain in the United States.

Reimbursement for Business Travel Expenses

If a client or customer reimburses you for all or part of your business travel expenses, you get no deduction for the amount of the reimbursement—the client gets the deduction. However, you don't have to count the reimbursed amounts as business income.

EXAMPLE: Clarence, a documents examiner, travels from Philadelphia to Nashville, Tennessee, to testify in a case for a client, Acme Corporation. He stays in Nashville for two weeks and incurs $5,000 in travel expenses. He bills Acme for this amount and receives the reimbursement. Clarence may not deduct the cost of the trip, but he also doesn't have to report the $5,000 reimbursement from Acme as business income. Acme may deduct the $5,000 as a business expense.

Travel Within the United States

Business travel within the United States is subject to an all or nothing rule: You may deduct 100% of your transportation expenses only if you spend *more than half of your time* on business activities while at your destination. In other words, your business days must outnumber your personal days. If you spend more time on personal activities than on business, you get no transportation deduction.

You may also deduct the destination expenses you incur on days when you do business. Expenses incurred on personal days at your destination are nondeductible personal expenses. (See "Calculating Time Spent on Business," below, for the rules used to determine what constitutes a business day.)

> **EXAMPLE:** Tom works out of his Atlanta home. He takes the train for a business trip to New Orleans. He spends six days in New Orleans, where he spends all of his time on business, and spends $400 for his hotel, meals, and other living expenses. On the way home, he stops in Mobile for three days to visit his parents and spends $100 for lodging and meals there. His round-trip train fare is $250. Tom's trip consisted of six business days and three personal days, so he spent more than half of the trip on business. He can deduct 100% of his train fare and the entire $400 he spent while on business in New Orleans. He may not, however, deduct the $100 he spent while visiting his parents.

If your trip is primarily a vacation—that is, you spend more than half of your time on personal activities—the entire cost of the trip is a nondeductible personal expense. However, you may deduct destination expenses that are directly related to your business. This includes things like phone calls or faxes to your office, or the cost of renting a computer for business work. It doesn't include transportation, lodging, or food.

> **EXAMPLE:** Tom (from the above example) spends two days in New Orleans on business and seven days visiting his parents in Mobile. His entire trip is a nondeductible personal expense.

However, while in New Orleans he spends $50 on long distance phone calls to his office; this expense is deductible.

As long as your trip is primarily for business, you can add a vacation to the end of the trip, make a side trip purely for fun, or enjoy evenings at the theater or ballet, and still deduct your entire airfare. What you spend while having fun is not deductible, but you can deduct all of your business and transportation expenses.

> **EXAMPLE:** Bill flies to Miami for a four-day business meeting. He spends three extra days in Miami swimming and enjoying the sights. Because he spent over half his time on business—four days out of seven—the cost of his flight is entirely deductible, as are his hotel and meal costs during the business meeting. He may not deduct his hotel, meal, or other expenses during his vacation days.

Travel Outside the United States

Travel outside the United States is subject to more flexible rules than travel within the country. The rules for deducting your transportation expenses depend on how long you stay at your destination.

Trips for Up to Seven Days

If you travel outside the United States for *no more than seven days,* you can deduct 100% of your airfare or other transportation expenses, as long as you spend part of the time on business. You can spend a majority of your time on personal activities, as long as you spend at least some time on business. Seven days means seven consecutive days, not counting the day you leave but counting the day you return to the United States. You may also deduct the destination expenses you incur on the days you do business. (See "Calculating Time Spent on Business," below, for the rules used to determine what constitutes a business day.)

EXAMPLE: Billie flies from Portland, Oregon, to Vancouver, Canada. She spends four days sightseeing in Vancouver and one day visiting suppliers for her import-export business. She may deduct 100% of her airfare, but she can deduct her lodging, meal, and other expenses from her stay in Vancouver for only the one day when she did business.

Trips for More Than Seven Days

The IRS does not want to subsidize foreign vacations, so more stringent rules apply if your foreign trip lasts more than one week. For these longer trips, the magic number is 75%: If you spend more than 75% of your time on business at your foreign destination, you can deduct what it would have cost to make the trip if you had not engaged in any personal activities. This means you may deduct 100% of your airfare or other transportation expenses, plus your living expenses while you were on business and any other business-related expenses:

EXAMPLE: Sean flies from Boston to Dublin, Ireland. He spends one day sightseeing and nine days in business meetings. He has spent 90% of his time on business, so he may deduct 100% of his airfare to Dublin and all of the living and other expenses he incurred during the nine days he spent on business. He may not deduct any of his expenses (including hotel charges) for the day he spent sightseeing.

If you spend more than 50%—but less than 75%—of your time on business, you can deduct only the business percentage of your transportation and other costs. You figure out this percentage by counting the number of business days and the number of personal days to come up with a fraction. The number of business days is the numerator (top number) and the total number of days away from home is the denominator (bottom number). For ease in determining the dollar amount of your deduction, you can convert this fraction into a percentage.

Requirements to Deduct Business Travel

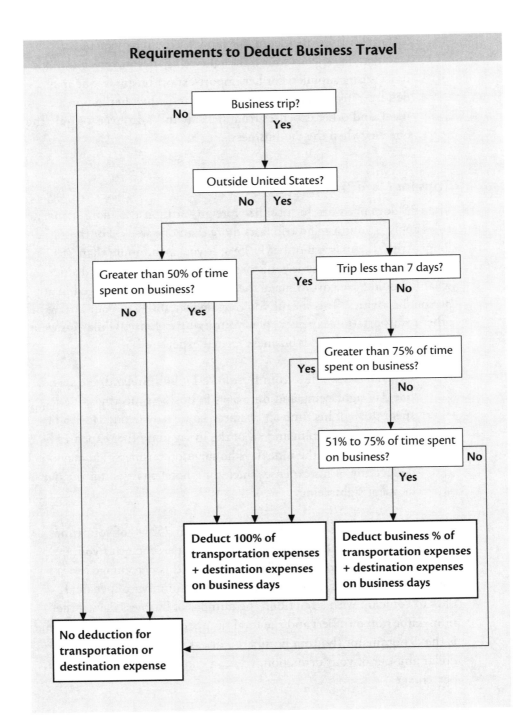

EXAMPLE: Sam flies from Las Vegas to London, where he spends six days on business and four days sightseeing. He spent 6/10 of his total time away from home on business. The fraction 6/10 converts to 60% (6 ÷ 10 = 0.60). He therefore spent 60% of his time on business. He can deduct 60% of his travel costs—that is, 60% of his round-trip airfare, hotel, and other expenses. The trip cost him $3,000, so he gets an $1,800 deduction.

If you spend 50% or less of your time doing business on a foreign trip that lasts more than seven days, you cannot deduct any of your costs.

Side Trips

You may not deduct expenses you incur if you stop at a nonbusiness (personal) destination en route to, or returning from, your business destination. For example, if you stop for three vacation days in Paris on your way to a weeklong business meeting in Bangladesh, you may not deduct your expenses from your Paris stay.

To determine how much of your airfare or other transportation costs are deductible when you make side trips, follow this three-step process:

1. Determine the percentage of the time you spent on vacation.
2. Multiply this vacation percentage by what it would have cost you to fly round-trip from your vacation destination to the United States.
3. Subtract this amount from your total airfare expense to arrive at your deductible airfare expense.

EXAMPLE: Jason lives in New York. On May 5, he flew to Paris to attend a business conference that began that same day. The conference ended on May 14. That evening, he flew from Paris to Dublin to visit friends until May 21, when he flew directly home to New York. The entire trip lasted 18 days—11 business days (the nine days in Paris and the two travel days) and seven vacation days. He spent 39% of his time on vacation (7 ÷ 18 = 39%). His total airfare was $2,000. Round trip airfare from New York to Dublin would have been $1,000. To determine his deductible airfare, he multiplies $1,000 by 39% and then subtracts this amount from his $2,000 airfare expense: $1,000 × 39% = $390; $2,000 − $390 = $1,610. His deductible airfare expense is $1,610.

Conventions

The cost of traveling to, and staying at, a convention are deductible just like the cost of any other business trip, as long as you satisfy the following rules.

Conventions Within North America

You may deduct the expense of attending a convention in North America if your attendance benefits your business. You may not, however, deduct any expenses for your family.

How do you know if a convention benefits your business? Look at the convention agenda or program (and be sure to save a copy). The agenda does not have to specifically address what you do in your business, but it must be sufficiently related to show that your attendance was for business purposes. Examples of conventions that don't benefit your business include those for investment, political, or social purposes.

You probably learned in school that North America consists of the United States, Canada, and Mexico. However, for convention expense purposes, North America includes much of the Caribbean and many other great vacation destinations.

Foreign Conventions

More stringent rules apply if you attend a convention outside of North America. You can take a deduction for a foreign convention only if:

- the convention is directly related to your business (rather than merely benefiting it), and
- it's as reasonable for the convention to be held outside of North America as in North America.

To determine whether it's reasonable to hold the convention outside of North America, the IRS looks at the purposes of the meeting and the sponsoring group, the activities at the convention, where the sponsors live, and where other meetings have been or will be held.

As a general rule, if you want a tax deduction, avoid attending a convention outside of North America unless there is a darn good reason for holding it there. For example, it would be hard to justify holding a convention for New York court reporters in Tahiti. On the other hand, it would probably be okay for a meeting of American travel writers to be held in Paris.

Travel by Ship

Forget about taking a tax deduction for a pure pleasure cruise. You may, however, be able to deduct part of the cost of a cruise if you attend business conventions, seminars, or similar meetings directly related to your business while on board. (Personal investment or financial planning seminars don't qualify.)

But there is a major restriction: You must travel on a U.S.-registered ship that stops only in ports in the United States or its possessions, such as Puerto Rico or the U.S. Virgin Islands. If a cruise sponsor promises you'll be able to deduct your trip, investigate carefully to make sure it meets these requirements.

To deduct your business-related cruise expenses, you must file a signed note with your tax return from the meeting or seminar sponsor listing the business meetings scheduled each day aboard ship and certifying how many hours you spent in attendance. Make sure to get this statement from the meeting sponsor. Your annual deduction for attending conventions, seminars, or similar meetings on ships cannot exceed $2,000.

Calculating Time Spent on Business

To calculate how much time you spend on business while on a trip, you must compare the number of days you spend on business to the number of days you spend on personal activities. A day is considered a business day if you:

- work for more than four hours

- must be at a particular place for your business—for example, to attend a business meeting—even if you spend most of the day on personal activities
- spend more than four hours on business travel (business travel time begins when you leave home and ends when you reach your hotel, or vice versa)
- drive at least 300 miles for business (you can average your mileage—for example, if you drive 600 miles to your destination in two days, you may claim two 300-mile days, even if you drove 500 miles on one day and 100 miles on the other)
- spend more than four hours on some combination of travel and work
- are prevented from working because of circumstances beyond your control, such as a transit strike or terrorist act
- stay at your destination between work days if it would have cost more to go home and return than to remain where you are (this "sandwich" rule allows you to count weekends as business days if you work at your travel destination during the previous and following week; see "Maximizing Your Business Travel Deductions," below).

EXAMPLE: Mike, a home-based inventor who hates flying, travels by car from his home in Reno, Nevada, to Cleveland, Ohio, for a meeting with a potential investor concerning his latest invention: diapers for pet birds. He makes the 2,100-mile drive in six days, arriving in Cleveland on Saturday night. He has his meeting with the investor for one hour on Monday. The investor is intrigued with his idea, but wants him to flesh out his business plan. Mike works on this for five hours on Tuesday and three hours on Wednesday, spending the rest of his time resting and sightseeing. He has his second investor meeting on Thursday, which lasts two hours. He spends the rest of the day sightseeing and then drives straight home on Friday. Mike's trip consisted of 15 business days: 11 travel days, one sandwiched day (the Sunday before his first meeting), two meeting days, and one day when he worked more than four hours. He had one personal day—the day when he spent only three hours working.

Be sure to keep track of your time while you're away. You can do this by taking notes on your calendar or travel diary. (See Chapter 15 for a detailed discussion of record keeping while traveling.)

Fifty Percent Limit on Meal Expenses

The IRS figures that you have to eat, whether you're at home or away on a business trip. Because meals you eat at home ordinarily aren't deductible, the IRS won't let you deduct all of your food expenses while traveling. Instead, you can deduct only 50% of your meal expenses while on a business trip. There are two ways to calculate your meal expense deduction: You can keep track of your actual expenses or use a daily rate set by the federal government.

Deducting Actual Meal Expenses

If you use the actual expense method, you must keep track of what you spend on meals (including tips and tax) while traveling and at your business destination. When you do your taxes, you add these amounts together and deduct half of the total.

> **EXAMPLE:** Frank goes on a business trip from Santa Fe, New Mexico, to Reno, Nevada. He gets there by car. While on the road, he spends $200 for meals. In Reno, he spends another $200. His total meal expense for the trip is $400. He may deduct half of this amount, or $200.

If you combine a business trip with a vacation, you may deduct only those meals you eat while on business—for example, meals you eat while attending business meetings or doing other business-related work. Meals that constitute business entertainment (for example, if you take a client out to a business lunch) are subject to the rules on entertainment expenses covered in Chapter 7.

You do not necessarily have to keep every receipt for your business meals, but you need to keep careful track of what you spend, and you should be able to prove that the meal was for business. See Chapter 15 for a detailed discussion of record keeping for meal expenses.

Using the Standard Meal Allowance

When you use the actual expense method, you must keep track of what you spend for each meal. This can be a lot of work, so the IRS provides an alternative method of deducting meals: Instead of deducting your actual expenses, you can deduct a set amount for each day of your business trip. This amount is called the standard meal allowance. It covers your expenses for business meals, beverages, tax, and tips. The amount of the allowance depends on where and when you travel.

The advantage of using the standard meal allowance is that you don't have to keep track of how much you spend on meals and tips. However, you have to keep records to prove the time, place, and business purpose of your travel. (See Chapter 15 for more on record keeping.)

The disadvantage is that the standard meal allowance is one-half of what federal workers are allowed to charge for meals while traveling, and is therefore relatively modest. In 2011, the full rate federal workers could charge for domestic travel ranged from $46 per day for travel in the least expensive areas to up to $71 for high-cost areas, which includes most major cities. And because you can generally deduct only half of your meal and entertainment expenses, your deduction is limited to one half of the federal meal allowance. While it is possible to eat on $35.50 per day in places like New York City or San Francisco, you probably won't be enjoying the finest culinary experience. If you use the standard meal allowance and spend more than the allowance, you get no deduction for the overage.

The standard meal allowance rates are generally higher for travel outside the continental United States—that is, Alaska, Hawaii, and foreign countries. For example, in 2011 the allowance for Tokyo was $205. In contrast, travelers to Baghdad were permitted only $11 per day.

The standard meal allowance includes $3 per day for incidental expenses—tips you pay to porters, bellhops, maids, and transportation workers. If you wish, you can use the actual expense method for your meal costs and the $3 incidental expense rate for your tips. However, you'd have to be a pretty stingy tipper for this amount to be adequate.

The standard meal allowance is revised each year. You can find the current rates for travel within the United States on the U.S. General Services Administration website at www.gsa.gov (look for the link to "Per Diem Rates"), or in IRS Publication 1542, *Per Diem Rates (for Travel Within the Continental United States)*. The rates for foreign travel are set by the U.S. State Department. When you look at these rate listings, you'll see several categories of numbers. You want the "M & IE Rate"—short for meals and incidental expenses. Rates are also provided for lodging, but these don't apply to nongovernmental travelers.

You can claim the standard meal allowance only for business days. If you travel to more than one location in one day, use the rate in effect for the area where you spend the night. Remember, you are allowed to deduct only 50% of the federal worker rate as a business expense.

> **EXAMPLE:** Art travels from Los Angeles to Chicago for a five-day business conference. Chicago is a high-cost locality, so the daily meal and incidental expense rate (M & IE) is $71. Art figures his deduction by multiplying the daily rate by five and dividing this in half: 5 days × $71 = $355; $355 × 50% = $177.50.

If you use the standard meal allowance, you must use it for *all of the business trips you take during the year.* You can't use it for some trips and use the actual expense method for others. For example, you can't use the standard allowance when you go to an inexpensive destination and the actual expense method when you go to a pricey one.

Because the standard meal allowance is relatively small, it's better to use it only if you travel exclusively to low-cost areas, or if you are simply unable or unwilling to keep track of what you actually spend for meals.

You Don't Have to Spend Your Whole Allowance

When you use the standard meal allowance, you get to deduct the whole amount, regardless of what you spend. If you spend more than the daily allowance, you are limited to the allowance amount. But if you spend less, you still get to deduct the full allowance amount. For example, if you travel to New York City and live on bread and water, you may still deduct $35.50 (half of the $71 per diem rate) for each business day. This strategy will not only save you money; you'll lose weight as well.

Maximizing Your Business Travel Deductions

Here are some simple strategies you can use to maximize your business travel deductions.

Plan Ahead

Plan your itinerary carefully before you leave to make sure your trip qualifies as a business trip. For example, if you're traveling within the United States, you must spend more than half of your time on business for your transportation to be deductible. If you know you're going to spend three days on business, arrange to spend no more than two days on personal activities so that your trip meets the requirements. If you're traveling overseas for more than 14 days, you'll have to spend at least 75% of your time on business to deduct your transportation—you may be able to do this by using strategies to maximize your business days (see "Maximize Your Business Days," below).

Make a Paper Trail

If you are audited by the IRS, you will probably be questioned about business travel deductions. Of course, you'll need to have records showing what you spent for your trips (see Chapter 15 for a detailed discussion). However, you'll also need documents proving that your trip was for your existing business. You can prove this by:

- making a note in your calendar or daily planner of every business meeting you attend or other business-related work you do—be sure to note the time you spend on each business activity
- obtaining and saving business cards from anyone you meet while on business
- noting in your calendar or daily planner the names of all the people you meet for business on your trip
- keeping the programs or agendas from any conventions or training seminars you attend, as well as any notes you made
- keeping copies of thank-you notes you send to the business contacts you met on your trips, and
- keeping copies of business-related correspondence or emails you sent or received before the trip.

Maximize Your Business Days

If you mix business with pleasure on your trip, you have to make sure that you have enough business days to deduct your transportation costs. You'll need to spend more than 50% of your days on business on domestic trips and more than 75% for foreign trips of more than 14 days.

You don't have to work all day for that day to count as a business day: Any day in which you work at least four hours is a business day, even if you goof off the rest of time. The day will count as a business day for purposes of determining whether your transportation expenses are deductible, and you can deduct your lodging, meal, and other expenses during the day, even though you worked only four hours.

You can easily maximize your business days by taking advantage of this rule. For example, you can:

- work no more than four hours in any one day whenever possible
- spread your business over several days—for example, if you need to be present at three meetings, try to spread them over two or three days instead of one, and
- avoid using the fastest form of transportation to your business destination—travel days count as business days, so you'll add business days to your trip if you drive instead of fly. Remember, there's no law that says you have to take the quickest means of transportation to your destination.

Take Advantage of the Sandwich Day Rule

Days when you do no business-related work still count as business days if they are sandwiched between workdays, as long as it was cheaper to spend that day away than to go back home for the off days. If you work on Friday and Monday, this rule allows you to count Saturday and Sunday as business days, even if you don't do any work.

> EXAMPLE: Kim flies from Houston to Honolulu, Hawaii, for a business convention. She arrives on Wednesday and returns the following Wednesday. She does not attend any convention activities during the weekend and goes to the beach instead. Nevertheless, because it was cheaper for her to stay in Hawaii than to fly back to Houston for the weekend and return to Hawaii, she may count Saturday and Sunday as business days. This means she can deduct her lodging and meal expenses for those days (but not the cost of renting a surfboard).

Travel Expenses Reimbursed by Clients or Customers

Business owners who travel while performing services for a client or customer often have their expenses reimbursed by the client. You need not include such reimbursements in your income if you provide an adequate accounting of the expenses to your client and comply with the accountable plan rules. Basically, this requires that you submit all your documentation to the client in a timely manner, and return any excess payments. Accountable plans are covered in detail in Chapter 11. Record-keeping rules for long-distance travel are covered in Chapter 15.

> **EXAMPLE:** Farley, a home-based architect, incurs $5,000 in travel expenses while working on a new shopping center for a client. He keeps complete and accurate records of his expenses which he provides to his client who reimburses him the $5,000. Farley need not include the $5,000 in his income for the year. Farley's client may deduct the reimbursement as a business expense.

If you do not adequately account to your client for these expenses, you must include any reimbursements or allowances in your income, and they should also be included in any 1099-MISC form the client is required to provide the IRS reporting how much you were paid (see Chapter 11). The client can still deduct the reimbursement as compensation paid to you. You may deduct the expenses on your own return, but you'll need documentation to back them up in the event of an audit.

Inventory

What Is Inventory?..234

    Supplies Are Not Inventory...235

    Incidental Supplies...236

    Long-Term Assets..236

Maintaining an Inventory...237

    When You Provide Services and Sell Merchandise..238

    Supplies for Providing a Service..239

Deducting Inventory Costs...239

    Computing the Cost of Goods Sold...240

    Determining the Value of Inventory..241

IRS Reporting...245

Barbee owns a home-based crafts business—she makes her own crafts and buys finished products from others, which she then sells at crafts fairs and on her website. This year, she spent $28,000 on inventory. You might think that she would be able to deduct all of these costs because she is a business owner. Well, think again—Barbee can deduct only a portion of her expenses because of the way the tax code treats inventories.

This chapter covers inventory, including how to determine which of your purchases constitute inventory, how to value your inventory, and how to calculate your deduction for inventory costs.

> **SKIP AHEAD**
>
> **Service providers can skip ahead.** If your home business involves making or buying goods to sell to customers—even if your primary business is to provide services—you need to read this chapter and learn about inventories. If you only provide services to your clients or customers, then you don't need to worry about inventories. You can skip ahead to Chapter 11.

What Is Inventory?

Inventory (also called merchandise) is the goods and products that a business owns to sell to customers in the ordinary course of business. It includes almost anything a business offers for sale, except for real estate. It makes no difference whether you manufacture the goods yourself or buy finished goods to resell to customers. Inventory includes not only finished merchandise, but also unfinished work in progress, as well as the raw materials and supplies that will become part of the finished merchandise.

Only things to which you hold title—that is, things you own—constitute inventory. Inventory includes items you haven't yet received or paid for, as long as you own them. For example, an item you buy with a credit card counts as inventory, even if you haven't paid the bill yet. However, if you buy merchandise that is sent C.O.D., you acquire ownership only after the goods are delivered and paid for. Similarly, goods that you hold on consignment are not part of your inventory because you don't own them.

> **EXAMPLE:** Barbee's inventory consists of the finished crafts she has for sale, the unfinished crafts she is working on, and the raw material she will eventually use to create finished crafts. Raw materials that she has on order (but has not paid for) are not inventory. Neither is Barbee's craft-making equipment, such as her leather hole punch and jewelry tools, nor the computer she uses to keep track of sales and maintain her website. These items are part of her business assets, not merchandise that she is offering for sale to customers. Jewelry pieces that Barbee is selling in her store on consignment also don't count as inventory because they still belong to the craftspeople who made them, not to Barbee.

Supplies Are Not Inventory

Materials and supplies that do not physically become part of the merchandise a business sells are not included in inventory. Unless they are incidental supplies (as described in "Incidental Supplies," below), the cost of these supplies must be deducted *in the year in which they are used or consumed*, which is not necessarily the year when you purchase them. This means that you must keep track of how much material you use each year.

> **EXAMPLE:** Barbee decides to tan her own leather, which she will use to create leather pouches to sell to customers. She orders large amounts of various expensive chemicals needed for the tanning process. In one year, she spent $5,000 for the tanning chemicals, but used only half of them. She may deduct $2,500 of the cost of the chemicals that year. She may not deduct the cost of the remaining chemicals until she uses them.

Incidental Supplies

There is an important exception to the rule that the cost of materials and supplies may be deducted only as they are used or consumed. You may deduct the entire cost of supplies that are *incidental* to your business in the year when you purchase them. Supplies are incidental if:

- they are of minor or secondary importance to your business (see "Maintaining an Inventory," below)—if you treat the cost of supplies on hand as an asset for financial reporting purposes, they are not incidental (IRS Private Letter Ruling 9209007)
- you do *not* keep a record of when you use the supplies
- you do not take a physical inventory of the supplies at the beginning and end of the tax year (Private Letter Ruling 8630003 and 9209007), and
- deducting the cost of supplies in the year you purchase them does not distort your taxable income (§ 1.162-3; Private Letter Ruling 9209007).

> EXAMPLE: This year, Barbee purchases $100 worth of lightbulbs to light her home workspace. She does not keep a record of how many lightbulbs she uses each year or take a physical inventory of how many she has on hand at year's end. The lightbulbs are incidental supplies. Barbee may deduct the entire $100 for the year, regardless of how many lightbulbs she actually used that year.

Long-Term Assets

Long-term assets are things that last for more than one year—for example, equipment, tools, office furniture, vehicles, and buildings. Long-term assets that you purchase to use in your business are not a part of your inventory. They are deductible capital expenses that you may depreciate over several years or, in many cases, deduct in a single year under Section 179. (See Chapter 5 for more on deducting long-term assets.)

EXAMPLE: Barbee buys a new computer to help her keep track of her sales. The computer is not part of Barbee's inventory because she bought it to use in her business, not to resell to customers. Because it will last for more than one year, it's a long-term asset, which she must either depreciate or expense under Section 179.

Maintaining an Inventory

A business is said to maintain or carry an inventory when it must include unsold inventory items as assets on its books, to be deducted only when the items are sold or become worthless. A business is required to carry an inventory if the production, purchase, or sale of merchandise produces income for the business—that is, if these activities account for a substantial amount of the business's revenues. And any business that wants to take an inventory deduction must carry an inventory and account to the IRS on inventory costs and sales.

> **TIP**
>
> **How big is "substantial"?** You must carry an inventory if buying, selling, or producing merchandise accounts for a substantial amount of your company's revenue. So how much is substantial? There's no exact figure, but many tax experts believe that a business that derives 8% or less of its revenue from the sale or production of merchandise need not maintain an inventory. A business that makes at least 15% of its money from selling or producing merchandise probably has to maintain an inventory, and a business that earns 9% to 14% of its money from merchandise is in a gray area.

Often, it's perfectly obvious when a business must carry an inventory. Barbee's crafts business is a perfect example. Barbee obtains all of her income from the manufacture and sale of crafts to customers, so she must maintain an inventory. On the other hand, a taxpayer who only provides a service to customers ordinarily doesn't have to maintain an inventory. For example, a bookkeeper who provides bookkeeping services to clients need not maintain an inventory of the paper he uses, nor does he need to compute the cost of goods sold each year for his taxes.

When You Provide Services and Sell Merchandise

Some home businesses provide services to customers and also sell merchandise. For example, a home-based plumbing contractor who provides plumbing services to customers may also supply various plumbing fixtures and materials. Separately billing clients or customers for an item tends to show it is merchandise that should be carried as inventory. However, this factor is not determinative in and of itself. The key is whether the sale of the merchandise is a substantial income-producing factor for the business. Thus, for example, a plumber who earns 15% or more of his business income from selling plumbing fixtures should probably treat the items as inventory.

Merchandise to Include in Inventory	
Include the following merchandise in inventory:	**Do not include the following items in inventory:**
Purchased merchandise if title has passed to you, even if the merchandise is in transit or you do not have physical possession of it for some other reason.	Goods you have sold, if title has passed to the buyer.
	Goods consigned to you.
Merchandise you've agreed to sell but have not separated from other similar merchandise you own to supply to the buyer.	Goods ordered for future delivery, if you do not yet have title.
Goods you have placed with another person or business to sell on consignment.	Assets such as land, buildings, and equipment used in your business.
Goods held for sale in display rooms, merchandise mart rooms, or booths located away from your place of business.	Supplies that do not physically become part of the item intended for sale.

> **CAUTION**
> **The standards are far from clear in this area.** If you sell services and goods, talk to a tax professional for advice on dealing with inventory.

Supplies for Providing a Service

Materials and property consumed or used up while providing services to customers or clients are supplies, not merchandise that must be included in inventory. Good examples are rubber gloves and disposable syringes used by doctors and nurses to provide medical services.

The same item can constitute supplies for one business and inventory for another. It all depends on whether the item is furnished to the customer or consumed in performing a service. For example, the paper used to prepare blueprints is inventory in the hands of a paper manufacturer, but supplies in the hands of an architect.

Deducting Inventory Costs

You cannot deduct inventory costs in the same way as other costs of doing business, such as your office rent or employee salaries. A business may deduct only the cost of goods it actually sells during a tax year—not the cost of its entire inventory. Inventory that remains unsold at the end of the year is a business asset, not a deductible expense.

You may deduct unsold inventory when you sell it in later years or in the year it becomes worthless (as a business loss). In contrast, you may deduct business expenses (such as home office expenses) entirely in the year when you incur them—in other words, they are currently deductible.

To figure out how much you can deduct for inventory, you must calculate the cost (to you) of the goods you sold during the year. You can then deduct this amount from your gross income when you do your taxes.

Computing the Cost of Goods Sold

The easiest way to calculate your inventory costs is to work backwards. Rather than trying to add up everything they sold during the year, most business owners figure out how much inventory they had available for sale during the year and how much they have left at the end of the year. The difference between these two numbers is the inventory sold that year.

To figure out the cost of goods sold, start with the cost of any inventory on hand at the beginning of your tax year. Add the cost of inventory that you purchased or manufactured during the year. Subtract the cost of any merchandise you withdrew for personal use. The sum of all this addition and subtraction is the cost of all goods available for sale during the tax year. Subtract from this amount the value of your inventory at the end of your tax year. (See "Determining the Value of Inventory," below, for information on how to calculate this value.) The cost of all goods sold during the year—and therefore, the amount you can deduct for inventory expenses on your taxes—is the remainder. This can be stated by the following equation:

	Inventory at beginning of year
Plus:	Purchases or additions during the year
Minus:	Goods withdrawn from sale for personal use
Equals:	Cost of goods available for sale
Minus:	Inventory at end of year
Equals:	Cost of goods sold

EXAMPLE: Barbee had $1,000 in inventory at the beginning of the year and purchased another $28,000 of inventory during the year. She removed $500 of inventory for her own personal use (to give away as Christmas presents). The cost of the inventory she had left at the end of the year is $10,500. She would calculate her cost of goods sold as follows:

Inventory at beginning of year		$ 1,000
Purchases or additions during the year	+	28,000
Goods withdrawn from sale for personal use	–	500
Cost of goods available for sale	=	28,500
Inventory at end of year	–	10,500
Cost of goods sold	=	$18,000

Note that all of these costs are based on what Barbee paid for her inventory, not what she sold it for (which was substantially greater).

Determining the Value of Inventory

To use the equation in "Computing the Cost of Goods Sold," above, you must be able to calculate the value of the inventory you have left at the end of the year. There is no single way to do this—standard methods for tracking inventory vary according to the type and size of business involved. As long as your inventory methods are consistent from year to year, the IRS doesn't care which method you use.

 RESOURCE

Need more information on how to value your inventory? This section provides only a small overview of a large subject. For more information on valuing inventory, refer to:

- *The Accounting Game*, by Darrell Mullis and Judith Orloff (Sourcebooks, Inc.)
- *Small Time Operator*, by Bernard B. Kamoroff (Bell Springs Publishing)
- IRS Publication 334, *Tax Guide for Small Business* (Chapter 7), and
- IRS Publication 538, *Accounting Periods and Methods*.

Taking Physical Inventory

You need to know how much inventory you have at the beginning and end of each tax year to figure your cost of goods sold. If, like most businesses, you use the calendar year as your tax year, this means that you need to figure out your inventory each December 31. Unless you hold a New Year's Eve sale, your inventory on January 1 will usually be the same as the prior year's ending inventory—your inventory on December 31. Any differences must be explained in a schedule attached to your tax return.

Until recently, the IRS required all businesses that sold or manufactured goods to make a physical inventory of the merchandise they owned—that is, to actually count it. This process, often called "taking inventory," is usually done at the end of the year, although it doesn't have to be. Nor is it necessary to count every single item in stock. Businesses can make a physical inventory of a portion of their total merchandise, then extrapolate their total inventory from the sample.

The IRS no longer requires small businesses to take physical inventories. (Small businesses are those that earn less than $1 million in gross receipts per year, and service businesses that earn up to $10 million per year.) But even small businesses must keep track of how much inventory they buy and sell to determine their cost of goods sold for the year. With modern inventory software, it is possible for a business to keep a continuous record of the goods on hand during the year. Keep copies of your invoices and receipts to prove to the IRS that you correctly accounted for your inventory, in case you are audited.

Identifying Inventory Items Sold During the Year

The second step in figuring out your cost of goods sold is to identify which inventory items were sold during the year. There are several ways to do this. You can specifically track each item that is sold during the year. This is generally done only by businesses that sell a relatively small number of high-cost items each year, such as automobile dealers or jewelers.

If you don't want to identify specific items by their invoices, you must make an assumption about which items were sold during the year and which items remain in stock. Small businesses ordinarily use the first-in, first-out (FIFO) method. The FIFO method assumes that the first items you purchased or produced are the first items that you sold, consumed, or otherwise disposed of.

EXAMPLE: Barbee purchased three leather pouches to sell to customers during 2011. She bought the first pouch on February 1 for $5, the second on March 1 for $6, and the third on April 1 for $7. At the end of the year, Barbee finds that she only has one of these pouches left in stock. Using the FIFO method, she assumes that the first two pouches that she bought were the first ones sold. This means that in 2011, she sold two pouches that cost her $11 and has one pouch left in her inventory that cost $7.

Another method of identifying inventory makes the opposite assumption. Under the last-in, first-out (LIFO) method, you assume that the last items purchased or produced were the first to sell. This method is not favored by the IRS. You may use it only if you use the accrual method of accounting (see Chapter 15) and take physical inventory. To use the LIFO method, you must file IRS Form 970, *Application to Use LIFO Inventory Method*, and follow some very complex tax rules.

Valuing Your Inventory

You must also determine the value of the inventory you sold during the year. The value of your inventory is a major factor in figuring out your taxable income, so the method that you use is very important. The two most common methods are the cost method and the lower of cost or market method. A new business that doesn't use LIFO to determine which goods were sold (see above) may choose either method to value its inventory. You must use the same method to value your entire inventory, and you cannot change the method from year to year without first obtaining IRS approval.

Cost Method

As the name indicates, when you use the cost method, your inventory cost is the amount that you paid for the merchandise. Note that this is not the same as what you sold it for, which will (hopefully!) be higher.

Using the cost method is relatively easy when you purchase goods to resell. To calculate the value of each item, start with the invoice price.

Add the cost of transportation, shipping, and other money you had to spend to acquire the items. Subtract any discounts you received.

Things get much more complicated if you manufacture goods to sell. In this situation, you must include all direct and indirect costs associated with the goods. This includes:

- the cost of products or raw materials, including the cost of having them shipped to you
- the cost of storing the products you sell, and
- direct labor costs (including contributions to pension or annuity plans) for workers who produce the products. This does not include your own salary, unless you are a corporate employee.

In addition, larger businesses (those with more than $10 million in gross receipts) must include an amount for depreciation on machinery used to produce the products and factory overhead expenses. If your home business makes this much money, obtain an accountant's help.

Lower of Cost or Market Method

What if the retail value of your inventory goes down during the year? This could happen, for example, if your inventory becomes obsolete or falls out of fashion. In this event, you may use the lower of cost or market method to value your inventory. Under this method, you compare the market (retail) value of each item on hand on the inventory date with its cost, and use the lower value as its inventory value. By using the lower of these two numbers, your inventory will be worth less and your deductible expenses will be greater, thereby reducing your taxable income.

> **EXAMPLE:** Barbee purchased a jeweled belt for $1,000. Due to a change in fashion, Barbee finds she can sell the belt for only $500. Using the lower of cost or market method, she may value the belt at $500.

However, you can't simply make up an inventory item's market value. You must establish the market value of your inventory through objective evidence, such as actual sales price for similar items.

> ⓘ **TIP**
>
> **Consider donating excess inventory to charity.** One way to get rid of inventory you can't sell is to donate it to charity. You'll benefit a worthwhile charity and, by removing the items from your shelves, generate a tax deduction as well.

IRS Reporting

You must report the cost of goods sold on your tax return. If you're a sole proprietor, the amount goes directly on your Schedule C. Part III of Schedule C tracks the cost of goods equation provided in "Deducting Inventory Costs," above. LLCs and partnerships report their cost of goods sold on Schedule A of IRS Form 1065, *U.S. Return of Partnership Income.* S corporations report cost of goods sold on Schedule A of Form 1120, *U.S. Income Tax Return for an S Corporation.* C corporations report this information on Schedule A of Form 1020, *U.S. Corporation Income Tax Return.*

Technically speaking, the cost of goods sold is not a business expense. Rather, it is subtracted from a business's gross income to determine its gross profit for the year. Business expenses are then subtracted from the gross profit to determine the business's taxable net profit, as shown by the following formula:

	Gross income
Minus:	Cost of goods sold
Equals:	Gross profit
Minus:	Deductible business expenses
Equals:	**Net profit**

As a practical matter, this is a distinction without a difference—both the cost of goods sold and business expenses are subtracted from your business income to calculate your taxable profit. However, you cannot deduct the cost of goods sold to determine your gross profit and then deduct it again as a business expense—this would result in a double deduction.

EXAMPLE: Barbee subtracts her $18,000 cost of goods sold from her gross income (all the money she earned from selling her crafts) to determine her gross profit. She earned $50,000 in total sales for the year and had $10,000 in business expenses, including rent, advertising costs, and business mileage. She calculates her net profit as follows:

Gross income		$ 50,000
Cost of goods sold	–	18,000
Gross profit	=	32,000
Business expenses	–	10,000
Net profit	=	$ 22,000

Barbee has to pay tax only on her $22,000 in net profit.

Obviously, the larger the cost of goods sold, the smaller your taxable income will be and the less tax you'll have to pay.

Hiring Help: Employees and Independent Contractors

Employees Versus Independent Contractors 248

Tax Deductions for Employee Pay and Benefits 252

    Employee Pay 252

    Payroll Taxes 255

    State Payroll Taxes 257

    Employee Fringe Benefits 259

Reimbursing Employees for Business-Related Expenditures 262

    Accountable Plans 262

    Unaccountable Plans 266

    Unreimbursed Employee Expenses 266

Employing Your Family or Yourself 268

    Employing Your Children 268

    Employing Your Spouse 271

    Rules to Follow When Employing Your Family 272

    Employing Yourself 276

Tax Deductions When You Hire Independent Contractors 278

    No Deductions for ICs' Taxes 279

    Paying Independent Contractors' Expenses 279

Anne has a highly successful home business selling used clothing on eBay. In fact, business is so good that she needs help keeping up with her orders. She hires John, a high school kid, to work ten hours per week helping her with fulfillment. Now, she has to figure out how to treat John—and the money she pays him—for tax purposes.

This chapter is about the host of tax rules that apply to home business owners like Anne who hire people, whether as employees or independent contractors. These rules apply when you hire strangers or family members, or when your incorporated business hires you.

Employees Versus Independent Contractors

As far as the IRS is concerned, there are only two types of people you can hire to help in your home business: employees and independent contractors. You must understand the difference between these two categories because the tax rules are very different for each. If you hire an employee, you become subject to a wide array of state and federal tax requirements. You must withhold taxes from your employee's earnings, and pay other taxes yourself. You must also comply with complex and burdensome bookkeeping and reporting requirements. If you hire an independent contractor, none of these requirements apply. Tax deductions related to the two types differ as well. Independent contractors (ICs) go by a variety of names: self-employed, freelancers, free agents, consultants, entrepreneurs, or business owners. What they all have in common is that they are people who are in business for themselves. In contrast, employees work for someone else's business.

Initially, it's up to you to determine whether any person you hire is an employee or an IC. However, your decision about how to classify a worker is subject to review by various government agencies, including:

- the IRS
- your state's tax department
- your state's unemployment compensation insurance agency, and
- your state's workers' compensation insurance agency.

These agencies are mostly interested in whether you have classified workers as independent contractors when you should have classified them as employees. The reason is that you must pay money to each of these agencies for employees, but not for independent contractors. The more workers that are classified as employees, the more money flows into the agencies' coffers. In the case of taxing agencies, employers must withhold tax from employees' paychecks and hand it over to the government; ICs pay their own taxes, which means the government must wait longer to get its money and faces the possibility that ICs won't declare their income or will otherwise cheat on their taxes. If an agency determines that you misclassified an employee as an IC, you may have to pay back taxes, fines, and penalties.

Scrutinizing agencies use various tests to determine whether a worker is an IC or an employee. The determining factor is usually whether you have the right to control the worker. If you have the right to *direct and control* the way a worker performs—both the final results of the job and the details of when, where, and how the work is done—then the worker is your employee. On the other hand, if you have only the right to accept or reject the final results the worker achieves, then that person is an IC.

An employer may not always exercise its right of control. For example, if an employee is experienced and well trained, the employer may not feel the need to closely supervise him or her. But the employer still has the right to step in at any time, which distinguishes an employment relationship from an IC arrangement.

EXAMPLE: Anne hires John to help her fill orders and ship her clothing items to customers. John works ten hours per week in Anne's home office and warehouse (which is located in her garage). Anne carefully trains John, a 17-year-old, in how to take orders and ship the ordered items. When John first starts work, Anne closely supervises how he does his job. Virtually every aspect of John's behavior on the job is under Anne's control, including what time he arrives at and leaves work, when he takes a lunch break, and the sequence of tasks he must perform. If John proves to be an able and conscientious worker, Anne may choose not to look over his shoulder very often. But Anne has the right to do so at any time. John is Anne's employee.

IRS Test for Worker Status		
	Workers will more likely be considered ICs if:	**Workers will more likely be considered employees if:**
Behavioral Control	• you do not give them instructions • you do not provide them with training	• you give them instructions they must follow about how to do the work • you give them detailed training
Financial Control	• they have a significant investment in equipment and facilities • they pay business or travel expenses themselves • they make their services available to the public • they are paid by the job • they have opportunity for profit or loss	• you provide them with equipment and facilities free of charge • you reimburse their business or travel expenses • they make no effort to market their services to the public • you pay them by the hour or other unit of time • they have no opportunity for profit or loss—for example, because they're paid by the hour and have all expenses reimbursed
Relationship Between You and the Worker	• they don't receive employee benefits such as health insurance • they sign a client agreement with the hiring firm • they can't quit or be fired at will • they perform services that are not part of your regular business activities	• they receive employee benefits • they have no written client agreement • they can quit at any time without incurring any liability to you • they can be fired at any time • they perform services that are part of your core business

In contrast, a worker is an independent contractor if the hiring business does not have the right to control the person on the job. Because the worker is an independent businessperson not solely dependent on you (the hiring party) for a living, your control is limited to accepting or rejecting the final results the IC achieves.

> **EXAMPLE:** Anne hires Mary, a bookkeeper, to keep her business's books. Anne is only one of Mary's many clients. Anne doesn't tell Mary how to do her bookkeeping tasks; Mary is a professional who already knows how to do her work. Mary sets her own hours, provides her own equipment, and works from her own home office. Mary is an independent contractor.
>
> Because Mary is clearly running her own business, it's virtually certain that Anne does not have the right to control the way Mary performs her bookkeeping services. Anne's control is limited to accepting or rejecting the final result. If Anne doesn't like the work Mary has done, she can refuse to pay her.

There's no clear cut way for auditors to figure out whether you have the right to control a worker you hire. After all, they can't look into your mind to see whether you are controlling a worker (or whether you believe that you have the right to do so). They rely instead on indirect or circumstantial evidence indicating control or lack of it—for example, whether you provide a worker with tools and equipment, where the work is performed, how the worker is paid, and whether you can fire the worker. The chart above shows the primary factors used by the IRS and most other government agencies to determine if you have the right to control a worker.

CAUTION

Part-time workers and temps can be employees. Don't assume that a person you hire to work part time or for a short period automatically qualifies as an IC. People who work for you only temporarily or part-time are your employees if you have the right to control the way they work.

RESOURCE

Need more information about independent contractors? For a detailed discussion of the practical and legal issues business owners face when hiring ICs, see *Working With Independent Contractors*, by Stephen Fishman (Nolo).

Tax Deductions for Employee Pay and Benefits

Only 9% of home businesses hire employees, according to a study sponsored by the Small Business Administration. However, the tax law provides valuable deductions for those who do have employees. You may deduct most or all of what you pay an employee as a business expense. Thus, for example, if you pay an employee $25,000 per year in salary and benefits, you'll ordinarily get a $25,000 tax deduction. You should factor this into your calculations whenever you're thinking about hiring employees or deciding how much to pay them.

Employee Pay

You may pay your employees in the form of salaries, sales commissions, bonuses, vacation allowances, sick pay (as long as it's not covered by insurance), or fringe benefits. For tax deduction purposes, it doesn't really matter how you measure or make the payments. The amounts you pay an employee may fall into any of the four basic categories of deductible business expenses:

- business operating expenses
- business start-up expenses
- long-term asset purchase expenses, or
- inventory costs.

The general rules for each of these types of expenses are discussed in earlier chapters; this section explains how employee pay can fall into each category.

Operating Expenses

Most of the time, amounts you pay employees to work in your business will be business operating expenses. These expenses are currently deductible as long as they are:

- ordinary and necessary
- reasonable in amount
- paid for services actually performed, and
- actually paid or incurred in the year the deduction is claimed (as shown by your payroll records).

(See Chapter 4 for more on business operating expenses.)

An employee's services are ordinary and necessary if they are common, accepted, helpful, and appropriate for your business; they don't have to be indispensable. An employee's pay is reasonable if the amount is within the range that other businesses pay for similar services. These requirements usually won't pose a problem when you hire an employee to perform any legitimate business function.

> **EXAMPLE:** Ken, a lawyer who works from home, hires Kim to work as a paralegal and pays her $2,500 per month—what such workers are typically paid in the area. Ken can deduct Kim's $2,500 monthly salary as a business operating expense. If Kim works a full year, Ken will get a $30,000 deduction.

Payments to employees for personal services are not deductible as business expenses.

> **EXAMPLE:** Ken hires Samantha to work as a live-in nanny for his three children. Samantha is Ken's employee, but her services are personal, not related to his business. Thus, Ken may not deduct her pay as a business expense.

Special rules (described in "Employing Your Family or Yourself," later in this chapter) apply if you hire family members to work in your business or hire yourself as an employee.

Start-Up Expenses

Anything you pay employees for services performed during the start-up phase of your business is a start-up expense. These expenses are not currently deductible, but you may deduct up to $5,000 in start-up expenses the first year you're in business, provided your expenses don't exceed $50,000. You can deduct any excess over 180 months. (See Chapter 3 for more information on deducting business start-up costs.)

> EXAMPLE: During 2011, Michelle hires Benjamin to work as her full-time personal assistant while she works to start up a Web-based home-schooling service. Benjamin helps Michelle deal with myriad details involved in starting the business. Benjamin worked for Michelle for four months before the website went online. His salary during this start-up phase—$10,000—is a business start-up expense. Michelle may deduct $5,000 of this amount the first year she's in business and the remaining $5,000 over 180 months ($333 per calendar year).

Long-Term Asset Expenses

If you pay an employee to help purchase, transport, install, or improve a long-term asset, the payments are not business operating expenses. Instead, they are added to the basis (cost) of the asset. As such, you may either depreciate them over several years or (in most situations) currently deduct them under Section 179. (See Chapter 5 for more on deducting long-term assets.)

> EXAMPLE: John owns a fleet of 50 used delivery trucks. He employs Martha, a mechanic, to install new engines in the trucks. The engines are long-term asset purchases. What John pays Martha to install the engines is added to their purchase price to arrive at their value for tax purposes (their taxable basis). John can depreciate this amount over five years or deduct the entire amount in one year under Section 179.

Inventory Costs

If you hire an employee to help you manufacture products for sale to customers, the employee's compensation is not a regular business expense. Instead, it is considered part of the cost of the products. These products are inventory, the cost of which may be deducted only as each item is sold. (See Chapter 10 for more on deducting inventory.)

> **EXAMPLE:** Richard owns a home pottery studio that manufactures pottery for sale to collectors. He pays Jean, his employee assistant, $25,000 a year. He adds this cost to the other costs he incurs to produce the pottery (materials, equipment, electricity, and so forth) to figure his total cost of goods sold. He deducts this amount from his gross income to determine his business's gross profit.

Payroll Taxes

Whenever you hire an employee, you become an unpaid tax collector for the government. You are required to withhold and pay both federal and state taxes for the worker. These taxes are called payroll taxes or employment taxes. Federal payroll taxes consist of:

- Social Security and Medicare taxes—also known as FICA
- unemployment taxes—also known as FUTA, and
- federal income taxes—also known as FITW.

You must periodically pay FICA, FUTA, and FITW to the IRS, either electronically or by making federal tax deposits at specified banks, which then transmit the money to the IRS. You are entitled to deduct as a business expense payroll taxes that you pay yourself. You get no deductions for taxes you withhold from employees' pay.

Every year, employers must file IRS Form W-2, *Wage and Tax Statement*, for each of their workers. The form shows the IRS how much the worker was paid and how much tax was withheld.

RESOURCE

Find out more about payroll taxes. IRS Circular E, *Employer's Tax Guide*, provides detailed information on payroll tax requirements. You can a get free copy by calling the IRS at 800-TAX-FORM, by calling or visiting your local IRS office, or by downloading it from the IRS website, www.irs.gov.

Employer's FICA Contributions

FICA is an acronym for Federal Income Contributions Act, the law requiring employers and employees to pay Social Security and Medicare taxes.

Ordinarily, FICA taxes consist of a 12.4% Social Security tax on income up to an annual ceiling; however, for 2011, this amount has been reduced to 10.4%. In 2011, the annual Social Security ceiling was $106,800. Medicare taxes are not subject to any income ceiling and are levied at a 2.9% rate. For 2011, this combines to a total 13.3% tax on employment income up to the Social Security tax ceiling. For all other years, the total tax is 15.3%.

Ordinarily, employers and employees split the cost of FICA taxes— the employer pays half and withholds the other half from the employee's pay. This means that each pay 7.65% up to the Social Security tax ceiling. However, for 2011 only, employers only need withhold 5.65% from their employees' pay. You are entitled to deduct (as a business operating expense) the portion of the tax that you pay yourself.

The ceiling for the Social Security tax changes annually. You can find out what the Social Security tax ceiling is for the current year from IRS Circular E, *Employer's Tax Guide*; the amount is printed right on the first page.

FUTA

FUTA is an acronym for the Federal Unemployment Tax Act, the law that establishes federal unemployment taxes. Most employers must pay both state and federal unemployment taxes. Even if you're exempt from the state tax, you may still have to pay the federal tax. Employers alone are responsible for FUTA—you may not collect or deduct it from employees' wages.

You must pay FUTA taxes if:

- you pay $1,500 or more to employees during any calendar quarter—that is, any three month period beginning with January, April, July, or October, or
- you had one or more employees for at least some part of a day in any 20 or more different weeks during the year. The weeks don't have to be consecutive, nor does the employee have to be the same each week.

For the past 35 years, the FUTA tax rate has been 6.2%. However, effective July 1, 2011 the rate fell to 6%. In practice, you rarely pay this much. You are given a credit of 5.4% if you pay the applicable state unemployment tax in full and on time. This means that the actual FUTA tax rate is usually 0.8% for the first half of 2011 and 0.6% for the second half of the year. In 2011, the FUTA tax was assessed on only the first $7,000 of an employee's annual wages. Therefore, the full amount of the tax is $49 per year per employee. This amount is a deductible business expense.

FITW

FITW is an acronym for Federal Income Tax Withholding. You must calculate and withhold federal income tax from your employees' paychecks. Employees are solely responsible for paying federal income tax. Your only responsibility is to withhold the funds and remit them to the government. You get no deductions for FITW; it wasn't your money to begin with.

State Payroll Taxes

Employers in every state are required to pay and withhold state payroll taxes. These taxes include:

- state unemployment compensation taxes in all states
- state income tax withholding in most states, and
- state disability taxes in a few states.

Employers in every state are required to contribute to a state unemployment insurance fund. Employees make no contributions, except in Alaska, New Jersey, Pennsylvania, and Rhode Island, where employers must withhold small employee contributions from employees' paychecks. The employer contributions are a deductible business expense.

If your payroll is very small—less than $1,500 per calendar quarter —you probably won't have to pay unemployment compensation taxes. In most states, you must pay state unemployment taxes for employees if you're paying federal FUTA taxes. However, some states have stricter requirements. Contact your state labor department for the exact rules and payroll amounts.

All states except Alaska, Florida, Nevada, South Dakota, Texas, Washington, and Wyoming have income taxation. If your state has income taxes, you must withhold the applicable amount from your employees' paychecks and pay it to the state taxing authority. Each state has its own income tax withholding forms and procedures. Contact your state tax department for information. Of course, employers get no deductions for withholding their employees' state income taxes.

California, Hawaii, New Jersey, New York, and Rhode Island have state disability insurance programs that provide employees with coverage for injuries or illnesses that are not related to work. Employers in these states must withhold their employees' disability insurance contributions from their pay. Employers must also make their own contributions in Hawaii, New Jersey, and New York—these employer contributions are deductible.

In addition, subject to some important exceptions, employers in all states must provide their employees with workers' compensation insurance to cover work-related injuries. Workers' compensation is not a payroll tax. Employers must purchase a workers' compensation policy from a private insurer or the state workers' compensation fund. Your workers' compensation insurance premiums are deductible as a business insurance expense (see Chapter 14).

CAUTION

Employers in California must withhold for parental leave.
California was the first state to require paid family leave. Employers in California must withhold money from their employees' paychecks (as part of the state's disability insurance program) to fund this leave program. For more information on the program, go to www.edd.ca.gov.

TIP

Bookkeeping expenses are deductible. Figuring out how much to withhold, doing the necessary record keeping, and filling out the required forms can be complicated. If you have a computer, software programs such as *QuickBooks* or *QuickPay* can help with all the calculations and print out your employees' checks and IRS forms. You can also hire a bookkeeper or payroll tax service to do the work. Amounts you pay a bookkeeper or payroll tax service are deductible business operating expenses. Moreover, the cost will be quite small if you only have a few employees. You can find these services in the phone book or on the Internet under payroll tax services. You can also find a list of payroll service providers on the IRS website at www.irs.gov/efile. Be aware, however, that even if you hire a payroll service, you remain personally liable if your payroll taxes are not paid on time. The IRS recommends that employers: (1) keep their company address on file with the IRS, rather than the address of the payroll service provider, so that the company will be contacted by the IRS if there are any problems; (2) require the payroll service provider to post a fiduciary bond in case it defaults on its obligation to pay any penalties and interest due to IRS deficiency notices; and (3) ask the service provider to enroll in and use the Electronic Federal Tax Payment System (EFTPS) so the employer can confirm payments made on its behalf. Such electronic filing is mandatory in the unlikely event your business's federal tax liability during a calendar year exceeds $200,000 (see www.eftps.gov for more information).

Employee Fringe Benefits

You don't have to provide any fringe benefits to your employees—not even health insurance (except in Hawaii and Massachusetts), sick pay, or vacation. But, starting in 2014, large employers (those with at least 50 more full-time employees) will be required to provide health insurance to their full-time employees or pay a penalty to the IRS. This shouldn't impact any home businesses. However, the tax law encourages you to provide employee benefits by allowing you to deduct the cost as a business expense. (You should deduct these expenses as employee benefits, not employee compensation.) Moreover, your employees do not have to treat the value of their fringe benefits as taxable income.

So you get a deduction and your employees get tax-free goodies. In contrast, if you're a business owner (a sole proprietor, partner in a partnership, an LLC member, or a greater than 2% shareholder of an S corporation), you must include in your income, and pay tax on, the value of any fringe benefits your company provides you—the only exception is for de minimis (minor) fringes. Tax-free employee fringe benefits include:

- health insurance
- accident insurance
- Health Savings Accounts (see Chapter 12)
- dependent care assistance
- educational assistance
- group term life insurance coverage—limits apply based on the policy value
- qualified employee benefit plans, including profit sharing plans, stock bonus plans, and money purchase plans
- employee stock options
- lodging on your business premises
- moving expense reimbursements
- achievement awards
- commuting benefits
- employee discounts on the goods or services you sell
- supplemental unemployment benefits
- de minimis (low-cost) fringe benefits such as low-value birthday or holiday gifts, event tickets, traditional awards (such as a retirement gift), other special occasion gifts, and coffee and soft drinks, and
- "cafeteria" plans that allow employees to choose among two or more of the tax-qualified benefits listed above, or receive reimbursement for specified expenses. Starting in 2011, small employers (those with 100 or fewer employees) can offer their employees a simple cafeteria plan—a plan not subject to the non-discrimination requirements of traditional cafeteria plans.

Health insurance is by far the most important tax-free employee fringe benefit; it is discussed in detail in Chapter 12. See IRS Publication 15-B, *Employer's Guide to Fringe Benefits*, for more information on the other types of benefits.

Employees may also be supplied with working condition fringe benefits. These are property and services you provide to an employee so that the employee can perform his or her job. A working condition fringe benefit is tax-free to an employee to the extent the employee would be able to deduct the cost of the property or services as a business or depreciation expense if he or she had paid for it. If the employee uses the benefit 100% for work, it is tax-free. But the value of any personal use of a working condition fringe benefit must be included in the employee's compensation and he or she must pay tax on it. The employee must meet any documentation requirements that apply to the deduction.

> **EXAMPLE:** Sam, the owner of a small architecture firm, leases a computer and gives it to his employee Paul so that he can perform design work at home. If Paul uses the computer 100% for his work, it is tax free to him. But if he uses it only 50% of the time for work and 50% of the time for personal purposes, he would have to pay income tax on 50% of its value.

The value of the personal use is determined according to its fair market value.

> **EXAMPLE:** It cost Sam $200 a month to rent the computer he gave Paul. If Paul uses the computer 50% of the time for work and 50% of the time for nondeductible personal uses, he would have to add $100 per month to his taxable compensation.

One of the most common working condition fringe benefits is a company car. If an employee uses a company car part of the time for personal driving, the value of the personal use must be included in the employee's income. The employer determines how to value the use of a car, and there are several methods that may be used. The most common is for the employer to report a percentage of the car's annual lease value as determined by IRS tables. For a detailed discussion of these valuation rules, refer to IRS Publication 15-B.

Reimbursing Employees for Business-Related Expenditures

When you own a business, you generally pay all of your business expenses yourself, including the cost of things you buy to enable your employees to do their work—for example, tools and equipment. However, there may be times when an employee must pay for a work-related expense. Most commonly, this occurs when an employee is traveling or entertaining while on the job. However, depending on the circumstances, an employee could end up paying for almost any work-related expense—for example, an employee might pay for office supplies or parking at a client's office.

These employee payments have important tax consequences, no matter what form they take. The rules discussed below apply whether the expenses are incurred by an employee who is not related to you or by an employee who is your spouse or child. They also apply to a business owner who has incorporated the business and works as its employee.

Accountable Plans

The best way to reimburse or otherwise pay your employees for work-related expenses is to use an accountable plan, as defined by the IRS (see "Requirements for an Accountable Plan," below). When you pay employees for their expenses under an accountable plan, two great things happen:

- you don't have to pay payroll taxes on the payments, and
- the employees won't have to include the payments in their taxable income.

Moreover, your business can deduct the amounts you pay, just like your other business expenses, subject to the same rules.

> EXAMPLE: Ken works as an employee for Amy's home-based wedding planning company. Amy decides that Ken should attend the Wonderful World of Weddings convention in Las Vegas. Ken pays his convention expenses out of his own pocket.

When he gets back, he documents his expenses as required by Amy's accountable plan. He paid $2,000 for transportation and hotel, and $1,000 in meal and entertainment expenses. Amy reimburses Ken $3,000. Amy may deduct the entire $2,000 cost of Ken's flight and hotel and deduct 50% of the cost of the meals and entertainment. Ken doesn't have to count the $3,000 reimbursement as income (or pay taxes on it), and Amy doesn't have to report that amount to the IRS on the W-2 form she files for Ken. Moreover, Amy need not withhold income tax or pay any Social Security or Medicare taxes on the $3,000.

Deductions for Employee Meals and Entertainment

Ordinarily, your employees' meal and entertainment expenses are only 50% deductible, just like your own meal and entertainment expenses. (Chapter 7 covers deductions for meals and entertainment.) However, you may take a 100% deduction for employee meals:

- provided as part of a company recreational or social activity—for example, a company picnic
- provided on company premises for your convenience—for example, if you provide lunch because your employees must remain in the office to be available to work, or
- if the cost is included as part of the employee's compensation and reported as such on his or her W-2.

Requirements for an Accountable Plan

An accountable plan is an arrangement by which you agree to reimburse or advance employee expenses only if the employee:

- pays or incurs expenses that qualify as deductible business expenses for your business while performing services as your employee

- adequately accounts to you for the expenses within a reasonable period of time, and
- returns to you (within a reasonable time) any amounts received in excess of the actual expenses incurred.

You can pay your employees' expenses in a variety of ways. For example, you can provide a cash advance the employee uses to pay expenses as they occur; you can have the employee pay the expenses out of his or her own pocket and then provide reimbursement; you can give the employee a company credit card; or, instead of the employee paying the expenses, you can have the bills sent directly to you for payment.

These strict rules are imposed to prevent employees from seeking reimbursement for personal expenses (or phony expenses) under the guise that they were business expenses. Employees used to do this all the time to avoid paying income tax on the reimbursed amounts (employees must count employer reimbursements for their personal expenses as income, but not reimbursements for the employer's business expenses).

An accountable plan need not be in writing (although it's not a bad idea). All you need to do is set up procedures for your employees to follow that meet these requirements.

Employees Must Document Expenses

Your employees must give you the same documentation for a work-related expense that the IRS requires of you when you claim that expense for your business. The employee should provide this documentation within 60 days after incurring the expense.

You need thorough documentation for car, travel, entertainment, and meal expenses—these are the expenses the IRS is really concerned about (see Chapters 7, 8, and 9). However, you can ease up on the documentation requirements if you pay employees a per diem (per day) allowance equal to or less than the per diem rates the federal government pays its workers while traveling. You can find these rates at www.gsa.gov (look for the link to "Per Diem Rates") or in IRS Publication 1542, *Per Diem Rates*. If you use this method, the IRS will assume that the amounts claimed for lodging, meals, and incidental expenses are accurate without any further documentation. The employee need only substantiate the time, place, and business purpose of the expense. The same is true if you pay the standard mileage rate for an employee who uses a personal car for business (see Chapter 8).

However, per diem rates may not be used for an employee who:

- owns more than 10% of the stock in an incorporated business, or
- is a close relative of a 10% or more owner—a brother, sister, parent, spouse, grandparent, or other lineal ancestor or descendent.

In these instances, the employee must keep track of the actual cost of all business-related expenses that he or she wants to get reimbursed for by the employer. Any per diem rate reimbursement for an owner or owner's relative must be counted as taxable wages for the employee.

The documentation requirements are less onerous for other types of expenses. Nevertheless, the employee still has to document the amount of money spent and show that it was for your business. For example, an employee who pays for a repair to his workplace computer out of his own pocket should save the receipt and write "repair of office computer" or something similar to show the business purpose of the payment. It's not sufficient for an employee to submit an expense report with vague categories or descriptions such as "travel" or "miscellaneous business expenses."

Returning Excess Payments

Employees who are advanced or reimbursed more than they actually spent for business expenses must return the excess to the employer within a reasonable time. The IRS says a reasonable time is within 120 days after an expense is incurred. Any amounts not returned are treated as taxable wages for the employee and must be added to the employee's income for tax purposes. This means that you, the employer, must pay payroll tax on those amounts.

> EXAMPLE: You give your employee a $1,000 advance to cover her expenses for a short business trip. When she gets back, she gives you an expense report and documentation showing she only spent $900 for business while on the trip. If she doesn't return the extra $100 within 120 days, it will be considered wages for tax purposes. The employee will have to report this extra money on her tax return, and you'll have to pay payroll tax on the $100.

Unaccountable Plans

If you don't comply with the accountable plan rule, any reimbursements you pay to employees for business-related expenses are deemed to be made under an unaccountable plan. These payments are treated as employee wages, which means that all of the following are true:

- The employee must report the payments as income on his or her tax return and pay tax on them.
- The employee may deduct the expenses—but only as a miscellaneous itemized deduction (see "Unreimbursed Employee Expenses," below).
- You may deduct the payments as wages paid to an employee.
- You must withhold income taxes and the employee's share of Social Security and Medicare taxes from the payments.
- You must pay the employer's 7.65% share of the employee's Social Security and Medicare taxes on the payments.

This is a tax disaster for the employee—and a pretty lousy result for the employer as well—because you will have to pay Social Security and Medicare tax that you could have avoided if the payments had been made under an accountable plan.

Unreimbursed Employee Expenses

Employees are entitled to deduct from their own income ordinary and necessary expenses arising from their employment that are not reimbursed by their employers. In this event, you (the employer) get no deduction, because you haven't paid for the expense.

CAUTION

Some states require reimbursement. Check with your state's labor department to find out the rules for reimbursing employee expenses. You might find that you are legally required to repay employees, rather than letting your employees deduct the expenses on their own tax returns. In California, for example, employers must reimburse employees for all expenses or losses they incur as a direct consequence of carrying out their job duties. (Cal. Labor Code § 2802.)

Employees may deduct essentially the same expenses as business owners, subject to some special rules. For example, there are special deduction rules for employee home office expenses (see Chapter 6), and employees who use the actual expense method for car expenses may not deduct car loan interest.

However, it's much better for the employees to be reimbursed by the employer under an accountable plan and let the employer take the deduction. Why? Because an employee can deduct unreimbursed employee expenses only if the employee itemizes deductions and only to the extent these deductions, along with the employee's other miscellaneous itemized deductions, exceed 2% of his or her adjusted gross income. Adjusted gross income (AGI) is the employee's total income minus deductions for IRA and pension contributions and a few other deductions (shown on Form 1040, line 35).

These rules apply to all employees, including family members who work as your employees, and to you if you've incorporated your business and work as its employee.

> **EXAMPLE:** Eric has formed a regular C corporation for his consulting business and works as its sole employee. In one year, he drives his own car 10,000 miles for his business. He pays all his car-related expenses out of his own pocket and does not seek reimbursement from his corporation. He may deduct his business mileage as an unreimbursed employee business expense on his individual tax return. However, he must keep track of his actual car expenses instead of using the standard mileage rate. His actual expenses are $5,000. He may deduct this amount to the extent that it and his other miscellaneous itemized deductions exceed 2% of his adjusted gross income. Eric's AGI for the year was $100,000, and he had no other miscellaneous itemized deductions, so he may only deduct his $5,000 car expense to the extent it exceeds $2,000 (2% × $100,000 = $2,000). Thus, he may only deduct $3,000 of his $5,000 car expense.

An employee's unreimbursed expenses must be listed on IRS Schedule A, Form 1040, as a miscellaneous itemized deduction. Employees must also file IRS Form 2106, *Employee Business Expenses*, reporting the amount of the expenses.

Employing Your Family or Yourself

Whoever said "never hire your relatives" must not have read the tax code. The tax law promotes family togetherness by making it highly advantageous for home business owners to hire family members. And when you have a home business, hiring your spouse, children, or other relatives can be very convenient for everyone (and eliminate the commute!).

Employing Your Children

Believe it or not, your children can be a great tax savings device. If you hire your children as employees to do legitimate work in your business, you may deduct their salaries from your business income as a business expense. Your child will have to pay tax on his or her salary only to the extent it exceeds the standard deduction amount for the year—$5,800 in 2011. Moreover, if your child is under the age of 18, you won't have to withhold or pay any FICA (Social Security or Medicare) tax on the salary (subject to a couple of exceptions).

These rules allow you to shift part of your business income from your own tax bracket to your child's bracket, which should be much lower than yours (unless you earn little or no income). This can result in substantial tax savings.

The chart below shows the federal income tax brackets for 2011. A child need only pay a 10% tax on taxable income up to $8,500—taxable income means total income minus the standard deduction. Thus, a child could earn up to $14,300 and pay only a 10% income tax. In contrast, if you were married and file jointly, you'd have to pay a 15% federal income tax on taxable income between $17,001 and $69,000, and a 25% tax on taxable income from $69,001 to $139,350. You'd also have to pay a 15.3% Social Security and Medicare tax (up to an annual ceiling), which your child under the age of 18 need not pay (for 2011, this tax is 13.3% up to the limit).

2011 Federal Personal Income Tax Brackets		
Tax Bracket	Income If Single	Income If Married Filing Jointly
10%	Up to $8,500	Up to $17,000
15%	From $8,501 to $34,500	$17,001 to $69,000
25%	$34,501 to $83,600	$69,001 to $139,350
28%	$83,601 to $174,400	$139,351 to $212,300
33%	$174,401 to $379,150	$212,301 to $379,150
35%	All over $379,150	All over $379,150

EXAMPLE: Carol hires Mark, her 16-year-old son, to perform computer inputting services for her medical record transcription business, which she owns as a sole proprietor. He works ten hours per week and she pays him $20 per hour (the going rate for such work). Over the course of a year, she pays him a total of $9,000. She need not pay FICA tax for Mark because he's not yet 18. When she does her taxes for the year, she may deduct his $9,000 salary from her business income as a business expense. Mark pays tax only on the portion of his income that exceeds the $5,800 standard deduction—so he pays federal income tax only on $3,200 of his $9,000 salary. With such a small amount of income, he is in the lowest federal income tax bracket—10%. He pays $320 in federal income tax for the year. Had Carol not hired Mark and done the work herself, she would have lost her $9,000 deduction and had to pay income tax and self-employment taxes on this amount—a 40% tax in her tax bracket (25% federal income tax + 15.3% self-employment tax = 40%). Thus, she would have had to pay an additional $3,600 in federal taxes. Depending on the state where Carol lives, she likely would have had to pay a state income tax as well.

What About Child Labor Laws?

You're probably aware that certain types of child labor are illegal under federal and state law. However, these laws generally don't apply to children under the age of 16 who are employed by their parents, unless the child is employed in mining, manufacturing, or a hazardous occupation. Hazardous occupations include driving a motor vehicle; being an outside helper on a motor vehicle; operating various power-driven machines, including machines for woodworking, metal forming, sawing, and baking; or roofing, wrecking, excavation, demolition, and shipbreaking operations.

A child who is at least 16 may be employed in any nonhazardous occupation. Children at least 17 years of age may spend up to 20% of their time driving cars and trucks weighing less than 6,000 pounds as part of their job if they have licenses and no tickets, drive only in daylight hours, and go no more than 30 miles from home. They may not perform dangerous driving maneuvers (such as towing) or do regular route deliveries. For detailed information, see the Department of Labor website, www.dol.gov.

No Payroll Taxes

One of the advantages of hiring your child is that you need not pay FICA taxes for your child under the age of 18 who works in your trade or business, or your partnership, if it's owned solely by you and your spouse.

> EXAMPLE: Lisa, a 16-year-old, makes deliveries for her mother's mail order business, which is operated as a sole proprietorship. Although Lisa is her mother's employee, her mother need not pay FICA taxes on her salary until she turns 18.

Moreover, you need not pay federal unemployment (FUTA) taxes for services performed by your child who is under 21 years old.

However, these rules do not apply—and you must pay both FICA and FUTA—if you hire your child to work for:

- your corporation, or
- your partnership, unless all the partners are parents of the child.

> EXAMPLE: Ron works in a home-based computer repair business that is co-owned by his mother and her partner, Ralph, who is no relation to the family. The business must pay FICA and FUTA taxes for Ron because he is working for a partnership and not all of the partners are his parents.

No Withholding

In addition, if your child has no unearned income (for example, interest or dividend income), you must withhold income taxes from your child's pay only if it exceeds the standard deduction for the year. The standard deduction was $5,800 in 2011 and is adjusted every year for inflation. Children who are paid less than this amount need not pay any income taxes on their earnings. However, you must withhold income taxes if your child has more than $300 in unearned income for the year and his or her total income exceeds $950 (2011).

> EXAMPLE: Connie, a 15-year-old girl, is paid $4,000 a year to help out in her parents' home business. She has no income from interest or any other unearned income. Her parents need not withhold income taxes from Connie's salary.
>
> If Connie is paid $4,000 in salary and has $500 in interest income, her parents must withhold income taxes from her salary because she has more than $300 in unearned income and her total income for the year was more than $950.

Employing Your Spouse

You don't get the benefits of income shifting when you employ your spouse in your business because your income is combined when you file a joint tax return. You'll also have to pay FICA taxes on your spouse's wages, so you get no savings there either. However, you need not pay

FUTA tax if you employ your spouse in your unincorporated business. This tax is usually less than $50 per year, so this is not much of a savings.

The real advantage of hiring your spouse is in the realm of employee benefits. You can provide your spouse with any or all of the employee benefits discussed in "Tax Deductions for Employee Pay and Benefits," above. You can take a tax deduction for the cost of the benefit, and your spouse doesn't have to declare the benefit as income, provided the IRS requirements are satisfied. This is a particularly valuable tool for health insurance—you can give your spouse health insurance coverage as an employee benefit. (See Chapter 12 for a detailed discussion.)

Another benefit of hiring your spouse is that you can take business trips together and deduct the cost as a business expense, as long as your spouse's presence was necessary (for your business, not for you, personally).

Rules to Follow When Employing Your Family

The IRS is well aware of the tax benefits of hiring a child or spouse, so it's on the lookout for taxpayers who claim the benefit without meeting the requirements. If the IRS concludes that your children or spouse aren't really employees, you'll lose your tax deductions for their salary and benefits. And they'll have to pay tax on their benefits. To avoid this, you should follow these simple rules:

Rule 1: Your Child or Spouse Must Be a Real Employee

First of all, your child or spouse must be a bona fide employee. Their work must be ordinary and necessary for your business, and their pay must be compensation for services actually performed. Their services don't have to be indispensable, but they must be common, accepted, helpful, and appropriate for your business. Any real work for your business can qualify—for example, you could employ your child or spouse to clean your office, answer the phone, stuff envelopes, input data, or make deliveries. You get no business deductions when you pay your child for personal services, such as babysitting or mowing your lawn at home. On the other hand, money you pay for yard work performed on business property could be deductible as a business expense.

The IRS won't believe that an extremely young child is a legitimate employee. How young is too young? The IRS has accepted that a seven-year-old child may be an employee (see "Hardworking Seven-Year-Old Was Parents' Employee," below), but probably won't believe that children younger than seven are performing any useful work for your business.

You should keep track of the work and hours your children or spouse perform by having them fill out time sheets or time cards. You can find these in stationery stores or you can create a time sheet yourself. It should list the date, the services performed, and the time spent performing the services. Although not legally required, it's also a good idea to have your spouse or child sign a written employment agreement specifying his or her job duties and hours. These duties should be related only to your business.

Rule 2: Compensation Must Be Reasonable

When you hire your children, it is advantageous (taxwise) to pay them as much as possible. That way, you can shift more of your income to your children, who are probably in a much lower income tax bracket. Conversely, you want to pay your spouse as little as possible, because you get no benefits from income shifting; you and your spouse are in the same income tax bracket (assuming you file a joint return, as the vast majority of married people do). Moreover, your spouse will have to pay the employee's share of Social Security taxes on his or her salary—an amount that is not tax deductible. This tax is ordinarily 7.65% up to the annual ceiling, but for 2011, it is only 5.65%. (As your spouse's employer, you'll have to pay employment taxes on your spouse's salary as well, but these taxes are deductible business expenses.) The absolute minimum you can pay your spouse is the minimum wage in your area.

However, you can't just pay whatever amount will result in the lowest tax bill: Your spouse's and/or your child's total compensation must be reasonable. Total compensation means the sum of the salary plus all the fringe benefits you provide your spouse, including health insurance and medical expense reimbursements, if any. You shouldn't have a problem as long as you don't pay more than you'd pay a stranger for the same work. In other words, don't try paying your child $100 per hour for office cleaning just to get a big tax deduction. Find out what workers who perform similar services in your area are being paid. For example, if you plan to hire your teenager to do computer inputting, call an employment agency or temp agency in your area to see what these workers are being paid.

To prove how much you paid (and that you actually paid it), you should pay your child or spouse by check, not cash. Do this once or twice a month, just as you would for any other employee. The funds should be deposited in a bank account in your child's or spouse's name. Your child's bank account may be a trust account.

Rule 3: Comply With Legal Requirements for Employers

You must comply with most of the same legal requirements when you hire a child or spouse as you do when you hire a stranger.

- **At the time you hire.** When you first hire your child or spouse, you must fill out IRS Form W-4. You (the employer) use it to determine how much tax you must withhold from the employee's salary. A child who is exempt from withholding should write "exempt" in the space provided and complete and sign the rest of the form. You must also complete U.S. Citizenship and Immigration Services Form I-9, *Employment Eligibility Verification*, verifying that the employee is a U.S. citizen or is otherwise eligible to work in the United States. Keep both forms. You must also record your employee's Social Security number. If your child doesn't have a number, you must apply for one. In addition, you must have an Employer Identification Number (EIN). If you don't have one, you may obtain it by filing IRS Form SS-4.
- **Every payday.** You'll need to withhold income tax from your child's pay only if it exceeds a specified amount (see "Employing Your Children," above). You don't have to withhold FICA taxes for children younger than 18. You must withhold income tax and FICA for your spouse, but not FUTA tax. If the amounts withheld plus the employer's share of payroll taxes exceed $2,500 during a calendar quarter, you must deposit the amounts monthly by making federal tax deposits at specified banks or electronically depositing them with the IRS.

- **Every calendar quarter.** If you withhold tax from your child's or spouse's pay, you must deposit it with the IRS or a specified bank. If you deposit more than $1,000 a year, you must file Form 941, *Employer's Quarterly Federal Tax Return*, with the IRS, showing how much the employee was paid during the quarter and how much tax you withheld and deposited. If you need to deposit less than $2,500 during a calendar quarter, you can make your payment along with the Form 941, instead of paying monthly. Employers with total employment tax liability of $1,000 or less may file employment tax returns once a year instead of quarterly. Use new IRS Form 944, *Employer's Annual Federal Tax Return*. You should be notified by the IRS if you're eligible to file Form 944. If you haven't been notified but believe you qualify to file Form 944, call the IRS at 800-829-0115.

- **Each year.** By January 31 of each year, you must complete and give your employee a copy of IRS Form W-2, *Wage and Tax Statement*, showing how much you paid the employee and how much tax was withheld. Starting with tax reporting for the 2011 tax year (so in early 2012), employers will be required to report on their W-2 forms the cost of providing group health insurance to their employees. This is required purely for informational purposes. These benefits will remain tax-free to employees. You must also file copies with the IRS and Social Security Administration by February 28. You must include IRS Form W-3, *Transmittal of Wage and Tax Statements*, with the copy you file with the Social Security Administration. If your child is exempt from withholding, a new W-4 form must be completed each year. You must also file Form 940 or Form 940-EZ, *Employer's Annual Federal Unemployment (FUTA) Tax Return*. The due date is January 31; however, if you deposited all of the FUTA tax when due, you have ten additional days to file. You must file a Form 940 for your child even though you are not required to withhold any unemployment taxes from his or her pay. If your child is your only employee, enter his or her wages as "exempt" from unemployment tax.

RESOURCE

Need more information on employing family members? IRS Circular E, *Employer's Tax Guide*, and Publication 929, *Tax Rules for Children and Dependents*, provide detailed information on these requirements. You can get free copies by calling the IRS at 800-TAX-FORM, by calling or visiting your local IRS office, or by downloading them from the IRS website, www.irs.gov.

Employing Yourself

If, like the vast majority of home business owners, you are a sole proprietor, partner in a partnership, or member of a limited liability company (LLC) taxed as a partnership, you are *not* an employee of your business. You are a business owner. However, if you have incorporated your business, whether as a regular C corporation or an S corporation, you are an employee of your corporation if you actively work in the business. In effect, you will be employing yourself. This has important tax consequences.

Your Company Must Pay Payroll Taxes

Your incorporated business must treat you just like any other employee for tax purposes. This means it must withhold income and FICA taxes from your pay, and pay half of your FICA tax itself. It must also pay FUTA taxes for you. It gets a tax deduction for its contributions, just like any other employer (see "Tax Deductions for Employee Pay and Benefits," above). Your corporation—not you personally—must pay these payroll taxes.

You can't avoid these payroll taxes by working for free. The corporation must pay you at least a reasonable salary—what similar companies pay for the same services.

Tax Deductions for Your Salary and Benefits

When you're an employee, your incorporated business can deduct your salary as a business expense. However, you will have to pay income tax on your salary, so you won't realize a net tax savings.

But being an employee can have a significant upside. You'll be eligible for all of the tax-advantaged employee benefits discussed in "Tax Deductions for Employee Pay and Benefits," above. This means that your corporation can provide you with benefits, like health insurance, and deduct the expense (see Chapter 12). If your corporation is a regular C corporation, you won't have to pay income tax on the value of your employee benefits. However, most employees of S corporations must pay tax on their employee benefits, so you probably won't get an overall tax savings. Employees of an S corporation who own less than 2% of the corporate stock don't have to pay tax on benefits, but it's unlikely you'll have this little stock in your own S corporation.

You Can't Deduct Your Draw

If you're a sole proprietor, partner, or LLC member, you do not pay yourself a salary. If you want money from your business, you simply withdraw it from your business bank account. This is called a "draw." Because you are not an employee of your business, your draws are not employee compensation and are not deductible as business expenses.

Your Employee Expenses

You have a couple of options for dealing with expenses you incur while working for your corporation—for example, when you travel on company business.

From a tax standpoint, the best option is to have your corporation reimburse you for your expenses. Whether you've formed a C or an S corporation, the rules regarding reimbursement of employee expenses (discussed in "Reimbursing Employees for Business-Related Expenditures," above) apply to you. If you comply with the requirements for an accountable plan, your corporation gets to deduct the expense and you don't have to count the reimbursement as income to you. If you fail to follow the rules, you must treat any reimbursements as employee income subject to tax.

Another option is simply to pay the expenses yourself and forgo reimbursement from your corporation. This is not a good idea, however—as an employee, you may deduct work-related expenses only to the extent they exceed 2% of your adjusted gross income (see "Unreimbursed Employee Expenses," above).

Tax Deductions When You Hire Independent Contractors

Anyone you hire to help in your home business who does not qualify as an employee is an independent contractor for tax purposes. As far as tax deductions are concerned, hiring independent contractors is very simple. Most of the time, the money you pay to an IC to perform services for your business will be deductible as a business operating expense. These expenses are deductible as long as they are ordinary, necessary, and reasonable in amount.

> EXAMPLE: Emily, a graphic designer, hires Don, an attorney, to sue a client who failed to pay her. He collects $5,000 and she pays him $1,500 of this amount. The $1,500 is an ordinary and necessary business operating expense—Emily may deduct it from her business income for the year.

Of course, you get no business deduction if you hire an IC to perform personal services.

> EXAMPLE: Emily pays lawyer Don $2,000 to write her personal will. Because this is a personal expense, Emily cannot deduct the $2,000 from her business income.

If you hire an IC to perform services during the start-up phase of your business, to manufacture inventory, or as part of a long-term asset purchase, you can't deduct payments to the IC as operating expenses. Instead, you must follow the rules to deduct these amounts as start-up expenses, inventory, or long-term assets, respectively. (See "Tax Deductions for Employee Pay and Benefits," above, for more on this rule.)

No Deductions for ICs' Taxes

When you hire an independent contractor, you don't have to withhold or pay any state or federal payroll taxes on the IC's behalf. Therefore, you get no deductions for the IC's taxes; the IC is responsible for paying them.

However, if you pay an unincorporated IC $600 or more during the year for business-related services, you must:

- obtain the IC's taxpayer identification number, and
- file IRS Form 1099-MISC, *Miscellaneous Income,* telling the IRS how much you paid the IC.

The IRS may impose a $250 fine if you intentionally fail to file a Form 1099 when required. You could also be subject to more severe penalties if the IRS later audits you and determines that you misclassified the worker.

If you're not sure whether you must file a Form 1099-MISC for a worker, go ahead and file one. You lose nothing by doing so—and you'll save yourself the consequences of failing to file if you were legally required to do so.

RESOURCE

Need more information on reporting requirements for ICs? For a detailed discussion of how to file a 1099 form—and the consequences of not filing one—see *Working With Independent Contractors,* by Stephen Fishman (Nolo).

Paying Independent Contractors' Expenses

Independent contractors often incur expenses while performing services for their clients—for example, for travel, photocopying, phone calls, or materials. Although many ICs want their clients to separately reimburse them for such expenses, it's better for you not to do so. ICs who pay their own expenses are less likely to be viewed as your employees by the IRS or other government agencies. Instead of reimbursing expenses, pay ICs enough so they can cover their own expenses.

However, it's customary in some businesses and professions for the client to reimburse the IC for expenses. For example, a lawyer who handles a business lawsuit will usually seek reimbursement for expenses such as photocopying, court reporters, and travel. If this is the case, you may pay these reimbursements without too much concern about misclassification problems.

When you reimburse an IC for a business-related expense, you get the deduction for the expense, not the IC. Unless the IC fails to follow the adequate accounting rules discussed below, you should not include the amount of the reimbursement on the 1099 form you file with the IRS reporting how much you paid the IC, because the reimbursement is not considered income for the IC. Make sure to require ICs to document expenses with receipts and save them in case the IRS questions the payments.

The rules differ depending on whether the IC provides you with an "adequate accounting."

Adequate Accounting for Travel and Entertainment Expenses

To make an adequate accounting of travel and entertainment expenses, an IC must comply with all the record-keeping rules applicable to business owners and employees. You must document the date, amount, place, and business purpose of the expense, and show the business relationship of the people at a business meal or entertainment event. (See Chapter 7.) The IRS is particularly suspicious of travel, meal, and entertainment expenses, so there are special documentation require-ments for these. (See Chapter 15 for more on record keeping.) You are not required to save the IC's expense records except for records for entertainment expenses. You may deduct the IC's travel, entertainment, and meal expenses as your own business expenses for these items. (But remember that meal and entertainment expenses are only 50% deductible.) You do not include the amount of the reimbursement you pay the IC on the Form 1099 you file with the IRS reporting how much you paid the IC.

EXAMPLE: Tim, a writer, hires Mary, a self-employed book publicity consultant, to help him promote his latest book. In the course of her work, Mary incurs $1,000 in meal and entertainment expenses while meeting potential contacts. She makes an adequate accounting of these expenses and Tim reimburses her the $1,000. Tim may deduct 50% of the $1,000 as a meal and entertainment expense for his business; Mary gets no deduction. When Tim fills out the 1099 form telling the IRS how much he paid Mary, he does not include the $1,000.

No Adequate Accounting for Travel and Entertainment Expenses

If an IC doesn't properly document travel, meal, or entertainment expenses, you are probably not under any legal obligation to pay them. However, if you decide to pay some of these expenses, you may deduct the full amount as IC payments, provided these expenses are ordinary, necessary, and reasonable in amount. The IC should provide you with some type of records to establish this. You are not deducting these expenses as travel, meal, or entertainment expenses, so the 50% limit on these deductions does not apply. However, you must include the amount of the reimbursement as income paid to the IC on the IC's 1099 form.

What If You Get Sick? Deducting Medical Expenses

The Health Care Reform Act 284

The Personal Deduction for Medical Expenses 287

Deducting Health Insurance Premiums 288

    Personal Income Tax Deduction for the Self-Employed 288

    Deducting Health Insurance as a Business Expense 291

Tax Credits for Employee Health Insurance 296

    Requirement #1: You Must Have Employees 297

    Requirement #2: Employee Compensation Must Average
    Less than $50,000 298

    Requirement #3: You Must Pay at Least 50% of Employee
    Health Insurance Premiums 298

    Amount of the Credit 299

Medical Reimbursement Plans 300

    What Is a Medical Reimbursement Plan? 300

    What Expenses May Be Reimbursed? 303

    Plan Requirements 303

    How to Establish a Plan 304

    Sample Plan 305

Health Savings Accounts 309

    What Are Health Savings Accounts? 309

    Establishing Your HSA 310

    Making Contributions to Your HSA 313

    Withdrawing HSA Funds 315

    Are HSAs a Good Deal? 316

    HSAs for Employees 317

    Tax Reporting for HSAs 319

f you own a home business or are thinking about starting one, one of the most important problems you face is how you'll pay for your health insurance and other medical expenses. There are at least four possibilities:

- If you have a job that provides health insurance coverage, you can keep it (and your coverage).
- If your spouse has a job that provides health coverage, you can obtain coverage through him or her (one-third of all home business owners obtain their health coverage this way).
- If you're under 27 years of age, your parents can cover you under their health insurance policy.
- You can purchase your own health insurance.

The last alternative is the most costly, but it will be your only choice if you don't have (or want to keep) your day job, or you don't have the benefit of a spouse's coverage. Fortunately, the tax law provides several deductions intended to help business owners pay their medical expenses. In addition, a tax-advantaged method of paying for medical expenses is available: the Health Savings Account.

The Health Care Reform Act

In March of 2010, Congress enacted a massive health care reform bill called the Patient Protection and Affordable Care Act. Among other things, this law contained several important tax changes for small businesses and small business owners, including home businesses. Most of these will be phased in over the next several years.

The most significant change created by the new law is the requirement that all Americans have health insurance coverage by 2014. Currently, there is no federal law requiring individuals to have health coverage; nor are employers required to provide it for their employees. This is all scheduled to change starting in 2014. By that year, all Americans must have at least minimal health coverage or they will have to pay a penalty to the IRS. To help everyone obtain coverage, starting in 2014, health insurers will not be allowed to deny coverage because of preexisting medical conditions.

The mandatory health coverage requirement will affect all businesses, large and small. But they will be affected in different ways. Larger employers—those with 50 or more full-time employees—will be required to provide their employees with minimum health coverage or pay a penalty to the IRS. Owners of smaller businesses with fewer than 50 employees will not be required to provide health coverage to their employees. But, to encourage them to do so voluntarily, small businesses with 25 or fewer employees will be entitled to a substantial health care insurance tax credit until 2016. And starting in 2014, all small business owners, including home business owners, will have to have at least minimal health insurance coverage for themselves and their families or pay a penalty to the IRS. This is true whether you're self-employed, a partner in a partnership or limited liability company, or an employee of your own small corporation. For most taxpayers, the annual penalty for each family member (up to three) will be $95 in 2014, $325 in 2015, and $695 in 2016 and later. The penalty is not applicable to people who can't afford coverage.

To help individuals and small businesses be able to afford health coverage, each state will be required to establish a health insurance exchange by 2014. These exchanges will be a competitive insurance marketplace where small businesses and individuals who might not otherwise be able to afford it, can buy qualified health benefit plans. The exchanges will offer a choice of health plans that meet certain benefits and cost standards. To help lower income people obtain coverage, a refundable premium assistance credit will be available for those who purchase health insurance from a state exchange and whose income is between 100% and 400% of the federal poverty line.

For more information on the new health care reform law, see www.healthcare.gov.

An Overview of the Health Care Reform Act

Here's a brief timeline of health care reforms. The changes are all covered in more detail later in this chapter or in the other chapters as noted below.

2010
- Small Employer Health Insurance Credit. A tax credit for certain small business employers of up to 35% of the contributions they pay for their employees' health insurance premiums. The percentage increases to 50% for 2014 and 2015, and ends in 2016.
- Adult children up to age 27 can remain on their parent's health insurance, regardless of whether or not they are dependent.

2011
- Health savings accounts, medical reimbursement arrangements, and flexible spending accounts can only be used for prescribed medicines—not over-the-counter medications.
- Value of health benefits must be reported on employee W-2 forms (see Chapter 11).
- Increased penalty taxes on nonqualified withdrawals from health savings accounts.

2012
- Expanded information reporting by businesses who hire independent contractors or purchase goods and services (see Chapter 11).

2013
- Medicare tax increase of 0.9% for wages or self-employment income in excess of $200,000 (single)/$250,000 (married filing jointly) (see Chapter 1).
- 3.8% tax on investment income of high income taxpayers (see Chapter 1).
- 10% floor on personal deduction for itemized medical expenses.

2014
- Large employers—those with at least 50 full-time employees—must provide health coverage or pay IRS penalties (see Chapter 12).
- Individuals must obtain health coverage or pay tax penalty.

The Personal Deduction for Medical Expenses

All taxpayers—whether or not they own a business—are entitled to a personal income tax deduction for medical and dental expenses for themselves and their dependents. Eligible expenses include both health insurance premiums and out-of-pocket expenses not covered by insurance (see "What HSA Funds Can Be Used For," later in this chapter, for a list of eligible expenses). However, there are two significant limitations on the deduction, which make it difficult to use for most taxpayers.

To take the personal deduction, you must comply with both of the following requirements:

- You must itemize your deductions on IRS Schedule A. (You can itemize deductions only if all of your itemized deductions exceed the standard deduction for the year—$11,600 for joint returns and $5,800 for single returns in 2011.)
- You can deduct only the amount of your medical and dental expenses that exceeds 7.5% of your adjusted gross income (AGI). Your AGI is your net business income and other taxable income, minus deductions for retirement contributions and one-half of your self-employment taxes, plus a few other items (as shown at the bottom of your Form 1040).

EXAMPLE: Al is a self-employed interior decorator whose adjusted gross income for 2011 is $80,000. He pays $350 per month for health insurance for himself and his wife. He spends another $2,000 in out-of-pocket medical and dental expenses for the year. Al may deduct his medical expenses only if all of his itemized deductions exceed the $11,600 standard deductions for the year. If they do exceed the standard deduction, his personal medical expense deduction is limited to the amount he paid that exceeds $6,000 (7.5% × $80,000 = $6,000). Because he paid a total of $6,200 in medical expenses for the year, he may deduct only $200.

As you can see, unless your medical expenses are substantial, the 7.5% limitation eats up most or all of your deduction. Moreover, starting in 2013, the threshold for the itemized medical expense deduction is scheduled to go up to 10% of AGI. However, people 65 or older will be exempt from the increase until 2017.

Thus, the more money you make, the less you'll be able to deduct. For this reason, most home business owners need to look elsewhere for meaningful medical expense deductions.

Deducting Health Insurance Premiums

Health insurance premiums are the largest medical expense most people pay. There are several ways that home business owners can deduct these premiums.

Personal Income Tax Deduction for the Self-Employed

Self-employed people, whether or not they work at home, are allowed to deduct health insurance premiums (including dental and long-term care coverage) for themselves, their spouses, and their dependents. Self-employed people who have Medicare coverage may deduct their Medicare Part B premiums as part of the self-employed health insurance deduction. In addition, this insurance can also cover your children up to age 27 (26 or younger as of the end of the year), whether or not they are your dependents. For these purposes, a child includes a son, daughter, stepchild, adopted child, or eligible foster child. This new age 27 standard replaces the lower age limits that applied under prior tax law, as well as the requirement that a child qualify as a dependent for tax purposes.

Sole proprietors, partners in partnerships, LLC members, and S corporation shareholders who own more than 2% of the company stock can use this deduction. Only owners of regular C corporations may not take this deduction. And you get the deduction whether you purchase your health insurance policy as an individual or have your business obtain it for you.

Self-Employment Tax Primer

Ordinarily, self-employment taxes consist of a 12.4% Social Security tax on income up to an annual ceiling; however, for 2011, this amount has been reduced to 10.4%. In 2011, the annual Social Security ceiling is $106,800. Medicare taxes are not subject to any income ceiling and are levied at a 2.9% rate. For 2011, this combines to a total 13.3% tax on employment or self-employment income up to the Social Security tax ceiling. For all other years, the total tax is 15.3%. If you earn more than the ceiling, deducting your health insurance costs from your self-employment income will not give you a very significant tax savings, because you would have had to pay only a 2.9% tax on that income.

EXAMPLE: Kim is a sole proprietor who pays $10,000 each year for health insurance for herself, her husband, and her three children. Her business earns approximately $50,000 in profit each year. Every year, she may deduct her $10,000 annual health insurance expense from her gross income for federal and state income tax purposes. Since her combined federal and state income tax rate is 30%, this saves her $3,000 in income taxes each year. Ordinarily, Kim may not deduct her premiums from her income when she figures her self-employment taxes.

Business Income Limitation

There is a significant limitation on the health insurance deduction for the self-employed: You may deduct only as much as you earn from your business. If your business earns no money or incurs a loss, you get no deduction. Thus, if Kim from the above example earned only $3,000 in profit from her business, her self-employed deduction would be limited to that amount; she wouldn't be able to deduct the remaining $7,000 in premiums she paid for the year.

If your business is organized as an S corporation, your deduction is limited to the amount of wages you are paid by your corporation.

If you have more than one business, you cannot combine the income from all your businesses for purposes of the income limit. You may only use the income from a single business you designate to be the health insurance plan sponsor.

Designating Your Plan Sponsor

If you purchase your health insurance plan in the name of one of your businesses, that business will be the sponsor. However, the IRS says you may purchase your health coverage in your own name and still get the self-employed health insurance deduction. (IRS Chief Counsel Memo 200524001.) This may be advantageous because it allows you to pick which of your businesses will be the sponsor at the start of each year. Obviously, you should pick the business you think will earn the most money that year.

Moreover, if you have more than one business, you can have one business purchase medical insurance and the other purchase dental insurance and deduct 100% of the premiums for each policy subject to the income limits discussed above. This will be helpful if no single business earns enough income for you to deduct both policies through one business.

EXAMPLE: Robert is a sole proprietor medical doctor who has a sideline business running a medical lab. He purchases a medical insurance policy for himself and his family with his medical practice as the sponsor. He also purchases a dental insurance plan with his lab business as the sponsor. He may deduct 100% of the premiums for each policy, subject to the income limits.

No Other Health Insurance Coverage

You may not take the self-employed health insurance deduction if you are eligible to participate in a subsidized health insurance plan maintained by your employer or your spouse's employer. This is so even if the plan requires copayments, or you have to pay additional premiums to obtain all the coverage you need.

EXAMPLE: Rich works as an employee editor at a publishing company and also has a part-time home business. He obtains insurance coverage for himself and his wife through his employer. However, he must pay $500 per month for his wife's coverage. This amount is not deductible under the self-employed health insurance deduction.

This rule applies separately to plans that provide long-term care insurance and those that do not. Thus, for example, if your spouse has employer-provided health insurance that does not include long-term care, you may purchase your own long-term care policy and deduct the premiums.

Tax Reporting

Because the self-employed health insurance deduction is a personal deduction, you take this deduction directly on your Form 1040 (it does not go on your Schedule C if you're a sole proprietor). If you itemize your deductions and do not claim 100% of your self-employed health insurance costs on your Form 1040, you may include the rest with your other medical expenses on Schedule A, subject to the 7.5% threshold (scheduled to increase to 10% in 2013 and later). You would have to do this, for example, if your health insurance premiums exceeded your business income.

Deducting Health Insurance as a Business Expense

You can deduct health insurance costs as a currently deductible business expense if your business pays them on behalf of an employee. The benefit to treating these costs as a business expense is that you can deduct them from your business income for tax purposes. The premiums are an employee fringe benefit and are not taxable income for the employee. Thus, if you are an employee of your business, you can have your business pay your health insurance premiums and then deduct the cost as a business expense, reducing both your income and your self-employment taxes.

EXAMPLE: Mona, a sole proprietor data miner, hires Milt to work as an employee in her business. She pays $250 per month to provide Milt with health insurance. The payments are a business expense that she can deduct from her business income. Milt need not count the value of the insurance as income or pay any tax on it. Mona deducts her $3,000 annual payments for Milt's insurance from her business income for both income tax and self-employment tax purposes. The $3,000 deduction saves her $750 in income taxes (she's in the 25% income tax bracket; 25% × $3,000 = $750). She also saves $459 in self-employment taxes (15.3% × $3,000 = $459).

Unfortunately, if (like the vast majority of home business owners) you are a sole proprietor, partner in a partnership, an LLC member, or S corporation shareholder with more than 2% of the company stock, you *cannot* be an employee of your own business for these purposes. Thus, you cannot have your business provide you with health insurance and deduct the cost as a business expense.

You can still take the self-employed health insurance tax deduction discussed above, which will effectively wipe out the extra income tax you had to pay. But the self-employed health insurance deduction is a personal deduction, not a business deduction, and thus does not reduce your business income for self-employment tax purposes.

Form a C Corporation and Hire Yourself

If you want to convert your own health insurance premiums to a business expense, you must form a C corporation to run your business and have the corporation hire you as its employee. You can do this even if you're running a one-person home business.

As an employee of a C corporation, your corporation must pay you a salary, as well as the employer's share of Social Security and Medicare taxes. Your corporation deducts your health insurance premiums from its taxes—you don't deduct them from your personal taxes. Because you own the corporation, you get the benefit of the deduction.

There are disadvantages to incorporating, however: Incorporating costs money, you'll have to comply with more burdensome bookkeeping requirements, and you will have a more complex tax return. You'll also have to pay state and federal unemployment taxes for yourself—a tax you don't have to pay if you're not an employee of your business. And, depending on your state's requirements, you may have to provide yourself with workers' compensation coverage.

Because your health insurance is 100% deductible from your income taxes, it may not be worthwhile to incorporate just to save on Social Security and Medicare taxes. This is particularly true if your employee income would substantially exceed the Social Security tax ceiling—$106,800 in 2011. If you're in this situation, think about obtaining a Health Savings Account instead (see "Health Savings Accounts," below).

Disability Insurance

Disability insurance pays a monthly benefit to employees who are unable to work due to sickness or injury. You may provide disability insurance as an employee benefit to your workers, including your spouse, and deduct the premiums as a business expense. If your business is a C corporation, it may deduct disability payments made for you, its employee. However, any employees who collect disability benefits must include them in their taxable income.

Employing Your Spouse

If, like 90% of home business owners, you're a sole proprietor (or have formed an entity other than an S corporation to run your business), there's another way you can deduct health insurance costs as a business expense: Hire your spouse to work in your business as an employee and provide him or her with health insurance. The insurance should be purchased in the name of the spouse/employee, not in the employer's name. The policy can cover your spouse, you, your children, and other dependents as well. Moreover, starting in 2010, the insurance can cover your children up to age 27 (26 or younger as of the end of the year), whether or not they are your dependents. Then you can deduct the cost of the health insurance as a business expense.

> **EXAMPLE:** Joe, a successful home-based financial consultant, hires his wife, Martha, to work as his employee assistant. He pays her $25,000 per year and provides her with a health insurance policy covering both of them and their two children. The annual policy premiums are $5,000. Joe may deduct the $5,000 as a business expense for his consulting practice, listing it as an expense on his Schedule C. He may deduct the $5,000 not only from his $80,000 income for income tax purposes, but also from his self-employment income.

If you do this and you're self-employed, do not take the health insurance deduction for self-employed people discussed in "Personal Income Tax Deduction for the Self-Employed," above. You're better off taxwise deducting all your health insurance premiums as a business expense because a business deduction reduces the amount of your income subject to self-employment taxes. The self-employed health insurance deduction is a personal deduction, not a business deduction, and thus does not reduce your business income for self-employment tax purposes.

There are a couple of catches to this deduction. This method ordinarily doesn't work if you have an S corporation because your spouse is deemed to be a shareholder of the corporation along with you and can't also be a corporate employee. In addition, your spouse must be a bona fide employee. In other words, he or she must do real work in your business, you must pay applicable payroll taxes, and you must otherwise treat your spouse like any other employee. (See Chapter 11 for a detailed discussion of your obligations to workers.)

You'll probably want to pay your spouse as low a salary as possible, because both of you will have to pay Social Security and Medicare taxes on that salary (but not on employee benefits like health insurance and medical expense reimbursements). You should, however, regularly pay your spouse at least some cash wages or the IRS could claim that your spouse is not a real employee. You can make the cash wages a relatively small part of your spouse's total compensation—wages plus fringe benefits like your medical reimbursement plan.

No matter how you pay your spouse, his or her total compensation must be reasonable—that is, you can't pay more than your spouse's services are worth. For example, you can't pay your spouse at a rate of $100 per hour for simple clerical work. Total compensation means the sum of the salary, plus all the fringe benefits you pay your spouse, including health insurance and medical expense reimbursements, if any (see "Medical Reimbursement Plans," below).

> **EXAMPLE:** Tina's husband, Tim, works part-time as a helper in her home-based wedding photography business. Tina calls a couple of employment agencies and learns that other wedding photography businesses in the area pay helpers like Tim about $10 per hour, so she decides to pay him at this rate. Tim will work 500 hours per year (ten hours per week, 50 weeks per year), so his total compensation should be about $5,000 (500 hours × $10/hr. = $5,000). Tina wants to provide Tim with a health insurance policy covering him and his family (including Tina) and a medical reimbursement plan. She would like to purchase a health insurance policy for $7,500 per year, but she knows she can't justify this expense since Tim's total annual compensation can't be more than about $5,000. Instead, Tina has her business provide Tim with $3,500 worth of health insurance, $500 worth of medical reimbursements, and $1,000 in salary. Tina and Tim must pay employment taxes on his $1,000 in wages. But Tina gets to deduct the wages and the $5,000 in health insurance and medical reimbursement costs as a business expense. This saves her (and Tim) $2,000 in federal and state taxes for the year.

Your Spouse May Not Be Your Partner

A marriage may be a partnership, but you can't be partners with your spouse in your business and also claim that he or she is your employee for purposes of health insurance deductions. If your spouse co-owns the business with you, he or she is treated as self-employed—not an employee—for purposes of health insurance. You and your spouse are co-owners if you file partnership returns for your business (IRS Form 1065) listing him or her as a partner, or if your spouse has made a substantial financial investment in your business with his or her own money.

Alternatively, starting in 2007, spouses who jointly own a business may elect to be taxed as a "qualified joint venture." When this is done, both spouses are treated as sole proprietors for tax purposes. See Chapter 1 for more details.

Of course, if you're single, you won't be able to hire a spouse to take advantage of this method for turning health insurance costs into a business expense. However, if you're a single parent, you could hire your child and deduct the cost of your child's health insurance as a business expense. But your child's policy cannot cover you or other family members.

Tax Credits for Employee Health Insurance

The previous section explained how you can deduct health insurance costs for employees—including your spouse—as a business expense. Tax deductions are all well and good, but there is something even better: tax credits. Unlike a deduction, a tax credit is a dollar-for-dollar reduction in the amount you owe the IRS. In other words, a $1,000 credit saves you $1,000 on your taxes. How much a $1,000 deduction saves you depends on your top tax bracket. As of 2011, however, it will be no more than $350 because the top federal income tax bracket is 35%.

The massive health insurance reform enacted by Congress in 2010 created a brand new tax credit for small employers who pay for health insurance for their employees. From 2010 through 2013, employers who qualify can claim a tax credit of up to 35% of their contributions to their employees' health insurance premiums, subject to certain limits. The percentage increases to 50% for 2014 and 2015. The credit ends in 2016. Obviously, if you qualify for the credit, you can save substantial taxes.

To qualify for the health insurance credit, you must satisfy three requirements.

Requirement #1: You Must Have Employees

You can qualify for the health insurance credit only if your business has non-owner employees who are not your relatives. In other words, you can forget about getting the credit if you're running a one-person home business. This eliminates the great majority of home businesses, but by no means all of them.

As is the case with the business tax deduction for health expenses, business owners don't count as employees for these purposes and don't qualify for the tax credit. This includes sole proprietors, partners in partnerships, shareholders owning more than 2% of an S corporation, and any owner of more than 5% of the business. In addition, family members don't count as employees. This includes a child (or descendant of a child); a spouse; a sibling or step-sibling; a parent (or ancestor of a parent); a step-parent; a niece or nephew; an aunt or uncle; or a son-in-law, daughter- in-law, father-in-law, mother-in-law, brother-in-law, or sister-in-law. Thus, you can't hire any of these people to work as employees in your business and qualify for the credit.

The credit is designed for smaller businesses. The full credit is available only to businesses with ten or fewer full-time employees. It is gradually phased out if you have more than ten full-time employees. It is phased out completely for a business with 25 full-time employees (something which should affect few home businesses).

Requirement #2: Employee Compensation Must Average Less than $50,000

The tax credit is intended to help employers pay for health insurance for employees with relatively low salaries. To qualify for the credit, the average annual wages of your employees for the year must be less than $50,000 per full-time employee. The credit is reduced by 4% for each $1,000 that the person's average annual compensation exceeds $25,000. Thus, the credit is completely phased out if your employees are paid $50,000 or more in annual wages.

The amount of average annual wages is determined by dividing (1) the total wages paid to employees during the tax year by (2) the number of the full-time employees for the year. For this purpose, wages means wages as defined for FICA purposes (without regard to the wage base limitation). Your employees can be full-time or part-time. If you have part-time employees, divide the total annual hours they work by 2080. The result will be the equivalent number of full-time employees.

> EXAMPLE: For the 2011 tax year, an employer pays $44,000 in wages and has two full-time employees. The employer's average annual wages would be $22,000 ($44,000 divided by 2 = $22,000).

Requirement #3: You Must Pay at Least 50% of Employee Health Insurance Premiums

Finally, you must pay at least 50% of the annual premiums for your employees' health insurance. Health insurance for purposes of the credit can take a variety of forms. It's up to the employer to decide what type of coverage to provide. You can pay for the insurance directly or reimburse your employees for their payments. The coverage can be under any hospital or medical service policy, or a health maintenance organization (HMO) contract offered by a health insurance company. Employers also have the option of providing dental or vision coverage, long-term care, nursing home care, home health care, community-based care, or any combination of these. Medicare supplemental health insurance also qualifies for the credit.

Only the health insurance premiums paid by the employer are counted in calculating the credit. If an employer pays only a portion of the premiums (with employees paying the rest), only that portion is counted. For example, if an employer pays 80% of the premiums for employees' coverage, only that 80% is counted in calculating the credit.

Amount of the Credit

For 2010 through 2013, the credit is equal to 35% of the employer's health insurance payments for its employees. This amount is increased to 50% for 2014 and 2015.

However, there is a cap on the amount of premiums that may be used to calculate the credit. This prevents employers from providing their employees with "Cadillac health care plans" and reaping huge tax credits. The cap is equal to the average premium charged in the state's small group health insurance market. This amount is determined by the Department of Health and Human Services (HHS). IRS Revenue Ruling 2010-13 lists the average premium for the small group market in each state. You can find it on the IRS website (www.irs.gov). For California, for example, the average premium for employee-only coverage is $4,628 per year, with $10,957 for family coverage. These are the maximum amounts that can be used to calculate the credit for California employers.

> **EXAMPLE:** During 2011, Joe hires his wife Jackie to work as a full-time employee in his home-based web design business. Jackie had not worked for the previous four months. He pays her a salary of $24,000 per year. He also pays for her health insurance which covers him as well, at a cost of $8,000 per year. This does not exceed the average premium for the small group market in the Joe's state and otherwise meets the requirements for the credit. Joe's health insurance credit for 2011 equals $2,800 (35% × $8,000 = $2,800). This means Joe may reduce his total tax liability for 2011 by $2,800.

The health credit is a general business credit you claim on your tax return. If the credit exceeds your tax liability for the year, the unused credit amount can be carried back for one year and carried forward for 20 years. However, an unused credit amount for 2010 can only be carried forward.

It's important to understand that, when you take the health credit, your tax deduction for employee health insurance expenditures is reduced by the amount of the credit. For example, if Joe from the example above took a $2,800 credit, he could deduct as a business expense only $5,200 of the $8,000 he paid for employee health insurance in 2011.

Medical Reimbursement Plans

Health insurance usually doesn't cover all of your medical expenses. For example, it doesn't cover preexisting conditions, or deductibles or copayments—that is, amounts you must pay yourself before your insurance coverage kicks in. Many costs aren't covered by insurance at all, including ongoing physical therapy, fertility treatment, and optometric care. As a result, the average American pays about $900 a year in out-of-pocket health-related expenses. One way to deduct these expenses is to establish a medical reimbursement plan. Another way is to use a Health Savings Account (discussed below).

Few home business owners take advantage of medical reimbursement plans. But you should definitely consider adopting one if you must obtain your own health insurance coverage, are married, and need or want your spouse to work as an employee in your home business. The potential tax benefits are substantial.

What Is a Medical Reimbursement Plan?

A medical reimbursement plan is an arrangement under which an employer reimburses its employees for health or dental expenses. These plans are usually self-funded—that is, the employer pays the expenses out of its own pocket, not through insurance.

Why would an employer do this? One good reason is that the reimbursements are deductible business expenses for the employer. Also, the employee doesn't have to include the reimbursements as taxable income (as long as the employee has not taken a deduction for these amounts as a personal medical expense).

So how does this help you? Again, your spouse (if you have one) comes to the rescue. You can hire your spouse as your employee and provide him or her with a medical reimbursement plan. The plan may cover not only your spouse, but also you, your children, and other dependents. Moreover, starting in 2010, your plan can cover your children up to age 27 (26 or younger as of the end of the year), whether or not they are your dependents. This allows your business to reimburse you and your family for out-of-pocket medical expenses and deduct the amounts as a business expense. And you don't have to include the reimbursements in your own taxable income. The IRS has ruled that this is perfectly legal. (Tax Advice Memo 9409006—see Chapter 18 for information on finding tax advice memoranda and other tax authorities.)

> **EXAMPLE 1:** Jennifer has her own public relations business. She hires her husband, Paul, to work as her part-time employee assistant. She establishes a medical reimbursement plan covering Paul, herself, and their young child. Paul spends $6,000 on medical expenses. Jennifer reimburses Paul for the $6,000 as provided by their plan. Jennifer may deduct the $6,000 from her business income for the year, meaning she pays neither income nor self-employment tax on that amount. Paul need not include the $6,000 in his income—it's tax free to him. The deduction saves Jennifer and Paul $2,000 in taxes for the year.

CAUTION

Your spouse must be a legitimate employee. Your spouse must be a legitimate employee for your medical reimbursement plan to pass muster with the IRS. You can't simply hire your spouse on paper—he or she must do real work in your business. If you can't prove your wife is a legitimate employee, the IRS will disallow your deductions in the event of an audit. If you're audited, the IRS will be particularly suspicious if your spouse is your only employee.

EXAMPLE 2: Mr. Haeder, a sole proprietor attorney who practiced law from his home, claimed that he hired his wife as his employee to answer the telephone, greet visitors, type legal papers, and clean his office. Mrs. Haeder had no employment contract or set work schedule, did not keep track of her hours, and did not directly or regularly receive a salary. Instead, Mr. Haeder paid her the maximum amount she could deduct as an IRA contribution. Annually, he transferred money in his brokerage account to an IRA in his wife's name. For all but one of the years eventually audited by the IRS, no W-2 was issued to Mrs. Haeder. Mr. Haeder sponsored a medical reimbursement plan that covered out-of-pocket expenses for his wife, her children, and her spouse—that is, himself. Mrs. Haeder submitted bills for out-of-pocket medical expenses to her husband, which he reimbursed and attempted to deduct as business expenses.

The IRS determined Mr. Haeder was not entitled to deduct the reimbursements under the medical reimbursement plan because Mrs. Haeder was not a bona fide employee. The tax court agreed, finding that there was no credible evidence that Mrs. Haeder performed any services other than those reasonably expected of a family member. (*Haeder v. Comm'r.*, TC Memo 2001-7 (2001).)

The medical expense reimbursement plan deduction is available only to your employees, not to you (the business owner). The only way you can qualify as an employee is if your business is a C corporation (see "Deducting Health Insurance as a Business Expense," above). If you don't have a spouse to employ, you could employ your child and provide him or her with a reimbursement plan. But the plan may not cover you or any other family members.

What Expenses May Be Reimbursed?

One of the great things about medical reimbursement plans is that they can be used to reimburse employees for a wide variety of health-related expenses. Deductible medical expenses include any expense for the diagnosis, cure, mitigation, treatment, or prevention of disease; or any expense paid to affect the structure or function of the human body. (IRS Reg. 1.213.1(e).)

This includes, of course, premiums for health and accident insurance, and health insurance deductibles and copayments. But it also includes expenses for acupuncture, chiropractors, eyeglasses and contact lenses, dental treatment, laser eye surgery, psychiatric care, and treatment for learning disabilities. (See "Withdrawing HSA Funds," below, for a list of expenses that can and cannot be deducted.) You can draft your plan to include only those expenses you wish to reimburse. Presumably, though, you'd want to include as many expenses as possible if the plan covers only your spouse, yourself, and your family.

Plan Requirements

If you decide to adopt a medical expense reimbursement plan, the plan must be in writing, it may not discriminate in favor of highly compensated employees, and it must reimburse employees only for medical expenses that are not paid for by insurance.

The nondiscrimination rule will affect you only if you have employees other than your spouse or children. If you do, a medical reimbursement plan may be too expensive for you, because you'll have to provide coverage to nonfamily members as well. A plan is nondiscriminatory under IRS rules if it:

- covers at least 70% of all employees
- covers at least 80% of all employees eligible to benefit from the plan, provided that 70% or more of all employees are eligible, or
- is found to be nondiscriminatory by the IRS based on the facts and circumstances.

EXAMPLE: Jim employs six people in his home-based crafts company. One works only 20 hours per week, while the other five work full-time. To be nondiscriminatory, Jim's medical expense reimbursement plan must cover 80% of his five employees eligible to participate—in other words, he must cover four of his five full-time employees.

However, the plan may exclude employees who:
- work fewer than 25 hours a week
- are not yet 25 years old
- work for you fewer than seven months in a year, or
- have worked for you less than three years.

If a plan is found to be discriminatory by the IRS, all or part of the medical benefits paid to highly compensated employees under the plan will be taxable to the employees. Highly compensated employees include:
- anyone among the top 25% highest-paid employees
- the five highest-paid corporate officers (if your business is incorporated), and
- shareholders who own more than 10% of the corporation stock.

How to Establish a Plan

If a medical expense reimbursement plan sounds attractive to you, you should establish one as early in the year as possible because it applies only to medical expenses incurred *after* the date the plan is adopted. (Rev. Rul. 2002-58.) Forget about using a plan to reimburse your spouse or yourself for expenses you have already incurred. If you do, the reimbursement must be added to your spouse's income for tax purposes and you must pay employment tax on it.

A written medical reimbursement plan must be drawn up and adopted by your business. If your business is incorporated, the plan should be adopted by a corporate resolution approved by the corporation's board of directors. You can find a form for this purpose in *The Corporate Records Handbook,* by Anthony Mancuso (Nolo).

Sample Plan

A sample medical expense reimbursement plan is provided below. To fill in the blanks, you will need to decide:

Eligibility

If you have employees other than your spouse (or think you may have them in the future), you must decide whether to place limitations on which employees may be covered by your plan. You may cover all your employees or exclude certain classes of employees as described in "Plan Requirements," above. It's up to you. But, be careful about who you exclude from your plan—make sure you don't eliminate your spouse. For example, if your plan excludes all employees who work fewer than 25 hours per week, your spouse will have to work at least 25 hours to qualify for your plan. If your spouse will only work 15 hours per week, your plan should exclude only those employees who work fewer than 15 hours.

Dollar Limits

You also have the option of placing an annual dollar limit on the reimbursements you'll make. If your spouse is your only employee, you probably won't want a limit. But, if you have other employees—or may have them in the future—a limit may be advisable.

Claims Submission

Finally, you must decide how often the employee must submit claims for reimbursement. Twice a year is fine, but you can make it more frequent if you wish.

Medical Expense Reimbursement Plan

Effective [_date_], [_your business name_] ("Employer") will reimburse all eligible employees for medical expenses incurred by themselves and their dependents, subject to the conditions and limitations set forth below.

1. Uninsured Expenses

Employer will reimburse eligible employees and their dependents only for medical expenses that are not covered by health or accident insurance.

2. Medical Expenses Defined

Medical expenses are those expenses defined by Internal Revenue Code § 213(d). They consist of any expense for the diagnosis, cure, mitigation, treatment, or prevention of disease; or any expense paid to affect the structure or function of the human body. Medical expenses include both prescription and non-prescription drugs and medicines.

3. Dependent Defined

Dependent is defined by I.R.C. § 152. It includes any member of an eligible employee's family for whom the employee and his or her spouse provides more than half of the financial support.

4. Eligibility

[_Choose Alternative A or B._]

Alternative A:
The plan shall be open to all employees.

Alternative B:
The plan shall be open to all employees who:

[_Check applicable boxes—you may check any number._]

☐ work more than [_specify—25 hrs/week is maximum_] hours per week

☐ are at least [_specify—25 years old is maximum_] years of age

☐ have completed [_specify—3 years is maximum_] years of service with Employer

☐ work [_specify—7 months is maximum_] months per year

5. Limitation *[Optional]*

Employer shall reimburse any eligible employee no more than [*dollar amount*] in any calendar year for medical expenses.

6. Submission of Claims

Any eligible employee seeking reimbursement under this plan shall submit to Employer, [*monthly, quarterly or at least twice a year (choose one)*] on [*date*] and [*date*], all bills for medical care, including those for accident or health insurance. Such bills and other claims for reimbursement shall be verified by Employer prior to reimbursement. Employer, in its sole discretion, may terminate the employee's right to reimbursement if the employee fails to comply.

7. Direct Payments

At its option, Employer may pay all or part of a covered employee's medical expenses directly, instead of making reimbursements to the employee. Such a direct payment shall relieve Employer of all further liability for the expense.

8. Termination

Employer may terminate this plan at any time. Medical expenses incurred prior to the date of termination shall be reimbursed by Employer. Employer is under no obligation to provide advance notice of termination.

9. Benefits Not Taxable

Employer intends that the benefits under this plan shall qualify under I.R.C. § 105 so as to be excludable from the gross income of the employees covered by the plan.

Employer's Signature: _____

Date: _____

Employee's Signature: _____

Date: _____

12 Steps to Audit-Proof Your Medical Reimbursement Plan

Your medical reimbursement plan is subject to attack by the IRS if it doesn't look like a legitimate business expense. Your spouse must be a real employee, you must treat him or her as such, and you must manage your plan in a businesslike manner.

1. Have your spouse sign a written employment agreement specifying his or her duties and work hours.
2. Adopt a written medical reimbursement plan for your business.
3. Keep track of the hours your spouse works, with time sheets.
4. Make sure your spouse's total compensation is reasonable.
5. Have your spouse open a separate bank account that he or she can use to pay medical expenses or receive reimbursements from your business.
6. Comply with all payroll tax, unemployment insurance, and workers' compensation requirements for your spouse-employee.
7. Reimburse your spouse for covered expenses by check from a separate business bank account or pay the health care provider directly from your business account. Make a notation on the check that the payment is made under your medical reimbursement plan.
8. Never pay your spouse in cash.
9. Your spouse should submit all bills to be reimbursed or paid by your business at least twice a year, or monthly or quarterly if you prefer. Keep all documentation showing the nature and amounts of the medical expenses paid for by your plan—receipts, canceled checks, and so on, to show that you didn't reimburse your spouse too much and that the payments were for legitimate business expenses.
10. Don't pay for expenses incurred before the date you adopted your plan.
11. If you have employees other than your spouse, make sure you meet the nondiscrimination requirements.
12. Claim your deduction on the correct tax form:
    - sole proprietors—Schedule C, line 14, "Employee benefit programs"
    - LLCs and partnerships—Form 1065, line 19, "Employee benefit programs," and
    - C corporations—Form 1120, Line 25, "Employee Benefit Programs."

Health Savings Accounts

Another tax-advantaged method of buying health insurance has been available since 2004: Health Savings Accounts (HSAs). HSAs can save you taxes, but they're not for everybody.

RESOURCE

Need more information on Health Savings Accounts? The IRS has set up an email address at hsainfo@do.treas.gov, and a voice mailbox at 202-622-4HSA, to answer questions about HSAs. You can also find HSA information on the IRS website at www.irs.gov. An informative private website is www. hsainsider.com.

What Are Health Savings Accounts?

The HSA concept is very simple: Instead of relying on health insurance to pay small or routine medical expenses, you pay them yourself. To help you do this, you establish a Health Savings Account with a health insurance company, bank, or other financial institution. Your contributions to the account are tax deductible, and you don't have to pay tax on the interest or other money you earn on the money in your account. You can withdraw the money in your HSA to pay almost any kind of health-related expense, and you don't have to pay any tax on these withdrawals.

In case you or a family member develops a serious health problem, you must also obtain a health insurance policy with a high deductible—for 2011, at least $1,200 for individuals and $2,400 for families. You can use the money in your HSA to pay this large deductible and any copayments you're required to make.

Using an HSA can save you money in two ways:

- you'll get a tax deduction for the money you deposit in your account, and
- the premiums for your high-deductible health insurance policy may be less than those for traditional comprehensive coverage policies or HMO coverage (you may save as much as 40%).

Establishing Your HSA

To participate in the HSA program, you need two things:
- a high-deductible health plan that qualifies under the HSA rules, and
- an HSA account.

HSA-Qualified Plans

You can't have an HSA if you're covered by health insurance other than a high-deductible HSA plan—for example, if your spouse has family coverage for you from his or her job. So you may have to change your existing coverage to qualify for an HSA. However, you may get your own HSA if you are not covered by your spouse's health insurance. In addition, people eligible to receive Medicare may not participate in the HSA program.

You need to obtain a bare-bones health plan that meets the HSA criteria (is "HSA-qualified"). You may obtain coverage from a health maintenance organization, preferred provider organization, or traditional plan. The key feature of an HSA-qualified health plan is that it has a relatively high annual deductible (the amount you must pay out of your own pocket before your insurance kicks in). In 2011, the minimum annual deductible for single people was $1,200, and $2,400 for families.

You can have a higher deductible if you wish, but there is an annual ceiling on the total amount you can have for your deductible plus other out-of-pocket expenses you're required to pay before your health plan provides coverage. (Such out-of-pocket expenses include co-payments, but do not include health insurance premiums.) For example, in 2011 the annual ceiling for an individual HSA plan was $5,950. This means that your annual deductible and other out-of-expenses you're required to pay before your insurance kicks in cannot exceed that amount. Thus, if your annual deductible was $3,000, your other annual out-of-pocket expenses would have to be limited to $2,950. In 2011, the maximum limits were $5,950 for single people and $11,900 for families. All these numbers are adjusted for inflation each year.

Family Deductibles

One attractive feature of HSA plans is that the annual deductible applies to the entire family, not each family member separately. With such a per-family deductible, expenses incurred by each family member accumulate and are credited toward the one family deductible. For example, a family of four would meet the $2,400 maximum annual deductible if each family member paid $600 in medical expenses during the year (4 × $600 = $2,400). This is a unique feature of HSA plans.

In addition, your health insurance plan must be "HSA-qualified." To become qualified, the insurer must agree to participate in the HSA program and give the roster of enrolled participants to the IRS. If your insurer fails to report to the IRS that you are enrolled in an HSA-qualified insurance plan, the IRS will not permit you to deduct your HSA contributions.

HSA-qualified health insurance policies should be clearly labeled as such on the cover page or declaration page of the policy. It might be possible to convert a high-deductible health insurance policy you already have to an HSA-qualified health insurance policy; ask your health insurer for details.

You can obtain an HSA-qualified health plan from health insurers that participate in the program. The following websites contain directories and contact information for insurers providing HSAs: www.hsainsider.com and www.hsafinder.com. The U.S. Treasury has an informative website on HSAs at www.treas.gov/offices/public-affairs/hsa. You can also contact your present health insurer to find out if it offers an HSA-qualified plan.

The premiums you pay for an HSA-qualified health plan are deductible to the same extent as any other health insurance premiums. This means that if you're self-employed, you may deduct your entire premium from your federal income tax as a special personal deduction. (See "Personal Income Tax Deduction for the Self-Employed," above.)

You can also deduct your contribution if your business is an LLC or partnership, or if you've formed an S corporation. If your partnership or

LLC makes the contribution for you as a distribution of partnership or LLC funds, it is reported as a cash distribution to you on your Schedule K-1 (Form 1065). You may take a personal deduction for the HSA contribution on your tax return (IRS Form 1040) and the contribution is not subject to income or self-employment taxes.

However, the tax result is very different if the contribution is made as a guaranteed payment to the partner or LLC member. A guaranteed payment is like a salary paid to a partner or an LLC member for services performed for the partnership or LLC. The amount of a guaranteed payment is determined without reference to the partnership's or LLC's income. The partnership or LLC deducts the guaranteed payment on its return and lists it as a guaranteed payment to you on your Schedule K-1 (Form 1065). You must pay income and self-employment tax on the amount. You may take a personal income tax deduction on your Form 1040 for the HSA contribution.

Contributions by an S corporation to a shareholder-employee's HSA are treated as wages subject to income tax, but they normally are not subject to employment taxes. The shareholder can deduct the contribution on his or her personal tax return (IRS Form 1040) as an HSA contribution.

If you've formed a C corporation and work as its employee, your corporation can make a contribution to your HSA and deduct the amount as employee compensation. The contribution is not taxable to you. (See "HSAs for Employees.")

HSA Account

Once you have an HSA-qualified health insurance policy, you may open your HSA account. You must establish your HSA with a trustee. The HSA trustee keeps track of your deposits and withdrawals, produces annual statements, and reports your HSA deposits to the IRS.

Any person, insurance company, bank, or financial institution already approved by the IRS to be a trustee or custodian of an IRA is automatically approved to serve as an HSA trustee. Others may apply for approval under IRS procedures for HSAs.

Health insurers can administer both the health plan and the HSA. However, you don't have to have your HSA administered by your insurer. You can establish an HSA with a bank, insurance company, mutual fund, or other financial institution offering HSA products.

Whoever administers your account will usually give you a checkbook or debit card to use to withdraw funds from the account. You can also make withdrawals by mail or in person.

Look at the plans offered by several companies to see which offers the best deal. Compare the fees charged to set up the account, as well as any other charges (some companies may charge an annual service fee, for example). Ask about special promotions and discounts, and find out how the account is invested.

Making Contributions to Your HSA

Once you set up your HSA-qualified health plan and HSA account, you can start making contributions to your account. There is no minimum amount you are required to contribute each year; you may contribute nothing if you wish. But there are maximum limits on how much you may contribute each year:

- If you have individual coverage, the maximum you may contribute to your HSA is $3,050.
- If you have family coverage, the maximum you may contribute to your HSA each year is $6,150.

These maximums are for 2011. They are adjusted for inflation each year.

Taxpayers who have HSAs may make a one-time tax-free rollover of funds from their Individual Retirement Accounts (IRAs) to their HSA. The rollover amount is limited to the maximum HSA contribution for the year (minus any HSA contributions you've already made for the year).

Catch-Up Contributions

Individuals who are 55 to 65 years old have the option of making additional tax-free catch-up contributions to their HSA accounts of up to $1,000. This rule is intended to compensate for the fact that older folks won't have as many years to fund their accounts as younger taxpayers. If you're in this age group, it's wise to make these contributions if you can afford them, so your HSA account will have enough money to pay for future health expenses.

	Self Only	Family
Maximum Contribution	$3,050	$6,150
Catch-Up Contribution (55 and over)	$1,000	$1,000
Minimum Deductible	$1,200	$2,400
Maximum Out-of-Pocket Payments	$5,950	$11,900

Deducting HSA Contributions

The amounts you contribute each year to your HSA account, up to the annual limit, are deductible from your federal income taxes. This is a personal deduction you take on the first page of your IRS Form 1040. You deduct it from your gross income, just like a business deduction. This means you get the full deduction, whether or not you itemize your personal deductions.

> **EXAMPLE:** Martin, a self-employed blacksmith, establishes an HSA for himself and his family with a $2,400 deductible. Every year, he contributes the maximum amount to his HSA account—$6,150 in 2011. Because he is in the 25% federal income tax bracket, this saves him $1,538 in federal income tax for 2011.

Where to Invest Your HSA Contributions

The contributions you make to your HSA account may be invested just like IRA contributions. You can invest in almost anything— money market accounts, bank certificates of deposit, stocks, bonds, mutual funds, Treasury bills, and notes. However, you can't invest in collectibles such as art, antiques, postage stamps, or other personal property. Most HSA funds are invested in money market accounts and certificates of deposit.

Withdrawing HSA Funds

If you or a family member needs health care, you can withdraw money from your HSA to pay your deductible or any other medical expenses. However, you cannot deduct qualified medical expenses as an itemized deduction on Schedule A (Form 1040) that are equal to the tax-free distribution from your HSA. You pay no federal tax on HSA withdrawals used to pay qualified medical expenses.

Qualified medical expenses are broadly defined to include many types of expenses ordinarily not covered by health insurance—for example, dental or optometric care. This is one of the great advantages of the HSA program over traditional health insurance.

No Approval Required

HSA participants don't have to obtain advance approval from their HSA trustee (whether their insurer or someone else) that an expense is a qualified medical expense before they withdraw funds from their accounts. You make that determination yourself. The trustee will report any distribution to you and the IRS on Form 1099-SA, *Distributions From an HSA, Archer MSA, or Medicare Advantage MSA.* You should keep records of your medical expenses to show that your withdrawals were for qualified medical expenses and are therefore excludable from your gross income.

However, you may not use HSA funds to purchase nonprescription medications. The only way to deduct these is to hire your spouse and establish a medical reimbursement plan. (See "Medical Reimbursement Plans," above.)

Tax-Free Withdrawals

If you withdraw funds from your HSA to use for something other than qualified medical expenses, you must pay regular income tax on the withdrawal, plus a 20% penalty. For example, if you were in the 25% federal income tax bracket, you'd have to pay a 45% tax on your nonqualified withdrawals.

Once you reach the age of 65 or become disabled, you can withdraw your HSA funds for any reason without penalty. If you use the money for nonmedical expenses, you will have to pay regular income tax on the withdrawals. When you die, the money in your HSA account is transferred to the beneficiary you've named for the account. The transfer is tax free if the beneficiary is your surviving spouse. Other transfers are taxable.

If you elect to leave the HSA program, you can keep your HSA account and withdraw money from it tax free for health care expenses. However, you won't be able to make any additional contributions to the account.

What HSA Funds Can Be Used For

Ordinarily, you may not use HSA funds to purchase health insurance. However, there are three exceptions to this general rule. You can use HSA funds to pay for:

- a health plan during any period of continuation coverage required under any federal law—for example, when you are terminated from your job and purchase continuing health insurance coverage from your employer's health insurer, which the insurer is legally required to make available to you under COBRA
- long-term health care insurance, or
- health insurance premiums you pay while you are receiving unemployment compensation.

For a list of all the expenses that may be paid with HSA funds, see IRS Publication 969, *Health Savings Accounts and Other Tax-Favored Health Plans.* You can download it from the IRS website at www.irs.gov.

Are HSAs a Good Deal?

Should you get an HSA? It depends. HSAs are a very good deal if you're young or in good health, and you don't go to the doctor often or take many expensive medications. You can purchase a health plan with a high deductible, pay substantially lower premiums, and have the security of knowing that you can dip into your HSA if you get sick and have to pay the deductible or other uncovered medical expenses.

If you don't tap into the money, it will keep accumulating free of taxes. You also get the benefit of deducting your HSA contributions from your income taxes. And you can use your HSA funds to pay for many health-related expenses that aren't covered by traditional health insurance.

If you enjoy good health while you have your HSA, you may end up with a substantial amount in your account that you can withdraw without penalty for any purpose once you turn 65. Unlike all other existing tax-advantaged savings or retirement accounts, HSAs provide a tax break when funds are deposited *and* when they are withdrawn. No other account provides both a "front-end" and "back-end" tax break. With IRAs, for example, you must pay tax either when you deposit or when you withdraw your money. This feature can make your HSA an extremely lucrative tax shelter—a kind of super IRA.

On the other hand, HSAs are not for everybody. You could be better off with traditional comprehensive health insurance if you or a member of your family has substantial medical expenses. When you are in this situation, you'll likely end up spending all or most of your HSA contributions each year and earn little or no interest on your account (but you'll still get a deduction for your contributions). Of course, whether traditional health insurance is better than an HSA depends on its cost, including the deductibles and copayments you must make. In addition, depending on your medical history and where you live, the cost of an HSA-qualified health insurance plan may be too great to make the program cost-effective for you. However, if your choice is an HSA or nothing, get an HSA.

HSAs for Employees

Employers may provide HSAs to their employees. Any business, no matter how small, may participate in the HSA program. The employer purchases an HSA-qualified health plan for its employees, who establish their own individual HSA accounts. The employer may pay all or part of its employees' insurance premiums and make contributions to their HSA accounts. Employees may also make their own contributions to their individual accounts. The combined annual contributions of the employer and employee may not exceed the limits listed in "Making Contributions to Your HSA," above.

HSAs are portable when an employee changes employers. Contributions and earnings belong to the account holder, not the employer. Employers are required to report amounts contributed to an HSA on the employee's Form W-2.

Health insurance payments and HSA contributions made by a business on behalf of its employees are currently deductible business expenses. The employees do not have to report employer contributions to their HSA accounts as income. You deduct them on the "Employee benefit programs" line of your business income tax return. If you're filing Schedule C, this is on Part II, line 14.

If you've formed a C corporation and work as its employee, your corporation may establish an HSA on your behalf and deduct its contributions on its own tax return. The contributions are not taxable to you, but you get no personal deduction for them. You do get a deduction, however, if you make contributions to your HSA account from your personal funds. You can't do this if you have an S corporation, LLC, or partnership because owners of these entities are not considered employees for employment benefit purposes.

Hiring Your Spouse

If you're a sole proprietor or have formed any business entity other than an S corporation, you may hire your spouse as your employee and have your business pay for an HSA-qualified family health plan for your spouse, you, and your children and other dependents. Moreover, starting in 2010, your HSA-qualified health plan can cover your children up to age 27 (26 or younger as of the end of the year), whether or not they are your dependents. Your spouse then establishes an HSA, which your business may fully fund each year. The money your business spends for your spouse's health insurance premiums and to fund the HSA is a fully deductible business expense. This allows you to reduce both your income and self-employment taxes. (See "Personal Income Tax Deduction for the Self-Employed," above.)

Nondiscrimination Rules

If you have employees other than yourself, your spouse, or other family members, you'll need to comply with nondiscrimination rules—that is, you'll have to make comparable HSA contributions for all employees with HSA-qualified health coverage during the year. Contributions are considered comparable if they are either of the same amount or the same percentage of the deductible under the plan. The rule is applied separately to employees who work fewer than 30 hours per week. Employers who do not comply with these nondiscrimination rules are subject to a 35% excise tax.

Tax Reporting for HSAs

You must report to the IRS how much you deposit to and withdraw from your HSA each year. You make the report using IRS Form 8889, *Health Savings Accounts*. You'll also have to keep a record of the name and address of each person or company you pay with funds from your HSA.

Deductions That Can Help You Retire

Why You Need a Retirement Plan (or Plans) 323

    Tax Deduction 324

    Tax Deferral 324

Individual Retirement Accounts (IRAs) 326

    Traditional IRAs 328

    Roth IRAs 330

Employer IRAs 332

    SEP-IRAs 332

    SIMPLE IRAs 333

Keogh Plans 334

    Types of Keogh Plans 334

    Setting Up a Keogh Plan 335

    Withdrawing Your Money 335

Solo 401(k) Plans 336

When you own your own business, it's up to you to establish and fund your own pension plan to supplement the Social Security benefits you'll receive when you retire. The tax law helps you do this by providing tax deductions and other income tax benefits for your retirement account contributions and earnings.

This chapter provides a general overview of the retirement plan choices you have as a small business owner. Deciding what type of account to establish is just as important as deciding how to invest your money once you open your account—if not more so. Once you set up your retirement account, you can always change your investments within the account with little or no difficulty. But changing the type of retirement account you have may prove difficult and costly. So it's best to spend some time up front learning about your choices and deciding which type of plan will best meet your needs.

RESOURCE

Need detailed information on retirement plans? For additional information on the tax aspects of retirement, check out these books and IRS guides:

- *Easy Ways to Lower Your Taxes*, by Sandra Block and Stephen Fishman (Nolo)
- *IRAs, 401(k)s & Other Retirement Plans*, by Twila Slesnick and John C. Suttle (Nolo)
- IRS Publication 560, *Retirement Plans for Small Business*, and
- IRS Publication 590, *Individual Retirement Arrangements*.

Two easy-to-understand guides on retirement investing are:

- *Get a Life: You Don't Need a Million to Retire Well*, by Ralph Warner (Nolo), and
- *Retire Happy: What You Can Do NOW to Guarantee a Great Retirement*, by Richard Stim and Ralph Warner (Nolo).

CAUTION

Get professional help if you have employees (other than your spouse). Having employees makes it much more complicated to set up a retirement plan (see "Having Employees Complicates Matters Tremendously," below). Because of the many complex issues that come up when you have employees, any business owner with employees should turn to a professional consultant for help in choosing, establishing, and administering a retirement plan.

Why You Need a Retirement Plan (or Plans)

In all likelihood, you will receive Social Security benefits when you retire. However, Social Security will probably cover only half of your needs when you retire—possibly less depending upon your retirement lifestyle. You'll need to make up this shortfall with your own retirement investments.

When it comes to saving for retirement, small business owners are better off than employees of most companies. This is because the federal government has created several types of retirement accounts specifically designed for small business owners. These accounts provide enormous tax benefits that are intended to maximize the amount of money you can save during your working years for your retirement years. The amount you are allowed to contribute each year to your retirement account depends upon the type of account you establish and how much money you earn. If your business doesn't earn money, you won't be able to make any contributions—you must have income to fund retirement accounts.

The two biggest benefits that most of these plans provide—tax deductions for plan contributions and tax deferral on investment earnings—are discussed in more detail below.

How Much Money Will You Need When You Retire?

The amount of money you'll need to live on when you retire depends on many factors, including your lifestyle. You could need anywhere from 50% to 100% of the amount you were earning while you were employed. On average, retirees need about 70% to 80% of their preretirement earnings.

Tax Deduction

Retirement accounts that comply with IRS requirements are called "tax qualified." You can deduct the amount you contribute to a tax-qualified retirement account from your income taxes (except for Roth IRAs and Roth 401(k)s—see "Traditional IRAs," below). If you are a sole proprietor, partner in a partnership, or an LLC member, you can deduct from your personal income all contributions you make to a retirement account. If you have incorporated your business, the corporation can deduct as a business expense contributions that it makes on your behalf. Either way, you or your business gets a substantial income tax savings.

> EXAMPLE: Art, a sole proprietor, contributes $10,000 this year to a qualified retirement account. He can deduct the entire amount from his personal income taxes. Because Art is in the 28% tax bracket, he saves $2,800 in income taxes for the year (28% × $10,000) and has also put away $10,000 toward his retirement.

Tax Deferral

In addition to the tax deduction you receive for putting money into a retirement account, there is another tremendous tax benefit to retirement accounts: tax deferral on earnings. When you earn money on an investment, you usually must pay taxes on those earnings in the year when you earn the money. For example, you must pay taxes on the interest you earn on a savings account or certificate of deposit in the year when the interest accrues. And when you sell an investment at a profit, you must pay income tax in that year on the gain you realize from the sale. For example, you must pay tax on the profit you earn from selling stock in the year when you sell the stock.

A different rule applies, however, for earnings you receive from a tax-qualified retirement account. You do not pay taxes on investment earnings from retirement accounts until you withdraw the funds. Most people withdraw these funds at retirement, so they are often in a lower income tax bracket when they pay tax on these earnings. This can result in substantial tax savings for people who would have had to pay higher taxes on these earnings if they had paid as the earnings accumulated.

EXAMPLE: Bill and Brian both invest in the same mutual fund. Bill has a taxable individual account, while Brian invests through a tax-deferred retirement account. They each invest $5,000 per year. They earn 8% on their investments each year and pay income tax at the 28% rate. At the end of 30 years, Brian has $566,416. Bill only has $272,869. Reason: Bill had to pay income taxes on the interest his investments earned each year, while Brian's interest accrued tax-free because he invested through a retirement account. Brian must pay tax on his earnings only when he withdraws the money (unless he withdraws before age 59½; see "Withdrawing Your Money," below).

The chart below compares the annual growth of a tax-deferred account and a taxable account.

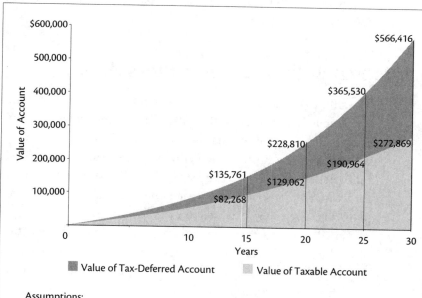

Assumptions:
- Investments earn 8% annually.
- $5,000 is invested annually in the tax-deferred account.
- $3,600 (what's left after $5,000 is taxed at 28%) is invested annually in the non-tax-deferred account.
- Income on the non-tax-deferred account is taxed annually at 28%, and recipient does not pay state income tax.

CAUTION

Retirement accounts have restrictions on withdrawals. The tax deferral benefits you receive by putting your money in a retirement account come at a price: You're not supposed to withdraw the money until you are 59½ years old; and, after you turn 70½, you must withdraw a certain minimum amount each year and pay tax on it. Stiff penalties are imposed if you fail to follow these rules. So, if you aren't prepared to give up your right to use this money freely, you should think about a taxable account instead, where there are no restrictions on your use of your money. You should also consider a Roth IRA or Roth 401(k)—you can withdraw your contributions to these accounts (but not earnings) at any time without penalty (see below).

RESOURCE

For detailed guidance on distributions from retirement accounts, refer to *IRAs, 401(k)s & Other Retirement Plans: Taking Your Money Out*, by Twila Slesnick and John C. Suttle (Nolo).

Individual Retirement Accounts (IRAs)

The simplest type of tax-deferred retirement account is the individual retirement arrangement (IRA). An IRA is a retirement account established by an individual, not a business. You can have an IRA whether you're a business owner or an employee in someone else's business. Moreover, you can establish an IRA for yourself as an individual and also set up one or more of the other types of retirement plans discussed below, which are just for businesses.

An IRA is a trust or custodial account set up for the benefit of an individual or his or her beneficiaries. The trustee or custodian administers the account. The trustee can be a bank, mutual fund, brokerage firm, or other financial institution (such as an insurance company).

IRAs are extremely easy to set up and administer. You need a written IRA agreement, but you don't have to file any tax forms with the IRS. The financial institution you use to set up your account will usually ask you to complete IRS Form 5305, *Traditional Individual Retirement Trust Account*, which serves as an IRA agreement and meets all of the IRS requirements. Keep the form in your records—you don't file it with the IRS.

Having Employees Complicates Matters Tremendously

If you own your own business and have no employees (other than your spouse), you can probably choose, establish, and administer your own retirement plan with little or no assistance. The instant you add employees to the mix, however, virtually every aspect of your plan becomes more complex. This is primarily due to legal requirements called nondiscrimination rules. These rules are designed to ensure that your retirement plan benefits all employees, not just you. In general, the laws prohibit you from doing the following:

- making disproportionately large contributions for some plan participants (like yourself) and not for others
- unfairly excluding certain employees from participating in the plan, and
- unfairly withholding benefits from former employees or their beneficiaries.

If the IRS finds a plan to be discriminatory at any time (usually during an audit), the plan could be disqualified—that is, determined not to satisfy IRS rules. If this happens, you and your employees will owe income tax and probably penalties, as well.

Having employees also increases the plan's reporting requirements. You must provide employees with a summary of the terms of the plan, notification of any changes you make, and an annual report of contributions. And you must file an annual tax return. Because of all the complex issues raised by having employees, any business owner with employees (other than a spouse) should seek professional help when creating a retirement plan.

Most financial institutions offer an array of IRA accounts that provide for different types of investments. You can invest your IRA money in just about anything—stocks, bonds, mutual funds, treasury bills and notes, and bank certificates of deposit. However, you can't invest in collectibles like art, antiques, stamps, or other personal property.

You can establish as many IRA accounts as you want, but there is a maximum combined amount of money you can contribute to all of your IRA accounts each year. The limit will be adjusted each year for inflation in $500 increments.

There are different limits for workers who are at least 50 years old. Anyone who is at least 50 years old at the end of the year can make increased annual contributions of $1,000 per year. This rule is intended to allow older people to catch up with younger folks who will have more years to make contributions at the higher levels.

Annual IRA Contribution Limits		
Tax Year	Under Age 50	Aged 50 or Over
2011	$5,000	$6,000

If you are married, you can double the contribution limits. For example, in 2010 each spouse can contribute up to $5,000 per year into their IRAs, for a total of $10,000. This is true even if one spouse isn't working. To take advantage of doubling, you must file a joint tax return, and the working spouse must earn at least as much as the combined IRA contribution.

Traditional IRAs

There are two different types of IRAs that you can choose from:
- traditional IRAs, and
- Roth IRAs.

Traditional IRAs have been around since 1974. Anybody who has earned income (income from a job, business, or alimony) can have a traditional IRA. As stated above, you can deduct your annual contributions to your IRA from your taxable income. If neither you nor your spouse (if you have one) has another retirement plan, you may deduct your contributions no matter how high your income is.

However, there are income limits on your deductions if you (or your spouse, if you have one) are covered by another retirement plan. For these purposes, being covered by another plan means you have one of the self-employed plans described below (or you or your spouse is covered by an employer plan).

These limits are based on your and your spouse's annual modified adjusted gross income (MAGI for short). Your MAGI is your adjusted gross income before it is reduced by your IRA contributions and certain other more unusual items.

Annual Income Limits for IRA Deductions				
Tax Year	Married Filing Jointly		Single Taxpayer	
	Full Deduction	Partial Deduction	Full Deduction	Partial Deduction
2011	$90,000	$90,000–$110,000	Under $56,000	$56,000–$66,000

If your income is in the phase-out range, you can use an online calculator at http://screen.morningstar.com/IRA/IRACalculator.html to determine how much you may deduct.

You can still contribute to an IRA even if you can't take a deduction. This is called a nondeductible IRA. Your money will grow in the account tax free, and, when you make withdrawals, you'll only have to pay tax on your account earnings, not the amount of your contributions (which have already been taxed). However, figuring out how much is taxable and how much is tax free can be a big accounting headache.

You may not make any more contributions to a traditional IRA after you reach age 70½. Moreover, you'll have to start taking distributions from the account after you reach that age.

There are time restrictions on when you can (and when you must) withdraw money from your IRA. You are not supposed to withdraw any money from your IRA until you reach age 59½, unless you die or become disabled. Under the normal tax rules, you are required to start withdrawing at least a minimum amount of your money by April 1 of the year after the year you turn 70. Once you start withdrawing money from your IRA, the amount you withdraw will be included in your regular income for income tax purposes.

As a general rule, if you make early withdrawals, you must pay regular income tax on the amount you take out, plus a 10% federal tax penalty. There are some exceptions to this early withdrawal penalty; for example, if you withdraw money to purchase a first home or pay educational expenses, the penalty doesn't apply to withdrawals up to a specified dollar limit. To learn about these and other exceptions in detail, see *IRAs, 401(k)s & Other Retirement Plans: Taking Your Money Out*, by Twila Slesnick and John Suttle (Nolo).

Roth IRAs

Like traditional IRAs, Roth IRAs are tax deferred and allow your retirement savings to grow without any tax burden. Unlike traditional IRAs, however, your contributions to Roth IRAs are *not* tax deductible. Instead, you get to withdraw your money from the account tax free when you retire.

Once you have established your account, your ability to contribute to it will be affected by changes in your income level. If you are single and your income reaches $107,000, your ability to contribute to your Roth IRA will begin to phase out. Once your income reaches $122,000, you will no longer be able to make contributions. If you are married and filing a joint return with your spouse, your ability to contribute to your account will start to phase out when your income reaches $169,000, and you will be prohibited from making any contributions at all when your income reaches $179,000. These are the 2011 limits. The limits are adjusted for inflation each year.

You can withdraw the money you contributed to a Roth IRA penalty-free anytime—you already paid tax on it so the government doesn't care. But the earnings on your investments in a Roth IRA are a different matter. You can't withdraw these until after five years. Early withdrawals of your earnings are subject to income tax and early distribution penalties. You are not, however, required to make withdrawals when you reach age 70½. Because Roth IRA withdrawals are tax free, the government doesn't care if you leave your money in your account indefinitely. However, your money will be tax free on withdrawal only if you leave it in your Roth IRA for at least five years.

Is the Roth IRA a good deal? If your tax rate when you retire is higher than your tax rate before retirement, you'll probably be better off with a Roth IRA than a traditional IRA because you won't have to pay tax on your withdrawals at the higher rates. The opposite is true if your taxes go down when you retire. The catch is that nobody can know for sure what their tax rate will be when they retire. You can find several online calculators that will help you compare your results with a Roth IRA versus traditional IRA at www.choosetosave.org/calculators. More information on Roth IRAs can be found at www.rothira.com.

Roth IRA Conversions

If the Roth IRA sounds attractive to you, and you already have a traditional IRA, you may convert it to a Roth IRA. This can vastly increase the amount of money in your Roth IRA.

However, when you convert to a Roth, you'll have to pay income tax on the amount of the conversion. For example, if you convert $20,000 from your traditional IRA to a Roth IRA, you'll have to add $20,000 to your taxable income for the year. If you were in the 25% bracket, this would add $5,000 to your income taxes. One way to keep these taxes down is to convert only a portion of your traditional IRAs into a Roth each year for several years instead of doing it all at once.

Whether a Roth conversion is a good idea or not depends on many factors including your age, your current tax rate, and your tax rate upon retirement. You can find an online calculator at http://dinkytown.com/java/RothTransfer.html that allows you to compare the results when you convert to a Roth versus leaving your traditional IRAs alone.

Employer IRAs

You can establish an employer IRA as long as you are in business and earn a profit. You don't have to have any employees, and it doesn't matter how your business is organized: You can be a sole proprietor, partner in a partnership, member of a limited liability company, or an owner of a regular or S corporation.

The great advantage of employer IRAs is that you can contribute more than you can to traditional IRAs and Roth IRAs. And as long as you meet the requirements for establishing an employer IRA, you can have one in addition to one or more individual IRAs.

There are two kinds of employer IRAs to choose from: SEP-IRAs and SIMPLE IRAs.

SEP-IRAs

SEP-IRAs are designed for the self-employed. Any person who receives self-employment income from providing a service can establish a SEP-IRA. It doesn't matter whether you work full time or part time. You can have a SEP-IRA even if you are also covered by a retirement plan at a full-time employee job.

A SEP-IRA is a simplified employee pension. It's very similar to an IRA except that you can contribute more money under this type of plan. Instead of a $5,000 to $6,000 annual contribution limit (2011), you can invest up to 20% of your net profit from self-employment every year, up to a maximum of $49,000 a year in 2011. You don't have to make contributions every year, and your contributions can vary from year to year. As with IRAs, you can invest your money in almost anything (stocks, bonds, notes, mutual funds, and so on).

You can deduct your contributions to SEP-IRAs from your income taxes, and the interest on your SEP-IRA investments accrues tax free until you withdraw the money. Withdrawals from SEP-IRAs are subject to the same rules that apply to traditional IRAs. If you withdraw money from your SEP-IRA before you reach age 59½, you'll have to pay a 10% tax penalty plus regular income taxes on your withdrawal, unless an exception applies. And you must begin to withdraw your money by April 1 of the year after the year you turn 70.

SIMPLE IRAs

Self-employed people and companies with fewer than 100 employees can set up SIMPLE IRAs. If you establish a SIMPLE IRA, you are not allowed to have any other retirement plans for your business (although you may still have your own individual IRA). SIMPLE IRAs are easy to set up and administer, and you will be able to make larger annual contributions than you could to a SEP or Keogh plan if you earn less than $10,000 per year from your business.

SIMPLE IRAs may be established only by an employer on behalf of its employees. If you are a sole proprietor, you are deemed to employ yourself for purposes of this rule, and you may establish a SIMPLE IRA in your own name as the employer. If you are a partner in a partnership, an LLC member, or the owner of an incorporated business, the SIMPLE IRA must be established by your business, not by you personally.

Contributions to SIMPLE IRAs are divided into two parts. You may contribute:

- up to 100% of your net income from your business up to an annual limit—the contribution limit is $11,500 for 2011 ($14,000 if you were born before 1955), and
- a matching contribution of up to 3% of your net business income.

If you're an employee of your incorporated business, your first contribution (called a salary reduction contribution) comes out of your salary, and the matching contribution is paid by your business.

The limits on contributions to SIMPLE IRAs might seem very low, but they could work to your advantage if you earn a small income from your business—for example, if you only work at it part time. This is because you can contribute an amount equal to 100% of your earnings, up to the $11,500 or $14,000 limits. Thus, for example, if your net earnings are only $10,000, you could contribute the entire amount (plus a 3% employer contribution). You can't do this with any of the other plans because their percentage limits are much lower. For example, you may contribute only 20% of your net self-employment income to a SEP-IRA or Keogh, so you would be limited to a $2,000 contribution if you had a $10,000 profit.

The money in a SIMPLE IRA can be invested like any other IRA. Withdrawals from SIMPLE IRAs are subject to the same rules as traditional IRAs with one big exception: Early withdrawals from SIMPLE IRAs are subject to a 25% tax penalty if you make the withdrawal within two years after the date you first contributed to your account. Other early withdrawals are subject to a 10% penalty, as with traditional IRAs, unless an exception applies.

Keogh Plans

Keogh plans—named after the Congressman who sponsored the legislation that created them—are only for business owners who are sole proprietors, partners in partnerships, or LLC members. You can't have a Keogh if you incorporate your business.

Keoghs require more paperwork to set up than employer IRAs, but they also offer more options: You can contribute more to these plans and still get an income tax deduction for your contributions.

Types of Keogh Plans

There are two basic types of Keogh plans:

- defined contribution plans, in which the amount you receive on retirement is based on how much you contribute to—and how much accumulates in—the plan, and
- defined benefit plans, which provide for payment of a set amount of money upon retirement.

There are two types of defined contribution plans: profit-sharing plans and money purchase plans. These plans can be used separately or in tandem with one other.

Profit-Sharing Plans

You can contribute up to 20% of your net self-employment income to a profit-sharing Keogh plan, up to a maximum of $49,000 per year in 2011. You can contribute any amount up to the limit each year or contribute nothing at all.

Money Purchase Plans

In a money purchase plan, you contribute a fixed percentage of your net self-employment earnings every year. You decide on the percentage when you establish your plan. Make sure you will be able to afford the contributions each year because you can't skip them, even if your business earns no profit for the year. In return for giving up flexibility, you can contribute a higher percentage of your earnings with a money purchase plan—the lesser of 25% of compensation or $49,000 in 2011 (the same maximum amount applies to profit-sharing plans).

Setting Up a Keogh Plan

As with individual IRAs and employer IRAs, you can set up a Keogh plan at most banks, brokerage houses, mutual funds, other financial institutions, and trade or professional organizations. You can also choose among a huge array of investments for your money.

To set up your plan, you must adopt a written Keogh plan and establish a trust or custodial account with your plan provider to invest your funds. Your provider should have an IRS-approved master or prototype Keogh plan for you to sign. You can also have a special plan drawn up for you, but this is expensive and unnecessary for most small business owners.

Withdrawing Your Money

You may begin to withdraw money from your Keogh plan after you reach the age of 59½. If you have a profit-sharing plan, early withdrawals are permitted without penalty if you suffer financial hardship, become disabled, or have to pay health expenses in excess of 7.5% of your adjusted gross income. If you have a money purchase plan, early withdrawals are permitted if you become disabled, leave your business after you turn 55, or make child support or alimony payments from the plan under a court order. Otherwise, early withdrawals from profit-sharing and money purchase Keogh plans are subject to a 10% penalty.

Solo 401(k) Plans

Most people have heard of 401(k) plans—they are retirement plans established by businesses for their employees. 401(k)s are a type of profit-sharing plan in which a business's employees make plan contributions from their salaries and the business makes a matching contribution. These plans are complex to establish and administer and are generally used only by larger businesses. Until recently, self-employed people and businesses without employees rarely used 401(k) plans, because they offered no benefit over other profit-sharing plans that are much easier to set up and run.

However, things have changed. Now, any business owner who has no employees (other than a spouse) can establish a solo self-employed 401(k) plan (also called a one-person or individual 401(k)). Solo 401(k) plans are designed specifically for business owners without employees.

Solo 401(k) plans have the following advantages over other retirement plans:

- You can make very large contributions—as much as 20% of your net profit from self-employment, plus an elective deferral contribution of up to $16,500 in 2011. The maximum contribution per year is $49,000 in 2011 (the same maximum amount that applies to the Keogh plans discussed above). Business owners who are at least 50 years old may make additional contributions of up to $5,000 per year; these catch-up contributions don't count toward the $49,000 annual limit.
- You can borrow up to $50,000 from your solo 401(k) plan penalty-free, as long as you repay the loan within five years (you cannot borrow from a traditional IRA, Roth IRA, SEP-IRA, or SIMPLE IRA).

As with other plans, you must pay a 10% penalty tax on withdrawals you make before the age of 59½, but you may make penalty-free early withdrawals for reasons of personal hardship (defined as an "immediate financial need" that you can't meet any other way).

You can set up a solo 401(k) plan at most banks, brokerage houses, mutual funds, and other financial institutions, and you can invest the money in a variety of ways. You must adopt a written plan and set up a trust or custodial account with your plan provider to invest your funds. Financial institutions that offer solo 401(k) plans have preapproved plans that you can use.

> CAUTION
> **Beware of retirement account deadlines.** If you want to establish any of the retirement accounts discussed in this chapter and take a tax deduction for the year, you must meet specific deadlines. The deadlines vary according to the type of account you set up, as shown in the following chart. Once you establish your account, you have until the due date of your tax return for the year (April 15 of the following year, or later if you receive a filing extension) to contribute to your account and take a deduction.

Retirement Account Deadlines	
Plan Type	Deadline for Establishing Plan
Traditional IRA	Due date of tax return (April 15 plus extensions)
Roth IRA	Due date of tax return (April 15 plus extensions)
SEP-IRA	Due date of tax return (April 15 plus extensions)
SIMPLE IRA	October 1
Keogh Profit-Sharing Plan	December 31
Keogh Money Purchase Plan	December 31
Keogh Defined Benefit Plan	December 31
401(k) Plan	December 31

More Home Business Deductions

Advertising 341

    Goodwill Advertising 341

    Giveaway Items 342

    Website Development and Maintenance 343

Business Bad Debts 343

    Requirements to Deduct Bad Debts 344

    Types of Bad Debts 346

Casualty Losses 349

    Amount of Deduction 350

    Damage to Your Home Office 352

    Tax Reporting 353

Charitable Contributions 353

Dues and Subscriptions 354

Education Expenses 355

    Starting a New Business 356

    Minimum Educational Requirements 357

    Traveling for Education 357

Gifts 358

Insurance for Your Business 359

    Homeowner's Insurance for Your Home Office 360

    Car Insurance 360

Interest on Business Loans 361

    Home Offices 362

    Car Loans 362

    Loans From Relatives and Friends 362

Loans to Buy a Business 362

Interest You Can't Deduct 363

Deducting Investment Interest 363

Keeping Track of Borrowed Money 364

Legal and Professional Services 366

Buying Long-Term Property 366

Starting a Business 367

Accounting Fees 367

Taxes and Licenses 367

Income Taxes 368

Self-Employment Taxes 368

Employment Taxes 369

Sales Taxes 369

Real Property Taxes 370

Other Taxes 371

License Fees 372

This chapter looks at some of the most common deductible operating expenses that you are likely to incur in the normal course of running your home business, such as advertising expenses, insurance, and legal fees. You can deduct these costs as business operating expenses as long as they are ordinary, necessary, and reasonable in amount, and meet the additional requirements discussed below.

Advertising

Almost any type of business-related advertising is a currently deductible business operating expense. You can deduct advertising to sell a particular product or service, to help establish goodwill for your business, or just to get your business known. Advertising costs include what you pay for:

- business cards
- brochures
- advertisements in the local yellow pages
- newspaper and magazine advertisements
- trade publication advertisements
- catalogs
- advertisements on the Internet
- fees you pay to advertising and public relations agencies
- package design costs, and
- signs and display racks.

However, advertising to influence government legislation is never deductible. And help-wanted ads you place to recruit workers are not advertising costs, but you can still deduct them as ordinary and necessary business operating expenses.

Goodwill Advertising

You can usually deduct the cost of goodwill advertising—ads intended to keep your name before the public—if it relates to business you reasonably expect to gain in the future. Examples of goodwill advertising include:

- advertisements that encourage people to contribute to charities, such as the Red Cross or similar causes
- sponsoring a little league baseball team, bowling team, or golf tournament
- giving away product samples, and
- holding contests and giving away prizes.

However, you can't deduct time and labor that you give away as an advertising expense, even though donating them often promotes goodwill. You must actually spend money to have an advertising expense. For example, a lawyer who does pro bono work for indigent clients to gain exposure for his law practice may not deduct the cost of his services as an advertising expense.

Giveaway Items

The cost of giveaway items that you use to publicize your business (such as pens, coffee cups, T-shirts, refrigerator magnets, calendars, tote bags, and key chains) are deductible. However, you are not allowed to deduct more than $25 in business gifts to any one person each year (see "Gifts," later in this chapter). This limitation applies to advertising giveaway items unless they:

- cost $4 or less
- have your name clearly and permanently imprinted on them, and
- are one of a number of identical items you distribute widely.

EXAMPLE 1: Jay has a home business selling rare wines. He orders 1,000 ballpoint pens with his name and contact information printed on them and distributes them at wine tastings and gourmet food and wine fairs. Each pen costs Jay $1. The pens do not count toward the $25 gift limit. Jay may deduct the entire $1,000 expense for the pens.

EXAMPLE 2: Jay buys a $200 fountain pen and gives it to his best customer. The pen is a business gift to an individual, so Jay can deduct only $25 of the cost.

Signs, display racks, and other promotional materials that you give to other businesses to use on their premises do not count as gifts.

Website Development and Maintenance

The cost of developing and maintaining a website for a business varies widely. It can be relatively inexpensive if you use a standard template you purchase from a template company. However, the cost will be much greater if you want to create a custom design for your website.

Many businesses currently deduct all website development and ongoing maintenance expenses as an advertising expense. However, some tax experts believe that the cost of initially setting up a website is a capital expense, not a currently deductible business operating expense, because the website is a long-term asset that benefits the business for more than one year. Under normal tax rules, capital expenses must be deducted over several years. Three years is the most common deduction period used for websites, because this is the period used for software.

However, even if website development costs are capital expenses, they may be currently deducted in a single year under Section 179 (see Chapter 5).

Most tax experts agree that ongoing website hosting, maintenance, and updating costs are a currently deductible operating expense. Money you spend to get people to view your website, such as SEO (search engine optimization) campaigns, is also a currently deductible advertising expense.

Business Bad Debts

Business bad debts are debts that won't be fully repaid and arise from your business activities. Examples include:
- money you lend for a business purpose
- sales you make on credit, or
- guaranteed business-related loans.

You can currently deduct business bad debts as business operating expenses when they become wholly or partly worthless. However, to claim the deduction, you must incur an actual loss of money or have previously included the amount of the debt as income on your tax return. Because of this limitation, many small businesses are unable to deduct bad debts.

Requirements to Deduct Bad Debts

You must meet three requirements to deduct a business bad debt as a business operating expense:

- you must have a bona fide business debt
- the debt must be wholly or partly worthless, and
- you must have suffered an economic loss from the debt.

A Bona Fide Business Debt

A bona fide debt exists when someone has a legal obligation to pay you a sum of money—for example, you sell goods or merchandise to a customer on credit. You will generally need some written evidence of the debt—for example, a signed promissory note or other writing stating the amount of the debt, when it is due, and the interest rate (if any)—in order to claim this deduction. An oral promise to pay may also be legally enforceable, but would be looked upon with suspicion by the IRS.

A business debt is a debt that is created or acquired in the course of your business or becomes worthless as part of your business. Your primary motive for incurring the debt must be related to your business. Debts you take on for personal or investment purposes are not business debts. (Remember, investing is not a business; see Chapter 2.)

EXAMPLE 1: Mark, an advertising agent, lends $10,000 to his brother-in-law, Scott, to help him develop his bird diaper invention. Mark will get 25% of the profits if the invention proves successful. This is an investment, not a business debt.

EXAMPLE 2: Mark lends $10,000 to one of his best business clients to keep the client's business running. Because the main reason for the loan is business related (to keep his client in business so he will continue as a client), the debt is a business debt.

A Worthless Debt

You may deduct a debt only if it is wholly or partly worthless. A debt becomes worthless when there is no longer any chance that it will be repaid. You don't have to wait until a debt is due to determine that it is worthless, nor do you have to go to court to try to collect it. You just have to be able to show that you have taken reasonable steps to try to collect the debt or that collection efforts would be futile. For example:

- you've made repeated collection efforts that have proven unsuccessful
- the debtor has filed for bankruptcy or has already been through bankruptcy and had all or part of the debt discharged (forgiven) by the bankruptcy court, or
- the debtor has gone out of business, gone broke, died, or disappeared.

Keep all documentation that shows a debt is worthless, such as copies of unpaid invoices, collection letters you've sent the debtor, logs of collection calls you've made, bankruptcy notices, and credit reports.

You must deduct the entire amount of a bad debt in the year it becomes totally worthless. If only part of a business debt becomes worthless—for example, you received a partial payment before the debt became uncollectible—you can deduct the unpaid portion that year or you can wait until the following year to deduct it. For example, if you think you might get paid more the next year, you can wait and see what your final bad debt amount is before you deduct it.

An Economic Loss

You are not automatically entitled to deduct a debt simply because the obligation has become worthless. To get a deduction, you must have suffered an economic loss. According to the IRS, you have suffered a loss only if you:

- already reported as business income the amount you were supposed to be paid
- paid out cash, or
- made credit sales of inventory for which you were not paid.

These rules make it impossible to deduct some types of business debts.

Types of Bad Debts

There are many different types of business debts that small businesses can incur. The sections that follow discuss some of the more common ones.

Sales of Services

Unfortunately, if you're a cash basis taxpayer who sells services to your clients (like many home businesses), you can't claim a bad debt deduction if a client fails to pay you. Cash basis taxpayers report income only when they actually receive it, not when they perform the services the client ordered. As a result, cash basis taxpayers don't have an economic loss (in the eyes of the IRS) when a client fails to pay.

> **EXAMPLE:** Bill, a home-based dog walker, works 20 hours walking a client's dogs and bills the client $250. The client never pays. Bill is a cash basis taxpayer, so he doesn't report the $250 as income because he never received it. As far as the IRS is concerned, Bill has no economic loss and cannot deduct the $250 the client failed to pay.

The IRS strictly enforces this rule (harsh as it may seem). Absent the rule, the IRS fears that businesses will inflate the value of their services in order to get a larger deduction.

Accrual basis taxpayers, on the other hand, report sales as income in the year the sales are made—not the year payment is received. These taxpayers can take a bad debt deduction if a client fails to pay for services rendered, because they have already reported the money due as income. Therefore, accrual taxpayers have an economic loss when they are not paid for their services.

> **EXAMPLE:** Andrea, a home-based financial consultant, bills a client $10,000 for consulting services she performed during the year. Andrea is an accrual basis taxpayer, so she characterizes the $10,000 as income on her books and includes this amount in her

gross income for the year in which she billed the services, even though she hasn't actually received payment. The client later files for bankruptcy, and the debt becomes worthless. Andrea may take a business bad debt deduction to wipe out the $10,000 in income she previously charged on her books.

There's no point in switching from cash basis to the accrual method to deduct bad debts. The accrual method doesn't result in lower taxes—the bad debt deduction merely wipes out a sale that was already reported as income and taxed.

RELATED TOPIC

Cash or accrual? Read all about it in Chapter 15, which includes a detailed discussion of the cash basis and accrual accounting methods.

Credit Sales of Inventory

Most deductible business bad debts result from credit sales of inventory to customers. If you sell goods on credit to a customer and are not paid, you can take a deduction whether you are an accrual or cash basis taxpayer. You deduct the cost of the inventory at the end of the year to determine the cost of goods sold for the year. (See Chapter 10 for more on inventory deductions.)

Cash Loans

Whether you are a cash basis or an accrual taxpayer, cash loans you make for a business purpose are deductible as bad debts in the year they become worthless.

EXAMPLE: John, an advertising agent, loaned $10,000 to one of his best clients to keep the client's business running. The client later went bankrupt and could not repay the loan. John may deduct the $10,000 as a business bad debt.

Business Loan Guarantees

If you guarantee a debt that becomes worthless, it qualifies as a business bad debt only if you:

- made the guarantee in the course of your business
- have a legal duty to pay the debt
- made the guarantee before the debt became worthless, and
- received reasonable consideration (compensation) for the guarantee—you meet this requirement if you make the guarantee for a good faith business purpose or according to normal business practices.

> **EXAMPLE:** Jane has a home business selling gourmet coffee and teas. She guaranteed payment of a $20,000 note for Pete's Coffee Bar, one of Jane's largest clients. Pete's later filed for bankruptcy and defaulted on the loan. Jane had to make full payment to the bank. She can take a business bad debt deduction because her guarantee was made for a good faith business purpose—her desire to retain one of her better clients and keep a sales outlet.

Loans or Guarantees to Your Corporation

If your business is incorporated, you cannot take a bad debt deduction for a loan to your corporation if the loan is actually a contribution to capital—that is, the money is part of your investment in the business. You must be careful to treat a loan to your corporation just as you would treat a loan made to a business in which you have no ownership interest. You should have a signed promissory note from your corporation setting forth:

- the loan amount
- the interest rate—which should be reasonable
- the due date, and
- a repayment schedule.

If you are a principal shareholder in a small corporation, you'll often be asked to personally guarantee corporate loans and other extensions of credit. Creditors demand these guarantees because they want to be able to go after your personal assets if they can't collect from your corporation. If you end up having to make good on your guarantee and can't get repaid from your corporation, you will have a bad debt. You can deduct this bad debt as a business debt if your dominant motive for making the loan or guarantee was to protect your employment status and ensure your continuing receipt of a salary. If your primary motive was to protect your investment in the corporation, the debt is a personal debt. The IRS is more likely to think you are protecting your investment if you receive little or no salary from the corporation or your salary is not a major source of your overall income.

Personal Debts

The fact that a debt doesn't arise from your business doesn't mean it's not deductible. Bona fide personal debts that become worthless are deductible as *short-term capital losses*. This means you can deduct them only as an offset to any capital gains you received from the sale of capital assets during the year. (Capital assets include items such as real estate, stocks, and bonds.) Your total deduction for personal debts is limited to $3,000 per year. Any loss in excess of this limit may be carried over to future years to offset future capital gains. Unlike business bad debts, personal debts are deductible only if they become wholly worthless.

Casualty Losses

Casualty losses are damage to property caused by fire, theft, vandalism, earthquake, storm, flood, terrorism, or some other "sudden, unexpected, or unusual event." There must be some external force involved in a casualty loss. Thus, you get no deduction if you simply lose property or it breaks or wears out over time.

You may take a deduction for casualty losses to business property only if—and only to the extent that—the loss is not covered by insurance. If the loss is fully covered, you can't take a deduction.

Amount of Deduction

How much you may deduct depends on whether the property involved was stolen, completely destroyed, or partially destroyed. However, you must always reduce your casualty losses by the amount of any insurance proceeds you receive (or reasonably expect to receive). If more than one item was stolen or destroyed, you must figure your deduction separately for each.

Total Loss

If the property is stolen or completely destroyed, your deduction is calculated as follows:

> Adjusted Basis
> − Salvage Value
> − Insurance Proceeds
> = Casualty Loss

(Your adjusted basis is the property's original cost, plus the value of any improvements, minus any deductions you took for depreciation or Section 179 expensing—see Chapter 5.) Obviously, if an item is stolen, there will be no salvage value.

> EXAMPLE: Sean's home computer is stolen by a burglar. The computer cost $2,000. Sean has taken no tax deductions for it because he purchased it only two months ago, so his adjusted basis is $2,000. Sean is a renter and has no insurance covering the loss. Sean's casualty loss is $2,000 ($2,000 Adjusted Basis − $0 Salvage Value − $0 Insurance Proceeds = $2,000).

Partial Loss

If the property is only partly destroyed, your casualty loss deduction is the lesser of the decrease in the property's fair market value or its adjusted basis, reduced by any insurance you receive or expect to receive.

EXAMPLE: Assume that Sean's computer from the example above is partly destroyed due to a small fire in his home. Its fair market value in its damaged state is $500. Because he spent $2,000 for the computer, the decrease in its fair market value is $1,500. The computer's adjusted basis is $2,000. He received no insurance proceeds. Thus, his casualty loss is $1,500.

Special Rules for Losses Related to Federally Declared Disasters

The cost of repairing damaged property is not part of a casualty loss. Neither is the cost of cleaning up after a casualty. Instead, these expenses are deductible in addition to any deductible casualty loss you have. Normally, you have to depreciate over several years the cost to clean-up hazardous waste on business property, or any repairs to property or equipment you make that make the property better than it was before it was repaired. However, special rules apply to damage or destruction to business property caused by a federally declared disaster during 2008 through 2011. Under those circumstances, you can currently deduct costs related to the repair of business property damaged by the disaster; the abatement or control of hazardous substances released due to the disaster; or the removal of debris from, or the demolition of structures on, real property damaged or destroyed by the disaster (I.R.C. § 198A). You can currently deduct these expenses, even though normally you would have to depreciate these costs under the regular tax rules.

Inventory

You don't have to treat damage to or loss of inventory as a casualty loss. Instead, you may deduct it on your Schedule C as part of the cost of your goods sold. (See Chapter 10 for more information on deducting inventory costs.) This is advantageous because it reduces your income for self-employment tax purposes, which casualty losses do not. However, if you do this, you must include any insurance proceeds you receive for the inventory loss in your gross income for the year.

Personal Property

You can deduct uninsured casualty losses to personal property—that is, property you don't use for your business—from your income tax. In 2010 and later, these losses are an itemized deduction and are deductible only to the extent they exceed 10% of your adjusted gross income for the year. For example, if you have $10,000 in total casualty losses and 10% of your AGI is $7,000, your loss is limited to $3,000. In addition, your loss for each item of individual or personal property is deductible only to the extent it exceeds $100—in other words, you must reduce your loss for each item by $100.

Damage to Your Home Office

You may deduct losses due to damage to or destruction of your home office as part of your home office deduction. However, your loss is reduced by any insurance proceeds you receive or expect to receive.

You can deduct casualty losses that affect your entire house as an indirect home office expense. The amount of your deduction is based on your home office use percentage.

> **EXAMPLE:** Dana's home, valued at $500,000, is completely destroyed by a fire. Her fire insurance covered only 80% of her loss, or $400,000, leaving her with a $100,000 loss. Her home office took up 20% of her home. She can deduct 20% of her $100,000 loss, or $20,000, as an indirect home office deduction.

You can fully deduct casualty losses that affect only your home office—for example, if only your home office is burned in a fire—as direct home office expenses. However, you can't take a business expense deduction for casualty losses that don't affect your home office at all—for example, if your kitchen is destroyed by fire. See Chapter 6 for a detailed discussion of the home office deduction.

If the loss involves business property that is in your home office, but is not part of your home—for example, a burglar steals your home office computer—you can deduct the entire value of that loss directly, rather than as part of the home office deduction.

Tax Reporting

You report casualty losses to business property on part B of IRS Form 4684, *Casualties and Thefts*, and then transfer the deductible casualty loss to Form 4797, *Sales of Business Property*, and the first page of your Form 1040. The amount of your deductible casualty loss is subtracted from your adjusted gross income for the year. However, casualty losses are not deducted from your self-employment income for purposes of calculating your Social Security and Medicare tax. These reporting requirements differ from those for other deductions covered in this chapter, which are reported on IRS Schedule C, Form 1040.

Partnerships, S corporations, and LLCs must also fill out Form 4797. The amount of the loss is subtracted when calculating the entity's total business income for the year. This amount is reported on the entity's information tax return (Form 1065 for partnerships and LLCs; Form 1120S for S corporations). C corporations deduct their casualty losses on their own tax returns (Form 1120).

If you take a casualty loss as part of your home office deduction, you must include the loss on Form 8829, *Expenses for Business Use of Your Home* (see Chapter 6).

Charitable Contributions

If, like the vast majority of home business owners, you are a sole proprietor, partner in a partnership, LLC member, or an S corporation shareholder, the IRS treats any charitable contributions your business makes as a personal contribution by you (and your co-owners, if any). As such, the contributions are not business expenses—you can deduct them only as a personal charitable contribution. You may deduct these contributions only if you itemize deductions on your personal tax return; they are subject to certain income limitations. The deduction is limited to the fair market value of the inventory on the date it is donated, reduced by any gain you would have realized had you sold the property at its fair market value instead of donating it.

> EXAMPLE: Barbee, who runs a crafts business out of her home, donates unsold inventory to a nursing home. The fair market value of the inventory is $1,000. Barbee spent $500 to acquire the inventory, so she would have had a $500 gain had she sold it at its fair market value. Her charitable deduction must be reduced by the amount of this gain, so she gets only a $500 deduction.

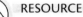 **RESOURCE**

For detailed guidance on tax deductions for charitable contributions, refer to *Every Nonprofit's Tax Guide* by Stephen Fishman (Nolo).

Dues and Subscriptions

Dues you pay to professional, business, and civic organizations are deductible business expenses, as long as the organization's main purpose is not to provide entertainment facilities to members. You can deduct dues paid to:

- bar associations, medical associations, and other professional organizations
- trade associations, local chambers of commerce, real estate boards, and business leagues, and
- civic or public service organizations, such as a Rotary or Lions club.

You get no deduction for dues you pay to belong to other types of social, business, or recreational clubs—for example, country clubs or athletic clubs (see Chapter 7). For this reason, it's best not to use the word "dues" on your tax return because the IRS may question the expense. Use other words to describe the deduction—for example, if you're deducting membership dues for a trade organization, list the expense as "trade association membership fees."

You may also deduct subscriptions to professional, technical, and trade journals that deal with your business field, as a business expense.

Education Expenses

What about deducting the cost of business-related education— for example, a college course or seminar? These expenses may be deductible, but only in strictly limited circumstances. To qualify for an education deduction, you must be able to show that the education:

- maintains or improves skills required in your existing business, or
- is required by law or regulation to maintain your professional status.

Because of these restrictions, it is usually not possible to deduct undergraduate and graduate tuition. Instead, this deduction is usually used by professionals like doctors and accountants who can deduct the cost of continuing professional education.

> **EXAMPLE:** Sue is a self-employed attorney who works from home. Every year, she is required by law to attend 12 hours of continuing legal education to maintain her status as an active member of the state bar. The legal seminars she attends to satisfy this requirement are deductible education expenses.

If you qualify, deductible education expenses include tuition, fees, books, and other learning materials. They also include transportation and travel (see below). You may also deduct expenses you pay to educate or train your employees.

Starting a New Business

You cannot currently deduct education expenses you incur to qualify for a *new* business or profession. For example, courts have held that IRS agents could not deduct the cost of going to law school, because a law degree would qualify them for a new business—being a lawyer (*Jeffrey L. Weiler*, 54 TC 398 (1970)). On the other hand, a practicing dentist was allowed to deduct the cost of being educated in orthodontia, because becoming an orthodontist did not constitute the practice of a new business or profession for a dentist. (Rev. Rul. 74-78.)

Can You Deduct Your MBA?

Ordinarily, you can't deduct the cost of obtaining a degree that leads to a professional license or certification—for example, a law degree, medical degree, or dental degree. However, it may be possible to deduct the cost of obtaining an MBA (a master's degree in business administration) because an MBA is a more general course of study that does not lead to a professional license or certification. The decisive factor is whether you were already established in your trade or business before you obtained the MBA. If so, it is deductible.

In one highly publicized case, for example, a registered nurse was allowed to deduct her $15,000 tuition cost of obtaining an MBA with a health care management specialization. The nurse worked for many years as a quality control coordinator at various hospitals. The court held that while the MBA may have improved her skill set, she was already performing the tasks and activities of her trade or business before commencing the MBA program, and continued to do so after receiving the degree. (*Lori A. Singleton-Clarke v. Comm'r*, T.C. Summ. Op. 2009-182 (2009).)

Minimum Educational Requirements

You cannot deduct the cost required to meet the minimum or basic level educational requirements for a business or profession. Thus, for example, you can't deduct the expense of going to law school or medical school.

Traveling for Education

Local transportation expenses you pay to travel to and from a deductible educational activity are deductible. This includes transportation between either your home or business and the educational activity. Going to or from home to an educational activity does not constitute nondeductible commuting. If you drive, you may deduct your actual expenses or use the standard mileage rate. (See Chapter 8 for more on deducting the cost of local travel.)

There's no law that says you must take your education courses as close to home as possible. You may travel outside your geographic area for education, even if the same or a similar educational activity is available near your home or place of business. Companies and groups that sponsor educational events are well aware of this rule and take advantage of it by offering courses and seminars at resorts and other enjoyable vacation spots such as Hawaii and California. Deductible travel expenses may include airfare or other transportation, lodging, and meals. (See Chapter 9 for more on business travel deductions.)

You cannot claim travel itself as an education deduction. You must travel *to* some sort of educational activity. For example, an architect could not deduct the cost of a trip to Paris because he studied the local architecture while he was there—but he could deduct a trip to Paris to attend a seminar on French architecture.

Lifetime Learning Credit

Instead of taking a tax deduction for your business-related education expenses, you may qualify for the lifetime learning credit. A tax credit is a dollar-for-dollar reduction in your tax liability, so it's even better than a tax deduction.

The lifetime learning credit can by used to help pay for any under-graduate or graduate level education, including nondegree education to acquire or improve job skills (for example a continuing education course). If you qualify, your credit equals 20% of the first $10,000 of postsecondary tuition and fees you pay during the year, for a maximum credit of $2,000 per tax return. However, the credit is phased out and then eliminated at the certain income levels: It begins to go down if your modified adjusted gross income is over $51,000 ($102,000 for a joint return), and you cannot claim the credit at all if your MAGI is over $61,000 ($122,000 for a joint return). These are the limits for 2011. The limits are adjusted for inflation each year.

You can take this credit not only for yourself, but for a dependent child (or children) for whom you claim a tax exemption, or your spouse as well (if you file jointly). And it can be taken any number of times. However, you can't take the credit if you've already deducted the education cost as a business expense.

> EXAMPLE: Bill, a self-employed real estate broker with a $40,000 AGI, spends $2,000 on continuing real estate education courses during 2011. He may take a $400 lifetime learning credit (20% × $2,000 = $400).

Gifts

If you give someone a gift for business purposes, your business expense deduction is limited to $25 per person per year. Any amount over the $25 limit is not deductible. If this amount seems low, that's because it was established in 1954!

EXAMPLE: Lisa, a self-employed marketing consultant, gives a $200 Christmas gift to her best client. She may deduct $25 of the cost.

A gift to a member of a customer's family is treated as a gift to the customer, unless you have a legitimate nonbusiness connection to the family member. If you and your spouse both give gifts, you are treated as one taxpayer—it doesn't matter if you work together or have separate businesses.

The $25 limit applies only to gifts to individuals. It doesn't apply if you give a gift to an entire company. Such companywide gifts are deductible in any amount, as long as they are reasonable. However, the $25 limit does apply if the gift is intended for a particular person or group of people within the company.

EXAMPLE: Bob sells products to the Acme Company. Just before Christmas, he drops off a $100 cheese basket at the company's reception area for use by all Acme employees. He also delivers an identical basket to Acme's president. The first basket left in the reception area is a companywide gift, not subject to the $25 limit. The basket for Acme's president is a personal gift and therefore is subject to the limit.

Insurance for Your Business

You can deduct the premiums you pay for any insurance you buy for your business as a business operating expense. This includes:
- fire, theft, and flood insurance for business property
- liability insurance
- medical insurance for your employees (see Chapter 12)
- professional malpractice insurance—for example, medical or legal malpractice insurance
- credit insurance that covers losses from business debts
- workers' compensation insurance you are required by state law to provide your employees (if you are an employee of an S corporation, the corporation can deduct worker's compensation

payments made on your behalf, but you must report them as part of your employee wages)

- business interruption insurance
- life insurance covering a corporation's officers and directors (unless you are a direct beneficiary under the policy), and
- unemployment insurance contributions (you deduct these either as insurance costs or as business taxes, depending on how they are characterized by your state's laws).

Homeowner's Insurance for Your Home Office

If you have a home office and qualify for the home office deduction, you may deduct the home office percentage of your homeowner's or renter's insurance premiums. For example, if your home office takes up 20% of your home, you may deduct 20% of the premiums. You can deduct 100% of any coverage that you add to your homeowner's or renter's policy specifically for your home office and/or business property. For example, if you add an endorsement to your policy to cover business property, you can deduct 100% of the cost.

Car Insurance

If you use the actual expense method to deduct your car expenses, you can deduct the cost of insurance that covers liability, damages, and other losses for vehicles used in your business as a business expense. If you use a vehicle only for business, you can deduct 100% of your insurance costs. If you operate a vehicle for both business and personal use, you can deduct only the part of the insurance premiums that applies to the business use of your vehicle. For example, if you use a car 60% for business and 40% for personal reasons, you can deduct 60% of your insurance costs.

If you use the standard mileage rate to deduct your car expenses, you can't take a separate deduction for insurance. The standard rate is intended to cover your insurance costs. (See Chapter 8 for more on vehicle deductions.)

Interest on Business Loans

Interest you pay on business loans is usually a currently deductible business expense. It makes no difference whether you pay the interest on a bank loan, personal loan, credit card, line of credit, car loan, or real estate mortgage. Nor does it matter whether the collateral you used to get the loan was business or personal property. If you use the money for business, the interest you pay to get that money is a deductible business expense. It's how you use the money that counts, not how you get it. Borrowed money is used for business when you buy something with the money that's deductible as a business expense.

> **EXAMPLE:** Max, the sole proprietor owner of a small construction company, borrows $50,000 from the bank to buy new construction equipment. He pays 6% interest on the loan. His annual interest expense is deductible.

Your deduction begins only when you spend the borrowed funds for business purposes. You get no business deduction for interest you pay on money that you keep in the bank. Money in the bank is considered an investment—at best, you might be able to deduct the interest you pay on the money as an investment expense.

How to Eliminate Nondeductible Personal Interest

Because interest on money you borrow for personal purposes—like buying clothes or taking vacations—is not deductible, you should avoid paying this type of interest whenever possible. If you own a business, you can do this by borrowing money to pay your business expenses, and then using the money your business earns to pay off your personal debt. By doing this, you "replace" your nondeductible personal interest expense with deductible business expenses.

Home Offices

If you are a homeowner and take the home office deduction, you can deduct the home office percentage of your home mortgage interest as a business expense. (See Chapter 6 for more on the home office deduction.)

Car Loans

If you use your car for business, you can deduct the interest that you pay on your car loan as an interest expense. You can take this deduction whether you deduct your car expenses using the actual expense method or the standard mileage rate, because the standard mileage rate was not intended to encompass interest on a car loan.

If you use your car only for business, you can deduct all of the interest you pay. If you use it for both business and personal reasons, you can deduct the business percentage of the interest. For example, if you use your car 60% of the time for business, you can deduct 60% of the interest you pay on your car loan.

Loans From Relatives and Friends

If you borrow money from a relative or friend and use it for business purposes, you may deduct the interest you pay on the loan as a business expense. However, the IRS is very suspicious of loans between family members and friends. You need to carefully document these transactions. Treat the loan like any other business loan: Sign a promissory note, pay a reasonable rate of interest, and follow a repayment schedule. Keep your canceled loan payment checks to prove you really paid the interest.

Loans to Buy a Business

If you borrow money to buy an interest in an S corporation, a partnership, or an LLC, it's wise to seek an accountant's help to figure out how to deduct the interest on your loan. You must allocate the money among the company's assets. Depending on what assets the business owns, the interest might be deductible as a business expense or as an investment expense, which is more limited (see "Interest on Business Loans," above).

Interest on money you borrow to buy stock in a C corporation is always treated as investment interest. This is true even if the corporation is small (also called closely held), and its stock is not publicly traded.

Interest You Can't Deduct

You can't deduct interest:

- on loans used for personal purposes
- on debts your business doesn't owe
- on overdue taxes (only C corporations can deduct this interest)
- that you pay with funds borrowed from the original lender through a second loan (but you can deduct interest on the new loan once you start making payments)
- that you prepay if you're a cash basis taxpayer (but you may deduct it the next year)
- on money borrowed to pay taxes or fund retirement plans, or
- on loans of more than $50,000 that are borrowed on a life insurance policy on yourself or another owner or employee of your business.

Points and other loan origination fees that you pay to get a mortgage on business property are not deductible business expenses. You must add these amounts to the cost of the building and deduct them over time using depreciation. The same is true for interest on construction loans if you are in the business of building houses or other real property.

Deducting Investment Interest

Investing is not a business, so you can't take a business expense deduction for interest that you pay on money borrowed to make personal investments. You may take a personal deduction for investment interest, but you may not deduct more than your net annual income from your investments. Any amount that you can't deduct in the current year can be carried over to the next year and deducted then.

EXAMPLE: Donald borrows $10,000 on his credit card to invest in the stock market. The interest he pays on the debt is deductible as an itemized personal deduction on Schedule A, Form 1040. He cannot deduct more than he earns during the year from his investments.

Get Separate Credit Cards for Your Business and Car Expenses

If you use the same credit card for your business and nonbusiness expenses, you are theoretically entitled to a business deduction for the credit card interest on your business expenses. However, you'll have a very difficult time calculating exactly how much of the interest you pay is for business expenses. To avoid this problem, use a separate credit card for business. This can be a special business credit card, but it doesn't have to be. You can simply designate one of your ordinary credit cards for business use. If you drive for business and use the actual expense method to take your deduction, it's a good idea to use another credit card just for car expenses. This will make it much easier to keep track of what you spend on your car.

Always pay your personal credit cards first, because you can't deduct the interest you pay on those cards.

Keeping Track of Borrowed Money

As mentioned above, you may deduct interest on borrowed money only if you use the money for business purposes. But if you deposit the money in a bank account that you use to pay both business and personal bills, how do you know what you spent the money on?

EXAMPLE: Linda borrows $10,000 from the bank and deposits it in her checking account. The account already contains $5,000. Over the next several months, she writes checks to pay for food, her mortgage, personal clothing, office furniture, and a computer for her business. How does Linda know whether the money she borrowed was used for her business expenses or personal expenses?

As you might expect, the IRS has plenty of rules to deal with this problem.

Thirty-Day Rule

If you buy something for your business within 30 days of borrowing money, the IRS presumes that the payment was made from those loan proceeds (up to the amount of the loan). This is true regardless of the method or bank account you use to pay the business expense. If you receive the loan proceeds in cash, you can treat the payment as made on the date you receive the cash instead of the date you actually make the payment.

> **EXAMPLE:** Frank gets a loan of $1,000 on August 4 and receives the proceeds in cash. Frank deposits $1,500 in his bank account on August 18, and on August 28 writes a check on the account for a business expense. Also, Frank deposits his paycheck and other loan proceeds into the account, and pays his personal bills from the account during the same period. Regardless of these other transactions, Frank can treat $1,000 of the deposit he made on August 18 as being paid on August 4 from the loan proceeds. In addition, Frank can treat the business expense he paid on August 28 as made from the $1,000 loan proceeds deposited in the account.

Allocation Rules

If you don't satisfy the 30-day rule, special allocation rules determine how loan proceeds deposited in a bank account were spent for tax purposes. Generally, the IRS will assume that loan proceeds were used (spent) before:

- any unborrowed amounts held in the same account, and
- any amounts deposited after the loan proceeds.

EXAMPLE: On January 9, Edith opened a checking account, depositing a $5,000 bank loan and $1,000 in unborrowed money. On February 13, Edith takes $1,000 from the account for personal purposes. On February 15, she takes out $5,000 to buy equipment for her business. Edith must treat the $1,000 used for personal purposes as made from the loan proceeds, leaving only $4,000 of the loan in the account for tax purposes. As a result, she may deduct as a business expense the interest she pays on only $4,000 of the $5,000 she used to buy the business equipment.

It's easy to avoid having to deal with these complex allocation rules: If you think you'll need to keep borrowed money in the bank for more than 30 days before you spend it on your business, place it in a separate account.

Legal and Professional Services

You can deduct fees that you pay to attorneys, accountants, consultants, and other professionals as business expenses if the fees are paid for work related to your business.

EXAMPLE: Ira, a freelance writer, hires attorney Jake to represent him in a libel suit. The legal fees Ira pays Jake are a deductible business expense.

Legal and professional fees that you pay for personal purposes generally are not deductible. For example, you can't deduct the legal fees you incur if you get divorced or you sue someone for a traffic accident injury. Nor are the fees that you pay to write your will deductible, even if the will covers business property that you own.

Buying Long-Term Property

If you pay legal or other fees in the course of buying long-term business property, you must add the amount of the fee to the tax basis (cost) of the property. You may deduct this cost over several years through depreciation or deduct it in one year under I.R.C. § 179. (See Chapter 5 for more on deducting long-term property.)

Starting a Business

Legal and accounting fees that you pay to start a business are deductible only as business start-up expenses. You can deduct $5,000 of start-up expenses the first year you're in business and any amounts over $5,000 over 180 months. The same holds true for incorporation fees or fees that you pay to form a partnership or an LLC. (See Chapter 3 for more on deducting start-up costs.)

Accounting Fees

You can deduct any accounting fees that you pay for your business as a deductible business expense—for example, fees you pay an accountant to set up or keep your business books, prepare your business tax return, or give you tax advice for your business.

Self-employed taxpayers may deduct the cost of having an accountant or other tax professional complete the business portion of their tax returns—Schedule C and other business tax forms—but they cannot deduct the time the preparer spends on the personal part of their returns. If you are self-employed and pay a tax preparer to complete your Form 1040 income tax return, make sure that you get an itemized bill showing the portion of the tax preparation fee allocated to preparing your Schedule C (and any other business tax forms you have to file).

Taxes and Licenses

Most taxes that you pay in the course of your business are deductible.

Income Taxes

Federal income taxes that you pay on your business income are not deductible. However, a corporation or partnership can deduct state or local income taxes it pays. Individuals may deduct state and local income taxes only as an itemized deduction on Schedule A, Form 1040. This is a personal, not a business deduction.

However, you can deduct state tax you pay on gross business income as a business expense. This tax is a federally deductible business operating expense. Of course, you can't deduct state taxes from your income for state income tax purposes.

Self-Employment Taxes

If you are a sole proprietor, partner in a partnership, or an LLC member, you may deduct one-half of your self-employment taxes from your total net business income. This deduction reduces the amount of income on which you must pay personal income tax. It's an adjustment to gross income, not a business deduction. You don't list it on your Schedule C; instead, you take it on page one of your Form 1040.

The self-employment tax is a 15.3% tax (3.3% for 2011), so your deduction is equal to 7.65% of your income (6.65% for 2011). To figure out your income after taking this deduction, multiply your net business income by 92.35% or 0.9235 (93.35% for 2011).

> EXAMPLE: Billie, a self-employed consultant, earned $70,000 from her business and had $20,000 in business expenses. Her net business income was $50,000. She multiplies this amount by 0.9235 to determine her net self-employment income, which is $46,175. This is the amount on which Billie must pay federal income tax.

This deduction is intended to help ease the tax burden on the self-employed.

Employment Taxes

If you have employees, you must pay half of their Social Security and Medicare taxes from your own funds and withhold the other half from their pay. Ordinarily, employment taxes consist of a 12.4% Social Security tax on income up to an annual ceiling; however, for 2011 only, this amount has been reduced to 10.4%. In 2011, the annual Social Security ceiling was $106,800. Medicare taxes are not subject to any income ceiling and are levied at a 2.9% rate. For 2011, this combines to a total 13.3% tax on employment income up to the Social Security tax ceiling. For all other years, the total tax is 15.3%. You may deduct half of this amount as a business expense. On your tax return, you should treat the taxes you withhold from your employees' pay as wages paid to your employees.

> **EXAMPLE:** You pay your employee $18,000 a year. However, after you withhold employment taxes, your employee receives $14,500. You also pay an additional $1,500 in employment taxes from your own funds. On your tax returns, should deduct the full $18,000 salary as employee wages and deduct the $1,500 as employment taxes paid.

Sales Taxes

You may not deduct state and local sales taxes that you are required to collect from the buyer and turn over to your state or local government. Do not include these taxes in your gross receipts or sales.

However, you may deduct sales taxes that you pay when you purchase goods or services for your business. The amount of the tax is added to the cost of the goods or services for purposes of your deduction for the item.

> **EXAMPLE:** Jean, a self-employed carpenter, buys $100 worth of nails from the local hardware store. She has to pay $7.50 in state and local sales taxes on the purchase. She may take a $107.50 deduction for the nails. She claims the deduction on her Schedule C as a purchase of supplies.

If you buy a long-term business asset, the sales taxes must be added to its basis (cost) for purposes of depreciation or expensing under I.R.C. § 179.

> **EXAMPLE:** Jean buys a $2,000 power saw for her carpentry business. She pays $150 in state and local sales tax. The saw has a useful life of more than one year and is therefore a long-term business asset for tax purposes. She can't currently deduct the cost as a business operating expense. Instead, Jean must depreciate the cost over several years or expense the cost (deduct the full cost in one year) under Section 179. The total cost to be depreciated or expensed is $2,150.

Real Property Taxes

You can deduct your current year's state and local property taxes on business real property as business expenses. However, if you prepay the next year's property taxes, you may not deduct the prepaid amount until the following year.

Home Offices

The only real property most home businesspeople own is their home. If you are a homeowner and take the home office deduction, you may deduct the home office percentage of your property taxes. However, as a homeowner, you are entitled to deduct all of your mortgage interest and property taxes, regardless of whether you have a home office. Taking the home office deduction won't increase your income tax deductions for your property taxes, but it will allow you to deduct them from your income for the purpose of calculating your self-employment taxes.

Charges for Services

Water bills, sewer charges, and other service charges assessed against your business property are not real estate taxes, but they are deductible as business expenses. If you have a home office, you can deduct your home office percentage of these items.

However, real estate taxes imposed to fund specific local benefits such as streets, sewer lines, and water mains, are not deductible as business expenses. Because these benefits increase the value of your property, you should add what you pay for them to the tax basis (cost for tax purposes) of your property.

Buying and Selling Real Estate

When real estate is sold, the real estate taxes must be divided between the buyer and seller according to how many days of the tax year each held ownership of the property. You'll usually find information on this in the settlement statement you receive at the property closing.

Other Taxes

Other deductible taxes include:

- excise taxes—for example, Hawaii imposes a general excise tax on businesses ranging from 0.5% to 4% of gross receipts
- state unemployment compensation taxes or state disability contributions
- corporate franchise taxes
- occupational taxes charged at a flat rate by your city or county for the privilege of doing business, and
- state and local taxes on personal property—for example, equipment or machinery that you use in your business.

You can deduct taxes on gasoline, diesel fuel, and other motor fuels that you use in your business. However, these taxes are usually included as part of the cost of the fuel. For this reason, you usually do not deduct these taxes separately on your return. However, you may be entitled to a tax credit for federal excise tax that you pay on fuels used for certain purposes—for example, farming or off-highway business use. See IRS Publication 378, *Fuel Tax Credits and Refunds* (available from the IRS website, www.irs.gov).

License Fees

License fees imposed on your business by your local or state government are deductible business expenses. For example, some cities and counties require home business owners to obtain business licenses; the fees for such licenses are deductible.

Record Keeping and Accounting

Basic Record Keeping for Tax Deductions.. 374

    Business Checkbook and Credit Cards 375

    Appointment Book... 377

    Expense Journal... 379

    Supporting Documents 384

Records Required for Specific Expenses 387

    Automobile Mileage and Expense Records 388

    Entertainment, Meal, Travel, and Gift Expenses 393

    Listed Property.. 399

How Long to Keep Records.. 401

What If You Don't Have Proper Tax Records?...................................... 403

Accounting Methods 404

    Cash Method 405

    Accrual Method 409

    Which Is Better—Accrual or Cash Method Accounting?........... 411

Tax Years... 413

When you incur business expenses, you can take tax deductions and save money on your taxes. But those deductions are only as good as the records you keep to back them up.

This is what Alton Williams, a schoolteacher with a sideline business selling new and used books, found out when he was audited by the IRS. Over a four-year period, he claimed over $70,000 in business deductions and inventory costs from his business. Unfortunately, he had no records or receipts tracking these expenses. His excuse: "A receipt is something I never thought I would actually need." The auditor reduced his deductions for each year by 50% to 70%, and Williams ended up owing the IRS almost $10,000 (*Williams v. Comm'r.*, 67 TC Memo 2185 (1994)).

Any expense you forget to deduct, or lose after an IRS audit because you can't back it up, costs you dearly. Every $100 in unclaimed deductions costs the average midlevel income person (in a 25% tax bracket) $43 in additional federal and state income and self-employment taxes.

Luckily, it's not difficult to keep records of your business expenses. This chapter shows you how to document your expenditures so you won't end up losing your hard-earned deductions.

Basic Record Keeping for Tax Deductions

This section explains how to set up a basic system for keeping track of your deductible expenses. All you need is:

- a business checking account
- an appointment book
- an expense journal, and
- supporting documents, such as receipts.

This system will get you started, but it is by no means everything you'll need for your business record keeping. For example, every business must keep track of its income. If you make or sell merchandise, you will have to also keep inventory records. And if you have employees, you must create and keep a number of records, including payroll tax records, withholding records, and employment tax returns.

RESOURCE

Need help with bookkeeping? For an excellent overall guide to small business bookkeeping, see *Small Time Operator,* by Bernard B. Kamoroff (Bell Springs Press).

Business Checkbook and Credit Cards

One of the first things you should do (if you haven't done it already) is set up a separate checking account for your business. Your business checkbook will serve as your basic source of information for recording your business expenses and income. Deposit all of your business receipts (checks you receive from clients, for example) into the account and make all business-related payments by check from the account. Don't use your business account to pay for personal expenses or your personal account to pay for business items.

You are legally required to have a separate business checkbook if you've formed a corporation, partnership, or an LLC. Keeping a separate business account is not legally required if you're a sole proprietor, but it will provide these important benefits:

- It will be much easier for you to keep track of your business income and expenses if you pay them from a separate account.
- Your business account will clearly separate your personal and business finances; this will prove very helpful if you're audited by the IRS.
- Your business account will help convince the IRS that you are running a business and not engaged in a hobby. Hobbyists don't generally have separate bank accounts to fund their pursuits. This is a huge benefit if your business incurs losses because losses from hobbies are not fully deductible. (See Chapter 2 for more on the hobby loss rule.)

Setting Up Your Bank Account

Your business checking account should be in your business name. If you're a sole proprietor (like the vast majority of home business owners), you can use your own name. If you've formed a corporation, partnership, or limited liability company, the account should be in your corporate, partnership, or company name. If you're a sole proprietor doing business under an assumed name, you'll probably have to give your bank a copy of your fictitious business name statement.

You don't have to open your business checking account at the same bank where you have your personal checking account. Shop around and open your account with the bank that offers you the best services at the lowest price. If you're doing business under your own name, consider opening up a second personal account in that name and using it solely for your business instead of creating a separate business account. You'll usually pay lower fees for a personal account than for a business account.

If you've incorporated your business, call your bank and ask what documentation you'll have to present to open the account. You will probably need to show the bank a corporate resolution authorizing the opening of a bank account and showing the names of the people authorized to sign checks. Typically, you will also have to fill out, and impress your corporate seal on, a separate bank account authorization form provided by your bank. You will also need to have a federal employer identification number. If you've established a partnership or limited liability company, you'll likely have to show the bank a resolution authorizing the account.

You may also want to establish interest-bearing accounts for your business, in which you can place cash you don't immediately need. For example, you may decide to set up a business savings account or a money market mutual fund in your business name.

When You Write Checks

If you already keep an accurate, updated personal checkbook, do the same for your business checkbook. If, however, you tend to be lax in keeping up your checkbook (as many of us are), you're going to have to change your habits. Now that you're in business, you can't afford this kind of carelessness. Unless you write large numbers of business checks, maintaining your checkbook won't take much time.

When you write business checks, you may have to make some extra notations besides the date, number, amount of the check, and the name of the person or company to which the check is written. If the purpose of the payment is not clear from the name of the payee, describe the business reason for the check—for example, the equipment or service you purchased.

You can use the register that comes with your checkbook and write in all this information manually, or you can use a computerized register. Either way works fine as long as the information is complete and up to date. (See "Records Required for Specific Expenses," below, to find out what information you need to record for various types of expenses.)

> **Don't Write Checks for Cash**
>
> Avoid writing checks payable to cash, because doing so makes it hard to tell whether you spent the money for a business purpose and may lead to questions from the IRS if you're audited. If you must write a check for cash to pay a business expense, be sure to include the receipt for the cash payment in your records.

Use a Separate Credit Card for Business

Use a separate credit card for business expenses instead of putting both personal and business items on one card. Credit card interest for business purchases is 100% deductible, while interest for personal purchases is not deductible at all (see Chapter 14). Using a separate card for business purchases will make it much easier for you to keep track of how much interest you've paid for business purchases. The card doesn't have to be in your business name; you can just use one of your personal credit cards.

Appointment Book

The next item you need is an appointment book, day planner, tax diary, or calendar. You can find inexpensive ones in any stationery store. Many computerized calendars are available as well. However, a calendar completed by hand in ink will always be more convincing to the IRS than one you create on a computer, because it is very easy to forge or alter a computerized calendar.

Properly used, this humble item will:

- provide solid evidence that you are serious about making a profit from your business, and thereby avoid an IRS claim that your activity is a hobby (see Chapter 2)
- help show that the expenses you incur are for business, not personal, purposes
- help verify entertainment, meal, and travel expenses
- enable you to use a sampling method to keep track of business mileage, instead of keeping track of every mile you drive all year (see "Records Required for Specific Expenses," below), and
- if you claim a home office deduction, help show that you use your office for business.

> **EXAMPLE:** Tom, a self-employed advertising copywriter who worked out of his Florida home, kept a detailed appointment book. He devoted a page to each day, listing all of his business activities. He also kept a mileage log to record his business mileage. When he was audited by the IRS, the auditor picked out a trip from his mileage log at random and asked him the purpose of the trip. Tom looked at his appointment book entry for that day, and was able to truthfully and credibly tell the auditor that the trip was to visit a client. The auditor accepted his explanation and the rest of his business mileage deductions.

Every day you work, you should write down in your appointment book (in ink):

- the name of every person you talk to for business
- the date, time, and place of every business meeting,
- every place you go for business
- the amount of all travel, meal, and entertainment expenses that are less than $75, and
- if you claim the home office deduction, the time you spend working in your office.

Below is a sample page from an appointment book for a self-employed real estate salesperson (you'll find information in "Records Required for Specific Expenses," below, on what information you need to list for different types of expenses).

Sunday	Monday	Tuesday	Wednesday	Thursday	Friday	Saturday
	1 Meeting with Earl Crowler	2	3 Show 111 Green St.	4 Answer phones	5 Sales Meeting	6 Prepare for open house— Green St.
7 Open House 111 Green St.	8	9 Sales Meeting	10 Lunch Gibbons	11	12 Meeting Kim Mann	13
14 Open House 222 Blue St.	15	16 Show Gibbons 222 Blue St.	17	18 Lunch Mortgage Broker	19 Sales Meeting	20
21 Open House 456 Main St.	22	23 Sales Meeting	24 Lunch Mortgage Broker	25 Breakfast Kiwanis Club	26 Sales Meeting	27
28 Open House 826 3rd St.	29 Continuing education seminar	30	31			

Expense Journal

You can track your expenses by creating what accountants call a chart of accounts—a listing of all your expenses by category. This will show what you buy for your business and how much you spent. It's very easy to do this. You can write your chart out on paper or you can set up a computer spreadsheet program, such as *Excel*, to do it. Or, if you already have or would prefer to use a financial computer program such as *Quicken*, you can do that instead.

Creating a Paper Expense Journal

You can easily create an expense journal by using paper divided into columns or a professional multicolumn book you can get from any stationery or office supply store. These multicolumn pages are also called "ledger sheets." Get ledger sheets with at least 12 or 14 columns.

Devote a separate column to each major category of expense you have. Alternatively, you can purchase accounting record books with the expense categories already printed on them. These cost more, however, and may not offer categories that meet your needs.

To decide what your expense categories should be, sit down with your bills and receipts and sort them into categorized piles. IRS Schedule C, *Profit or Loss From Business,* the tax form sole proprietors must use to claim their deductions, lists common categories of business expenses. These categories are a good place to start when you devise your own list, because you'll have to use them when you complete your Schedule C for your taxes. The Schedule C categories include:

- advertising
- bad debts
- car and truck expenses
- commissions and fees
- depletion (rarely used by most small businesses)
- depreciation and Section 179 expense deductions
- employee benefit programs
- insurance (other than health)
- interest
- legal and professional services
- meals and entertainment
- office expenses
- pension and profit-sharing plans
- rent or lease—vehicles, machinery, and equipment
- rent or lease—other business property
- repairs and maintenance
- supplies
- taxes and licenses
- travel
- utilities, and
- wages.

The Schedule C list of business categories is by no means exclusive. (In fact, it used to contain more categories.) It just gives you an idea of how to break down your expenses. Depending on the nature of your business, you may not need all these categories or you might have others. For example, a graphic designer might have categories for printing and typesetting expenses, or a writer might have a category for agent fees. Be sure not to use multiple categories for the same expenses—for example, you don't need both an "office supplies" and an "office expenses" category; one will do.

You should always include a final category called "miscellaneous" for various and sundry expenses that are not easily pigeonholed. However, you should use this category sparingly, to account for less than 10% of your total expenses. Unlike travel or advertising, miscellaneous is not a type of business expense. It's just a heading under which you can lump together different types of expenses that don't fit into another category.

You can add or delete expense categories as you go along—for example, if you find that your miscellaneous category contains many items for a particular type of expense, add it as an expense category. You don't need a category for automobile expenses, because these expenses require a different kind of documentation for tax purposes.

In separate columns, list the check number, date, and name of the person or company paid for each payment. If you pay by credit card or check, indicate it in the check number column.

Once a month, go through your check register, credit card slips, receipts, and other expense records and record the required information for each transaction. Also, total the amounts for each category when you come to the end of the page and keep a running total of what you've spent for each category for the year to date.

The following example shows a portion of an expense journal.

Expense Journal

Date	Check No.	Transaction	Amount	Advertising	Outside Contractors	Utilities	Supplies	Rent	Travel	Equipment	Meals & Entertainment	Misc.
5/1	123	ABC Properties	500					500				
5/1	124	Office Warehouse	150				150					
5/10	VISA	Computer World	1,000							1,000		
5/15	VISA	Cafe Ole'	50									50
5/16	Cash	Sam's Stationery	50				50					
5/18	125	Electric Co.	50			50						
5/30	126	Bill Carter	500		500							
Total This Page			2,300		500	50	200	500		1,000	50	
Total Year to Date			7,900	200	2,000	250	400	2,500	300	1,500	250	500

Using Computer Financial Programs

There are many computer programs designed to help people and businesses keep track of their finances. These range from relatively simple checkbook programs like *Quicken*, to complex and sophisticated accounting programs like *QuickBooks Pro* and *MYOB*. You can use these in place of the handwritten ledger sheets or simple spreadsheets described above. However, you'll be better off using handwritten ledger sheets, which are easy to create and simple to keep up to date, instead of a complicated computer program that you can't understand or use properly. So, if you're not prepared to invest the time to use a computer program correctly, don't do it!

This book doesn't explain how to use these programs in detail. You'll need to read the manual and/or tutorial that comes with the program you choose. There are also books that explain how to use them—for example, *Using Quicken in a Business*, by Stephen Nelson, CPA (Redmond Technology Press).

Before You Purchase a Program

You don't want to spend your hard-earned money on a financial program only to discover that you don't like it. Before you purchase a program:
- Talk to others in similar businesses to find out what they use. (If they don't like a program, ask them why.)
- Think carefully about how many features you need—the more complex the program, the harder it will be to learn and use it.
- Obtain a free demo version to see if you like it—you can usually download one from the software company's website.

The simplest financial programs are those that work off of a computerized checkbook, like *Quicken*. When you buy something for your business, you write a check using the program. It automatically inputs the data into a computerized check register, and you print out the check using your computer (payments can also be made online). You'll have to input credit card and cash payments separately.

You create a list of expense categories just like you do when you create a ledger sheet or spreadsheet. Programs like *Quicken* come with preselected categories, but these are not adequate for many businesses, so you'll probably have to create your own. The expense category is automatically noted in your register when you write a check.

The program can then take this information and automatically create income and expense reports—that is, it will show you how much you've spent or earned for each category. This serves the same function as the expense journal. It can also create profit and loss statements. You can even import these amounts into tax preparation software, such as *TurboTax*, when it's time to do your income taxes.

Quicken provides all the tools many small service businesses need. However, if your business involves selling goods or maintaining an inventory, or if you have employees, you'll need a more sophisticated program. Other programs (such as *MYOB Account Edge* and *Plus* by MYOB, *Sage Peachtree Accounting* by Peachtree Software, and

QuickBooks by Intuit) can accomplish more complex bookkeeping tasks, such as double-entry bookkeeping, tracking inventory, payroll, invoicing, handling accounts receivable, and maintaining fixed asset records.

Supporting Documents

The IRS lives by the maxim that "figures lie and liars figure." It knows very well that you can claim anything in your books and on your tax returns, because you create or complete them yourself. For this reason, the IRS requires that you have documents to support the deductions you claim on your tax return. In the absence of a supporting document, an IRS auditor may conclude that an item you claim as a business expense is really a personal expense, or that you never bought the item at all. Either way, your deduction will be disallowed.

The supporting documents you need depend on the type of deduction. However, at a minimum, every deduction should be supported by documentation showing:

- what you purchased for your business
- how much you paid for it, and
- who (or what company) you bought it from.

You must meet additional record-keeping requirements for local transportation, travel, entertainment, meal, and gift deductions, as well as for certain long-term assets that you buy for your business ("Records Required for Specific Expenses," below, covers these rules).

You can meet the basic requirements by keeping the following types of documentation:

- canceled checks
- sales receipts
- account statements
- credit card sales slips
- invoices, or
- petty cash slips for small cash payments.

Keep your supporting documents in a safe place. If you don't have a lot of receipts and other documents to save, you can simply keep them all in a single folder. If you have a lot of supporting documents to save or are the type of person who likes to be extremely well organized, separate your documents by category—for example, income, travel expenses, or equipment purchases. You can use a separate file folder for each category or get an accordion file with multiple pockets.

Canceled Check + Receipt = Proof of Deduction

Manny, a self-employed photographer, buys a $500 digital camera for his business from the local electronics store. He writes a check for the amount and is given a receipt. How does he prove to the IRS that he has a $500 business expense?

Could Manny simply save his canceled check when it's returned from his bank? Many people carefully save all their canceled checks (some keep them for decades), apparently believing that a canceled check is all the proof they need to show that a purchase was a legitimate business expense. This is not the case. All a canceled check proves is that you spent money for something. It doesn't show what you bought. Of course, you can write a note on your check stating what you purchased, but why should the IRS believe what you write on your checks yourself?

Does Manny's sales receipt prove that he bought his camera for his business? Again, no. A sales receipt only proves that somebody purchased the item listed in the receipt. It does not show who purchased it. You could write a note on the receipt stating that you bought the item, but you could easily lie. Indeed, for all the IRS knows, you could hang around stores and pick up receipts people throw away to give yourself tax deductions. There are also websites that, for a fee, will create legitimate-looking fake receipts.

However, when you put a canceled check together with a sales receipt (or an invoice, a cash register tape, or a similar document), you have concrete proof that you purchased the item listed in the receipt. The check proves that you bought something, and the receipt proves what that something is.

This doesn't necessarily prove that you bought the item for your business, but it's a good start. Often, the face of a receipt, sales slip, or the payee's name on your canceled check will strongly indicate that the item you purchased was for your business. But if it's not clear, note the purpose of the purchase on the document. Such a note is not proof of how you used the item, but it will be helpful. For some types of items that you use for both business and personal purposes—cameras are one example—you might be required to keep careful records of your use. (See "Records Required for Specific Expenses," below, for the stricter rules that apply to these types of expenses.)

Credit Cards

Using a credit card is a great way to pay business expenses. The credit card slip will prove that you bought the item listed on the slip. You'll also have a monthly statement to back up your credit card slips. You should use a separate credit card for your business.

Account Statements

Sometimes, you'll need to use an account statement to prove an expense. Some banks no longer return canceled checks, or you may pay for something with an ATM card or another electronic funds transfer method. Moreover, you may not always have a credit card slip when you pay by credit card—for example, when you buy an item over the Internet. In these situations, the IRS will accept an account statement as proof that you purchased the item. The chart below shows what type of information you need on an account statement.

Proving Payments With Bank Statements	
If payment is by:	**The statement must show:**
Check	Check number
	Amount
	Payee's name
	Date the check amount was posted to the account by the bank
Electronic funds transfer	Amount transferred
	Payee's name
	Date the amount transferred was posted to the account by the bank
Credit card	Amount charged
	Payee's name
	Transaction date

Records Required for Specific Expenses

The IRS is particularly suspicious of business deductions people take for local transportation, travel, meals, gift, and entertainment expenses. It knows that many people wildly inflate these deductions—either because they're dishonest or because they haven't kept good records and instead estimate how much they think they must have spent. For this reason, special record-keeping requirements apply to these deductions. Likewise, there are special requirements for long-term assets that can be used for both personal and business purposes. If you fail to comply with the requirements discussed below, the IRS may disallow the deduction, even if it was legitimate.

Automobile Mileage and Expense Records

If you use a car or other vehicle for business purposes, you're entitled to take a deduction for gas and other auto expenses. You can either deduct the actual cost of your gas and other expenses or take the standard rate deduction based on the number of business miles you drive. (See Chapter 8 for more on car expenses.)

Either way, you must keep a record of:

- your mileage
- the dates of your business trips
- the places you drove for business, and
- the business purpose for your trips.

The last three items are relatively easy to keep track of. You can record the information in your appointment book, calendar, or day planner. Or, you can record it in a mileage logbook—you can get one for a few dollars from any stationery store and stash it in your car glove compartment.

No Documentation Needed for Utilitarian Vehicles

All this documentation is not required for vehicles that ordinarily are not driven for personal use—for example, ambulances, hearses, trucks weighing more than 14,000 pounds, cement mixers, cranes, tractors, garbage trucks, dump trucks, forklifts, moving vans, and delivery trucks with seating for only the driver (with or without a folding jump seat). But you still need to keep track of your gas, repair, and other expenses.

Calculating your mileage takes more work. The IRS wants to know the total number of miles you drove during the year for business, commuting, and personal driving other than commuting. Commuting is travel between home and your office or other principal place of business. If you work from a home office, you'll have no commuting mileage. Personal miles include, for example, trips to the grocery store, personal vacations, or visits to friends or relatives.

Claiming a Car Is Used Solely for Business

If you use a car 100% for business, you don't need to keep track of your personal or commuting miles. However, you can successfully claim to use a car 100% for business only if you:

- work out of a tax deductible home office
- have at least two cars, and
- use one car just for business trips.

There are several ways to keep track of your mileage; some are easy and some are a bit more complicated.

Fifty-Two-Week Mileage Book

The hardest way to track your mileage—and the way the IRS would like you to do it—is to keep track of every mile you drive every day, 52 weeks a year, using a mileage logbook or business diary. This means you'll list every trip you take, whether for business, or personal reasons. If you enjoy record keeping, go ahead and use this method. But there are easier ways.

Tracking Business Mileage

An easier way to keep track of your mileage is to record your mileage only when you use your car for business. Here's what to do:

- Obtain a mileage logbook and keep it in your car with a pen attached.

- Note your odometer reading in the logbook at the beginning and end of every year that you use the car for business. (If you don't know your January 1 odometer reading for this year, you might be able to estimate it by looking at auto repair receipts that note your mileage.)
- Record your mileage and note the business purpose for the trip every time you use your car for business.
- Add up your business mileage when you get to the end of each page in the logbook (this way, you'll only have to add the page totals at the end of the year instead of all the individual entries).

Here's an example of a portion of a page from a mileage logbook.

Mileage Log

Date	Business Purpose	Odometer Reading Begin	End	Business Miles
5/1	Visit Art Andrews—potential client	10,111	10,196	85
5/4	Delivered documents to Bill James in Stockton	10,422	10,476	54
5/5	Picked up office supplies	10,479	10,489	10
5/8	Meeting—Acme Corp.—Sacramento	10,617	10,734	117
5/10	Lunch with Stu Smith—client	10,804	10,841	37
5/13	Meeting—Acme Corp.—Sacramento	10,987	11,104	117
5/15	Breakfast—Mary Moss—client	11,201	11,222	21
5/15	Lunch—Sam Simpson—potential client	11,222	11,247	25
5/15	Attend sales seminar—Hilton Hotel	11,247	11,301	54
5/17	Bank	11,399	11,408	9
5/18	Meeting—ABC Company	11,408	11,436	28
5/20	Sales presentation—Smith Bros. & Co.	11,544	11,589	45
Total				602

At the end of the year, your logbook will show the total business miles you drove during the year. You calculate the total miles you drove during the year by subtracting your January 1 odometer reading from your December 31 reading.

If you use the actual expense method, you must also calculate your percentage of business use of the car. You do this by dividing your business miles by your total miles.

> EXAMPLE: Yolanda uses her car extensively for her home business. At the beginning of the year, her odometer reading was 34,201 miles. On December 31, it was 58,907 miles. Her total mileage for the year was therefore 24,706. She recorded 62 business trips in her mileage logbook for a total of 9,280 miles. Her business use percentage of her car is 38% (9,280 ÷ 24,706 = 0.376).

Record Your Mileage Electronically

If writing your mileage down in a paper mileage logbook seems too primitive, you can keep your records in electronic form. There is special software available for recording business mileage. However, be warned: Although the IRS's official policy is that electronic records are acceptable, many IRS auditors are old-fashioned. They like to see paper and ink mileage records because they are much harder to alter, forge, or create in a hurry than electronic records.

Sampling Method

There is an even easier way to track your mileage: Use a sampling method. Under this method, you keep track of your business mileage for a sample portion of the year and use your figures for that period to extrapolate your business mileage for the whole year.

This method assumes that you drive about the same amount for business throughout the year. To back up this assumption, you must scrupulously keep an appointment book showing your business appointments all year long. If you don't want to keep an appointment book, don't use the sampling method.

Your sample period must be at least 90 days—for example, the first three months of the year. Alternatively, you may sample one week each month—for example, the first week of every month. You don't have to use the first three months of the year or the first week of every month; you could use any other three-month period or the second, third, or fourth week of every month. Use whatever works best for you—you want your sample period to be as representative as possible of the business travel you do throughout the year.

You must keep track of the total miles you drove during the year by taking odometer readings on January 1 and December 31 and deducting any atypical mileage before applying your sample results.

> EXAMPLE: Tom, a traveling salesman, uses the sample method to compute his mileage, keeping track of his business miles for the first three months of the year. He drove 6,000 miles during that time, and had 4,000 business miles. The business percentage of his car use was 67%. From his January 1 and December 31 odometer readings, Tom knows he drove a total of 27,000 miles during the year. However, Tom drove to the Grand Canyon for vacation, so he deducts this 1,000 mile trip from his total. This leaves him with 26,000 total miles for the year. To calculate his total business miles, he multiplies the yearlong total by the business use percentage of his car: 67% × 26,000 = 17,420. Tom claims 17,420 business miles on his tax return.

Keeping Track of Actual Expenses

If you take the deduction for your actual auto expenses instead of using the standard rate (or if you are thinking about switching to this method), keep receipts for all of your auto-related expenses, including gasoline, oil, tires, repairs, and insurance. You don't need to include these expenses in your ledger sheets; just keep them in a folder or envelope. At tax time, add them up to determine how large your deduction will be if you use the actual expense method. Also add in the amount you're entitled to deduct for depreciation of your auto. (See Chapter 8 for more on using the actual expense method, including vehicle depreciation.)

Use a Credit Card for Gas

If you use the actual expense method for car expenses, you should use a credit card when you buy gas. It's best to designate a separate card for this purpose. The monthly statements you receive will serve as your gas receipts. If you pay cash for gas, you must either get a receipt or make a note of the amount in your mileage logbook.

Costs for business-related parking (other than at your office) and for tolls are separately deductible whether you use the standard rate or the actual expense method. Get and keep receipts for these expenses.

Entertainment, Meal, Travel, and Gift Expenses

Deductions for business-related entertainment, meals, and travel are hot-button items for the IRS because they have been greatly abused by many taxpayers. You need to have more records for these expenses than for almost any others, and they will be closely scrutinized if you're audited.

Whenever you incur an expense for business-related entertainment, meals, gifts, or travel, you must document the following five facts:

- The date: The date you incurred the expense will usually be listed on a receipt or credit card slip. Appointment books, day planners, and similar documents have the dates preprinted on each page, so entries on the appropriate page automatically date the expense.
- The amount: How much you spent, including tax and tip for meals.
- The place: The nature and place of the entertainment or meal will usually be shown on a receipt, or you can record it in an appointment book.

- The business purpose: Show that the expense was incurred for your business—for example, to obtain future business, encourage existing business relationships, and so on. It is not sufficient merely to write "lunch with client" on a receipt. What you need to show depends on whether the business conversation occurred before, during, or after entertainment or a meal. (See Chapter 7 for more information about these rules.)
- The business relationship: If entertainment or meals are involved, you should record the business relationship among the people at the event—for example, list their names and occupations and any other information needed to establish their business relation to you.

The IRS does not require you to keep receipts, canceled checks, credit card slips, or any other supporting documents for entertainment, meal, gift, or travel expenses that cost less than $75. However, *you must still document the five facts listed above.* This exception does not apply to lodging—that is, hotel or similar costs—when you travel for business. You do need receipts for these expenses, even if they cost less than $75.

CAUTION

The $75 rule applies only to travel, meals, gifts, and entertainment. The rule that you don't need receipts for expenses of less than $75 applies *only* to travel, gift, meal, and entertainment expenses. It does not apply to other types of business expenses. For example, if you go to the office supply store and buy $50 worth of supplies for your business and then spend $70 for lunch with a client, you need a receipt for the office supplies, but not the business lunch. If you find this rule hard to remember, simply keep all of your receipts.

All this record keeping is not as hard as it sounds. You can record the five facts you have to document in a variety of ways, and the information doesn't have to be all in one place. Information that is shown on a receipt, canceled check, or other item need not be duplicated in a log, appointment book, calendar, or account book. Thus, for example, you can record the five facts with:

- a receipt, credit card slip, or similar document alone
- a receipt combined with an appointment book entry, or
- an appointment book entry alone (for expenses less than $75).

However you document your expense, you are supposed to do it in a timely manner. You don't need to record the details of every expense on the day you incur it. It is sufficient to record them on a weekly basis. However, if you're prone to forgetting details, it's best to get everything you need in writing within a day or two.

Using Electronic Records to Document Travel Deductions

These days, many of us fly without an actual airline ticket, using "paperless travel." When you book a flight this way, you will receive a receipt and an itinerary (via download from a website, email, or fax), but no actual ticket. The IRS says it's perfectly fine to use copies of these types of electronic records to document a travel deduction, as long as they show the amount spent, date, location, and business purpose of the expenditure. Make sure you save these records, in either digital or hard copy format. (Ltr. Ruling 98050007.)

Receipt or Credit Card Slip Alone

An easy way to document an entertainment, gift, travel, or meal expense is to use your receipt, credit card slip, invoice, or bill. A receipt or credit card slip will ordinarily contain the name and location of the place where the expense was incurred, the date, and the amount charged. Thus, three of the five facts you must document are already covered. You just need to describe the business purpose and business relationship (if entertainment or meals are involved). You can write this directly on your receipt or credit card slip.

Proof Required for Travel, Entertainment, and Gift Deductions				
Records must show:	**Amount**	**Time**	**Place or Description**	**Business Purpose and Relationship**
Travel	Cost of each separate expense for travel, lodging, meals. Incidental expenses may be totaled in categories such as taxis, daily meals, and so on.	Dates you left and returned for each trip, and the number of days spent on business.	Name of city, town, or other destination.	Business purpose for the expense, or the benefit gained or expected to be gained.
Entertainment (including meals)	Cost of each separate expense. Incidental expenses such as taxis, telephones, etc. may be totaled on a daily basis.	Date of entertainment.	Name and address or location of place of entertainment. Type of entertainment, if not otherwise apparent. For entertainment directly before or after business discussion: date, place, nature, and duration.	Nature of business discussion or activity. Identities of people who took part in discussion and entertainment. Occupations or other information (such as names or titles) about the recipients that shows their business relationship to you. Proof you or your employee was present at business meal.
Gifts	Cost of gift.	Date of gift.	Description of gift.	Same as for Entertainment.

EXAMPLE: Mary, a freelance computer programmer, has lunch with Harold, president of Acme Technologies, Inc., to discuss doing some programming work for Acme. Her restaurant bill shows the date, the name and location of the restaurant, the number of people served, and the amount of the expense. Mary just has to document the business purpose for the lunch and identify her dining companion. She writes on the receipt: "Lunch with Harold Lipshitz, President, Acme Technologies, Inc. Discussed signing contract for programming services." All five facts Mary must prove are on the receipt. This is all Mary needs. She need not duplicate the information elsewhere—for example, in an appointment book or day planner.

```
        GREENS RESTAURANT
        FORT MASON, BLDG A
           SF, CA 94123
          (415)771-6222
  Server: LES              05/26/2011
  Table 28/1                 1:35 PM
  Guests: 2                    30005

  Bowl of soup                  6.50
  Sampler                      12.00
  Filo                         19.75
  Ravioli                      21.00

  Sub Total                    59.25
  Tax                           5.04

  Total                        64.29

  Balance Due            64.29

                    $10.00 tip

  Lunch with Harold Lipshitz,
  president, Acme Technologies, Inc.
  Discussed signing contract for
  programming services.
```

Receipt Plus Appointment Book

You can also document the five facts you need to record for an expense by combining the information on a receipt with entries in an appointment book, day planner, calendar, diary, or similar record.

EXAMPLE: Assume that Mary from the above example saves her receipt from the restaurant where she had her business lunch. She writes nothing on the receipt. She still needs to document the five facts. Her receipt contains the date, the name and location of the restaurant, and the cost of the lunch. She records who she ate with and the business purpose of the lunch by writing a note in her appointment book: "Lunch with Harold Lipshitz, President, Acme Technologies, Inc. Discussed signing contract for programming services."

Appointment Book		
19 *Thursday*	*232/134*	
7		
8		
9		
10		
11		
12	Lunch—Harold Lipshitz, President, Acme Technologies. Greens Restaurant.	
1	Discussed signing contract for programming services. $74.	
2		
3		
4		
5		
6		
20 *Friday*	*233/133*	
7		
8		

Appointment Book Alone

If your expense is for less than $75, you don't need to keep a receipt (unless the expense is for lodging). You may record the five facts in your appointment book, day planner, daily diary, calendar, or on any other sheet of paper.

EXAMPLE: Assume that Mary from the above examples doesn't keep her receipt from her lunch. Because lunch cost less than $75, she does not need it. Instead, she documents the five facts she needs to record in her appointment book. She writes: "Lunch—Harold Lipshitz, President, Acme Technologies, Inc., Green's Restaurant. Discussed signing contract for programming services. $74." This short entry records the place of the lunch, who she ate with, the business purpose, and the amount. She doesn't need to add the date because this is already shown by her appointment book.

Listed Property

Listed property refers to certain types of long-term business assets that can easily be used for personal as well as business purposes. Listed property includes:

- cars, boats, airplanes, motorcycles, and other vehicles
- computers, and
- any other property generally used for entertainment, recreation, or amusement—for example, VCRs, cameras, and camcorders.

Because all listed property is long-term business property, you cannot deduct it like a business expense. Instead, you must depreciate it over several years or deduct it in one year under Section 179. (See Chapter 5 for detailed information on deducting listed property.)

Special Record Keeping Requirements

The IRS fears that taxpayers might claim business deductions for listed property, but use it for personal reasons. That's why you're required to document how you use listed property. Keep an appointment book, logbook, business diary, or calendar showing the dates, times, and reasons for which the property is used—both business and personal. You also can purchase logbooks for this purpose at stationery or office supply stores.

Receipts to Keep	
Type of Expense	**Receipts to Save**
Travel	Airplane, train, or bus ticket stubs; travel agency receipts; rental car; and so on.
Meals	Meal check, credit card slip.
Lodging	Statement or bill from hotel or other lodging provider. Your own written records for cleaning, laundry, telephone charges, tips, and other charges not shown separately on hotel statement.
Entertainment	Bill from entertainment provider; ticket stubs for sporting event, theatre, or other event; credit card slips.

EXAMPLE: Bill, an accountant, purchases a computer he uses 50% for business and 50% to play games. He must keep a log showing his business use of the computer. Shown below is a sample from one week in his log.

Usage Log for Personal Computer			
Date	Time of Business Use	Reason for Business Use	Time of Personal Use
5/1	4.5 hours	Prepared client tax returns	1.5 hours
5/2			3 hours
5/3	2 hours	Prepared client tax returns	
5/4			2 hours

Exception to Record Keeping Rule for Computers

You usually have to document your use of listed property even if you use it only for business. However, there is an exception to this rule for computers: If you use a computer or computer peripheral (such as a printer) only for business and keep it at your business location, you need not comply with the record-keeping requirement. This includes computers that you keep at your home office if the office qualifies for the home office deduction. (The home office deduction is covered in Chapter 6.)

> **EXAMPLE:** John, a freelance writer, works full time in his home office, which he uses exclusively for writing. The office is clearly his principal place of business and qualifies for the home office deduction. He buys a $4,000 computer for his office and uses it exclusively for his writing business. He does not have to keep records showing how he uses the computer.

This exception applies only to computers and computer peripheral equipment. It doesn't apply to other items such as calculators, copiers, fax machines, or typewriters.

TIP

Rules for cell phones. Cell phones and similar personal communication devices are no longer considered listed property. Thus, the strict record keeping requirements for listed property do not apply to these devices. In addition, you don't have to include the fair market value of a cell phone provided to an employee for business purposes in the employee's gross income for tax purposes, as long as the cell phone is provided to the employee for noncompensatory purposes (meaning business purposes not related to providing additional compensation).

How Long to Keep Records

You need to have copies of your tax returns and supporting documents available in case you are audited by the IRS or another taxing agency. You might also need them for other purposes—for example, to get a loan, mortgage, or insurance.

You should keep your records for as long as the IRS has to audit you after you file your returns for the year. These statutes of limitation range from three years to forever—they are listed in the table below.

To be on the safe side, you should keep your tax returns indefinitely. They usually don't take up much space, so this shouldn't be a big hardship. Your supporting documents probably take up more space. You should keep these for at least six years after you file your return. If you file a fraudulent return, keep your supporting documents indefinitely (if you have any). If you're audited, they will show that at least some of your deductions were legitimate.

Keep your long-term asset records for three years after the depreciable life of the asset ends. For example, keep records for five-year property (such as computers) for eight years. You should keep your ledger sheets for as long as you're in business, because a potential buyer of your business might want to see them.

IRS Statutes of Limitations	
If:	The limitations period is:
You failed to pay all the tax due	3 years
You underreported your gross income for the year by more than 25%	6 years
You filed a fraudulent return	No limit
You did not file a return	No limit

Scanning Your Records

If you don't want to keep paper copies of your tax records, you can make digital copies by scanning them and storing them on a computer hard disk or CD-ROM. The IRS has approved the use of electronic storage systems for this purpose. (Rev. Proc. 97-22, 1997-1 CB 652.)

What If You Don't Have Proper Tax Records?

Because you're human, you may not have kept all the records required to back up your tax deductions. Don't despair, all is not lost—you may be able to fall back on the *Cohan* rule. This rule (named after the Broadway entertainer George M. Cohan, who was involved in a tax case in the 1930s) is the taxpayer's best friend. The *Cohan* rule recognizes that all business people must spend at least some money to stay in business, and so must have at least some deductible expenses, even if they don't have adequate records to back them up.

If you're audited and lack adequate records for a claimed deduction, the IRS can use the *Cohan* rule to make an estimate of how much you must have spent, and allow you to deduct that amount. However, you must provide at least some credible evidence on which to base this estimate, such as receipts, canceled checks, notes in your appointment book, or other records. Moreover, the IRS will allow you to deduct only the smallest amount you must have spent, based on the records you provide. In addition, the *Cohan* rule cannot be used for travel, meal, entertainment, or gift expenses, or for listed property.

If an auditor claims you lack sufficient records to back up a deduction, you should always bring up the *Cohan* rule and argue that you should still get the deduction based on the records you do have. At best, you'll probably get only part of your claimed deductions. If the IRS auditor disallows your deductions entirely or doesn't give you as much as you think you deserve, you can appeal in court and bring up the *Cohan* rule again there. You might have more success with a judge. However, you can't compel an IRS auditor or a court to apply the *Cohan* rule in your favor. They have discretion to decide whether to apply the rule and how large a deduction to give you.

> **EXAMPLE:** Ajuba Gaylord had a part-time business as a home-based salesperson. One year, she took a $474 deduction for postage and over $1,100 for meals and entertainment. The IRS disallowed both deductions because she had no documentary evidence showing that the expenses were for her business. However, the tax court applied the *Cohan* Rule and allowed

her a $75 deduction for postage. It reasoned that this was the least that she must have spent, given the nature of her business. However, the court would not use the *Cohan* Rule to grant her a deduction for meal and entertainment expenses. (*Gaylord v. Comm'r.*, TC Memo 2003-273.)

Reconstructing Tax Records

If you can show that you possessed adequate records at one time, but now lack them due to circumstances beyond your control, you may reconstruct your records for an IRS audit. Circumstances beyond your control include acts of nature such as floods, fires, earthquakes, or theft. (Treas. Reg. 1.275.5(c)(5).) If you lose your tax records while moving, that doesn't constitute circumstances beyond your control. Reconstructing records means you either create brand new records just for your audit or obtain other evidence to corroborate your deductions—for example, statements from people or companies from whom you purchased items for your business.

Accounting Methods

An accounting method is a set of rules used to determine when and how your income and expenses are reported. Accounting methods might sound like a rather dry subject, but your choice about how to account for your business expenses and income will have a huge impact on your tax deductions. You don't have to become as expert as a CPA on this topic, but you should understand the basics.

You must choose an accounting method when you file your first tax return. If you later want to change your accounting method, you must get IRS approval. The IRS requires some types of businesses to use the accrual method. If your business doesn't fall into this group, you are free to choose the method you want, as long as it clearly shows your income and expenses. If you operate two or more separate businesses, you can use a different accounting method for each. (A business is separate for tax purposes only if you keep a separate set of books and records for it.)

There are two basic methods of accounting: cash basis and accrual basis. Most home businesses can use either method.

Personal and Business Accounting Methods May Differ

You can account for business and personal items using different accounting methods. For example, you can figure your business income under an accrual method, even if you use the cash method to figure personal items. Almost everyone uses the cash basis method of accounting for personal finances, so it might be convenient to continue to use it for personal items even if you the accrual method for your business.

Cash Method

The cash method is the simplest method. It is used by individuals who are not in business and by most small businesses that provide services and do not maintain inventory or offer credit. The cash method is based on this commonsense idea: You haven't earned income for tax purposes until you actually receive the money, and you haven't incurred an expense until you actually pay the money. Using the cash basis method, then, is like maintaining a checkbook. You record income only when the money is received and expenses only when they are actually paid. If you borrow money to pay business expenses, you incur an expense under the cash method only when you make payments on the loan.

> EXAMPLE 1: Helen, a home-based marketing consultant, completes a market research report on September 1, 2011 but isn't paid by the client until February 1, 2012. Using the cash method, Helen records the payment as income in February 2012—when she receives it.

EXAMPLE 2: On December 1, 2011, Helen goes to the Acme electronics store and buys a laser printer for her consulting business. She buys the item on credit from Acme—she's not required to make any payments until March 1, 2012. Helen does not record the expense until 2012 when she actually pays for the printer.

The Cash Method of Paying Expenses

Although it's called the cash method, this method for paying business expenses includes payments by check, credit card, or electronic funds transfer, as well as by cash. If you pay by check, the amount is deemed paid during the year in which the check is drawn and postal mailed or emailed—for example, a check dated December 31, 2011 is considered paid during 2011 only if it has a December 31, 2011 postmark or it's electronically paid by that date.

Constructive Receipt

Under the cash method, payments are "constructively received" when an amount is credited to your account or otherwise made available to you without restrictions. Constructive receipt is as good as actual receipt. If you authorize someone to be your agent and receive income for you, you are considered to have received it when your agent receives it.

EXAMPLE: Interest is credited to your business bank account in December 2011, but you do not withdraw it or enter it into your passbook until 2012. You must include the amount in gross business income for 2011, not 2012.

No Postponing Income

You cannot hold checks or other payments from one tax year to another to avoid paying tax on the income. You must report the income in the year the payment is received or made available to you without restriction.

> **EXAMPLE:** On December 1, 2011, Helen receives a $5,000 check from a client. She holds the check and doesn't cash it until January 10, 2012. She still has to report the $5,000 as income for 2011 because she constructively received it that year.

No Prepayment of Expenses

The general rule is that you can't prepay expenses when you use the cash method—you can't hurry up the payment of expenses by paying them in advance. An expense you pay in advance can be deducted only in the year to which it applies.

> **EXAMPLE:** Helen pays $1,000 in 2011 for a business insurance policy that is effective for one year, beginning July 1. She can deduct $500 in 2011 and $500 in 2012.

However, there is an important exception to the general rule called the 12-month rule. Under this rule you may deduct a prepaid expense in the current year if the expense is for a right or benefit that extends no longer than the earlier of:

- 12 months, or
- until the end of the tax year after the tax year in which you made the payment.

> **EXAMPLE 1:** You are a calendar year taxpayer and you pay $10,000 for a business insurance policy that is effective for one year beginning July 1, 2011. The 12-month rule applies because the benefit you've paid for—a business insurance policy— extends only 12 months into the future. Therefore, the full $10,000 is deductible in 2011.

EXAMPLE 2: You are a calendar year taxpayer and you pay $3,000 in 2011 for a business insurance policy that is effective for three years, beginning July 1, 2011. This payment does not qualify for the 12-month rule because the benefit extends more than 12 months. Therefore, you must use the general rule: $500 is deductible in 2011, $1,000 is deductible in 2012, $1,000 is deductible in 2013, and $500 is deductible in 2014.

This type of prepayment is fully deductible in the year it was made, provided it complies with the 12-month rule. Under this rule, cash basis taxpayers (which includes most small landlords) may deduct a prepaid expense such as insurance in the current year if the term of the insurance coverage extends no longer than the earlier of: 12 months, or the end of the tax year after the tax year in which the payment was made.

EXAMPLE: On July 1, 2011, Irving pays $2,000 for a new insurance policy for his rental building. The policy covers the period from July 1, 2011 through the end of 2012. Irving can deduct the entire $2,000 payment in 2011 because the coverage ends within 12 months.

There is one small catch: If you previously followed the old rule, under which expenses prepaid beyond the calendar year were not currently deductible, you must get IRS approval to use the 12-month rule. Approval is granted automatically by the IRS upon filing of IRS Form 3115, *Application for Change in Accounting Method.* You should attach one copy of the form to the return for the year of the change and send another copy to the IRS national office (not the service center where you file your return). The address is on the instructions for the form.

It is a good idea to get a tax pro to help you with this form because it may require some adjustment of the deductions you've taken for prepaid expenses in previous years under the old rule.

Accrual Method

In accrual basis accounting, you report income or expenses as they are earned or incurred, rather than when they are actually collected or paid. With the accrual method, you count income when a sale occurs and expenses when you receive the goods or services. You don't have to wait until you see the money or actually pay money out of your checking account. The accrual method can be difficult to use because complex rules determine when income or expenses accrue.

When Expenses Are Incurred

Under the accrual method, you generally deduct a business expense when:

- you are legally obligated to pay the expense
- the amount you owe can be determined with reasonable accuracy, and
- you have received or used the property or services involved.

> EXAMPLE: Bill, the owner of a home-based furniture refinishing business, borrows $10,000 from his bank to help pay his business operating expenses. He signs a promissory note on December 15, 2011 and receives the money the same day, but doesn't start making payments to the bank until the following January. Bill can deduct the expense in 2011 because he became legally obligated to pay the expense upon signing the note, the amount of the expense can be determined from the note, and he received the money that day.

Thus, when you use the accrual method, you can take a deduction for an expense you incur even if you don't actually pay for it until the following year. You can't do this under the cash basis method. There are obvious advantages to getting a tax deduction this year without actually having to shell out any money until a future year.

When Income Is Received

While the accrual method lets you deduct expenses that you haven't paid for yet, it also requires you to report payments you haven't yet received as income. Transactions are counted as income when an order is made, an item is delivered, or services are provided, regardless of when the money for them (receivables) is actually received or paid.

> EXAMPLE: Andrea repairs watches in her home workshop as a part-time business. She is hired to repair an antique watch and finishes the job on December 15, 2011. She bills the customer for $250, which she receives on January 20, 2012. Because she uses the accrual method of accounting, Andrea must count the $250 as income in December 2011, because that's when she earned the money by finishing the job. She must report this income in her 2011 tax return, even though she did not receive the money that year.

Businesses That Must Use the Accrual Method

Any business, however small, may use the accrual method. Some types of businesses are required to use it, including C corporations with average annual gross receipts exceeding $5 million. As a general rule, you are required to use the accrual method if you produce, purchase, or sell merchandise and are required to maintain an inventory (see Chapter 10). However, there are two big exceptions that relieve most home businesses from having to use the accrual method.

Exception #1—Businesses That Earn Less Than $1 Million. Even if you deal in merchandise, you may use the cash basis method if your average annual gross receipts were $1 million or less for the three tax years ending with the prior tax year. This includes the vast majority of home businesses that have inventories.

Exception #2—Some Businesses That Earn Less Than $10 Million. Even if your home business earns more than $1 million per year, you may use the cash basis method if your average annual gross receipts were $10 million or less for the three tax years ending with the prior tax year, *and*:

- your principal business is providing services
- your principal business is making or modifying personal property according to customers' specifications, or
- your business does not involve mining, manufacturing, wholesale or retail trade, or certain information services (see IRS Publication 538, *Accounting Periods and Methods,* for more details).

Obtaining IRS Permission to Change Your Accounting Method

You choose your accounting method by checking a box on your tax form when you file your tax return. Once you choose a method, you can't change it without getting permission from the IRS. Permission is granted automatically for many types of changes, including using the 12-month rule to deduct prepaid expenses. You must file IRS Form 3115, *Application for Change in Accounting Method,* with your tax return for the year you want to make the change (if the change is automatically granted).

Automatic approval can also be obtained to change to the cash method if you've been using the accrual method and come within one of the exceptions discussed above. However, changing your accounting method can have serious consequences, so consult a tax professional before doing so.

Which Is Better—Accrual or Cash Method Accounting?

There is no single best accounting method. Each method has its advantages and disadvantages. The cash basis method is much simpler to use and easier to understand. Because you don't report income until it's actually received, it's more advantageous than the accrual method if you're in a business in which you are paid slowly.

EXAMPLE: Tom is a freelance writer who usually must wait months until he is paid for his articles by magazines and newspapers. He contracts with the *Podunk Review* to write an article about inventions created by people in jail. He is to be paid $1,000 within 60 days after the article is accepted. The article is accepted by the *Podunk Review* on September 1, 2011, but Tom doesn't receive his check until March 2012. If he used the accrual method, he would have to recognize the $1,000 as income for 2011 even though he didn't receive it that year. If he used the cash basis method, he wouldn't recognize the income until 2012, when he gets the check.

The accrual method is more complicated than the cash basis method and harder to use, but it shows the ebb and flow of business income and debts more accurately than the cash basis method. You get a truer picture of your net profits for any given time period with the accrual method because income earned in one time period is accurately matched against the expenses for that period. Moreover, the accrual method is more advantageous than the cash basis method if you are paid promptly by your clients or customers, because you are allowed to deduct expenses when you incur them, not when you actually pay for them. When you are paid promptly, the cash method's actual receipt rule is not important; and using the accrual method you may prepay business expenses in advance to offset the income you received for the year—something you can't do with the cash method.

EXAMPLE: Dick is a home-based consultant who makes his clients pay within 30 days. He received $100,000 in consulting income by December 1, 2011 and had no outstanding receivables. To offset his business income, he purchases $10,000 worth of business equipment on credit in December. He doesn't have to pay for the equipment until the end of January 2012, but he can still deduct the $10,000 from his 2011 business income because he uses the accrual method of accounting.

Tax Years

You are required to pay taxes for a 12-month period, also known as the tax year. Sole proprietors, partnerships, limited liability companies, S corporations, and personal service corporations (see Chapter 1) are required to use the calendar year as their tax year—that is, January 1 through December 31.

However, there are exceptions that permit some small businesses to use a tax year that does not end in December (also known as a fiscal year). You need to get the IRS's permission to use a fiscal year. The IRS doesn't want businesses to use a fiscal year, but it might grant you permission if you can show a good business reason for it.

One good reason to use a fiscal year is that your business is seasonal. For example, if you earn most of your income in the spring and incur most of your expenses in the fall, a tax year ending in July or August might be better than a calendar tax year ending in December because the income and expenses on each tax return will be more closely related. To get permission to use a fiscal year, you must file IRS Form 8716, *Election to Have a Tax Year Other Than a Required Tax Year.*

Claiming Tax Deductions for Prior Years

Reasons for Amending Your Tax Return 416

    Net Operating Losses 417

    Retroactive Tax Laws 419

    Casualty Losses 420

Time Limits for Filing Amended Returns 420

    Three-Year Amendment Period 420

    Section 179 Deductions 421

    Net Operating Losses 422

    Bad Debts.. 422

How to Amend Your Return 423

How the IRS Processes Refund Claims 424

Sam, a self-employed genealogy researcher, has worked out of his home office for the last four years. However, he has never taken the home office deduction because he was afraid it would increase his chances of being audited. After reading this book, he realizes that he should have claimed the deduction on his last three tax returns. Had he done so, he would have saved thousands on his taxes. But what can he do now?

Fortunately, tax returns are not engraved in stone. If, like Sam, you realize that you failed to claim tax deductions to which you were entitled, you may be able to amend your tax returns for those years and get the IRS to send you a refund check.

Reasons for Amending Your Tax Return

It's very common for taxpayers to file amended tax returns. Here are some reasons why you might want to amend a tax return:

- You forgot to take a deduction.
- You have a net operating loss for the year and want to apply it to prior years.
- You claimed a deduction to which you were not entitled.
- You entered incorrect information on your return.
- A retroactive change in the tax laws makes you eligible for an additional deduction.

You need not amend your return if you discover that you made a simple math error. These will be corrected by the IRS computers, and you'll be notified of the change by mail.

However, if you made a mistake in your favor, failed to report income, or took deductions to which you were not entitled, amending your return may avoid all or some fines, interest, and penalties if you're later audited by the IRS.

 CAUTION
Filing an amended return makes an audit more likely. You don't have to file an amended return if you don't want to. Filing an amended tax return increases the chances that your tax return for the year involved will be

audited by the IRS. Thus, it may not be worth doing unless you are entitled to a substantial refund. If you're not sure whether to amend, consult a tax professional for advice.

Net Operating Losses

Unfortunately, many home business owners don't earn a profit from their business. You have a business loss for the year if your total business expenses exceed your total business income. If, like the vast majority of home business owners, you're a sole proprietor, you may deduct any loss your business incurs from your other income for the year—for example, income from a job, investment income, or your spouse's income (if you file a joint return).

If your business is operated as an LLC, S corporation, or a partnership, your share of the business's losses are passed through the business to your individual return and deducted from your other personal income in the same way as a sole proprietor. However, if you're one of the few home business owners who operate through a C corporation, you can't deduct a business loss on your personal return. It belongs to your corporation.

If your losses exceed your income from all sources for the year, you have a "net operating loss" (NOL for short). While it's not pleasant to lose money, an NOL can provide important tax benefits: It may be used to reduce your tax liability for both past and future years.

Figuring the Amount of an NOL

Figuring the amount of an NOL is not as simple as deducting your losses from your annual income. Instead, you start with your adjusted gross income on your tax return for the year reduced by your itemized deductions or standard deduction (but not your personal exemption). This must be a negative number or you won't have any NOL for the year. Your adjusted gross income already includes all the deductions you have for your business losses. You then add back to this amount any nonbusiness deductions you have that exceed your nonbusiness income. These include the standard deduction or itemized deductions, deduction for the personal exemption, nonbusiness capital losses,

IRA contributions, and charitable contributions. If the result is still a negative number, you have an NOL for the year. Schedule A of IRS Form 1045, *Application for Tentative Refund*, may be used to calculate an NOL.

Carrying a Loss Back and Forward

Ordinarily, you may carry back an NOL for the two years before the year you incurred the loss. However, in the case of business losses incurred during 2008 or 2009, the carryback period is extended up to five years—that is, you may carry back a 2008 or 2009 NOL for three, four, or five years. In addition, the carryback period is increased to three years if the NOL is due to a casualty or theft, or if you have a qualified small business and the loss is in a presidentially declared disaster area. (A qualified small business is a sole proprietorship or a partnership that has average annual gross receipts of $5 million or less during the three-year period ending with the tax year of the NOL.) For a list of presidentially declared disaster areas, see www.fema.gov/news/disasters.fema.

This is called carrying back an NOL. The IRS will send you a refund of all or part of the taxes you paid for one or both of those years, depending on the size of the NOL and your income for those years. You must first carry the entire NOL to the earliest carryback year. If your NOL is not used up, you can carry the rest to the next earliest carryback year.

If you still have part of your NOL left, you then use it to reduce your income in future years—this is called carrying forward an NOL. You can carry forward an NOL for up to 20 years after the NOL year. You start by carrying it to the first tax year after the NOL year. If you do not use it up, you carry the unused part to the next year. You continue to carry any unused part of the NOL forward until the NOL is used up or you complete the 20-year carryforward period.

Electing to Only Carry Forward an NOL

Under the ordinary IRS rule, you first carry back an NOL as described above. However, you can choose not to carry back your NOL at all.

Instead, you can elect only to carry it forward to future years. Some people do this because they are afraid they'll get audited if they carry an NOL back and receive a refund of taxes they've already paid. You may also want to carry an NOL forward if you expect your income to rise substantially in future years and want to use your NOL in the future, when you'll be subject to a higher tax rate.

To make this choice, you must attach a statement to your original return filed by the due date (including extensions) for the NOL year. This statement must show that you are choosing to waive the carryback period under Section 172(b)(3) of the Internal Revenue Code. Write "Filed pursuant to Section 301.9100-2" at the top of the statement. File the amended return at the same address you used for your original return.

If you filed your return timely but did not file the statement with it, you must file the statement with an amended return for the NOL year within six months of the due date of your original return (excluding extensions). If you do not file this statement on time, you cannot waive the carryback period.

RESOURCE

Need to know more about NOLs? Refer to IRS Publication 536, *Net Operating Losses*, for more information. You can download it from the IRS website at www.irs.gov, or obtain a paper copy by calling the IRS at 800-TAX-FORM.

Retroactive Tax Laws

Sometimes, Congress or the IRS changes the tax laws or regulations and makes the change retroactive—that is, the change applies to returns filed some time before the change was made. If a retroactive change is more favorable to you than the laws that were in effect when you filed your return, you might be entitled to a refund for prior years.

Casualty Losses

There is a special rule for certain types of casualty losses—losses to business property caused by things like fire, floods, or earthquakes. If you suffer a loss to your business property or home office due to a disaster that occurs in an area the president declares to be a disaster area, you have the option of deducting the loss from your previous year's taxes. You do this by filing an amended tax return for the year and deducting the amount of the loss from your taxable income for that year. This will reduce the taxes you had to pay for the year, and the IRS will send you a refund check for the difference. Alternatively, you can wait and deduct your loss from the current year's taxes. But if you want to get some money from the IRS quickly, you should file an amended return (unless you paid no tax the prior year). (See Chapter 14 for a detailed discussion of casualty losses.)

Time Limits for Filing Amended Returns

Unfortunately, you can't wait forever to amend a tax return for a prior year. If you wait too long, you'll forever lose your right to file an amended return for the year, even if it means you'll be forced to give up a deduction for that year to which you were legally entitled.

Three-Year Amendment Period

The general rule is that you must file an amended return within three years after the date you filed the original return, or two years after the date you paid the tax, whichever is later. The three-year period applies in most cases. Even if you filed your return for the year before April 15, it is deemed to be filed on that date for amendment purposes. For example, you have until April 15, 2013 to file an amended return for your 2009 taxes, which are deemed to have been filed on April 15, 2010 (even if you filed them earlier).

> **EXAMPLE:** Sam failed to claim a deduction for the interest he paid on a loan for a car he used in his business during 2009. He

filed his 2009 taxes on April 1, 2010. How long does Sam have to amend his 2009 tax return to claim the deduction? Until April 15, 2013, three years after he is deemed to have filed his original tax return for 2009 (April 15, 2010). If he fails to meet the deadline, he loses his right to claim the deduction and obtain a tax refund.

However, if you obtained an extension of time to file your original return for the year involved, you may add that time to the three-year period. You can get an automatic extension of time to file your return until October 15. (Partnerships and S corporations may receive an automatic extension only until September 15.)

EXAMPLE: Assume that Sam from the above example obtained an extension of time to file his 2009 tax return to October 15, 2010. He would have until October 15, 2013 to amend his tax return for 2009.

Section 179 Deductions

To claim or disclaim a Section 179 deduction, you must file your amended return within six months after the due date for the return for the tax year involved, including any extensions of time you received. Because tax returns are ordinarily due on April 15, you must file your amended return by October 15 to claim a Section 179 deduction for the prior year, unless you received an extension of time to file your return, in which case you have until April 15 of the following year.

EXAMPLE: Jill bought a $3,000 computer for her home medical record transcription business during 2011. When she did her taxes for the year in early 2012, she thought she had to depreciate the computer's cost over five years. She took a depreciation deduction for the computer on her 2011 tax return. However, she learns later that she could have deducted the entire cost in one year using Section 179. She has until October 15, 2012 to file an amended 2011 return to claim the deduction. If she fails to do so, she loses the right to claim a Section 179 deduction for the property and must use depreciation instead.

Net Operating Losses

There are two ways to claim a refund of a prior year's taxes due to a later net operating loss: you can file IRS Form 1040X, *Amended U.S. Individual Income Tax Return* (see "How to Amend Your Return," below), within the usual three-year limitation period, or you can seek a quick refund by filing IRS Form 1045, *Application for Tentative Refund.* If you file Form 1045, the IRS is required to send your refund within 90 days. However, you must file Form 1045 within one year after the end of the year in which the NOL arose.

Should You File Your Amendment as Late as Possible?

The IRS ordinarily has only three years after a return is filed to audit the return. Filing a Form 1040X does not extend this period. Thus, if you file your Form 1040X near the end of the three-year period, the IRS will have very little time to audit your return for the year involved. As a result, it might accept your claim without auditing your return. However, it might also refuse to accept your 1040X unless you agree to extend the time it has to audit your return for the year.

Bad Debts

In some instances, you may be able to deduct a business bad debt as a business operating expense. A debt doesn't become "bad" until it is clearly worthless. This may occur years after the loan was originally made. (See Chapter 14 for more on the requirements for deducting bad debts.) If you failed to claim a bad debt deduction on your original tax return for the year the debt became totally worthless, you have up to seven years to file an amended return listing the bad debt. However, the seven-year term applies only to debts that are completely worthless. If a debt is only partially worthless, you must amend your return within the usual three-year period.

How to Amend Your Return

If you, like the vast majority of home business owners, are a sole proprietor, you amend your income tax return by filing IRS Form 1040X, *Amended U.S. Individual Income Tax Return*. When you file Form 1040X to obtain a refund of taxes you've already paid, it is called a "claim for refund."

Filing an amended tax return is not terribly difficult. You can usually do it yourself, with or without the aid of a computer tax preparation program. The heart of the form consists of three columns: A, B, and C. You record the relevant figures from your original tax return in Column A; the corrected information is listed in Column C; and the difference between the two is listed in Column B. You must also provide a brief explanation for the changes.

If you're amending your previous year's tax return and are entitled to an additional refund for that year, tax experts suggest that you wait until you receive your original refund check for that year. You can go ahead and cash the first refund check as soon as you receive it. Of course, you can file your amended return immediately if you were not entitled to a refund on your original return.

You must mail or hand deliver Form 1040X to the IRS. You can't file it electronically. If you mail it, send it by certified mail, with postal return receipt requested. This will let you know when the IRS received it. If you amend your returns for more than one year, mail each 1040X in a separate envelope. The 1040X instructions show where to mail the form.

You may also hand deliver the form to the IRS service center where you file your tax returns. If you do this, be sure to get a stamped copy as your filing receipt.

To obtain a refund due to an NOL, you may file IRS Form 1045 either alone or along with Form 1040X. You can often get your refund faster by using Form 1045 alone. The calculations required to figure out how much you can deduct from your income in prior years can be complicated. Tax preparation programs like *TurboTax* aren't designed to handle net operating losses, so it's a good idea to get some help from a tax professional. Refer to IRS Publication 536, *Net Operating Losses*, for more information.

> CAUTION
> **Don't forget your state tax returns.** The IRS routinely shares information with states that impose income taxes (every state except Alaska, Florida, Nevada, South Dakota, Texas, Washington, and Wyoming). Thus, your state tax department will probably learn that you amended your federal tax return. For this reason, tax experts advise that you also amend your state tax returns for the years affected.

How the IRS Processes Refund Claims

The IRS doesn't like paying back money to taxpayers. When you file a Form 1040X, your tax return for that year will receive extra special attention. An IRS employee will pull your return and examine it and your 1040X to decide whether you're really entitled to a refund and if so, how much. Your claim may be denied or accepted as filed, or the amended items may be audited. If a claim is audited, the procedures are almost the same as in the audit of a regular tax return. Moreover, the IRS has the option of extending the audit to your entire tax return, not just the amended items. Thus, *filing an amended tax return increases your chances of an audit.*

You should receive your refund, if you're entitled to one, in about 12 weeks. However, your refund may be reduced by amounts you owe for past due child support, debts you owe to another federal agency, or past due state income tax obligations. You will be notified if this happens.

If the IRS denies your claim, it must explain why—for example, because you filed it late. You have the right to appeal such a denial. For a detailed discussion of IRS appeals, refer to *Stand Up to the IRS*, by Frederick W. Daily (Nolo).

Staying Out of Trouble With the IRS

What Every Home Business Owner Needs to Know About the IRS.............426

  Anatomy of an Audit..426

  The IRS: Clear and Present Danger or Phantom Menace? 428

  You Are the IRS's Number One Target..430

  How Tax Returns Are Selected for Audits...431

Ten Tips for Avoiding an Audit..434

  Tip #1: Be Neat, Thorough, and Exact...434

  Tip #2: Mail Your Return by Certified Mail......................................434

  Tip #3: Don't File Early..435

  Tip #4: Don't File Electronically..435

  Tip #5: Form a Business Entity..436

  Tip #6: Explain Items the IRS Will Question....................................436

  Tip #7: Avoid Ambiguous or General Expenses 437

  Tip #8: Report All of Your Income..437

  Tip #9: Watch Your Income-to-Deduction Ratio..............................437

  Tip #10: Beware of Abnormally Large Deductions 438

Most taxpayers have at least some concern about the possibility of facing an IRS audit. You may be wondering how the IRS decides to audit, how likely it is that you'll be audited, and what you can do to avoid being one of the unlucky ones. This chapter explains IRS audits and provides tips and strategies that will help you avoid attracting the attention of the IRS—or come out of an audit unscathed, if you find yourself in the government's crosshairs.

RESOURCE

Need more information on dealing with the IRS? For a detailed discussion of audits and other IRS procedures, see *Stand Up to the IRS*, by Frederick Daily (Nolo).

What Every Home Business Owner Needs to Know About the IRS

Just as you should never go into battle without knowing your enemy, you should never file a tax return without understanding what the IRS plans to do with it.

Anatomy of an Audit

You can claim any deductions you want to take on your tax return— after all, you (or your tax preparer) fill it out, not the government. However, all the deductions you claim are subject to review by the IRS. This review is called a tax audit. There are three types of audits: correspondence, office, and field audits.

- **Correspondence audits.** As the name indicates, correspondence audits are handled entirely by mail. These are the simplest and shortest type of IRS audit, usually involving a single issue. They are by far the most common type of IRS audit. The IRS sends you written questions about a perceived problem, and may request additional information and/or documentation. If you don't provide satisfactory answers or information, you'll be assessed additional taxes. Correspondence audits are often used to question a home business about unreported income—income the IRS knows the taxpayer received because an IRS Form 1099 listing the payment has been filed by a client or customer.

- **Office audits.** Office audits take place face-to-face with an IRS auditor at one of the 33 IRS district offices. These are more complex than correspondence audits, often involving more than one issue or more than one tax year. If you make less than $100,000 per year, this is the type of in-person audit you're likely to face.

- **Field audits.** The field audit is the most comprehensive IRS audit, conducted by an experienced revenue officer. In a field audit, the officer examines your finances, your business, your tax returns, and the records you used to create the returns. As the name implies, a field audit is normally conducted at the taxpayer's place of business; this allows the auditor to learn as much about your business as possible. Field audits are ordinarily reserved for taxpayers who earn a lot of money. You probably won't be subjected to one unless your home business earns more than $100,000 per year.

How Home Business Owners Get in Trouble With the IRS

When auditing self-employed home business owners, the IRS is most concerned about whether you have:

- **Underreported your income.** Unlike employees who have their taxes withheld, sole proprietor business owners have no withholding—and many opportunities to underreport how much they earn, particularly if they run a cash business.

- **Claimed tax deductions to which you were not entitled.** For example, you claimed that nondeductible personal expenses, such as a personal vacation, were deductible business expenses.

- **Properly documented the amount of your deductions.** If you don't have paperwork to back up the amount of a deduction, the IRS may reduce it, either entirely or in part. Lack of documentation is the main reason small business owners lose deductions when they get audited.

- **Taken business deductions for a hobby.** If you continually lose money, or you are involved in a fun activity such as art, photography, crafts, or writing and don't earn profits every year, the auditor may also question whether you are really in business. If the IRS claims you are engaged in a hobby, you could lose every single deduction for the activity. (See Chapter 2 for more on the hobby loss rule.)

Records Available to Auditors

An IRS auditor is entitled to examine the business records you used to prepare your tax returns, including your books, check registers, canceled checks, and receipts. The auditor can also ask to see records supporting your business tax deductions, such as a mileage record if you took a deduction for business use of your car. The auditor can also get copies of your bank records, either from you or your bank, and check them to see whether your deposits match the income you reported on your tax return. If you deposited a lot more money than you reported earning, the auditor will assume that you didn't report all of your income, unless you can show that the deposits you didn't include in your tax return weren't income. For example, you might be able to show that they were loans, inheritances, or transfers from other accounts. This is why you need to keep good financial records.

The IRS: Clear and Present Danger or Phantom Menace?

A generation ago, the three letters Americans feared most were I-R-S. There was a simple reason for this: The IRS, the nation's tax police, enforced the tax laws like crazy. In 1963, an incredible 5.6% of all Americans had their tax returns audited. Everybody knew someone who had been audited. Jokes about IRS audits were a staple topic of nightclub comedians and cartoonists.

In 2009, only 0.9% of all Americans were audited, and an IRS audit was a relatively rare event. There are several reasons for the change:

- A decline in the IRS workforce: Between 1997 and 2006, the IRS workforce declined by 14%.
- An increase in workload: At the same time the IRS workforce was declining, its workload was increasing. Between 1995 and 2004, the number of returns filed increased 12%, reaching 174 million.
- A new emphasis on taxpayer service, rather than enforcement: Starting in the mid-1990s, the IRS began to emphasize taxpayer service rather than enforcement. Staff was shifted from doing audits to performing service functions like answering taxpayer questions.
- Legal changes: Congress enacted new laws in 1998 that were intended to prevent perceived abuses by IRS agents and auditors. These new protections also made it more difficult for the IRS to go after tax cheats.

According to the IRS Oversight Board, the IRS does not have the resources to pursue at least $30 billion worth of known taxes that are incorrectly reported or not paid. In 2005, the nation's tax gap—the total inventory of taxes that are known and not paid—was estimated at $345 billion.

Both the IRS and the Congress are aware of the IRS's enforcement problems and have taken some steps to ameliorate them. The IRS has received moderate budget increases in the past few years and has placed a renewed emphasis on enforcement. Staff has been shifted from performing service functions like answering taxpayer questions to doing audits.

The precipitous decline in audit rates that began in the mid-1990s has been stopped, but audit rates remain at relatively low levels. However, the IRS Commissioner promises that audit rates will go up in the next few years, with small businesses one of the main targets. With huge federal budget deficits yawning as far as the eye can see, it seems likely that this is one government promise that will be kept.

Aggressive or Dishonest?

Given the relatively low audit rates in recent years, many tax experts say that this is a good time to be aggressive about taking tax deductions. In this context, aggressive means taking every deduction to which you might arguably be entitled. If a deduction falls into a gray area of law, you would decide the question in your favor. This is *tax avoidance*, which is perfectly legal.

However, being aggressive does not mean being dishonest—that is, taking phony deductions that you are clearly not entitled to take or falsely increasing the amount of the deductions to which you are entitled. This is *tax evasion*, which is a crime.

You Are the IRS's Number One Target

Although the IRS is a troubled agency and audit rates are at or near all-time lows, tens of thousands of people still get audited every year. Moreover, the sad fact is that self-employed people, including home business owners, are the IRS's number one target. This is shown by audit rate statistics: In 2011, the IRS audited 277,945 of the 15,442,712 tax returns filed by Schedule C filers—the category that includes 90% of all home business owners.

Every year, the IRS releases statistics about who got audited the previous year. Here are the most recently available audit statistics.

This chart shows that in 2010, 4.7% of sole proprietors earning $100,000 to $200,000 were audited. Not even corporations with assets worth between $5 million and $10 million were audited as often.

These statistics undoubtedly reflect the IRS's belief that sole proprietors habitually underreport their income, take deductions to which they are not entitled, or otherwise cheat on their taxes. The lesson these numbers teach is that you need to take the IRS seriously. This doesn't mean that you shouldn't take all the deductions you're legally entitled to take, but you should understand the rules and be able to back up the deductions you do take with proper records.

IRS Audit Rates		
	2009 Audit Rate	2010 Audit Rate
Sole Proprietors		
Income under $25,000	1.1%	1.2%
$25,000 to $100,000	1.9%	2.5%
$100,000 to $200,000	4.2%	4.7%
over $200,000	3.2%	3.3%
Partnerships	0.4%	0.4%
S Corporations	0.4%	0.4%
C Corporations		
Assets under $250,000	0.7%	0.8%
$250,000 to $1 million	1.3%	1.4%
$1 million to $5 million	1.8%	1.7%
$5 million to $10 million	2.7%	3%

How Tax Returns Are Selected for Audits

It's useful to understand how tax returns are selected for audit by the IRS. (By the way, if you are audited, you are entitled to know why you were selected. You ordinarily have to ask to find out.)

DIF Scores

One way the IRS decides who to audit is by plugging the information from your tax return into a complex formula to calculate a "discriminate function" (DIF) score. Returns with high DIFs have a far higher chance of being flagged for an audit, regardless of whether or not you have done anything obviously wrong. Anywhere from 25% to 60% of audited returns are selected this way.

Exactly how the DIF is calculated is a closely guarded secret. Some of the known factors the formula takes into account are:

- **The nature of your business.** Businesses that deal with large amounts of cash are scrutinized more closely than those that don't.

- **Where you live.** Audit rates differ widely according to where you live. In 2000, for example, taxpayers in Southern California were almost five times more likely to be audited than taxpayers in Georgia. The IRS no longer releases information on audit rates by region, but according to the latest available data, the state with the highest audit rate is Nevada; other high-audit states include Alaska, California, and Colorado. Low-audit states include Illinois, Indiana, Iowa, Maryland, Massachusetts, Michigan, New York (not including Manhattan), Ohio, Pennsylvania, and West Virginia.

- **The amount of your deductions.** Returns with extremely large deductions in relation to income are more likely to be audited. For example, if your tax return shows that your business is earning $25,000, you are more likely to be audited if you claim $20,000 in deductions than if you claim $2,000.

- **Hot-button deductions.** Certain types of deductions have long been thought to be hot buttons for the IRS, especially auto, travel, and entertainment expenses. Casualty losses and bad debt deductions may also increase your DIF score. Some people believe that claiming the home office deduction makes an audit more likely, but the IRS denies this.

- **Businesses that lose money.** Businesses that show losses are more likely to be audited, especially if the losses are recurring. The IRS may suspect that you must be making more money than you are reporting—otherwise, why would you stay in business?

- **Peculiar deductions.** Deductions that seem odd or out of character for your business could increase your DIF score—for example, a plumber who deducts the cost of foreign travel might raise a few eyebrows at the IRS.

- **How you organize your business.** Sole proprietors get higher DIF scores than businesses that are incorporated or owned by partnerships or limited liability companies. As a result, sole proprietors generally are most likely to be audited by the IRS.

Partnerships and small C corporations are ten times less likely to be audited than sole proprietors.

IRS Matching Program

Whenever a client pays you $600 or more for your services during the year, it must report the payments to the IRS on IRS Form 1099. IRS computers match the information on 1099s with the amount of income reported on tax returns, using Social Security and other identifying numbers. Discrepancies usually generate correspondence audits.

Groups Targeted for Audit

Every year, the IRS gives special attention to specific industries or groups of taxpayers that it believes to be tax cheats. Businesses that receive a lot of cash are a perennial audit favorite. Other IRS favorites include doctors, dentists, lawyers, CPAs, and salespeople.

The IRS also targets taxpayers who use certain tax shelters or have offshore bank accounts or trusts. But you don't have to be rich to be an audit target. The IRS also heavily audits low-income taxpayers who claim the earned income tax credit.

Tips and Referrals

You could also get audited as a result of a referral from another government agency, such as your state tax department. The IRS also receives tips from private citizens—for example, a former business partner or ex-spouse.

Bad Luck

A certain number of tax returns are randomly selected for audit every year. If you find yourself in this category, there's not much you can do about it. As long as you have adequate documentation to support your deductions, you should do just fine.

State Tax Audits Grow Increasingly Common

Although most people (and books) focus on IRS audits, audits by state income tax agencies are becoming increasingly common. Many states have increased fines and late-payment penalties. Others have adopted severe—and highly effective—punishments against delinquent taxpayers. For example, some states refuse to issue drivers' licenses to people who owe back taxes. Others are hiring private tax collectors and publishing names of tax evaders online.

Ten Tips for Avoiding an Audit

Here are ten things you can do to minimize your chances of getting audited.

Tip #1: Be Neat, Thorough, and Exact

If you file by mail (as you should), submit a tax return that looks professional; this will help you avoid unwanted attention from the IRS. Your return shouldn't contain erasures or be difficult to read. Your math should be correct. Avoid round numbers on your return (like $100 or $5,000). This looks like you're making up the numbers instead of taking them from accurate records. You should include, and completely fill out, all necessary forms and schedules. Moreover, your state tax return should be consistent with your federal return. If you do your own taxes, using a tax preparation computer program will help you produce an accurate return that looks professional.

Tip #2: Mail Your Return by Certified Mail

Mail your tax return by certified mail, return receipt requested. In case the IRS loses or misplaces your return, your receipt will prove that you submitted it. The IRS also accepts returns from private delivery services including Federal Express, Airborne Express, and United Parcel Service.

Contact these companies for details on which of their service options qualify and how to get proof of timely filing.

Tip #3: Don't File Early

Unless you're owed a substantial refund, you shouldn't file your taxes early. The IRS generally has three years after April 15 to decide whether to audit your return. Filing early just gives the IRS more time to think about whether you should be audited. You can reduce your audit chances even more by getting an automatic extension to file until October 15. (Partnerships and S corporations may receive an automatic extension only until September 15.) Note, however, that filing an extension does not extend the date by which you have to pay any taxes due for the prior year—these must be paid by April 15.

Tip #4: Don't File Electronically

The IRS would like all taxpayers to file their returns electronically— that is, by email. There is a good reason for this: It saves the agency substantial time and money. Every year, the IRS must hire thousands of temp workers to enter the numbers from millions of paper returns into its computer system. This is expensive, so the IRS has only about 40% of the data on paper returns transcribed. The paper returns are then sent to a warehouse where they are kept for six years and then destroyed. The IRS makes its audit decisions based on this transcribed data. By filing electronically, you give the IRS easy access to 100% of the data on your return instead of just 40%. Moreover, if you file electronically, you cannot add written explanations of any deductions the IRS might question (see Tip #6). No one can say for sure whether filing a paper return lessens your chance of an audit, but why make life easier for the IRS if you don't have to? New IRS rules that went into effect in 2011 require professional tax preparers to file their clients' returns electronically unless the client elects to opt out of electronic filing. To opt out, you have to file a special form with your paper tax return. Ask your tax preparer about this.

Tip #5: Form a Business Entity

The audit rate statistics in the table "IRS Audit Rates," above, show that partnerships and small corporations are audited far less often than sole proprietors. In 2010, for example, the IRS audited .40% of partnerships, .40% of S corporations, and only .70% of regular C corporations with assets worth less than $250,000. In contrast, 2.5% of sole proprietors earning $25,000 to $100,000 were audited. Ninety percent of home business owners are sole proprietors, but no law says they have to be. Incorporating your business or forming a limited liability company will greatly reduce your audit risk. However, you must balance this against the time and expense involved in forming a corporation or an LLC. Moreover, in some states—most notably California—corporations and LLCs have to pay additional state taxes.

Tip #6: Explain Items the IRS Will Question

If your return contains an item that the IRS may question or that could increase the likelihood of an audit, include an explanation to help show everything is on the up and up. For example, if your return contains a substantial bad debt deduction, explain the circumstances showing that the debt is a legitimate business expense. This won't necessarily avoid an audit, but it may reduce your chances. Here's why: If the IRS computer gives your return a high DIF score, an IRS classifier screens it to see whether it warrants an audit. If your explanations look reasonable, the screener may decide you shouldn't be audited after all.

Such explanations ("disclosures" in tax parlance) can be made on plain white paper and attached to your return, or you can use special IRS forms. IRS Form 8275, *Disclosure Statement*, can be used to explain or disclose any information that there isn't room to include on your other tax forms. Another IRS form, Form 8275-R, *Regulation Disclosure Statement*, must be used to disclose tax positions that are contrary to IRS regulations or other rules. You shouldn't file Form 8275-R without professional help.

Tip #7: Avoid Ambiguous or General Expenses

Don't list expenses under vague categories such as "miscellaneous" or "general expense." Be specific. IRS Schedule C lists specific categories for the most common small business expenses. If an expense doesn't fall within one of these classifications, create a specific name for it.

Tip #8: Report All of Your Income

The IRS is convinced that self-employed people, including many home business owners, don't report all of their income. Finding such hidden income is a high priority. As mentioned above, IRS computers compare 1099 forms with tax returns to determine whether there are any discrepancies. Not all income home business owners receive is reported to the IRS on Form 1099—for example, if you sell a product to customers rather than providing a service, your receipts will not be reported on Form 1099. However, if you are audited, the auditor may examine your bank records to see whether you received any unreported income.

Tip #9: Watch Your Income-to-Deduction Ratio

Back in the 1990s, a statistics professor named Amir D. Aczel got audited by the IRS. The experience proved so unpleasant that he decided to conduct a statistical study of how and why people get selected for IRS audits. He carefully examined more than 1,200 returns that were audited and reported his findings in a book (now out of print) called *How to Beat the IRS At Its Own Game* (Four Walls Eight Windows, 1995). He concluded that the key factor leading to an audit was the ratio of a taxpayer's expenses to his or her income.

According to Aczel, if your total business expenses amount to less than 52% of your gross business income, you are "not very likely" to be audited. If your business expenses are 52% to 63% of your business income, there is a "relatively high probability" that the IRS computer will tag you for an audit. Finally, if your expenses are more than 63% of your income, Aczel claims you are "certain to be computer tagged for audit." Of course, this doesn't necessarily mean that you *will* be audited. Less than 10% of returns that are computer tagged for audit are actually audited. But being tagged considerably increases the odds that you'll be audited.

Whether Aczel's precise numbers are correct or not is anyone's guess. However, his basic conclusion—that your income-to-deduction ratio is an important factor in determining whether you'll be audited—is undoubtedly true. (A former IRS commissioner admitted as much in a CNN interview in 1995.)

Tip #10: Beware of Abnormally Large Deductions

It is not just the total amount of your deductions that is important. Very large individual deductions can also increase your audit chances. How much is too much? It depends in part on the nature of your business. A $2,000 foreign travel deduction might look abnormal for a plumber, but not for a person in the import-export business.

The Government Accountability Office released a report in 2004 that shows the dollar range for common deductions claimed by sole proprietors in 2001 who earned less than $25,000 from their businesses.

Looking at this chart, you can see that in 2001, the home office deduction ranged from a low of $40 (the amount claimed by taxpayers in the 1st percentile) to a high of $10,130 (the amount claimed by taxpayers in the 99th percentile). The average deduction (mean) was $1,800. The median deduction (half of the sample size claimed more than this number, while the other half claimed less) was $1,120. This tells you that if you claim a $15,000 home office deduction, the IRS will think something is wrong. This does not necessarily mean you will get audited, but it increases your chances. Of course, if you're entitled to a $15,000 home office deduction, you should claim it. But be prepared to back it up with good documentation.

The second chart below shows the amounts for the same deductions claimed in 2001 by sole proprietors who earned $25,000 to $100,000. As you'd expect, these amounts are somewhat higher than the deductions claimed by proprietors who earned less than $25,000. For example, the average home office deduction claimed by these taxpayers was $3,000.

These deductions were claimed back in 2001, so you must correct for inflation when using the charts today. You'd expect these deductions to be about 20%–25% higher for sole proprietors in 2011.

Range of Expenses for Sole Proprietorships With Gross Income Less Than $25,000 (Tax Year 2001)

Expense category	Mean	1st	10th	Median	90th	99th
Advertising	$ 600	$ 10	$ 40	$ 220	$1,200	$ 5,290
Bad debts	1,700	10	50	300	2,020	18,480
Car/truck	2,300	30	190	1,420	5,480	12,530
Commissions	1,600	10	60	440	3,480	14,060
Depletion	1,400	0	70	770	2,850	6,060
Depreciation	2,000	20	130	950	4,560	17,150
Employee benefit programs	2,300	180	310	1,540	4,460	7,300
Insurance	800	20	100	460	1,780	4,830
Interest on mortgage	3,400	10	320	1,840	7,210	25,960
Interest on other business debt	1,800	10	70	480	2,830	11,770
Legal/professional services	400	20	50	160	680	3,790
Office	600	10	40	250	1,360	4,510
Pension/profit sharing plans	1,500	0	10	800	3,480	6,950
Rent on machinery/equipment	1,800	10	100	750	4,810	9,120
Rent on other business property	2,800	30	200	1,990	6,170	13,970
Repairs	900	10	60	370	2,330	7,110
Supplies	1,100	10	70	500	2,710	8,410
Taxes	400	10	30	140	860	2,960
Travel	1,200	20	80	560	2,800	8,520
Meals/entertainment	500	10	30	200	1,140	3,560
Utilities	900	10	110	580	2,030	5,370
Wages	4,500	30	190	1,190	8,000	29,940
Other	2,200	10	110	860	4,480	16,320
Home office	1,800	40	280	1,120	3,900	10,130
All categories	$7,000	$ 60	$ 590	$4,400	$14,970	$36,260

Source: GAO analysis of IRS data

Range of Expenses for Sole Proprietorships With Gross Income From $25,000 to $100,000 (Tax Year 2001)						
Expense category	Mean	1st	10th	Median	90th	99th
Advertising	$1,600	$ 20	$ 80	$ 680	$4,290	$10,920
Bad debts	1,500	20	70	580	2,680	15,530
Car/truck	6,100	100	880	4,200	12,990	30,910
Commissions	5,200	20	140	1,670	13,910	51,330
Depletion	6,000	40	280	4,960	13,780	24,490
Depreciation	4,300	50	330	2,400	9,900	27,870
Employee benefit programs	2,700	90	160	1,830	6,890	10,500
Insurance	1,600	60	250	990	3,610	8,060
Interest on mortgage	4,100	30	410	2,190	9,020	32,400
Interest on other business debt	1,900	10	140	970	4,750	11,910
Legal/professional services	700	40	90	250	1,290	7,820
Office	1,300	20	100	580	3,020	10,150
Pension/profit sharing plans	3,100	0	100	1,170	9,020	10,440
Rent on machinery/ equipment	3,100	20	130	1,260	7,600	21,950
Rent on other business property	6,400	40	600	4,790	14,400	26,610
Repairs	2,200	30	110	900	5,700	18,250
Supplies	3,000	30	180	1,250	7,110	26,840
Taxes	1,000	10	50	400	2,540	7,520
Travel	2,300	30	140	1,070	5,490	17,930
Meals/entertainment	1,000	20	70	500	2,440	6,070
Utilities	2,100	60	370	1,500	4,400	11,690
Wages	10,500	100	750	6,640	26,160	48,090
Other	6,200	40	410	2,880	15,110	45,530
Home office	3,000	110	550	2,060	6,910	12,960
All categories	$26,200	$1,560	$ 7,240	$21,420	$51,140	$90,100

Source: GAO analysis of IRS data

Help Beyond This Book

Secondary Sources of Tax Information 442

   Information From the IRS 443

   Other Online Tax Resources 445

   Tax Publications 446

   Tax Software 449

The Tax Law 449

   Internal Revenue Code 450

   IRS Regulations 452

   Court Cases 452

   IRS Rulings, Interpretations, and Tax Advice 454

Consulting a Tax Professional 457

   Types of Tax Pros 457

   Finding a Tax Pro 458

There are many resources available to supplement and explain more fully the tax information covered in this book. Many of these resources are free; others are reasonably priced. The more expensive tax publications for professionals are often available at public libraries or law libraries—and a lot of tax information is available free on the Internet.

If you have a question about a specific tax deduction or any other tax-related matter, you can:

- consult a secondary tax source
- review the tax law, or
- see a tax professional.

You can do these suggested steps in any order you wish, depending on how much time and money you want to spend. For example, you can see a tax professional right away instead of doing any research yourself. Although this will save you time, it will cost you money.

 RESOURCE

Need more information on legal research? Before you try to research tax law on your own, it's a good idea to learn how to do legal research first. An excellent resource is *Legal Research: How to Find & Understand the Law*, by Stephen Elias and Susan Levinkind (Nolo). You can also find information at Nolo's website at www.nolo.com.

Secondary Sources of Tax Information

You might think that the easiest place to find answers to your tax questions is in the tax code—after all, that's where the actual laws are collected. However, the tax code can be dry and difficult to decipher—particularly if you're trying to figure out how a particular law or rule applies to your situation. Instead of diving right into the code books, your best bet is usually to start with one of the many secondary sources that try to make the tax law more understandable.

Unlike the primary sources listed in "The Tax Law," below, these sources are not the law itself or the IRS's official pronouncements on the law. Instead, they are interpretations and explanations of the law, which are intended to make it more understandable to those who aren't tax experts. Often, you'll be able to find the answer to your question in one or more of these sources. You can also learn about topics not covered in this book—for example, what constitutes income for tax purposes, how to complete your tax returns, or how to deal with an IRS audit.

Information From the IRS

The IRS has made a huge effort to inform the public about the tax law, creating hundreds of informative publications, an excellent website, and a telephone answering service. However, unlike the regulations and rulings issued by the IRS, these secondary publications and assistance are for informational purposes only. They are not official IRS pronouncements, and the IRS is not legally bound by them.

Reading IRS publications is a useful way to get information on IRS procedures and learn how the agency views the tax law. But keep in mind that these publications only present the IRS's interpretation of the law, which may be different from how a court might rule on the same issue. That's why you shouldn't rely exclusively on IRS publications for information.

IRS Website

The IRS has one of the most useful websites of any federal government agency. Among other things, almost every IRS form and informational publication can be downloaded from the site. The Internet address is www.irs.gov.

The IRS website has a special section for small businesses and the self-employed, categories that include virtually all home businesses (www.irs.gov/businesses/small/index.html). It includes:

- answers to basic tax questions and a calendar of tax deadlines
- online access to most IRS forms and information booklets
- industry-specific tax information for certain industries like construction and child care
- tips on how to avoid common tax problems

- announcements of new IRS policies and procedures of particular interest to small businesses
- links to court opinions and to rulings and regulations on specific industries
- links to non-IRS sites for general tax information, and
- links to helpful small business resources.

IRS Booklets

The IRS publishes over 350 free booklets explaining the tax code, called IRS Publications ("Pubs," for short). Many of these publications are referenced in this book. Some are relatively easy to understand, others are incomprehensible or misleading. As with all IRS publications, they only present the IRS's interpretation of the tax laws—which may or may not be upheld by the federal courts.

You can download all of the booklets from the IRS website at www. irs.gov.

IRS Telephone Information

The IRS offers a series of prerecorded tapes of information on various tax topics on a toll-free telephone service called TELETAX (800-829-4477). See IRS Publication 910, *Guide to Free Tax Services,* for a list of topics.

You can talk to an IRS representative on the telephone by calling 800-829-1040. (It is difficult to get though to someone from January through May.) Be sure to double check anything an IRS representative tells you over the phone—the IRS is notorious for giving misleading or outright wrong answers to taxpayers' questions, and the agency will not stand behind oral advice that turns out to be incorrect.

Videos

The IRS also has a number of informational videos available for online viewing at its own YouTube channel at www.youtube.com/IRSVideos.

Free IRS Programs

In larger metropolitan areas, the IRS offers small business seminars on various topics, such as payroll tax reporting. You can ask questions at these half-day meetings, which are often held at schools or federal buildings. Call the IRS at 800-829-1040 to find out whether programs are offered near you and to get on the IRS small business mailing list. The IRS also has an online tax workshop for small businesses; you can find it at the online classroom on the IRS website. You can also order a free CD-ROM with a video presentation of the workshop through the IRS website.

Other Online Tax Resources

In addition to the IRS website, there are hundreds of privately created websites on the Internet that provide tax information and advice. Some of this information is good; some is execrable. A comprehensive collection of Web links about all aspects of taxation can be found at: www.taxsites.com. Here are some other pages listing links to sites that offer tax information:

Some useful tax-related websites include:
- www.accountantsworld.com (Accountants World website)
- www.unclefed.com (Uncle Fed's Tax Board website)
- www.smbiz.com/sbwday.html (Small Business Taxes & Management website)
- http://taxes.alltop.com/ (Alltop tax aggregator).

Nolo's Website

Nolo maintains a website that is useful for small businesses and the self-employed. The site contains helpful articles, information about new legislation, book excerpts, and the Nolo catalog. The site also includes a legal encyclopedia with specific information for businesspeople, as well as a legal research center you can use to find state and federal statutes, including the Internal Revenue Code. The Internet address is www.nolo.com.

Tax Publications

If you like to read books, you'll be happy to know that there are enough books about tax law to fill a library. Tax publications vary from the broadly focused to the highly detailed. You can find answers to most tax questions in one or more of these resources.

Publications for the Nonexpert

There are many books (like this one) that attempt to make the tax law comprehensible to the average person. The best known are the paperback tax preparation books published every year. These books emphasize individual taxes, but also have useful information for small businesses. Two of the best are:
- *The Ernst & Young Tax Guide* (John Wiley & Sons), and
- *J.K. Lasser's Your Income Tax* (John Wiley & Sons).

J.K. Lasser publishes other useful tax guides, many of which are targeted at small businesses. You can find a list of these publications at: www.wiley.com (search "small business taxes").

Tax guides designed for college courses can also be extremely helpful. Two good guides to all aspects of income taxes that are updated each year are:
- *Prentice Hall's Federal Taxation Comprehensive* (Prentice Hall), and
- *CCH Federal Taxation Comprehensive Topics* (Commerce Clearing House).

Nolo also publishes several books that deal with tax issues:
- *Tax Deductions for Professionals*, by Stephen Fishman (Nolo), covers deductions for those with professional practices, such as doctors, lawyers, architects, dentists, and others.
- *Easy Ways to Lower Your Taxes*, by Sandra Block and Stephen Fishman (Nolo), is a guide to tax planning for both business owners and non-owners.
- *Stand Up to the IRS*, by Frederick W. Daily (Nolo), explains how to handle an IRS audit.

- *Tax Savvy for Small Business*, by Frederick W. Daily (Nolo), provides an overview of the entire subject of taxation, geared to the small business owner.
- *Working With Independent Contractors*, by Stephen Fishman (Nolo), shows small businesses how to hire independent contractors without running afoul of the IRS or other government agencies.
- *Working for Yourself*, by Stephen Fishman (Nolo), covers the whole gamut of legal issues facing the one-person business.
- *IRAs, 401(k)s & Other Retirement Plans: Taking Your Money Out*, by Twila Slesnick and John C. Suttle (Nolo), covers the tax implications of withdrawing funds from retirement accounts.
- *Every Landlord's Tax Deduction Guide*, by Stephen Fishman (Nolo), provides detailed guidance on tax deductions for small residential landlords.
- *The Real Estate Agent's Tax Deduction Guide*, by Stephen Fishman (Nolo).

Publications for Tax Professionals

You may have a question that you can't answer by looking at websites or tax publications for the layperson. In this event, you can consult one or more publications for tax professionals—accountants, CPAs, and attorneys. These are the most detailed and comprehensive secondary sources available.

There are six main publishing companies that publish reference materials for tax professionals:

- Business News Association (BNA); www.bna.com
- Commerce Clearing House (CCH); www.cch.com
- Kleinrock Publishing
- Research Institute of America (RIA); www.riahome.com
- Tax Analysts; www.taxanalysts.com, and
- West Group; http://west.thomson.com.

These publishers produce an incredible volume of tax information, ranging from detailed analyses of the most arcane tax questions to brief, one-volume guides to the entire federal tax law. Among their publications are:

Tax Services. These are highly detailed discussions of the tax law, organized by I.R.C. section or topic and updated frequently—every week, or at least every month. The most authoritative is *The Law of Federal Income Taxation*, published by West Group (it's also called "Mertens" by tax professionals because it was originally edited by Jacob Mertens). Other tax services include the *United States Tax Reporter* (published by RIA) and *Standard Federal Tax Reporter* (published by CCH).

Tax Treatises. Tax treatises provide in-depth, book-length treatment of a particular tax topic. Among the most useful are the *Tax Management Portfolios*, a series of paperback booklets published by BNA. If you're looking for information on a very precise tax issue, you might find what you need in a portfolio.

Tax Citators. Tax citators summarize tax cases and compile and organize them by subject matter and I.R.C. section. By using a citator, you can find all the tax cases that have addressed a specific tax topic. Both CCH and RIA publish citators.

Tax Deskbooks. CCH publishes a well-known one-volume tax deskbook called the *Master Tax Guide* that provides an overview of the tax law. It's updated each year.

You can find a good discussion on how to use these tax materials in *West's Federal Tax Research* (South-Western College Publishing).

All of these publications are available in print form, on CD-ROMs, and on subscriber websites (notably, Westlaw and Lexis, subscriber databases containing legal information). As you might expect, they are generally very expensive. You can also find them in a law library, some large public libraries, or a tax professional's office.

Trade Association Publications

There are hundreds of trade associations and organizations representing every conceivable occupation—for example, the American Society of Home Inspectors, the Association of Independent Video and Film-makers, and the Graphic Artists Guild. Most of these have specialized publications and newsletters that track tax issues of common interest. You can learn about specific tax issues in your industry that even your tax professional might not know about—perhaps a new case or IRS ruling. Also, you can often find speakers on tax topics at programs offered to members at conventions and trade shows.

If you don't know the name and address of an association relevant to your business, ask other businesspeople in your field. Or check out the *Encyclopedia of Associations* (Gale Research); it should be available at your public library. Also, many of these associations have websites on the Internet, so you may be able to find the one you want by doing an Internet search.

Tax Software

Today, millions of taxpayers use tax preparation software to complete their own income tax returns. The best-known programs are *TurboTax* and *TaxCut*. These programs contain most IRS tax forms, publications, and other tax guidance. Both have helpful websites—www.turbotax. com and www.taxcut.com.

The Tax Law

If you can't find an answer to your question in a secondary source, you might be able to find help in the tax law itself. Or, you may want to consult the tax law to verify (or clarify) what you've learned from secondary sources.

The tax law of the United States comes from several sources:
- the Internal Revenue Code
- IRS regulations
- court cases, and
- IRS rulings, interpretations, and tax advice.

Every branch of the federal government is involved in creating the tax law. The Internal Revenue Code is enacted by Congress (the legislative branch), IRS regulations and rulings are issued by the IRS (a department of the executive branch), and taxpayers may appeal the IRS's actions to the federal courts (the judicial branch).

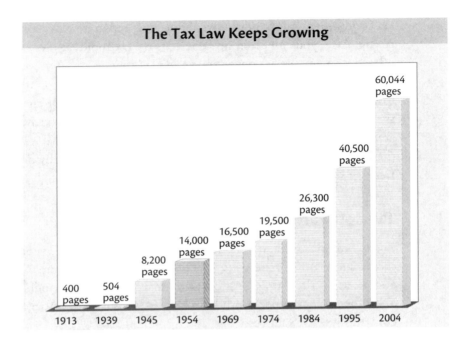

The Tax Law Keeps Growing

	Number of pages
The Tax Law Versus *War and Peace*	
Internal Revenue Code	3,653
IRS Regulations	13,079
War and Peace, by Leo Tolstoy	1,444

Internal Revenue Code

The Internal Revenue Code (I.R.C.) is the supreme tax law of the land. The I.R.C. (also called "the code" or "the tax code") is written, and frequently rewritten, by Congress. The first tax code, adopted in 1913, contained 14 pages. Today, the tax code is more than 3,500 pages long.

The I.R.C. is found in Title 26 of the United States Code (USC, for short). The USC encompasses all of our federal laws. "Title" simply refers to the place within the massive USC where the I.R.C. is found.

The entire tax code covers income taxes, Social Security taxes, excise taxes, estate and gift taxes, and tax procedure. It is organized by category and broken down into subtitles, chapters, subchapters, parts, subparts, sections, subsections, paragraphs, subparagraphs, and clauses. The income tax laws are in Chapter 1 of Subtitle A of the Tax Code. Most of the laws dealing with tax deductions are found in Parts VI and VII of Subchapter B of Chapter 1.

For our purposes, the most important thing to remember about the organization of the tax code is that each specific tax law is contained in a separate numbered section. For example, Section 179 covers first-year expensing of long-term business assets. For the sake of convenience, tax professionals will often refer to these numbered sections of the tax code.

> EXAMPLE: "I.R.C. § 179(b)(4)(A)" means that this particular tax law is found in Title 26 of the USC (the Internal Revenue Code), Section 179, Subsection b, Paragraph 4, Subparagraph A.

The tax code is published each year in a two-volume set (usually in paperback). You should be able to find it in the reference section of any public library. You can also purchase a set from various tax publishers, such as Commerce Clearing House and Research Institute of America. A complete set of the tax code costs more than $80. You can also purchase a one-volume abridged version for much less. This will likely contain all the tax code provisions you'll want to read. The entire United States Code (including the I.R.C.) is also available on CD-ROM from the Government Printing Office for less than $40.

Fortunately, the I.R.C. is available free on the Internet. You can get to the entire I.R.C. from Nolo's website at www.nolo.com. Portions are also available on the IRS website (www.irs.gov) and several other websites, including www.legalbitstream.com.

CAUTION

Make sure your tax code is current. The I.R.C. is amended every year; in recent years, these amendments have made major changes to the law. Make sure that any copy of the I.R.C. you use in your research is current.

IRS Regulations

Even though the Internal Revenue Code contains over 3,600 pages, it does not provide adequate guidance for every situation that arises in real life. To supplement the I.R.C., the IRS issues regulations, called "Treasury Regulations," "Regulations," or "Regs." Although written by the IRS, not Congress, these regulations have almost the same authoritative weight as the tax code itself.

While the tax code is usually written in broad and general terms, the regulations get down and dirty, providing details about how tax code provisions are intended to operate in the real world. Regulations are slightly easier to read than the tax code on which they are based and often include examples that can be helpful. The regulations cover many (but not all) of the tax code provisions.

To see if a particular I.R.C. section is supplemented by a regulation, start with the number of the I.R.C. section. If there is a corresponding regulation, it will bear the same number, usually preceded by the number "1."

> EXAMPLE: "Reg. 1.179" refers to a Treasury regulation interpreting I.R.C. § 179.

The regulations are published in a multivolume set by the Government Printing Office and tax publishers such as CCH and RIA. These are available in law libraries and in some large public libraries. You can download many (though not all) regulations from the IRS website and from the website www.legalbitstream.com.

Court Cases

When a dispute arises between a taxpayer and the IRS, the taxpayer may take the matter to federal court. The courts are the final arbiters of tax disputes. A court may overrule the IRS if the court concludes that the IRS applied the tax code in a manner contrary to the United States Constitution or differently from what Congress intended.

Tax disputes are tried in three different courts: a special tax court that handles only tax disputes; the regular federal trial courts (called

U.S. District Courts); and the Court of Federal Claims. If either the taxpayer or the IRS doesn't like the outcome of the trial, it may appeal to the federal appellate courts (called the U.S. Courts of Appeals), and even to the U.S. Supreme Court.

Decisions of these courts are published, along with explanations and discussions of the tax law. These court decisions provide valuable interpretations of the tax laws. Many, but not all, of these court interpretations are binding on the IRS. Thousands of court decisions dealing with tax law have been published, so chances are good that there is at least one decision on the issue that interests you.

To locate a published court decision, you must understand how to read a case citation. A citation provides the names of the people or companies involved on each side of the case, the volume of the legal publication (called a reporter) in which the case can be found, the page number on which it begins, and the year in which the case was decided. Here is an example of what a legal citation looks like: *Smith v. Jones*, 123 F.3d 456 (1995). Smith and Jones are the names of the people in the legal dispute. The case is reported in Volume 123 of the Federal Reporter, Third Series, beginning on page 456; the court issued the decision in 1995.

Opinions by the federal district courts are in a series of reporters called the Federal Supplement, abbreviated as F.Supp. Any case decided by a federal court of appeals is found in a series of books called the Federal Reporter. Older cases are contained in the first series of the Federal Reporter, or F. More recent cases are contained in the second or third series of the Federal Reporter, F.2d or F.3d. Cases decided by the U.S. Supreme Court are found in three publications: United States Reports (identified as U.S.), the Supreme Court Reporter (identified as S.Ct.), and the Supreme Court Reports, Lawyer's Edition (identified as L.Ed.). Supreme Court case citations often refer to all three publications.

Many, but not all, of these legal decisions are available free on the Internet. Tax court decisions and tax decisions from other courts, from 1990 to date, can be accessed for free at www.legalbitstream.com. Tax court decisions from 1999 on can also be accessed at www.ustaxcourt .gov. The website www.findlaw.com contains links to all types of law-related websites. Virtually all legal decisions are available on the subscriber websites Lexis.com and Westlaw.com. You may be able to access these websites through a library or tax professional's office.

Hard copies of published decisions by the United States Tax Court can be found in the Tax Court Reports, or TC, published by the U.S. Government Printing Office. You can also find tax court decisions in a reporter called Tax Court Memorandum Decisions, or TCM, published by Commerce Clearing House, Inc. You can find tax decisions from all federal courts in a reporter called U.S. Tax Cases, or USTC, published by Commerce Clearing House, Inc. These are available in law libraries.

For a detailed discussion of how to research court cases, see *Legal Research: How to Find & Understand the Law*, by Stephen Elias and Susan Levinkind (Nolo), or go to Nolo's website at www.nolo.com.

IRS Rulings, Interpretations, and Tax Advice

It might seem like the tax code, regulations, and court decisions would provide everything anyone ever wanted to know about tax law. But even more IRS guidance is available. The IRS publishes several types of statements (besides Regs) of its position on various tax matters. These pronouncements guide IRS personnel and taxpayers as to how the IRS will apply specific tax laws.

Unlike the tax code and regulations, these statements do not have the force of law. Rather, they are the IRS's own interpretation of the tax law, which is not necessarily binding on the courts (or on you, should you choose to challenge the IRS's interpretation in court). However, they give you a good idea of how the IRS would handle the situation involved.

Revenue Rulings

IRS Revenue Rulings (Rev. Rul.) are IRS announcements of how the tax law applies to a hypothetical set of facts. The IRS publishes over 100 of these rulings every year. These rulings represent the IRS's view of the tax law, and the IRS presumes that they are correct. If an auditor discovers that you have violated a revenue ruling, you will probably have to pay additional tax. On the other hand, if you can show an auditor that a revenue ruling supports your position, you probably won't have to pay more tax. Even if you have violated a revenue ruling, all is not necessarily lost. Revenue rulings are not binding on the courts, which can (and do) disregard them from time to time. Thus, it's possible you could win your case on appeal even if a revenue ruling goes against you.

You can download free copies of all IRS Revenue Rulings from 1954 to date from: www.taxlinks.com. Revenue rulings also appear in the weekly *Internal Revenue Cumulative Bulletin*, which is published by the U.S. Government Printing Office. Tax book publishers Prentice-Hall, Commerce Clearing House, and Research Institute of America also reprint IRS Revenue Rulings. They are indexed by I.R.C. section and subject matter.

> **EXAMPLE:** "Rev. Rul. 03-41" refers to IRS Revenue Ruling number 41, issued in 2003.

Revenue Procedures

Revenue procedures ("Rev. Procs.") are IRS announcements dealing with procedural aspects of tax practice. Rev. Procs. are used primarily by tax return preparers. They often explain when and how to report tax items, such as how to claim a net operating loss on a tax form or return. You can obtain free copies of many revenue procedures at www.legalbitstream.com. Revenue procedures are contained in the weekly *Internal Revenue Cumulative Bulletin*, which you can find in larger public and law libraries, and also are reprinted by tax book publishers and on the IRS website.

> **EXAMPLE:** "Rev. Proc. 99-15" refers to a published Revenue Procedure number 15, issued in 1999.

Letter Rulings

IRS letter rulings are IRS answers to specific written questions from taxpayers about complex tax situations. The only person who is entitled to rely on the ruling as legal authority is the taxpayer to whom the ruling is addressed; even if you find yourself in a similar position, the IRS is not legally required to follow the guidance it gave in the letter. However, letter rulings offer valuable insight into the IRS's position on tax treatment of complex transactions. Since 1976, letter rulings have been made available to the general public. You can access free copies of many letter rulings at www.legalbitstream.com.

> EXAMPLE: "Ltr. Ruling 9913043 (April 3, 1999)" refers to a letter ruling issued on April 3, 1999. The first two numbers of the seven-digit identifier show the year it was issued, the next two indicate the week of the year, and the last three show the ruling for that week. Thus, this letter ruling was the 43rd issued during the 13th week of 1999.

IRS General Guidance

From time to time, the IRS gives general guidance and statements of policy in official announcements and notices similar to press releases. You can access many of these for free at www.legalbitstream.com. They appear in the weekly *Internal Revenue Cumulative Bulletin*. It usually doesn't pay to search IRS announcements or notices because they are too broad to answer specific questions.

Internal Revenue Manual

The *Internal Revenue Manual* (IRM) is a series of handbooks that serve as guides to IRS employees on tax law and procedure. The IRM tells IRS employees (usually auditors or collectors) how specific tax code provisions should be enforced. The manual is for IRS internal use, but most of it is public and reprinted by private tax book publishers. It is available to the public in the Freedom of Information Act reading rooms of larger IRS offices, and in law libraries and some tax professionals' offices. Portions of the IRM are also available on the IRS website.

The IRM is revealing of IRS attitudes in certain areas—for example, Section 4.10.3 of the *Manual* describes the techniques IRS auditors are supposed to use when they examine the depreciation deductions claimed by a business.

IRS Forms and Instructions

IRS forms are well known to us all, especially Form 1040, the annual personal income tax return. There are more than 650 other IRS forms, listed at www.irs.gov/formspub/index.html. You can get them free at IRS offices or by calling 800-829-FORM or 800-829-1040. You can also download them from the IRS website, www.irs.gov. Many IRS forms come with instructions and explanations of the tax law.

Consulting a Tax Professional

You don't have to do your own tax research. There are hundreds of thousands of tax professionals (tax pros) in the United States ready and eager to help you—for a price. A tax pro can answer your questions, provide guidance to help you make key tax decisions, prepare your tax returns, and help you deal with the IRS if you get into tax trouble.

Types of Tax Pros

There are several different types of tax pros. They differ widely in training, experience, and cost.

- **Tax preparers.** As the name implies, tax preparers prepare tax returns. The largest tax preparation firm is H & R Block, but many mom-and-pop operations open for business in store-front offices during tax time. In most states, anybody can be a tax preparer; no licensing is required. However, the IRS is now requiring paid tax preparers other than CPAs, enrolled agents, or attorneys, to register with the IRS. Starting in 2011, registered preparers will also be required to take continuing education courses and pass a competency exam. Nevertheless, most tax preparers don't have the training or experience to handle taxes for businesses and, therefore, are probably not a wise choice for tax preparation services or advice. A 2006 study by the Government Accountability Office underscores this. Posing as taxpayers, GAO investigators visited 19 outlets of several unidentified commercial tax-preparation firms and asked them to prepare returns based on two hypothetical situations. The 19 preparers arrived at the correct refund amount only twice. The GAO said that several of the preparers gave very bad tax advice, particularly when it came to reporting business income.

- **Enrolled agents.** Enrolled agents (EAs) are tax advisers and preparers who are licensed by the IRS. They must have at least five years of experience or pass a difficult IRS test. They can represent taxpayers before the IRS, and in administrative proceedings, circuit court, and, possibly, tax court, if they pass the appropriate tests. Enrolled agents are the least expensive of the true tax pros but are reliable for tax return preparation and more routine tax matters. They can be quite adequate for many home businesses.

- **Certified public accountants.** Certified public accountants (CPAs) are licensed and regulated by each state. They undergo lengthy training and must pass a comprehensive exam. CPAs represent the high end of the tax pro spectrum. In addition to preparing tax returns, they perform sophisticated accounting and tax work. CPAs are found in large national firms or in small local outfits. The large national firms are used primarily by large businesses. Some states also license public accountants. These are competent, but are not as highly regarded as CPAs.

- **Tax attorneys.** Tax attorneys are lawyers who specialize in tax matters. The only time you'll ever need a tax attorney is if you get into serious trouble with the IRS or another tax agency and need legal representation before the IRS or in court. Some tax attorneys also give tax advice, but they are usually too expensive for home businesses. You're probably better off hiring a CPA if you need specialized tax help.

Finding a Tax Pro

The best way to find a tax pro is to obtain referrals from business associates, friends, or professional associations. If none of these sources can give you a suitable lead, try contacting the National Association of Enrolled Agents or one of its state affiliates. You can find a listing of affiliates at the NAEA website at www.naea.org. Local CPA societies can give you referrals to local CPAs. You can also find tax pros in the telephone book under "Accountants, Tax Return." Local bar associations can refer you to a tax attorney. Be aware that CPA societies and local bar associations refer from a list on a rotating basis, so you shouldn't construe a referral as a recommendation or certification of competence.

Your relationship with your tax pro will be one of your most important business relationships, so be picky about the person you choose. Talk with at least three tax pros before hiring one. You want a tax pro who takes the time to listen to you, answers your questions fully and in plain English, seems knowledgeable, and makes you feel comfortable. Make sure the tax pro works frequently with small businesses. It can also be helpful if the tax pro already has clients in businesses similar to yours. A tax pro already familiar with the tax problems posed by your type of business can often give you the best advice for the least money.

Index

A

Abandoned business property, 83
Accelerated depreciation, 106, 107–109
Accountable plans, 171, 203, 262–265, 267
Accountants, 2, 458, 459
Accounting fees, 48, 56, 61, 367
Accounting methods, 404–412
    accrual method, 243, 346–347, 405,
       409–412
    cash method, 56, 346, 347, 405–408,
       410–412
    changing, 411
    overview of, 404–405, 411–412
    personal and business differing, 405
    12-month rule, 407–408
Accrual accounting method, 243, 346–347,
    405, 409–412
Actual expense method
    auto expenses, 183–185, 198, 200, 201,
       360, 364, 392–393
    meal expenses, 225–226
    See also Vehicle depreciation
Adjusted basis, 83, 187–188
Adjusted gross income (AGI), 35, 267, 287,
    329
ADS (Alternative Depreciation System),
    106, 110
Advertising
    expense deductions, 48, 65, 159, 341–343
    as proof of start date, 52
AGI (adjusted gross income), 35, 267, 287,
    329
Allocation rules, loan proceeds, 365–366
Alternative Depreciation System (ADS),
    106, 110

Amended returns, 415–424
    capital gains taxes on home office portion
       of home, 152
    how to complete form and file, 423–424
    IRS audits and, 416–417, 424
    net operating losses (NOLs), 417–419,
       422, 424–425
    reasons for, 416–420
    refund claims processing, 424
    Section 179 deduction claims, 93
    time limits for filing, 420–423
Amortization, 53, 111, 113
Appointment books, record keeping with,
    229, 377–379, 388, 391–392, 397–399
Assets. *See* Long-term assets
Athletic club dues, 169
Attorneys, tax, 458, 459
Audits, IRS. *See* IRS audits
Audits, state, 434
Autos. *See* Cars

B

Bad debts, 343–349
    amended return for, 422–423
    requirements to deduct, 343–345
    types of, 346–349
Bank accounts, 32, 61, 375–377, 385–386,
    387
Bar exam fees, 69
Barns, 85, 123, 133
Basis. *See* Tax basis
Behavior test, 29–34
Benefits. *See* Fringe benefits
Bicycles, 183, 201
Bonus depreciation

heavy weight vehicles, 195
how to calculate, 98–100
overview of, 95–100
passenger automobiles, 189, 190, 192–193
Section 179 deduction vs., 75–76
when not to use, 102–103
Bookkeeping, 259, 375, 382–384
Borden, Linda, 26
Business, legal forms of
    audit rates, 431, 436
    overview of, 7–11
    tax treatment, 11–14
    See also Corporations; Limited liability
        companies (LLCs); Partnerships; Sole
        proprietorships
Business assets. *See* Long-term assets
Business cards, 33, 52
Business checking accounts, 32, 61,
    375–377, 385–386, 387
Business credit cards, 364, 377, 386, 393,
    395, 397
Business deductions, 5
Business equipment, 64, 85, 93–94, 105,
    144, 149
    See also Computers and peripheral
        equipment
Businesses
    hobby loss rule, 6, 24–25, 28, 34–35,
        375, 428
    income-producing activities vs., 35–43
    making sure you are in business, 6,
        125–126
    multiple businesses, 115, 125–126, 290
    proving you are in business, 24–34,
        155–156
    start date, 51–53
    that never begin, 55–56
    See also Existing businesses
Business expenses
    average/range of deductions for, 21,
        438–440
    categories of, 14–16, 380–381, 383

direct expenses, 142, 149, 150
indirect expenses, 142–143, 145–147, 149,
    150
prepaying, 370, 407–408, 412
See also Inventory; Long-term assets;
    Operating expenses; Start-up expenses
Business licenses, 33, 48, 61, 372
Business loans, 61, 347–349, 361, 362–363,
    364–366
Business owners
    as employees, 276–278, 292–293
    spouses as, 9–10, 296
Business plans, 32
Business travel expenses, 205–231
    for businesses that never begin, 55
    business purpose requirement, 211–213,
        229
    calculating time spent on business,
        223–225, 229–230
    conventions, 222–223
    deductible expenses, 214–216
    destination vs. transportation expenses, 214
    entertainment expenses, 214
    expenses reimbursed by clients/customers,
        214, 230–231
    how to maximize deductions, 228–230
    independent contractors, 280–281
    IRS audits, 229, 432
    meal expenses, 159–160, 214, 225–228
    per diem rates, 226–228, 264–265
    record keeping, 225, 229, 280, 393–399,
        400
    sandwich day rule, 230
    ship travel, 223
    tax home and, 207–211
    travel outside U.S., 218–223, 226, 227
    travel with family or employees, 215–216,
        272
    travel within U.S., 217–218, 220, 222,
        227
    trips qualifying as business travel,
        206–213, 357

See also Car and local travel expenses
Buying existing businesses, 50, 53, 55–56, 362–363

C

C (regular) corporations
  audit rates, 431, 433, 436
  business owners as employees, 276–278
  deduction for health insurance, 292–293
  disability insurance, 293
  HSA-qualified health insurance plan, 312
  HSAs for employees, 318
  inventory costs deduction, 245
  overview of, 13–14
  renting home office to, 136–137
  S corporations vs., 8
Cafeteria benefit plans, 266
Calendars, record keeping with, 229, 377–379, 388, 391–392, 397–399
California, parental leave program, 258
Capital expenses
  current expenses vs., 63–64, 73–74, 76–78
  overview of, 15
  See also Long-term assets
Capital gains taxes, 42, 151–152, 349
Car and local travel expenses, 175–204
  actual expense method, 183–185, 198, 200, 201, 360, 364, 392–393
  commuting expenses, 179, 197, 201, 389
  corporation employees, 176, 203
  how to maximize deduction, 199–201
  IRS audits, 176, 202
  IRS requirements for deducting, 176–179
  before new business starts, 177
  record keeping, 176, 200–201, 388–393
  reimbursed by clients/customers, 203–204
  standard mileage rate, 179–182, 198, 199, 265, 360
  tax reporting, 201–203

  transportation other than by car, 201
  trips from your office, 147, 178–179
  See also Cars; Vehicle depreciation
Cars
  claiming car used solely for business, 389
  company cars, 261
  converted from personal to business use, 188
  credit card for expenses, 364
  driven by other people, 177–178
  electric cars, 189
  fair market value, 188, 199
  insurance costs, 360
  interest on car loans, 181, 202, 362, 420–421
  leasing, 197–199
  luxury cars, 199
  mileage and expense records, 388–393
  passenger automobile definition, 185–186
  repairs and improvements, 196–197
  used for both business and personal purposes, 181, 186, 190, 191, 193, 261
  using two, for business, 200
  See also Car and local travel expenses; Vehicle depreciation
Case citations, 453
Case law, 452–454
Cash accounting method, 56, 346, 347, 405–408, 410–412
Casualty losses, 146, 349–353, 418, 420
Cell phones, 33, 144, 401
Certified public accountants (CPAs), 458, 459
Charitable contributions, 353–354
Checking accounts, business, 32, 61, 375–377, 385–386
Checks
  as proof of deduction, 384, 385–386
  written for cash, 377
Child labor laws, 270
Children
  business travel with, 215–216

as employees, 268–271, 272–276, 302
health insurance, 293, 296, 297
lifetime learning credit, 358
medical reimbursement plans, 301, 302
salaries, 273–274
Classifying workers, 248–251
Clients or customers
bad debts from credit sales to, 347
entertainment expenses split with, 167
expenses reimbursed by, 171–172,
203–204, 214, 230–231
met at home office, 133, 146
travel to meet, 147, 224–225
Closing your business, 53–54
Cohan rule, 403–404
Community property states, 9, 10
Commuting expenses, 179, 197, 201, 389
Company cars, 261
Computers and peripheral equipment
depreciating, 88, 103, 106–107, 110
home office deduction, 146–147
as listed property, 80
as long-term asset, 74, 80
record keeping rules, 147, 400–401
Section 179 deduction, 85, 88
supplied to employees, 261
Computer software
for bookkeeping, 259, 382–384
computerized calendars, 377–378
depreciating, 111–112
for expense journals, 379, 382–384
Section 179 deduction, 85
tax preparation software, 2, 115, 383, 449
Conditional sales contracts, 118–119,
198–199
Condominium association fees, 146
Constructive receipt, cash accounting
method, 406
Convention expenses
entertainment expenses, 161, 166
nondeductible expenses, 37
reimbursing employees for, 262–263

travel to, 212, 222–223, 230
Conventions, depreciation, 103–106, 107,
108, 109, 193
Co-ownership, spouses in, 9–10, 296
Copyright depreciation, 85, 102, 113
Corporation employees
business expense deduction for health
insurance, 292–293
business owners as, 276–278, 292–293
Health Savings Accounts (HSAs), 318
home office deduction, 135, 153
local travel deduction, 176, 203
reimbursed for business expenses, 153
Corporations
business checking accounts, 375–376
business owners as employees, 276–278,
292–293
deducting costs of forming, 49
deducting general start-up costs, 56
franchise taxes, 371
income-producing activities expenses, 37
loans or guarantees to, 348–349
overview of, 8
reporting entertainment expenses, 173
See also C (regular) corporations;
Corporation employees; S (small
business) corporations
Correspondence audits, 426–427
Cost method, valuing inventory, 243–244
Cost of goods sold, 240–241, 245–246, 347
Country club dues, 69, 169, 354
Court cases, 452–454
Crafts businesses, 31, 51, 234, 235
Credit cards, business, 364, 377, 386, 393,
395, 397
Current expenses
capital expenses vs., 73–74, 76–78
overview of, 63–64
See also Operating expenses
Customers. *See* Clients or customers

D

Date business begins, 51–53

Day care centers, 135, 139

Day planners, record keeping with, 229, 377–379, 388, 391–392, 397–399

Day traders, 40–41

Defined benefit Keogh plans, 334, 337

Defined contribution Keogh plans, 334–335, 337

De minimis (minor) fringe benefits, 260

Dental expenses or insurance, 287, 288, 290, 298, 300, 303, 315

Depreciation, 100–114

    Alternative Depreciation System (ADS), 106, 110

    computer software, 111–112

    defined, 100

    first-year depreciation, 103–104, 106

    half-year convention, 103–104, 193–194

    home office, 112–113, 145

    intangible assets, 113–114

    listed property, 109–110

    long-term assets, 75–76

    midquarter convention, 104–106

    Modified Accelerated Cost Recovery System (MACRS), 106, 110

    real property, 76, 112–113

    tax reporting and record keeping, 115–116

    when begins/ends, 81–82

    when to use, 101, 102

    See also Bonus depreciation; Vehicle depreciation

Depreciation methods, 106–109

    accelerated depreciation, 106, 107–109

    150% declining balance depreciation, 194

    overview of, 106

    straight-line depreciation, 106–107, 193, 194

    200% double declining balance depreciation, 94, 99, 107–109, 194

Depreciation periods, 103, 105, 110, 112, 194–195

Depreciation recapture, 101, 114

Depreciation tables, 108, 109

Destination expenses, business travel, 214, 216, 217, 218–219, 220

DIF scores, 431–433

Direct expenses, 142, 149, 150

Disability insurance, 258, 293, 371

Disasters, federally declared, 98, 351

Draws, business owner, 277

Dues, 169–170, 354

E

Earned income tax credit, 433

EAs (enrolled agents), 458

EBay, buying and selling on, 42, 48

Educational seminars, 33, 37

Education expenses, 61, 211, 213, 355–358

Electric cars, 189

Electronic records

    auto mileage, 391

    calendars, 377–378

    expense journals, 382–384

    tax record storage, 402

    travel deduction documentation, 395

Electronic tax filing, 53, 259, 435

Employee fringe benefits. *See* Fringe benefits

Employee health care

    deducting health insurance expense, 291–296

    Health Care Reform Act and, 284–286, 297

    health insurance for spouse as employee, 272, 293–296

    Health Savings Accounts (HSAs), 317–319

    medical reimbursement plans, 300–308

    tax credits for health insurance, 285, 286, 296–300

Employee reimbursement, 262–268

accountable plans, 153, 262–265, 267

business owners as employees, 153, 173, 277

meals and entertainment expenses, 263

overview of, 262

state requirements, 266

unaccountable plans, 266

unreimbursed expenses, 266–268, 278

See also Medical reimbursement plans

Employees

business owners as, 276–278, 292–293

business travel with, 215

car loan interest as nondeductible, 181

children as, 268–271, 272–276, 302

deductions for pay/benefits to, 13–14, 252–255, 272

independent contractors vs., 248–252

part-time and temporary workers, 251

professional help for retirement plans for, 322–323, 327

spouses as, 11, 271–276, 293–296, 301–302, 318

See also Corporation employees; Employee health care; Employee reimbursement; Fringe benefits; Payroll taxes

Employer Identification Number (EIN), 274

Employer IRAs, 332–334, 337

Employment taxes. *See* Payroll taxes

Enrolled agents (EAs), 458

Entertainment expenses deduction, 157–173

activities considered/not considered business entertainment, 158–159

business discussions before, during or after entertainment, 161–164

business travel, 214

calculating, 166–172

employee entertainment, 263

entertaining at home, 164–165

entertaining in business settings, 166

entertainment expenses split with client, 167

entertainment tickets, 170–171

expenses reimbursed by client, 171–172, 173

independent contractors, 280–281

IRS audits, 161

IRS requirements, 160–166, 167

meal expenses, 158, 159–160, 163, 225, 263

nondeductible expenses, 167–170

record keeping, 393–399, 400

tax reporting, 173

who you can entertain, 160

See also Meal expenses

Excise taxes, 319, 371

Exclusive business use requirement, home office deduction, 126–128

Existing businesses

buying, 50, 53, 55–56, 362–363

expanding, 50

Expense journals, 379–384

electronic journals, 382–384

paper journals, 379–382

Expenses. *See* Business expenses

Expertise, proof of business, 30, 33

F

Family

business travel with, 215–216, 272

employing, and health insurance tax credit, 297

health insurance coverage, 291, 293–296

HSAs for, 311, 313, 314

interest on loans from, 362

IRS rules on employing, 272–276

medical reimbursement plan coverage, 301–302

See also Children; Spouses

Family leave, 258

Federal income taxes

children as employees, 268–269, 271

deductibility of, 368

FITW (Federal Income Tax Withholding), 257, 271, 274–275

legal forms of business and, 11–14
self-employed health insurance deduction, 288–291, 311–312
   spouses co-owning business, 9–11
   tax brackets, 16–17, 268–269
Federal payroll taxes, 255–257
FICA (Federal Income Contributions Act), 256, 270–271, 274, 276
Fictitious business names, 376
Field audits, 128, 427
FIFO (first-in, first-out) inventory method, 242–243
Filing tax returns. *See* Tax reporting
Fines and penalties, 69, 184
First-year depreciation, 103–104, 106
First-year expensing. *See* Section 179 deduction
FITW (Federal Income Tax Withholding), 257, 271, 274–275
Foreign travel
   conventions, 222–223
   as education expense, 213
   IRS requirements for deducting expenses, 218–222
   ship travel, 223
   side trips, 221–222
Form of business. *See* Business, legal forms of
401(k) plans, solo, 336–337
Friends, interest on loans from, 362
Fringe benefits
   business owners as employees, 277
   de minimis (minor) benefits, 260
   for employees, 259–261
   spouses as employees, 272
   working condition benefits, 261
   See also Employee health care; Retirement plans
Fuel taxes, 371
Furniture, 15, 85, 93, 105, 127–128, 144
FUTA (Federal Unemployment Tax Act), 256–257, 270–271, 275, 276

G

Gift, property obtained as, 87, 97, 102
Gift deductions, 170–171, 342–343, 358–359, 393–399, 400
Giveaway items, 342–343
Goodwill advertising, 341–342
Guaranteed business loans, 348–349
Guaranteed payments, 312
GVWR (Gross Vehicle Weight Rating), 186

H

Half-year convention, 103–104, 193–194
Hazardous occupations, 270
Health Care Reform Act, 284–286
Health insurance
   for children, 293, 296, 297
   designating sponsors, 290
   for employees, 259, 260
   Health Care Reform Act and, 284–286
   HSA-qualified plans, 310–311
   Medicare expenses, 288, 298
   options for purchasing, 284
   self-employed health insurance deduction, 288–291
   for spouses, 272, 291, 293–296
   using HSA funds to purchase, 316
   See also Employee health care
Health Savings Accounts (HSAs), 309–319
   contributing to, 313–314
   for employees, 317–319
   establishing, 310–313
   health insurance purchased with, 316
   online resources, 309, 311
   overview of, 309
   pros and cons, 309, 316–317
   record keeping, 315, 319
   tax reporting, 319
   withdrawals from, 315–316
Heavy weight vehicles, 186, 195–196

Hobby loss rule, 6, 24–25, 28, 34–35, 375, 428

Home, entertaining at, 164–165

Home business tax scams, 25, 26

Home maintenance expenses, 146

Home office
  deductible/nondeductible expenses, 150
  depreciating business portion of home, 112–113, 145
  IRS entering, 128, 427
  local travel from, 147, 178–179
  people having no main place of business, 178–179, 208–209
  renting to corporation, 136–137
  separate structure as, 133–134
  size of, 127
  telephone, 33, 155

Home office deduction, 121–156
  deductible expenses, 140, 142–143, 145–147
  IRS audits, 122, 155–156
  not allowed for income-producing activities, 36
  record keeping, 156
  rental property managers, 42–43
  selling your home, 151–152
  tax reporting, 154–155
  when renting home, 154–155, 156

Home office deduction, calculating, 136–153
  day care centers, 139
  determining percentage of home used for business, 136, 138–140, 141
  direct expenses, 142, 149, 150
  indirect expenses, 142–143, 145–147, 149, 150
  overview of, 136, 138
  profit limit on, 125–126, 147–149, 151
  room method, 139–140, 141
  square footage method, 139, 141

Home office deduction requirements, 122–135

administrative/management activities conducted from home, 130–133
  being in business, 125–126
  clients or customers met at home, 133
  corporation employees, 135, 153
  day care center at home, 135
  exclusive business use, 126–128
  inventory/product samples stored at home, 134
  office must be part of home, 138
  overview of, 122–123, 124
  principal place of business, 129–130
  regular business use, 129
  separate structure used for business, 133–134

Homeowner's insurance, 145, 360

HSAs. *See* Health Savings Accounts (HSAs)

I

ICs. *See* Independent contractors (ICs)

Improvements. *See* Repairs and improvements

Incidental supplies, 236

Inclusion amount, 199

Income
  adjusted gross income (AGI), 267, 287
  behavior test and, 31
  business expenses paid by employees and, 262–263, 265, 266, 267–268, 277–278
  modified adjusted gross income (MAGI), 329
  unreported income, 402, 427, 433, 437
  use of Section 179 deduction and, 90–92, 102, 192

Income-producing activities, 35–43
  investment interest expense, 37, 363–364
  Medicare tax increase, 19
  no home office deduction, 125
  overview of, 35–36
  self-employment taxes, 37–38
  tax deduction restrictions, 5, 36–37

types of, 38–43

Income taxes, state, 17–18, 258, 368, 434
See also Federal income taxes

Income-to-deduction ratio, 437–438

Independent contractors (ICs)
deductions when hiring, 61, 278–281
employees vs., 248–252
entertaining, 160
filing Form 1099, 279, 280, 281

Indirect expenses, 142–143, 145–147, 149, 150

Individual retirement accounts. *See* IRAs (individual retirement accounts)

Inherited property, 87, 97, 102

Installment purchases, 118–119, 198–199

Insurance
car insurance, 360
disability insurance, 258, 293, 371
homeowner's insurance, 145, 360
liability insurance, 359
long-term care insurance, 291, 298
overview of deducting, 145–146, 359–360
renter's insurance, 145, 360
12-month rule on prepaying, 407–408
workers' compensation insurance, 258
See also Health insurance

Intangible assets, 102, 113–114

Interest
business loans, 61, 361, 362–363
car loans, 181, 202, 362, 420–421
credit cards, 364, 377
home mortgage interest, 143, 156, 362, 370
investment interest, 5, 37, 363–364
nondeductible interest, 361, 363, 364

Internal Revenue Code (I.R.C.), 450–451

Internal Revenue Cumulative Bulletin, 455, 456

Internal Revenue Manual (IRM), 456

Internal Revenue Service. *See* IRS (Internal Revenue Service)

Internet resources. *See* Online resources

Inventors, 49, 52, 113

Inventory, 233–246
donating excess to charity, 245
items qualifying as, 16, 234–237, 238
maintaining (carrying), 237–239
stored at home, 134
when starting business, 48

Inventory, valuing, 241–245
cost method, 243–244
first-in, first-out (FIFO) inventory method, 242–243
last-in, first-out (LIFO) inventory method, 243
lower of cost (market) method, 244

Inventory costs deduction
bad debts for credit sales, 347
computing cost of goods sold, 240–241
damaged or lost inventory, 351–352
determining value of inventory, 241–245
for employee pay, 255
overview of, 16, 239
tax reporting, 245–246

Investing. *See* Personal investing

Investment deductions, 5

Investment interest, 37, 363–364

IRAs (individual retirement accounts), 326–334
deadlines for establishing, 337
employer IRAs, 332–334
overview of, 326–328
Roth IRAs, 330–331
SEP-IRAs, 332
SIMPLE IRAs, 333–334
traditional IRAs, 328–330

IRS (Internal Revenue Service)
behavior test, 29–34
entering home office, 128, 427
obtaining tax forms from, 457
profit test, 27–29, 30
recommendations on payroll service providers, 259

refund claims processing, 424
standard mileage rates for 2011, 180
tax information, 443–445
telephone, 444, 457
test for worker status, 250
website, 38, 443–444
IRS 1040, 10
IRS audits, 425–440
  amended returns, 416–417, 424
  business travel deductions, 229
  chances of, 416–417, 424, 428–431, 432, 436, 437–438
  chief concerns, 393, 427–428, 432, 433
  Cohan rule, 403–404
  DIF scores, 431–433
  entertainment expenses deduction, 161
  home office deduction, 122, 155–156
  how returns are selected, 431–433
  medical reimbursement plans, 308
  postponing, 28–29
  providing legal basis for deductions, 6
  range of common deductions, 438–440
  record keeping and, 374, 404, 427, 428
  statutes of limitations, 402
  tips for avoiding, 434–440
  transportation deduction, 176, 202
  types of, 426–427
  when auditors can enter your home, 128
IRS Circular E, *Employer's Tax Guide*, 256, 276
IRS Form 940 or 940-EZ, *Employer's Annual Federal Unemployment (FUTA) Tax Return*, 275
IRS Form 941, *Employer's Quarterly Federal Tax Return*, 275
IRS Form 944, *Employer's Annual Federal Tax Return*, 275
IRS Form 970, *Application to Use LIFO Inventory Method*, 243
IRS Form 1020, *U.S. Corporation Income Tax Return*, inventory costs deduction, 245
IRS Form 1040, 291, 312

IRS Form 1040X, *Amended U.S. Individual Income Tax Return*, 422, 423, 424
IRS Form 1045, *Application for Tentative Refund*, 418, 422
IRS Form 1065, *U.S. Return of Partnership Income*, 12, 13, 70, 154, 203, 245
IRS Form 1098, *Mortgage Interest Statement*, 156
IRS Form 1099-MISC, *Miscellaneous Income*
  business travel expenses reimbursed by client or customers, 231
  entertainment expenses reimbursed by client, 171, 172
  home office deduction for renters, 154–155
  independent contractors, 279, 280, 281
  IRS audit triggered by, 427, 433, 437
  transportation expenses reimbursed by client or customers, 203
IRS Form 1099-SA, *Distributions from an HSA, Archer MSA, or Medicare Advantage MSA*, 315
IRS Form 1120, *U.S. Corporation Income Tax Return*, 13
IRS Form 1120S, *U.S. Income Tax Return for an S Corporation*, 13, 70
IRS Form 2106, *Employee Business Expenses*, 268
IRS Form 3115, *Application for Change in Accounting Method*, 408, 411
IRS Form 4562, *Depreciation and Amortization*, 93, 115, 116, 186, 202
IRS Form 4684, *Casualties and Thefts*, 353
IRS Form 4797, *Sales of Business Property*, 353
IRS Form 5213, *Election to Postpone Determination as to Whether the Presumption Applies That an Activity Is Engaged in for Profit*, 28–29
IRS Form 5305, *Traditional Individual Retirement Trust Account*, 326–327

IRS Form 8275, *Disclosure Statement*, 436

IRS Form 8275-R, *Regulation Disclosure Statement*, 436

IRS Form 8716, *Election to Have a Tax Year Other Than a Required Tax Year*, 413

IRS Form 8829, *Expenses for Business Use of Your Home*, 140, 148, 154, 353

IRS Form 8889, *Health Savings Accounts*, 319

IRS Form SS-4, 274

IRS Form W-2, *Wage and Tax Statement*, 255, 263, 275, 318

IRS Form W-3, *Transmittal of Wage and Tax Statements*, 275

IRS Form W-4, 274

IRS letter rulings, 455–456

IRS Publication 15-B, *Employer's Guide to Fringe Benefits*, 260, 261

IRS Publication 378, *Fuel Tax Credits and Refunds*, 371

IRS Publication 463, *Travel, Entertainment, Gift, and Car Expenses*, 189, 199

IRS Publication 505, *Tax Withholding and Estimated Tax*, 17

IRS Publication 523, *Selling Your Home*, 152

IRS Publication 536, *Net Operating Losses*, 419

IRS Publication 538, *Accounting Periods and Methods*, 411

IRS Publication 544, *Sales and Other Dispositions of Assets*, 83

IRS Publication 550, *Investment Income and Expenses*, 38

IRS Publication 560, *Retirement Plans for Small Business*, 322

IRS Publication 587, *Business Use of Your Home*, 154

IRS Publication 590, *Individual Retirement Arrangements*, 322

IRS Publication 910, *Guide to Free Tax Services*, 444

IRS Publication 929, *Tax Rules for Children and Dependents*, 276

IRS Publication 946, *How to Depreciate Property*, 100, 108, 109, 189

IRS Publication 969, *Health Savings Accounts and Other Tax-Favored Health Plans*, 316

IRS Publication 1542, *Per Diem Rates*, 227, 264

IRS regulations, 452

IRS reporting requirements. *See* Tax reporting

IRS Revenue Procedures (Rev. Procs.), 455

IRS Revenue Rulings (Rev. Ruls.), 454–455

IRS Schedule A, *Itemized Deductions*
  employee's unreimbursed expenses, 267
  hobby expenses, 35
  home office expenses for corporation employees, 153
  income-producing activity expenses/ income, 38
  inventory costs deduction, 245
  medical expenses, 287–288
  mortgage interest and property taxes, 143
  self-employed health insurance costs, 291
  state and local income taxes, 368
  transportation expenses of corporation employees, 203

IRS Schedule C, *Profit or Loss From Business*
  business equipment and furniture expense, 144
  car expenses, 202
  entertainment expenses deduction, 173
  expense categories, 380, 437
  inventory costs deduction, 245
  operating expenses on, 69–70
  rental property managers, 43
  sole proprietorships, 12
  stock traders, 40

IRS Schedule D, *Capital Gains and Losses*, 38, 40

IRS Schedule E, *Supplemental Income and Loss*, 12–13, 38, 43, 203
IRS Schedule K-1, *Partner's Share of Income, Credits, Deductions, etc.*, 12, 70, 312
IRS Schedule SE, 9

K

Keogh plans, 334–335, 337
Knowledge workers, 51–52

L

Land, 76, 79, 85, 112
Leasing
    cars, 182, 197–198
    long-term assets, 79, 117–119
Legal fees, 48, 56, 61, 366–367
Legal forms of business. *See* Business, legal forms of
Legal research, 442–457
    consulting tax professionals, 457–459
    information from IRS, 443–445
    Nolo's website, 445
    online tax resources, 445
    tax law, 449–457
    tax preparation software, 449
    tax publications, 446–449
Legislative grace, 6
Letterhead, 33
Liability insurance, 359
Licenses, 33, 48, 61, 372
Lifetime learning credit, 358
LIFO (last-in, first-out) inventory method, 243
Limited liability companies (LLCs)
    business profit limitation on Section 179 deduction, 92
    car and local travel expenses reporting, 203
    deducting costs of forming, 49
    entertainment expenses reporting, 173

home office deduction reporting requirements, 154
income-producing activities expenses, 37
inventory costs deduction, 245
overview of, 9, 11–12, 13
self-employed health insurance deduction, 288–291, 292, 311–312
Listed property
    depreciating, 81, 106, 109–110
    overview of, 80–81
    qualifying for bonus depreciation, 97, 102
    recapture, 114
    record keeping, 116, 399–401
    vehicles as, 186–187
LLCs. *See* Limited liability companies (LLCs)
Loans
    bad debt deductions for, 347–349
    business loans, 61, 361, 362–363, 364–366
    car loans, 181, 202, 362, 420–421
    from family or friends, 362
Lobbying expenses, 69
Local travel expenses. *See* Car and local travel expenses
Logbooks
    business mileage, 388–392, 393
    client visits to home, 133
    listed property, 116, 399–401
    shared-use items, 147
    time spent working, 34
Long-term assets, 71–119
    abandoning, 83
    bonus depreciation, 75–76, 95–100
    bought before business starts, 49
    defined, 73
    employee pay, 254
    inventory vs., 236–237
    IRS behavior test and, 30–31
    leasing, 117–119
    overview of deducting, 15, 75–76
    repairs and improvements to, 76–77

selling, 79, 83

tax basis, 82, 366–367, 370

tax reporting and record keeping, 115–116, 402

See also Capital expenses; Depreciation; Listed property; Section 179 deduction

Long-term care insurance, 291, 298, 316

Losses

casualty losses, 146, 349–353, 418, 420

home businesses incurring, 91

net operating losses (NOLs), 417–419, 422, 424–425

profit motive and, 24–25, 27–28

Section 179 deduction and, 90–91

short-term capital losses, 349

unsold inventory as, 239

vehicle depreciation deduction and, 192–193

when abandoning long-term assets, 83

when selling or closing business, 54

See also Hobby loss rule

Lower of cost method, valuing inventory, 244

M

MACRS (Modified Accelerated Cost Recovery System), 106, 110

MAGI (modified adjusted gross income), 329, 358

Marginal tax brackets, 17

Market method, valuing inventory, 244

Married couples. *See* Spouses

Material participation requirement, spouses co-owning business, 9

Materials. *See* Supplies

MBA expenses, 356

Meal expenses

actual expense method, 225–226

as business travel deduction, 159–160, 214, 225–228

employee meals, 263

entertainment expense deduction, 158, 159–160, 163, 225

IRS breakdown for dinner, lunch and breakfast, 167

record keeping, 225–226, 393–399, 400

standard meal allowance, 226–228, 264–265

See also Entertainment expenses deduction

Medical expenses

Health Care Reform Act and, 284–286

personal deduction, 287–288

See also Employee health care; Health insurance; Health Savings Accounts (HSAs); Medical reimbursement plans

Medical reimbursement plans, 300–308

audit-proofing, 308

for children, 302

how to establish, 304

IRS rules, 303–304

overview of, 300–302

reimbursable expenses, 303

sample plan, 305–307

for spouses, 301–302, 308

Medicare expenses, 288, 298

Medicare taxes, 10, 11, 18, 19, 255, 256, 289

See also FICA (Federal Income Contributions Act)

Midquarter convention, 104, 106

Midyear convention, 103–104, 193–194

Mixed-use property, 80

Modified Accelerated Cost Recovery System (MACRS), 106, 110

Modified adjusted gross income (MAGI), 329, 358

Money purchase Keogh plans, 335, 337

Mortgage interest, 143, 156, 362, 370

Motorcycles, 183, 187, 201

Multiple businesses, 115, 125–126, 290

Multiple business locations, 129–130, 147

N

Net operating losses (NOLs), 417–419, 422, 424–425
Nondiscrimination rule, 303–304, 319, 322–323, 327

O

Occupational taxes, 371
Office audits, 427
Office furniture, 15, 85, 93, 105, 127–128, 144
Office supplies, 14, 21, 47, 63
150% declining balance depreciation method, 194
Online resources
  car price guides, 188
  health care reform law, 285
  Health Savings Accounts (HSAs), 309, 311
  Internal Revenue Code (I.R.C.), 451
  IRS website, 38, 443–444
  leasing cars, 198
  Nolo's website, 2, 445
  premiums for small group health insurance, 299
  standard meal allowance, 227
  state income tax information, 18
  tax information, 445
  tax preparation software, 449
Operating expenses
  bookkeeping expenses, 259
  common expenses, 61, 63
  employee pay, 253
  expenses for expanding existing business, 50
  nondeductible expenses, 61, 62, 66, 68–69
  overview of, 15
  payments to independent contractors, 278
  qualifying as start-up expenses, 47, 48

  requirements to deduct, 60–68
  tax reporting, 69–70
  See also Current expenses
Ordinary and necessary requirement
  business travel expenses, 215
  entertainment expenses, 160
  operating expenses, 60–63, 253
  transportation deduction, 176–177
Organizational costs, when starting business, 49

P

Parental leave withholding, California, 258
Parking fees, 166, 181, 183, 184, 185, 393
Parking tickets, 69, 181, 184
Partnerships
  audit rates, 431, 433, 436
  business profit limitation on Section 179 deduction, 92
  car and local travel expenses reporting, 203
  deducting costs of forming, 49
  entertainment expenses reporting, 173
  health insurance for spouse, 296
  home office deduction reporting requirements, 154
  income-producing activities expenses, 37
  inventory costs deduction, 245
  overview of, 8, 11–13
  self-employed health insurance deduction, 288–291, 292, 311–312
  spouses co-owning business taxed as, 9, 296
Part-time work, 24, 33–34, 251, 298
Pass-through taxation, 11–13
Patents, 85, 102, 113
Patient Protection and Affordable Care Act, 284–286
Payroll service providers, 259
Payroll taxes
  bookkeeping expenses, 259

business owners as employees, 276
children as employees, 270–271, 274, 275
deducting, 369
federal taxes, 255–257
reimbursements to employees, 262, 263, 265, 266
spouses as employees, 11, 273, 274, 275
spouses co-owning business, 10
state taxes, 257–258, 371
Per diem rates, 226–228, 264–265
Personal debts, 349
Personal deductions
    HSA contributions, 311, 312, 314, 318
    investment interest, 37, 363–364
    medical expenses, 287–288
    overview of, 4–5
    self-employed health insurance, 288–291, 294, 311
Personal guarantees, 348–349
Personal investing, 5, 27, 35–36, 37, 38–39, 363–364
    See also Income-producing activities
Personal property
    casualty loss deductions, 352
    state and local taxes, 371
    tangible, 85–86
    See also Long-term assets
Personal wealth, 31
Physical inventory, 236, 241–242
Political contributions, 69
Principal place of business requirement, home office deduction, 129–130
Professional fees, 48, 366–367
Professional organization memberships, 33, 61, 169–170, 354
Professional stock traders, 40–41
Profits
    behavior test, 29–34
    home businesses earning, 91
    limits for home office deduction, 125–126, 147–149, 151

limits on Section 179 deduction, 90–92, 102, 192
limits on self-employed health insurance deduction, 289–290
operating expense deduction and, 64
profit motive requirement, 24–25
taxes paid only on, 5–6
Profit-sharing Keogh plans, 334, 337
Profit test, 27–29, 30
Property
    abandoned property, 83
    depreciation periods, 103, 105
    gift/inherited property, 87, 97, 102
    intangible assets, 102, 113–114
    mixed-use property, 80
    qualifying for bonus depreciation, 97–98
    real property, 112–113, 143, 370–371
    useful life of, 93–94
    See also Listed property; Long-term assets; Personal property; Real property
Property tax deductions, 143, 156, 181, 370–371
Public transportation expenses, 214

Q

Qualified joint ventures, 9–10, 296

R

Real estate dealers, 42
Real estate investing, 5, 39, 42–43, 371
Real property
    depreciating, 112–113
    taxes, 143, 370–371
Reasonable requirement
    compensation for employed family members, 273–274
    employee pay, 253
    employees returning excess reimbursements, 265
    entertainment expenses, 167

operating expenses, 68
Recapture
    depreciation, 101, 114, 152
    Section 179, 88, 93–95, 191
Receipts
    constructive receipt, cash accounting
        method, 406
    as proof of deduction, 385–386
    as proof of travel, entertainment, or gift
        deductions, 395–398, 400
Record keeping, 373–404
    actual expense method, 185, 201
    appointment book, 377–379
    business checkbook, 375–377
    business credit card, 377
    business expenses, 14
    business travel deductions, 225, 229,
        280–281
    car mileage and expense records,
        388–393
    Cohan rule, 403–404
    computer usage, 147, 400–401
    depreciation and Section 179 deductions,
        115–116
    documentation for employee
        reimbursements, 264–265
    electronic records, 377–378, 391, 395
    entertainment, meal, travel, and gift
        expenses, 393–399, 400
    entertainment expenses, 161
    expense journal, 379–384
    Health Savings Accounts (HSAs), 315,
        319
    home office expenses, 156
    IRS audits and, 374, 404, 427, 428
    listed property, 116, 399–401
    meal expenses, 225–226, 393–399, 400
    overview of, 374
    to pass behavior test, 31–32
    $75 rule, 394, 398–399
    start-up expenses, 54
    supporting documents, 382–387

transportation deduction, 176, 200–201
Records, how long to keep, 401–402
Recovery classes/periods, 103, 105, 110, 112,
    194–195
Regular business use requirement, home
    office deduction, 129
Regular corporations. *See* C corporations
Regular depreciation. *See* Depreciation
Reimbursement
    by business entity, 153, 173
    by clients/customers, 171–172, 203–204,
        214, 230–231
    of independent contractors, 279–281
    See also Employee reimbursement
Relatives. *See* Family
Rent, deducting, 143, 156
Rental property management, 37, 42–43
Renter's insurance, 145, 360
Renting home office to corporation,
    136–137
Repairs and improvements
    automobile deductions, 196–197
    as capital vs. operating expense, 61, 63,
        76–78
    home office deduction, 146
    to land, 112
    as start-up expense, 47
Repair tools, 197
Reporting. *See* Tax reporting
Research and development expenses, 49
Retirement plans, 321–337
    deadlines for establishing, 337
    how much money you'll need in
        retirement, 323
    information sources, 322
    Keogh plans, 334–335
    overview of, 322–323
    solo 401(k) plans, 336–337
    tax benefits, 323–325
    withdrawal restrictions, 326
    See also IRAs (individual retirement
        accounts)

Retroactive tax laws, 419
Room method, home office deduction, 139–140, 141
Roth IRAs, 330–331, 337
Royalties, 37

S

S (small business) corporations
  audit rates, 431, 436
  business owners as employees, 276–278
  business profit limitation on Section 179 deduction, 92
  C corporations vs., 8
  entertainment expenses reporting, 173
  home office deduction reporting requirements, 154
  inventory costs deduction, 245
  overview of, 11, 12, 13
  self-employed health insurance deduction, 288–291, 292, 311, 312
  spouse as shareholder, 294
Salaries
  business owners as employees, 276, 277
  employee, and health insurance tax credit, 298
  family members as employees, 273–274, 294–295
Sales taxes, 369–370
Sampling method, tracking mileage, 391
Sandwich day rule, business travel, 230
Section 174 deduction, 49, 111–112
Section 179 deduction, 84–95
  advantages of, 84, 92
  amended returns, 93, 421–422
  annual limit, 15, 89–90
  bicycles or motorcycles, 183
  bonus depreciation and, 75–76, 95–98
  business income limit, 90–92, 102, 192
  computer software, 111
  date of purchase and, 92–93
  how to calculate, 87–93

income-producing activities, 36
  long-term assets bought before business starts, 49
  property deductible/nondeductible under, 85–87
  property used for both business and personal purposes, 86–87, 88, 94–95
  recapture, 88, 93–95, 191
  tax reporting and record keeping, 115–116
  vehicles, 191–192, 195, 196, 202
  when not to use, 101–102
Securities dealers, 40
Security system costs, 146
Self-employed health insurance deduction, 288–291, 311–312
Self-employment taxes
  deducting, 368
  income-producing activities, 37–38
  overview of, 18–19, 289
  spouses co-owning business, 10
  See also Medicare taxes; Social Security taxes
Selling long-term assets, 83, 93–95, 101, 114
Selling your business, 54
Selling your home, 151–152, 371
Seminars
  educational seminars, 33, 355
  IRS seminars, 445
  travel to, 178, 212, 223, 357
SEP-IRAs, 332, 337
Service providers, 52, 234, 238–239, 346–347
$75 record keeping rule, 394, 398–399
Short-term capital losses, 349
SIMPLE IRAs, 333–334, 337
Small business corporations. See S (small business) corporations
Small Employer Health Insurance Credit, 285, 286, 296–300
Social Security taxes, 10, 11, 18, 255, 256, 289

See also FICA (Federal Income
Contributions Act)
Software. *See* Computer software
Sole proprietorships
   audit rates, 431, 432, 436
   business checking accounts, 375, 376
   business profit limitation on Section 179
      deduction, 91–92
   car and local travel expenses reporting,
      185, 202
   common operating expenses, 63
   entertainment expenses reporting, 173
   home office deduction reporting
      requirements, 154
   inventory costs deduction, 245
   overview of, 7–8, 11, 12
   self-employed health insurance deduction,
      288–291, 292, 311–312
   spouses co-owning business electing
      taxation as, 9–10
   value and range of common deductions,
      21, 438–440
Solo 401(k) plans, 336–337
Sponsors, health insurance plans, 290
Spouses
   business travel with, 215–216, 272
   community property states, 10
   compensation for, 273–274, 294–295
   co-owning business, 9–11, 296
   deducting expenses for entertaining, 164,
      169
   as employees, 11, 271–276, 293–296, 297,
      301–302, 318
   health insurance for, 272, 291, 293–296
   Health Savings Accounts (HSAs), 318
   lifetime learning credit, 358
   medical reimbursement plans, 301–302,
      308
Square footage method, home office
   deduction, 139, 141
Standard meal allowance, 226–228,
   264–265

Standard mileage rate, 179–182, 198, 199,
   265, 360
Start-up expenses, 45–54
   businesses not lasting 15 years, 53–54
   businesses that never begin, 55–56, 213
   business travel expenses, 212–213
   buying/expanding existing business, 50
   common deductible expenses, 47–48
   determining date business begins, 51–53
   employee pay, 254
   expenses nondeductible as, 48–49
   for income-producing activities, 37
   legal and accounting fees, 367
   limits on amount deducted, 46, 53,
      56–57
   local travel expenses before business
      starts, 177
   overview of, 14, 46–47
   payments to independent contractors, 278
   record keeping, 54
   tax reporting, 53
State taxes
   disability insurance programs, 258, 371
   income taxes, 17–18, 258, 368, 434
   payroll taxes, 257–258, 371
   on personal property, 371
   unemployment compensation taxes,
      257–258, 371
   workers' compensation insurance
      programs, 258
Stationery, 33
Stock trading, 39–41
Straight-line depreciation method, 106–107,
   193, 194
Subscriptions, 61, 355
Supplies
   average deduction for, 21
   as deductible business expense, 144, 147
   incidental supplies, 236
   inventory vs., 235–236, 239
   office supplies, 14, 21, 47, 63
SUVs, 186, 188, 195–196

T

Tangible personal property, 85–86
Tax attorneys, 458, 459
Tax avoidance, 430
Tax basis
  adjusted basis, 83, 187–188
  cars, 187–188
  defined, 50, 82
  long-term assets, 82, 366–367, 370
  midquarter convention for first-year
    depreciation and 104, 106
  real estate taxes and, 371
  sales tax added to, 54
Tax brackets, 16–17, 268–269
Tax citators, 448
Tax code, 442
Tax credits
  earned income tax credit, 433
  employee health insurance, 285, 286,
    296–300
  fuel taxes, 371
  lifetime learning credit, 358
Tax deduction basics, 3–21
  aggressive vs. dishonest deductions, 430
  average/range of deductions for common
    expenses, 21, 434–440
  caution on buying things to get
    deduction, 20
  deductible business expenses, 14–16
  definition of tax deduction, 4
  how deductions work, 4–6
  income-to-deduction ratio, 437–438
  learning about home business tax
    deductions, 2
  legal forms of business, 7–14
  tax savings from deductions, 1, 16–21
  types of deductions, 4–5
Tax deferral, retirement plans, 324–326
Tax deskbooks, 448
Taxes, overview of deductibility, 367–371
  See also specific types of taxes

Tax evasion, 430
Tax home, 207–211
  defined, 207
  no main place of business, 208–209
  temporary work locations, 209–211
Tax law
  amended return for retroactive changes
    in, 419
  court cases, 452–454
  Internal Revenue Code (I.R.C.), 450–451
  IRS regulations, 452
  IRS rulings, interpretations, and tax
    advice, 454–457
  overview of, 449–450
  secondary sources on, 442–449
  See also Legal research
Tax preparation fees, 367
Tax preparation software, 2, 115, 383, 449
Tax preparers, 457–458
Tax professionals, 2, 447–448, 457–459
Tax publications
  IRS publications, 444
  for nonexperts, 446–447
  for tax professionals, 447–448
  trade association publications, 448–449
Tax rates
  federal income taxes, 16–17, 268–269
  federal unemployment taxes (FUTA), 257
  FICA taxes, 256
  Medicare taxes, 18, 19, 256
  self-employment taxes, 368
  Social Security taxes, 18, 256
  state income taxes, 17–18
Tax reporting
  casualty losses, 353
  depreciation and Section 179 deductions,
    115–116
  entertainment expenses deduction, 173
  Health Savings Accounts (HSAs), 319
  home office deduction, 154–155
  inventory costs deduction, 245–246
  local travel deduction, 201–203

long-term assets, 1115–1116
operating expenses, 69–70
self-employed health insurance deduction, 291
Tax returns
errors on, 416
filing electronically, 53, 259, 435
tips for avoiding IRS audit, 434–440
See also Amended returns
Tax scams, 25, 26
Tax services, 448
Tax treatises, 448
Tax withholding
California's parental leave program, 258
federal income taxes (FITW), 257, 271, 274–275
state disability insurance programs, 258
state income taxes, 258
Tax years, 413
Telephones, 33, 144, 155, 401
Thirty-day rule, 365
Three-of-five test, 27–29, 30
Three-year amendment period, 420–421
Trade association publications, 448–449
Trademarks, 85, 102, 113
Transient status, 209
Transportation expenses, business travel, 214, 217–218, 219, 220, 221–223, 228, 229–230
Travel expenses. *See* Business travel expenses; Car and local travel expenses
Trucks, 186, 187, 188–189, 195–196
12-month rule, 407–408
200% double declining balance depreciation method, 94, 99, 107–109, 194

U

Unaccountable plans, employee reimbursements, 266

Unemployment taxes
FUTA (Federal Unemployment Tax Act), 256–257, 270–271, 275, 276
state unemployment compensation taxes, 257–258, 371
U.S. Citizenship and Immigration Services Form I-9, *Employment Eligibility Verification*, 274
Useful life of property, 93–94
Utilitarian vehicles, 186, 388
Utilities, 21, 63, 145, 380

V

Vans, 186, 187, 188–189, 195–196
Vehicle depreciation
auto repairs and improvements, 196–197
beyond five-year limit, 194–195
car repair tools, 197
depreciation limits for passenger automobiles, 189–194
determining business vs. personal miles, 190
heavy weight vehicles, 195–196
leased cars, 199
overview of, 185
passenger automobile requirement, 185–186
standard mileage rate method and, 182
tax reporting, 202
what you can depreciate, 187–188

W

Websites, business, 33, 52, 343
See also Online resources
Workers' compensation insurance, 258
Write-offs, 4

NOLO *Keep Up to Date*

1 Go to Nolo.com/newsletters to sign up for free newsletters and discounts on Nolo products.

- **Nolo's Special Offer.** A monthly newsletter with the biggest Nolo discounts around.

- **Landlord's Quarterly.** Deals and free tips for landlords and property managers.

2 Don't forget to check for updates. Find this book at **Nolo.com** and click "Legal Updates."

Let Us Hear From You

3 Register your Nolo product and give us your feedback at Nolo.com/book-registration.

- Once you've registered, you qualify for technical support if you have any trouble with a download or CD (though most folks don't).

- We'll send you a coupon for 15% off your next Nolo.com order!

DEHB8

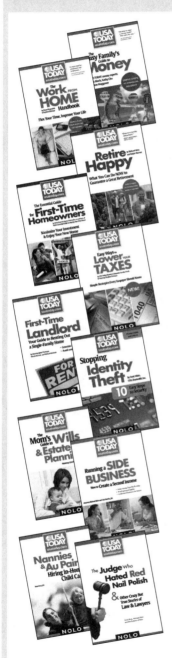

⚖️ NOLO *Online Legal Forms*

Nolo offers a large library of legal solutions and forms, created by Nolo's in-house legal staff. These reliable documents can be prepared in minutes.

Create a Document

- **Incorporation.** Incorporate your business in any state.
- **LLC Formations.** Gain asset protection and pass-through tax status in any state.
- **Wills.** Nolo has helped people make over 2 million wills. Is it time to make or revise yours?
- **Living Trust (avoid probate).** Plan now to save your family the cost, delays, and hassle of probate.
- **Trademark.** Protect the name of your business or product.
- **Provisional Patent.** Preserve your rights under patent law and claim "patent pending" status.

Download a Legal Form

Nolo.com has hundreds of top quality legal forms available for download—bills of sale, promissory notes, nondisclosure agreements, LLC operating vagreements, corporate minutes, commercial lease and sublease, motor vehicle bill of sale, consignment agreements and many more.

Review Your Documents

Many lawyers in Nolo's consumer-friendly lawyer directory will review Nolo documents for a very reasonable fee. Check their detailed profiles at **Nolo.com/lawyers**.